World Religions

Paperback edition
Published in 2004 by
TIMES BOOKS
HarperCollins Publishers
77-85 Fulham Palace Road
London W6 8JB

The Collins website address is
www.collins.co.uk

First published by Times Books 2002

Printed and bound in Singapore

British Library Cataloguing in Publication Dad
A catalogue record for this book is available from
the British Library

ISBN 0 0071 9991 0

General Editor
Martin Palmer
*Director of the International Consultancy
on Religion, Education and Culture
(ICOREC)*

Contributors
See pages 4–5

Editorial and Design Team for Flame Tree
Jennifer Bishop, Michelle Clare, Vicky
Garrard, Dave Jones, Nicki Marshall,
Sonya Newland, Nick Wells, Polly Willis,
Tom Worsley

Editorial and Design Team for HarperCollins
Philip Parker, Martin Brown

World Religions

Martin Palmer

Contributors

MARTIN PALMER
General Editor; Roots of Religion; Taoism
Martin Palmer is the Director of the International Consultancy on Religion, Education and Culture (ICOREC). ICOREC specialises in projects related to religious, environmental and development issues and works with a variety of international organisations such as The World Wide Fund for Nature (WWF), The World Bank, UNESCO, and the World Council of Churches. He was also instrumental in the creation of the Alliance of Religions and Conservation first launched in 1995 by HRH the Prince Philip of which he is now Secretary General. In 1997 he founded the Sacred Land Project which works world wide preserving sacred sites from Mongolia to Mexico.

Martin is the author of many books including *Travels through Sacred China, Sacred Britain, Christianity and Ecology, Sacred Gardens* and the forthcoming *Jesus Sutras* which is a translation of the sacred texts of the Nestorian Christians, China's first Christian community dating from AD 635. He frequently appears on television and radio, has presented a number of series on sacred topics and also writes for a wide variety of publications.

Martin studied theology at Cambridge, with a special emphasis on Chinese and Japanese studies. He founded the Centre for the Study of Religion and Education in inner city Manchester and has been a pioneer in the areas of interfaith environmental education.

BRENDA RALPH-LEWIS
The Ancient Near East; Zorastrianism
Brenda Ralph Lewis is a freelance author specializing in history, with particular reference to ancient civilizations. Her most recent book (out of a total of more than 90), published in 2001, deals with the philosophy and practice of ritual sacrifice in both ancient and modern religion. Mrs Lewis has also written over 25 TV and video scripts on the history and culture of ancient civilisations. She is married with one son and lives in Buckinghamshire.

ROBERT MORKOT
Ancient Egypt
Robert Morkot is an ancient historian specialising in North-East Africa. He studied at London University and the Humboldt-University, Berlin, and currently teaches at Exeter University. As well as many academic publications he is author of *The Penguin Historical Atlas of Ancient Greece* (1996), *The Black Pharaohs: Egypt's Nubian Rulers* (2000) and *The Empires of Ancient Egypt (2001).*

MICHAEL KERRIGAN
Greece and Rome
An Edinburgh-based freelance writer specializing in the civilizations of ancient times, Michael Kerrigan has written on almost every aspect of archaeology, ancient history and culture, covering subjects from the origins of agriculture to the icons of Byzantium, from the rise of the Greek city-state to the fall of Rome. A regular contributor to such journals as the *Times Literary Supplement* and the *Scotsman*, his recent books include *Ancient Greece and the Mediterranean* (2001), *Ancient Rome and the Roman Empire* (2001) and *The Instruments of Torture* (2001).

NIGEL CAMPBELL PENNICK
Northern Europe
Nigel Pennick was born in Surrey in 1946. Trained in biology, he published descriptions of eight new species of marine algae before moving on to become a writer and illustrator. He is author of over 40 books on European spiritual traditions, arts and landscapes.

SUSANNA ROSTAS
Central and South America
Susanna Rostas has a D.Phil in Social Anthropology and has taught at both Goldsmiths' College and Durham University. She is currently a Research Associate in the Department of Social Anthropology in Cambridge. Her publications include *The Popular Use of Popular Religion in Latin America* with Andre Droogers.

TARA LEWIS
Shamanism
Having obtained a joint Honours degree in Comparative Religions and History of Art, and researched a thesis on 'Shamans in the work of Siyah Qalam', after travelling widely in Asia for her studies, Tara Lewis went on to work for the Alliance of Religions and Conservation (a UK-based charity). She established ARC Asia, organising and developing conservation projects with religious communities in Cambodia, Thailand, Indonesia, Mongolia and China. She is currently editing *Mongolian Sacred Legends of the Land*.

JIMMY WEINER
Oceania; Australian Aboriginals
Dr. James F. Weiner received his PhD from Australian National University in 1984. He has held teaching and research positions in anthropology at Australian National University, University of Manchester and University of Adelaide. He has worked for over three years in Papua New Guinea with the Foi people and has published two books on New Guinea mythology. Currently he is working as an independent consultant in native title for Aboriginal communities throughout Australia. He is also working on a book about the Hindmarsh Island sacred site case in South Australia.

GRAHAM HARVEY
The Maoris
Graham Harvey is Reader in Religious Studies at King Alfred's College, Winchester. He is particularly interested in Maori and Ojibwe spirituality, but has also published books about contemporary Paganism and ancient Judaism. His (edited) *Indigenous Religions: a Companion* brings together excellent writing about issues in indigenous religious and their study.

FREDA RAJOTTE
Native North Americans
Rev Dr Freda Rajotte has always been dedicated to both justice issues and to preserving the integrity of creation. As a Geography professor she focused upon the related issues of economic development and environmental conservation. She also gave courses in Comparative Religion. Freda has numerous First Nation colleagues, relatives and friends. Always interested in encouraging better understanding between people of different cultures and faiths, for seven years she was the director of the Canadian Coalition for Ecology, Ethics and Religion. During this time, thanks to the contributions and assistance of many First Nation leaders, she compiled and published *First Nations Faith and Ecology*. Freda is married and has six children.

KEVIN WARD
African Traditional Religions
Dr Kevin Ward teaches African Religious Studies in the Department of Theology and Religious Studies at the University of Leeds. He worked for over 20 years in East Africa, as a teacher in Kenya and as a lecturer at a seminary in Uganda. He is ordained in the Church of Uganda.

MICHAEL SHACKLETON
Shinto
Michael Shackleton studied at Cambridge University, and also at the University of Manchester from which he received a post-graduate diploma in Social Anthropology. At present he is Associate Professor of Social Anthropology at Osaka Gakuin University in Japan with a special interest in Japanese Religion (in particular New Religions and traditional mountain cults, or 'shugendo'). He undertakes research, which has recently taken him to Southern Ethiopia and Southern Sudan. Michael is also involved in working with Martin Palmer (General Editor) on the Alliance of Religions and Conservation (ARC) scheme. He currently lives in Japan with his wife and two children.

JIM PYM
Buddhism
Jim Pym has been a Buddhist for over 40 years. He is the author of *You Don't Have to Sit on the Floor*; a book on practical Buddhism in Western culture (Rider Books 2001), editor of *Pure Land Notes*, a Buddhist journal, and a member of the Council of the Buddhist Society, London.

ALAN BROWN
Christianity
Alan Brown is director of the National Society's Kensington R. E. Centre and R. E. (Schools) Officer of the General Synod Board of Education. He has written a great many books about the Christian faith and world religions, as well as numerous articles, reviews and booklets. He is also tutor and examiner for The Open University course, 'The Religious Quest'.

JOHN CHINNERY
Confucianism
Dr John Chinnery formerly headed the Department of East Asian Studies at the University of Edinburgh. He is a frequent visitor to China and has written on a wide range of Chinese subjects, from philosophy to the theatre. He is currently Honorary President of the Scotland China Association.

RAMESHCHANDRA MAJITHIA
Hinduism
Rameshchandra Majithia was born in Tanzania. He graduated with a BSc in Engineering from the University of London and followed a career as a teacher of mathematics and graphic communication at secondary level. He was responsible for informing organised groups to Shree Sanatan Mandir, the first Hindu temple to be established, about Hinduism; he is also editor of the bimonthly magazine published by the temple. He gave Hinduism input to Religious Education students in teacher training, and has co-ordinated Hindu religious education for children aged five to 16 for the last seven years at his local temple in Leicester.

AMAR HEGEDÜS
Islam
Writer, reviewer, broadcaster and lecturer on Islamic subjects, Amar Hegedüs established the Islam in English Press (IEP) to provide ready access, in comprehensible style and language, to this frequently misrepresented subject. He networks with other faiths in common initiatives to create better understanding between peoples, and provides spiritual and pastoral care to the community. He is Chaplaincy Imam to the South London and Maudsley NHS Trust.

DR SHAH
Jainism
Professor Natubhai Shah teaches Jainism at the FVG Antwerp, Selly Oak Colleges University of Birmingham and occasionally at the SOAS London University. He represents Jainism at the highest level and was responsible for the creation of the beautiful Jain temple in Leicester, and for establishing Jain Academy and Jain Studies courses in the UK and Mumbai University. He was awarded *Jain Ratna* by the Prime Minister of India in 2001. He is the author of *Jainism: The World of Conquerors* (1998).

RACHEL MONTAGU
Judaism
Rabbi Rachel Montagu is Assistant Education Officer for the Council of Christians and Jews and teaches Judaism and Biblical Hebrew at Birkbeck College and Allen Hall. She read Classics at Newnham College, Cambridge and studied Judaism at Leo Baeck College, London and Machon Pardes, Jerusalem. She is married and has two sons.

RAJWANT SINGH
Sikhism
Dr Rajwant Singh was born in Calcutta, India, and emigrated to the United States. In 1984 he helped initiate the Sikh Association of America, and he is a founding member of the Guru Gobind Singh Foundation, a Sikh congregation based in Maryland. As well as serving as a special advisor to Jathedar Manjit Singh, one of the spiritual heads of the worldwide Sikh community, he has also served as a board member for the North American Interfaith Network. Dr Singh founded the Sikh Council on Religion and Education (SCORE) in 1998, based in Washington DC, of which he is currently the chairman. Acting on behalf of SCORE, he has been invited to speak at the White House, the US Congress, the Vatican and by various non-governmental organizations to present the Sikh perspective.

MARK TULLY
East Meets West; Multi-faith Societies
Mark Tully was born in Calcutta, India, and was educated at Cambridge University where he did a Masters in History and Theology. He worked as a correspondent for the BBC for 30 years, and for 22 years of that time was the Delhi correspondent. Since 1994, Mark has been a freelance broadcaster and writer. His most recent publications include *Amritsar – Mrs Gandhi's Last Battle* (1985), *Raj to Rajiv* (1985), *No Full Stops In India* (1988), *The Heart of India* (1995) and *Lives of Jesus* (1996). In 1992 he was awarded the Padma Shri by the Government of India, and in 2002 received the KBE.

ELIZABETH PUTTICK
New Religious Movements; Women and Religion
Dr Elizabeth Puttick is a sociologist of religion, specializing in women's spirituality and new religions (including New Age, shamanism and paganism). Her publications include *Women in New Religions* (Macmillan/St Martin's Press). She teaches religious studies at the British American College, London, and also works as a literary agent and publishing consultant.

RACHEL STORM
Rastafari; Scientific Religions; Glossary
Rachel Storm has studied and written about mythology and religion since the 1980s. She is the author of three books in the area and has contributed to a number of encyclopedias, as well as to national and international magazines and newspapers.

SUSAN GREENWOOD
Contemporary Paganism
Susan Greenwood is lecturer is the School of Cultural and Community Studies at the University of Sussex, an Open University Associate Lecturer and Visiting Fellow at Goldsmiths College, University of London. She gained her doctorate from research on Paganism, and her recent publications include *Magic, Witchcraft and the Otherworld: an anthropology* (2000).

PAUL VALLELY
The Culture of the West; Conflicts of Ideology
Paul Vallely writes on religion for *The Independent* newspaper, of which he is associate editor. He is chair of the Catholic Institute for International Relations and is the editor of *The New Politics: Catholic Social Teaching for the 21st century* (1999) and is the author of *Bad Samaritans: First World Ethics and Third World Debt* (1990) and various other books.

Contents

Introduction

Since the earliest days of humanity, religion has played a part in both structuring life and explaining life. Through ritual, myths and legends, dance, art, buildings, beliefs, teachings and daily practices, faith has guided, inspired and shaped the way people have lived. As with all things human, even those perhaps touched by the divine, this has led to great acts of generosity and great acts of arrogance; it has brought peace and has created wars; it has held those who are suffering wiping away their tears and it has been the very cause of tears. Religion, like any human endeavour, brings out the best and the worst in people. However, for most people, throughout history and today, religion has made the mundane sacred; given meaning to what could otherwise be experienced as a meaningless world and has taught that small acts of kindness and thoughtfulness are the true fruits of religion.

In this Encyclopedia, we explore what this means and has meant. Our notion, and to some degree definition, of what is religion ranges from the vast arrays of indigenous religions still to be found today to the great missionary faiths such as Buddhism and Islam. It travels from the great ancient faiths of antiquity such as Egypt or Greece to the most modern of faiths – such as the Baha'is or some of the new pagan movements. Together and over time these ideas, thoughts, beliefs and practices, have, for better or worse, made the world we live in today.

A fertility statuette from the Baoule culture of the Ivory Coast.

A sixteenth-century Italian fresco depicting the gods of Olympus.

Where it has been possible, we have asked that members of the living faiths of our contemporary world be our guides. For ultimately, faith is personal and thus to understand its significance we need to do more than just stand outside and examine its shape and form. We also need to know something of what it feels like to live within a worldview such as, for example, Hinduism or African Traditional religion. Buildings and rituals are important but more important is the reason why they exist. To understand this we need to hear the voice of faith as well as see its outward manifestations.

Such a voice comes from allowing the faith itself to determine that which is important and significant, and this is something we asked the contributors to do, albeit in dialogue with those of us with overall responsibility for this book. What can appear to outsiders as the most important aspect of a faith can upon closer examination be of less significance to the believer. For example, most outsiders view Christmas as the most important Christian festival. While it is very important and through the stories, activities, symbols and celebrations one can indeed gain a good idea of Christianity, it is not the most important festival. That falls to

Easter and without understanding why Easter is the more significant, an understanding of Christianity would be incomplete, indeed rather lopsided.

The decision was taken early on in the construction of this Encyclopedia to include faiths which have died. Religion is always changing and although the great faiths of today may seem unaltered through time, in fact they are constantly adapting. The faiths of the world are the oldest surviving human institutions in the world. As such they have learnt a thing or two about continuity. But some faiths have not survived. They have become part of the rich tapestry of our world but only as now fading colours in the background. Yet without an understanding of the shifting ideas, which are manifested in the changes, for example, the insignificant role of humanity in Egyptian religion to the nuanced role of humanity in for example Middle Eastern religions of ancient

Above: A giant thirteenth-century stone Buddha from Kamakura, Japan.

Left: An image of Shiva from Madras in India.

years, has re-emerged as a major player on the world scene. This is for good, bad and indifferent reasons. The good is the increasing role of religions in social and environmental issues. Where once science and the state were seen as having taken over the traditional role of faiths as guides through social and ecological upheavals, now increasingly, religion is being included as a partner once again. In part this is due to the collapse of ideologies such as Marxism and state control. In part it is because in the end people relate better to locally led initiatives rather than governmental and especially inter-governmental initiatives. The faiths have the best network for reaching virtually all-local communities, in the world. They are now beginning to offer this in partnership with humanitarian movements and environmental and social concerns.

The bad is the rise of extremism within so many faiths. Labelled as 'fundamentalism' – a phrase which is usually insulting to all major faiths – extremism is religion with its back to the wall and fighting back. It arises from the sense of helplessness, which so many who lie outside the sphere of the benefits of modern technology and economics feel. It is often a cry of pain and frustration from the most powerless and as such demands serious attention from the world. Sadly, however, it is often then forced or chooses to take the path of violence in order to be heard. The rise of extremism in the world's faiths – there is no major faith without such a movement

Left: An eighteenth-century wall painting portrays an imaginary meeting between Lao Zi, the founder of Taoism, Confucius and Buddha.

Below: This limestone relief from the ninth century BC shows the Babylonian king Marduk.

Mesopotamia, our current notion of what it means to be human cannot adequately be understood.

The need for an Encyclopedia, which thus opens up the worlds of faiths, has perhaps never been so urgent. It was conventional wisdom in the twentieth century to assume that religion was dying. Science, modern secular political movements and the growth of pluralism were seen as the potential death knells of religion. This was especially so for writers – who were the majority writers on religion – from the West where in many European countries, overt practice of traditional religion was in decline.

The reality in the twenty-first century is that religion, having suffered the most extensive period of persecution in history in the last 100

Left: An illuminated Hebrew Bible manuscript from 1299.

– is a challenge to the rest of the world to listen carefully to the root concerns and to offer help before the movement feels completely isolated and literally at war with the rest of the world.

The indifferent is the increasing recognition that, far from fading, religion is transmogrifying in many cultures. Pluralism has led many whose grandparents were of one faith to embrace either another faith or to include into their religious worldview, elements of different faiths. This pluralism has weakened some traditional faiths, but it may be that from such an interaction, new religions are beginning to emerge as well as new expressions of the older faiths.

Finally, religion embodies the wisdom and experience of humanity through countless generations. It contains some of the most wonderful poetry and literature the world has ever seen. Through its rituals and liturgies, prayers and actions it brings hope to many and offers vehicles for living, which aid billions in making sense of a difficult world. Its understandings of what it means to be human and its recognition that the world is more than just that which can be observed, noted and catalogued means that its approach is truly encyclopaedic. What, therefore, could be more appropriate than an encyclopedia of world religions.

Martin Palmer
2002

Below: The yin-yang symbol. Together, yin and yang form the two halves of the Tao, or universal whole, in Taoism.

The Roots of Religion

Religion Before History

Our knowledge of prehistoric religion is, of necessity, scant and uncertain. Our only evidence is archaeological, and the range of interpretations possible from any one artefact or site is enormous. For many years there was a tendency to interpret virtually any prehistoric object as religious – no matter what its nature – and for evidence to be twisted and bent to fit the pet theories of the researcher, commonly extrapolated back from anthropological theories which are often now discredited themselves. In the final analysis, our best theories are only speculation.

THE FAMOUS CHAUVET cave paintings, over 30,000 years old, discovered in France in 1994, depict in vivid and splendid detail animals which now long extinct, are perhaps our earliest evidence of religious activity. Undisturbed patterns in the dirt of the floor seem to show signs of dancing; there is a bear skull on a stone block which might be a shrine; and a strange figure at the back of the cave seems, possibly, to combine aspects of beast and man.

The depiction of the animals may represent a symbolic invocation of the animal spirits to fill the hunters with power, or an attempt to increase the numbers of the animals to be hunted, or even direct worship of the animals themselves. Possibly, though, their purpose is simply artistic; perhaps the men and women who painted these wonderful paintings did so purely in order to celebrate and delight in beauty and their own ability to create. We simply do not, and cannot, know.

PALEOLITHIC VENUS

Perhaps the most striking prehistoric artefacts are the so-called 'Venuses': carved female stone figures with prominent and exaggerated breasts and genitalia, sometimes headless, which appear all over Europe from 40,000 to 25,000 BC. Again, it is hard to know what

The Venus of Malta. This figurine was discovered at the ancient Maltese temple of Hagar Qim and dates from around 3400–3000 BC. Little is known about the prehistoric people who built these temples, but the discovery of this statuette and others of similar type suggest that they worshipped a mother goddess. The Venus is made from hard-fired clay and stands 13 cm (5 in) high.

It is believed that caves, such as those at Chauvet and Lascaux, south-west France, were sacred for the people who lived nearby, and that they expressed their religious beliefs on the walls of these natural galleries. Depicted here is a multitude of animals, including horses, bulls and deer, on the cave walls at Lascaux.

interpretation to place upon these figures. Do they represent the exultation or the degradation of the female form? Were they intended to celebrate or perhaps increase female fertility? Or were they simply pornographic? After all, drawing naughty pictures has been commonplace in virtually all cultures.

WAS THERE A GODDESS?

These figures are a keystone of a powerful modern myth – the 'Cult of the Great Goddess'. First proposed in the nineteenth century, the belief that prehistoric societies were united in their worship of a single 'Goddess' became an orthodoxy of the study of prehistoric religion until the 1970s, and virtually any figure, dot, spiral or curve was interpreted as representing the Goddess. Although now discredited academically, it is still a common belief in both feminist and neo-pagan circles. The hard truth of it is that there is absolutely no evidence of a universal prehistoric 'Goddess', it is a projection back of our own need for a figure to counteract the masculine God of the Judeo-Christian tradition, and highlights the problems of how to interpret a silent religious prehistory.

Stonehenge in Wiltshire, UK. This megalithic monument was constructed in phases, probably beginning around 2950 BC. It comprises an outer circle surrounded by a ditch, an inner circle of bluestones and a central horseshoe shape with its axis aligned to the midsummer solstice. Like similar structures across Europe, little is known of its purpose, but it is likely to have had a ritual function.

THE GREAT SITES

There are spectacular prehistoric sites, such as the long barrows and stone circles of England, or the mound cultures of North and South America, which may have had a strongly religious purpose. In the case of the long barrows, dating from around 4000–3000 BC, they may have been part of a tradition of ancestor-worship; skulls seem to have been regularly moved in and out of them, probably for some ritual purpose. Perhaps the spirits of the ancestors watched over the tribe, or joined them at festivals.

As for the stone circles – easily the most impressive and awesome prehistoric sites in Europe – their purpose remains essentially unknown. Certainly at the larger sites, such as Stonehenge, they probably had a ceremonial or dramatic function. They have often been associated with astrology, but the evidence for this is scant, and what conjunctions and alignments there are may be for purely dramatic or architectural purposes; after all, the windows of many cathedrals are aligned to light up the altar in sunlight, but nobody would claim this was their primary purpose. Many of the stone circles are near areas that show signs of trade and industry; perhaps they were boundaries within which making a deal was sacred. Again, we simply cannot tell.

Really, all we can be sure of is that some form of religious activity, some form of veneration and worship, was taking place. The dead were certainly buried with some respect for their future fate; perhaps this is the most telling sign of religion. The nature of religious activity, towards whom or what it was directed, the cosmology into which it fitted, and the nature of the ceremonies involved all remain hidden behind a veil that will never be lifted.

The Nature of Religion

Religion, for billions of people, is a vital way of making sense of their life, and of giving purpose and meaning to existence. Through ethical and metaphysical theology, and through ceremony and liturgy, religion imbues people with a powerful sense of meaning. Many attempts have been made to define religion, most of which fail before its vast diversity, but one factor that links almost all religions is their belief in a reality beyond the material world, that there is something greater than just the here and now.

THERE IS A strong argument about the etymology of the word 'religion' itself, which reflects two rather different views of the purpose of religion. It may be derived from the Latin *religare*, 'to bind', suggesting that the first concern of religion is to bind humanity and the divine together, and to bind us together in community; to those opposed to religion, this binding can seem like an imprisonment. On the other hand, it may be derived from *relegare*, 'to tread carefully', reflecting a respect and care for both the natural and supernatural worlds, which for many is the primary concern of religion – to provide us with guidance as to how to live.

Indeed, religion provides us with a purpose greater and more profound than simple survival, forging a bridge between the world of human experience and the supposed greater realm of the divine. For some religious people, this means forsaking the temporal pleasures of this world in search of a transcendent meta-reality, through fasting, celibacy and so forth. For others, it leads to a desire to improve this world, to bring the material closer to the divine and to honour the presence of God in everything.

A PERSONAL OR PUBLIC APPROACH?

There has always been something of a tension in religion between the community and the individual. Structured communities, from the Catholic Church to the Hindu caste system, have always been a part of religion, as have communities bound by less formal ties, and many people find that the experience of worshipping as a community – and the support that a community can provide – powerful and profound. Others find religious communities stifling, sometimes even oppressive, and approach the divine in a more individual way. Generally speaking, the shift in the West over the last century has been towards the second approach; religion is increasingly seen as a matter of personal conscience, not public commitment.

ATTITUDES TOWARDS RELIGION

Religion has often been attacked as essentially an oppressive, even tyrannical force. It has been linked to racism, war, dictatorship, sexism and

Community worship in a Christian church. For many people the practice of community worship is fundamental to their faith, providing a focus and support. The last 100 years, however, have seen a shift in approach to religious worship: people are increasingly seeing it as a case of personal commitment rather than public demonstration.

slavery, and every religion has its fair share of guilt here, from the cruelty of the Inquisition to the slave-keeping Buddhist monks of China. Karl Marx (1818–83) famously wrote that 'religion is the opium of the people' and many have seen religion as essentially soporific, designed to keep the oppressed and downtrodden quiet before their masters.

However, Marx also wrote that religion was the 'heart of a heartless world, the soul of soulless conditions'. As much as religion has been used to justify human horrors, it is also often a profoundly redemptive and powerful force, providing hope and liberation for billions of people. In the end, the success of religion lies, perhaps, in its providing powerful explanations, or legitimising the asking of questions about, the issues of existence, the cosmos and good and evil. It may not settle all questions, but it gives many people a way of coping with the problems of their lives, and a means to explore even deeper questions about the universe.

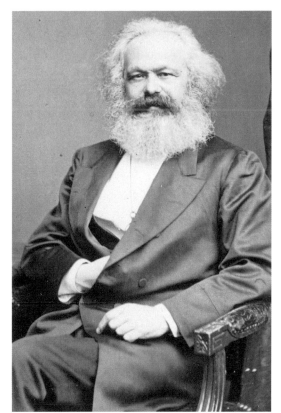

The German philosopher Karl Marx. Marx – a Jew – saw in religion both a tool of oppression of the people and their own frustrated attempts at redemption, which could only truthfully be fulfilled through socialism.

Fresco depicting Christ in judgement. In most faiths one supreme power is worshipped – although in different guises and by different names – and is often seen as forgiving of human weakness and benevolent. However, this attribute has raised questions about the presence of worldly suffering.

THE ULTIMATE POWER

Broadly speaking, almost all religions claim to worship or venerate one ultimate power – God, Buddha, Tao – the names change. For some faiths, especially Islam and Judaism, the being of God is so unknowable that it is forbidden even to try to depict 'God'. In other faiths, such as Hinduism and Taoism, this power is depicted in many different ways and is accompanied by a wide range of gods and goddesses. In faiths such as Christianity and Islam, there is a strong emphasis on the relationship between God and humanity, with humanity's proper role being seen generally as submission and acceptance before God's might. God is generally seen as omnipotent, omniscient, and benevolent; reconciling these three attributes with the reality of suffering is often a problematic concern.

Other religions, however, such as Shinto and Hinduism, have a more practical focus. They often have a profound side, but there is also the simple question of 'What can this god do for us?' In Chinese folk religion, for instance, the gods are essentially seen as being useful patrons to whom one makes offerings in return for favour. Something of this same pragmatism can also be seen in ancient Greek and Roman religion.

A Religious World-view

Although degrees of devotion vary widely between worshippers, from the monk or nun who dedicates their entire life to meditation and prayer, to the casual worshipper who attends services maybe once a week – or perhaps only on the most important holidays – religion is a major aspect of many lives. For many religious people, there is no difference between religion and life; every aspect of their life is guided by their faith.

I T IS SOMETIMES easy to think of religion as something confined to certain times and places: the church, the mosque, the synagogue, Sunday services or morning prayers. Many people, however, attempt to apply the principles of their religion to their every action, using it as the cornerstone of their own morality.

This can have all kinds of implications. Some Catholics, for example, will refuse to work for organizations that promote or sanction abortion. Because of the prohibition on usury in the Qur'an, many Muslims prefer to bank only with Muslim-owned banks that don't charge interest on loans, or to set up small community banks that have the same purpose. Private and public charity is a major concern for many religious people because the values of almost all religions include a concern for the poor and stress the virtue of almsgiving. Schooling is perhaps the most obvious example of this: many religious parents prefer to send their children to a school which promotes their faith, rather than a secular one which may teach them 'unacceptable' values.

RELIGION AND SCIENCE

The West has become increasingly used to thinking of religion and science as essentially opposed forces. This has not been helped either by the extremism of American creationists, or by the tendency of some scientists to make overly grandiose claims about 'knowing the mind of God'. For many, however, there is no distinction between religion and science; many

The Central Mosque in Regent's Park, London. Although providing a focal point for religion, mosques, churches, synagogues and other places of worship they remain only physical manifestations of faith. Religious followers worldwide apply their faith to every thought and action.

Living Religions Worldwide
Although many indigenous religions exist in isolated areas, there has been a global dissemination of other beliefs, in particular the spread of Eastern religions, such as Buddhism, to the West in recent years. Many countries are also seeing a further integration between Church and State as religion and politics become interwoven. This map shows the distribution of majority religions across the globe.

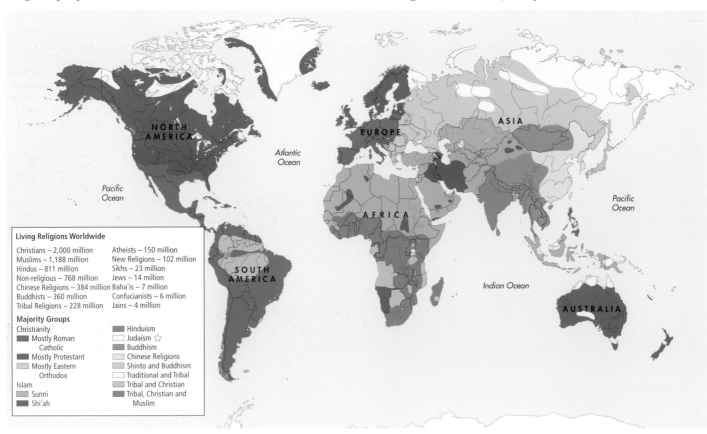

Living Religions Worldwide

Christians – 2,000 million
Muslims – 1,188 million
Hindus – 811 million
Non-religious – 768 million
Chinese Religions – 384 million
Buddhists – 360 million
Tribal Religions – 228 million

Atheists – 150 million
New Religions – 102 million
Sikhs – 23 million
Jews – 14 million
Baha'is – 7 million
Confucianists – 6 million
Jains – 4 million

Majority Groups

Christianity
- Mostly Roman Catholic
- Mostly Protestant
- Mostly Eastern Orthodox

Islam
- Sunni
- Shi'ah

- Hinduism
- Judaism ☆
- Buddhism
- Chinese Religions
- Shinto and Buddhism
- Traditional and Tribal
- Tribal and Christian
- Tribal, Christian and Muslim

famous scientists have been religious and have seen the discovery of the laws of nature as a sacred charge from God.

Science has seemed to answer some questions about the origins of life and the nature of the mind better, perhaps, than religion, and some people believe that the sphere of influence of religion will shrink as our knowledge of science grows. Many, however, believe that there are certain questions, particularly concerning the meaning and purpose of existence – if there is one – that science simply cannot answer, and that religion provides far more powerful answers to such questions.

RELIGION AND POLITICS

As with science, there is little distinction between religion and politics for many people. Indeed, the separation of Church and State is essentially a product of the eighteenth century, following terrible European religious wars between Catholic and Protestant. Before that, the State was strongly associated with a particular religion, and followers of other religions were frequently persecuted, such as Cathars and Jews in medieval France, or Christians in Shinto-dominated Japan. Wars were often religiously motivated, from the Crusades to the Hindu extermination of Buddhism during the ninth to the twelfth centuries in India.

A religious world-view, however, also often leads to a powerful motivation for social change. The socialist movement in England, for example,

had strong associations with the nonconformist churches, and the support of religious leaders is often essential in elections. Two-thirds of American Jews consistently vote Democrat, reflecting the Jewish commitment to social justice and a concern for minority rights.

Even now, some states are entirely committed to one religion. This is particularly common in Islamic countries such as Iran and Saudi Arabia, where Islamic religious law is used as the basis for the justice system, and the rights of members of other religions are circumscribed; for instance, non-Muslims can only worship in private in Saudi Arabia and cannot attempt to convert others. Communist states, dominated by an atheist ideology, often carried out terrible religious persecution, such as Stalin's purges of the Jews, and the Cultural Revolution in China. The situation in China eased after 1977, though the government retains a cautious attitude to religious activity.

In recent years, faiths have found themselves being brought more strongly into partnership with secular structures that formerly thought religion obsolete. The environment movement now has a strong involvement with all the major religions, while the World Bank is working with faiths to try and find new economic and developmental models.

Alongside this runs the quest for deeper spiritual meaning. It is not without significance that, worldwide, the practice of spiritual retreats is growing. While patterns of religious observance are changing, the quest goes on.

Illuminated manuscript depicting the capture of Montségur Castle in France, where over 200 Cathars were burnt alive as heretics by Crusader knights. From earliest times religion has been associated with tyranny and the imposition of one faith on others. Even today many still regard religion as a form of oppression.

Soldiers of the Communist Chinese army jeer as alleged anti-revolutionary prisoners are paraded through the streets wearing dunces caps in 1967. The Cultural Revolution (1966–76) was the culmination of Mao Zedong's beliefs and fears during the last decade of his power. During this time, persecution was commonplace and extended to religious groups.

Ancient Religions

THE ANCIENT NEAR EAST

The Sumerians

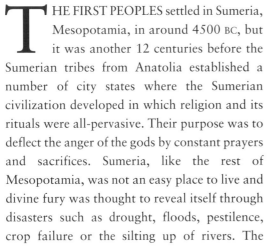

Sumeria, the earliest known city civilization, set the religious tone for the rest of Mesopotamia. Sumeria seemed to be saturated with divine presence and its concept of myriad gods and goddesses, each controlling their own aspect of life, together with the sacrifices required to humour them, greatly influenced other Mesopotamian religions.

THE FIRST PEOPLES settled in Sumeria, Mesopotamia, in around 4500 BC, but it was another 12 centuries before the Sumerian tribes from Anatolia established a number of city states where the Sumerian civilization developed in which religion and its rituals were all-pervasive. Their purpose was to deflect the anger of the gods by constant prayers and sacrifices. Sumeria, like the rest of Mesopotamia, was not an easy place to live and divine fury was thought to reveal itself through disasters such as drought, floods, pestilence, crop failure or the silting up of rivers. The

Sumerians believed that humans had been created out of clay in order to relieve the gods of their workload. It followed that humans were the servants of the gods. Nevertheless, the gods were envisaged as much like humans, with similar physical form, needs, appetites and characteristics. This was why food became the most frequent form of sacrificial offering.

GODS AND GHOSTS

The vast Sumerian pantheon represented aspects of the world – the harvest, the wind or the sun – in divine form. The principal deity

3300 BC	Immigrants from Anatolia arrive in Sumeria and build city-states
3100 BC	Temples built at Uruk, along the ancient course of the Euphrates
2600 BC	Sumerian king list (a list of the names of Sumerian kings, discovered by archeologists)
2200 BC	*Ziggurats* built in Sumeria
2000 BC	Myths of Gilgamesh, King of Uruk, written in the Sumerian language on clay tablets
1720 BC	Shift in the position of the Euphrates River leads to collapse of Nippur and other Sumerian cities

The Spread of Ancient Near Eastern Peoples
The area of the Ancient Near East comprises part of what is now known as the Middle East, a section of western Asia encompassing the eastern Mediterranean to the Iranian plateau. The Sumerians built the region's first-known civilization between the Tigris and Euphrates rivers from the fourth millennium BC. By the eighteenth century BC the new state of Babylonia had been formed and this gradually overtook that of Sumeria. The Babylonian Empire eventually absorbed that of Assyria.

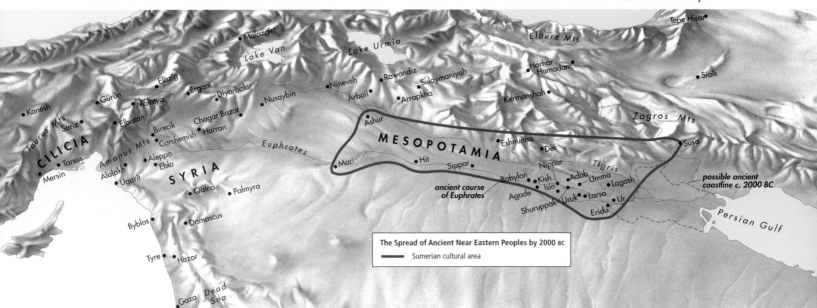

The Spread of Ancient Near Eastern Peoples by 2000 BC
— Sumerian cultural area

was Anu, ruler of Heaven, who was later replaced by Enlil, Lord of the Winds. There were also some 3,000 other deities in Sumeria. In addition, individual villages had their own local gods, as did inanimate objects. Enlil, for instance, was god of the hoe through his connection with the moist spring wind and the planting season. Enlil's son, Ninurta, was god of the plough. Concepts of reincarnation and the afterlife were alien to Sumerian theology. The dead, Sumerians believed, had no specific place in which to continue in the same style they had known while living. Consequently, the living were thought to be constantly at risk from their presence and only by regular offerings of food and drink could these ghosts be dissuaded from haunting them.

THE PRIESTS

Priests in the Sumerian temples acted as conduits between the gods and human beings. They conducted the daily services and presided over festivals, such as Akitu, the festival of the new year, which fell approximately at the time of the Spring equinox. They interpreted the entrails of sacrificed animals, usually sheep, in order to learn the divine will. They performed the public sacrifices which usually consisted of goats, cattle and birds, as well as sheep. The divine portion of an animal sacrifice comprised the right leg, the kidneys and a piece of meat for roasting. The rest of the animal sacrifices were consumed at the temple feast. In addition,

The Epic of Gilgamesh

Gilgamesh, the fifth king of the first dynasty of Uruk, in present-day southern Iraq, reigned in around 2600 BC, and was the subject of five Sumerian poems probably written six centuries later. Gilgamesh became the hero not only of Sumerian, but also of Hittite, Akkadian and Assyrian legend. The Epic tells how Gilgamesh searches for immortality, but after many adventures, he fails and is forced to recognize the reality of death.

libations of water were poured over sheaves of grain or bunches of dates so that the gods of fertility would grant rain for healthy crops. All manner of offerings were brought to the priests in the temples for use by the gods: clothing, beds, chairs, drinking vessels, jewels, ornaments or weapons. All these were classed as divine property and were placed in the temple treasuries. Clothing was first offered to the gods, then distributed among the priests and other officials who staffed the temples. The high priest had first pick, and the last went to the lowly sweepers of the temple courtyards.

Gilgamesh between two demi-gods supporting the sun. Gilgamesh was a legendary king of the Sumerians, but his tale was adopted by later peoples of the Ancient Near East and the Babylonian Epic of Gilgamesh – telling of Gilgamesh's quest for immortality – has become one of the best-known works of ancient literature.

Sumerian mosaic depicting a sacrifice. This mosaic dates from the third millennium BC and is crafted from ivory and mother-of-pearl. Sacrifices were performed by the priests, who were seen to be the link between humans and the gods. After a sacrifice had been made, the entrails of the animals were studied by the priests as a means of divining the will of the gods.

ZIGGURATS

The high temple towers known as *ziggurats*, which were topped by a small temple dedicated to one of the Mesopotamian deities, were a feature of religious architecture around 2200 BC and 500 BC. The practice of building *ziggurats* began in Sumeria, spreading later to Babylonia and Assyria. The step-sided *ziggurat* bore little resemblance to the later pyramids of Ancient Egypt. There were no internal rooms or passageways and the core was made of mud brick, with baked brick covering the exterior. The shape was either square or rectangular, with measurements averaging 40 or 50 sq m (130 or 165 sq ft) at the base. The most complete extant *ziggurat*, now named Tall al-Muqayyar, was built at Ur in south-west Sumeria (present-day southern Iraq). The most famous was

the Tower of Babel, which is popularly believed to have had links with the *ziggurat* at the temple of Marduk, the national god of Babylonia. The Tower of Babel, having been built in the vicinity of Babylon, is regarded by some archaeologists and anthropologists as an extension of the worship of Marduk at his *ziggurat* temple in the city.

The Tower of Babel. This is the most famous of the *ziggurat* temple towers built by the Sumerians. Some 25 *ziggurats* have been discovered in southern Iraq; originally, *ziggurats* were higher than their remains now suggest. It was possible to climb up a *ziggurat* by means of the stairs or a spiral ramp, but just under half either lost these features over time or were not provided with them to start with.

The Babylonians

There were two empires of Babylonia – the Old Empire (*c.* 2200–1750 BC) and the Neo-Babylonian Empire (625–539 BC). Both the Babylonian and Assyrian religions, which bore a close resemblance to one another, originally derived from that of Sumeria. However, differences between them evolved over time. The Babylonian religion stressed goodness, truth, law and order, justice and freedom, wisdom and learning, courage and loyalty. The chief Babylonian god was Marduk, 'king over the universe entire'.

BABYLONIAN FAITH encompassed the whole universe and each sector of it was under the rule of a particular deity. Heaven, earth, sea and air comprised one sector, the sun, the moon and the planets another. Nature, as manifested in rivers, mountains, plains and other geographical features was a further sector and the fourth was the city state of Babylon. Marduk, the chief god, presided over the pantheon. Like the Sumerians, the Babylonians believed that tools and implements – bricks, ploughs, axes, hoes – had their own particular deities. In addition, individuals had their own personal gods to whom they prayed and looked for salvation. Magic was prominent in Babylonian religion and Ea, god of wisdom, was also god of spells and incantations. The sun and the moon had their own gods, Shamash and Sin respectively. Shamash was also the god of justice. Adad was the god of wind, storm and flood and Ishtar, a dynamic, but cruel deity, was goddess of love and war. Although the general tenor of Babylonian religion was beneficent, there was also a negative, fearful side to it. This was represented by underworld gods, demons, devils and monsters who posed an ongoing threat to the wellbeing of humanity.

WORSHIP AND RITUAL IN BABYLONIA

Worship and ritual at the Babylonian temples usually took place out of doors, in courtyards where there were fountains for washing before prayers and altars where sacrifices were offered. The private areas of a temple, the monopoly of the high priest, the clergy and royalty, were indoors. The occult tendency in Babylonian religion was fully represented among the clergy. They included astrologers, soothsayers, diviners, the interpreters of dreams, musicians and singers. Sacrifices took place daily. One Babylonian temple kept a stock of 7,000 head of cattle and 150,000 head of other animals for this purpose alone. Apart from animals, sacrifices consisted of vegetables, incense or libations of water, beer and wine. There were numerous festivals, including a feast for the new moon and the most important, Akitu, which lasted 11 days and involved lively processions. At Akitu, worshippers purified themselves, propitiated the gods, offered sacrifices, performed penance and obtained absolution.

A limestone relief showing the Babylonian king Marduk greeting a scribe, dating from the ninth century BC. The symbols of the gods can be seen around the two figures. Marduk was the chief Babylonian god, and achieved this status after he had conquered Tiamut, the monster of primeval chaos.

King Hammurabi, the Babylonian king who made the city of Babylon his capital in the eighteenth century BC and introduced a code of laws.

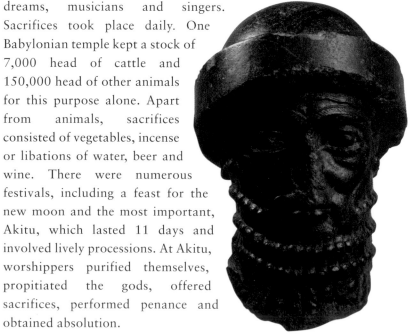

BABYLONIAN BELIEF

The ethos of Babylonia was essentially philanthropic. Compassion and mercy were prime virtues. The poor and unfortunate, widows and orphans, were accorded special protection. No one, however virtuous, was considered to be faultless so that suffering, where it occurred, was never entirely undeserved. The gods handed out punishment for unethical or immoral behaviour. To obtain the help of the gods in solving problems, it was necessary first of all to confess sin and admit to failings. Only then would an individual's personal god intercede for them with the greater Babylonian deities. There was no comfortable afterlife in Babylonian belief. After death, the spirit parted from the body and all that awaited it was descent into the dark underworld. There was no protection from a wretched existence after death, not even for those who had led righteous and ethical lives.

A relief showing a Babylonian map of the world. The Babylonians were a learned people and during the height of their empire Babylonian knowledge and literature was disseminated across a vast area. Cuneiform script became a standard 'language' and Babylonian scribes were employed in the key cities across the Ancient Near East.

THE COSMOLOGY OF BABYLON

The renowned Babylonian skill in astronomy and mathematics developed from the interest in the heavens that was an integral part of their religion. Using only the naked eye, astronomers would observe the movements of heavenly bodies and use them to make prophecies or cast horoscopes. In Babylonian times, the seven planets visible in the sky – the Sun, Moon, Mercury, Venus, Mars, Jupiter and Saturn – were wanderers among the fixed constellations of the zodiac. Each of them had its own god or goddess. In common with the Sumerians, the Babylonians believed that heaven and earth had once been joined as a single enormous mountain. This was imitated by *ziggurat* temple towers which were regarded as cosmic mountains. Apart from the Tower of Babel, whose construction was detailed in the Biblical Book of Genesis, the most apposite was the *ziggurat* built by King Nebuchadnezzar (*c.* 630–562 BC), the Temple of Seven Spheres of the World. This had seven tiers, one for each stage of heaven, as represented by the seven visible planets. Inside was a vault, also constructed in seven levels, which represented the seven gates through which Ishtar, goddess of sex and war, passed during her regular descents into the underworld.

c. **2200–1750 BC**	Old Babylonian Empire
c. **1900 BC**	Epic of Gilgamesh
c. **1790 BC**	Code (of laws) of Hammurabi, sixth king of the Amorite dynasty of Babylon
c. **1750 BC**	Death of Hammurabi
625 BC	Establishment of New Babylonian Empire by King Nabopolassar
c. **587 BC**	Marduk as chief god of Babylonia
c. **539 BC**	Persian conquest of the Babylonian Empire

When Anu the Sublime ... and Bel, the lord of Heaven and earth ... assigned to Marduk ... God of righteousness, dominion over earthly humanity ... they made [Babylon] great on earth, and founded an everlasting kingdom, whose foundations are laid as solidly as those of heaven and earth.

From the Prologue to the Laws of Hammurabi, king of Babylon

The Assyrians

Religion had important political significance in Assyria. Kings were believed to derive their power from Assur, the chief god, and both divination and astrology were initially facilities for the use of the monarch. Underlying this though, was a popular religion based on fear and superstition.

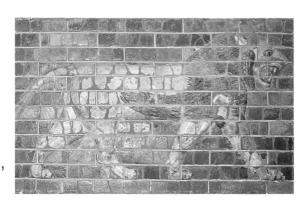

RELIGION WAS A VITAL factor in unifying and strengthening the Assyrian Empire (746–612 BC). This was a state religion, with the king himself as chief priest and representative on earth of Assur the chief Assyrian god, from whom Assyria likely takes its name. Divination and prophecy were religious functions of the State, designed to aid the king by revealing the destiny of the Empire. Even the libraries of Assyrian cities had a god of their own: Nabu, son of Marduk, principle god of Babylonia, and the god of scribes. Considering the importance of scribes and their records, this made Nabu effectively the deity overseeing Assyrian government administration. Assyrian temples, modelled on those of Babylonia, tended to be monolithic. Unlike the more ascetic Babylonians, Assyrians favoured rich decorations, large statues and elaborate reliefs on their temple buildings. The temples were the scene of daily rituals that included feeding the gods. To judge by Assyrian records, the expense was considerable.

ASSUR, NATIONAL GOD OF ASSYRIA

Four of the six major Assyrian deities – Ishtar, Shamash, Adad and Sin – were identical in both name and function with those worshipped in Babylonia. However, Assur replaced Marduk as the chief deity and Ninurta, god of hunting and war, was Assur's eldest son. Assur was raised to prominence by King Sennacherib of Assyria (d. 681 BC). Originally, it was Marduk, chief god of Babylonia, who featured in the great ritual at

Ceramic art depicting a lion, symbol of Ishtar. Like the other major gods of Assyria, Ishtar was shared by the Babylonians and it is often difficult to separate the mythology and beliefs of the two civilizations. In the Assyrian version of the creation myth, Marduk is replaced by Assur.

The Near East 1000–600 BC At its height the Assyrian Empre was focused around the capital at Nineveh, but other cities were also great centres of learning. This map shows the key cities of the empire. With the destruction of Nineveh in 612 BC by the combined forces of the Babylonians, Syrians and Medes, the empire of Assyria finally fell.

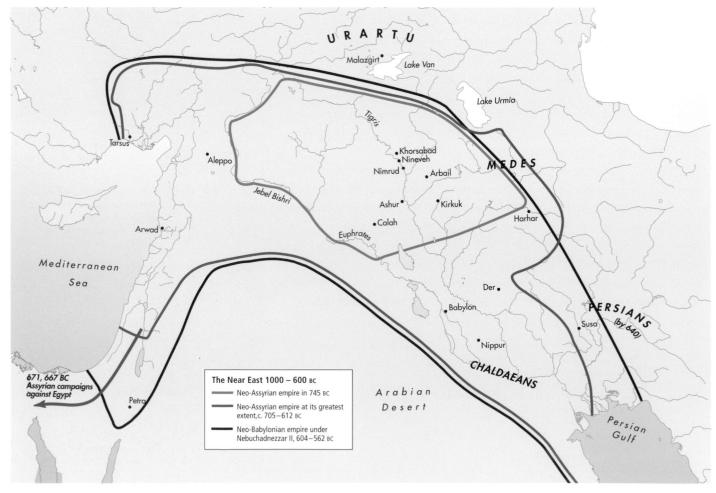

The Near East 1000 – 600 BC
— Neo-Assyrian empire in 745 BC
— Neo-Assyrian empire at its greatest extent, c. 705–612 BC
— Neo-Babylonian empire under Nebuchadnezzar II, 604–562 BC

671, 667 BC Assyrian campaigns against Egypt

THE LIBRARY OF KING ASHURBANIPAL

King Ashurbanipal of Assyria, who reigned between 668 BC and 627 BC, gathered together a collection of texts, written in cuneiform (a wedge-shaped script) that represented the first systematically catalogued library in the Ancient Near East. Much of present-day knowledge concerning Assyria comes from tablets preserved from this library, including the text of the Epic of Gilgamesh. An important purpose of the library was to furnish information for priests and diviners in their work of advising the king and seeing to his spiritual needs. Ashurbanipal's sources were the libraries of temples all over Mesopotamia, together with tablets from Ashur, Calah (an ancient Assyrian city south of Mosul in present-day Iraq) and the king's great capital at Nineveh. Scribes were ordered to copy texts concerning a wide variety of religious and other subjects: omens, the motions of the sun, moon, planets and stars, prayers, incantations, rituals, proverbs and creation stories. Scientific texts were also stored in Ashurbanipal's library, together with folk tales, one of which, 'The Poor Man of Nippur' prefigured the famous stories of 'One Thousand and One Nights' from Baghdad. The library was discovered by Sir Henry Layard during excavations at the palace of King Sennacherib between 1845 and 1851. More than 20,000 tablets from Ashurbanipal's collection were later placed in the British Museum.

An Assyrian relief from the palace at the great capital Nineveh, dating from around 650 BC. The relief shows King Ashurbanipal on his chariot. His reign was characterized by sumptuous living, and many of the reliefs at Nineveh depict lion hunting.

the Akitu festival, which celebrated his victory over Tiamat. Tiamat was a primordial creature who had created monsters to avenge the death of her 'husband' Apsu at the hands of Ea, one of their children, the younger gods. In his role as champion of the younger gods, however, Marduk killed the monsters and Tiamat as well.

Sennacherib, however, ascribed the deed to Assur after he conquered and destroyed Babylon in 689 BC and so gave the god his central place in both the festival and the Assyrian pantheon. This was a political rather than a religious move. It was believed that Assyria had been granted its empire by Assur and that its armies were under his protection. Assyrian kings used to present Assur with their reports on campaigns they had conducted, virtually making the god a divine commander-in-chief.

RELIGION AND SUPERSTITION

Assyria was an extremely harsh land, with few natural advantages and much arid desert.

The struggle for survival imposed on those who lived there produced a popular religion permeated with the power of the supernatural and dominated by superstition. Devils and evil spirits lurked everywhere and charms and incantations were frequently used to exorcise them. To the Assyrians, devils and demons had the power to enter the human body and the clay and metal charms worn to fend them off included human heads and monstrous animals. Repeating seven times the seven magical words inscribed on stone tablets was another commonly used means of averting evil. The supernatural appeared so all-pervading in Assyria that a series of omens was developed, listing every conceivable piece of bad luck, with instructions on how to avoid them. A special class of priests – the *baru*, or seers – dealt with the science of omens and portents.

May all the gods curse anyone who breaks, defaces, or removes this tablet with a curse which cannot be relieved, terrible and merciless as long as he lives, may they let his name, his seed be carried off from the land, and may they put his flesh in a dog's mouth.

Curse on book-thieves, from the library of King Ashurbanipal

A reconstruction of a wall painting found in the house of a senior Assyrian official at Khorsabad. The painting shows winged figures and bulls separated by stylized roses.

745 BC	Succession of King Tiglath-Pileser III, who turned Assyria into an empire and a military state
732–722 BC	Assyrian conquest of Palestine and Syria
710 BC	King Sargon II conquers Babylon
705 BC	Nineveh, rebuilt by King Sennacherib, becomes capital of Assyria
689 BC	Assur made national god of Assyria
668–627 BC	Reign of King Ashurbanipal
612 BC	Destruction of Nineveh by Babylonians, Syrians and Medes; fall of the Assyrian Empire.

The Canaanites

The Canaanites are the earliest recorded settlers of ancient Palestine, with a history in the region dating back to 3000 BC. Canaanite religion and Canaanite gods were synonymous with nature. For instance, the end of the rainy, fertile season was their sign that Mot, the god of death, had killed Baal in his guise as storm god. According to the Bible, however, the Canaanites' abominable religious practices marked them for destruction.

BAAL, WHO WAS worshipped not only in Canaan, but throughout the surrounding area, was not a name, but a title meaning 'lord' or 'master'. This did not describe a single god or divine function. Baal could be lord of trees, rocks, streams, mountains and other natural phenomena, but was most frequently identified with storms, rain and fertility. The fertility of an area frequently threatened by drought and desert was the main preoccupation of Canaanite religion and the gods were often associated with the manifestations of nature. Baal, for instance, was called 'rider of the clouds', 'god of lightning and thunder' or 'lord of the sky and the earth'. Likewise, Yarikh, the moon god, was called illuminator of myriads of stars, lamp of heaven or lord of the sickle. The Canaanite pantheon was based around a family unit, with the gods envisaged as kings presiding over royal courts. The supreme god, and father of Baal, was El, creator of creatures. Shachar, the dawn, and Shalim, the dusk were his twin offspring. Apart from Baal, there were several fertility deities, such as Baalat, goddesses of conception and childbirth, sea-deities and hunter-deities.

THE CANAANITES AND THE BIBLE

The Canaanites had gods with more sinister representations: death, sterility, destruction, chaos and the underworld. However, the worship of these and other gods as idols was not the only aspect of the Canaanite religion that earned such a pejorative image in the Bible. There is also the controversial assertion that many Canaanite religious practices were barbaric, together with what biblical scribes saw as abominations: incest, bestiality and human sacrifice. The practice of offering their children as sacrifices to Baal came under special censure. So did

A statuette of the Canaanite god Baal, fashioned from bronze and gold, and dating from around 1400–1200 BC. The name of Baal comes from the ancient Hebrew word *ba'al*, meaning 'lord'. Baal was a fertility god with a widespread cult following not only by the Canaanites, but also by the Phoenicians.

Kingdoms and Empires
Canaan is the Biblical name for the area of ancient Palestine west of the river Jordan. This map shows Egyptian dominated Canaan and its surrounding kingdoms and empires in the period from 1500–1100 BC.

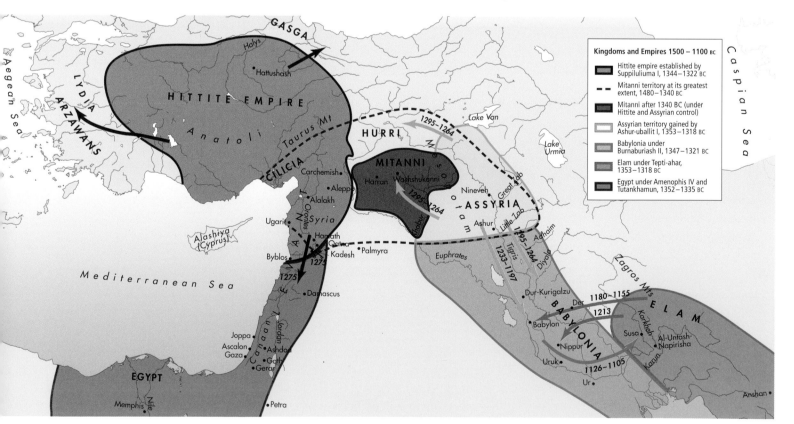

Kingdoms and Empires 1500 – 1100 BC

- Hittite empire established by Suppiluliuma I, 1344–1322 BC
- Mitanni territory at its greatest extent, 1480–1340 BC
- Mitanni after 1340 BC (under Hittite and Assyrian control)
- Assyrian territory gained by Ashur-uballit I, 1353–1318 BC
- Babylonia under Burnaburiash II, 1347–1321 BC
- Elam under Tepti-ahar, 1353–1318 BC
- Egypt under Amenophis IV and Tutankhamun, 1352–1335 BC

the essentially orgiastic, sensual atmosphere of Canaanite religion and its fertility cults and serpent symbols. The biblical view of God and worship was vastly different from that of the Canaanites. The Canaanites viewed worship as a means of controlling the gods, rather than serving them and the sexual nature of Canaanite deities was in complete contrast to the spiritual qualities of the biblical God who occupied a lofty place, far beyond such earthly temptations. The biblical representation certainly has elements of the polemic and archeology and anthropology show a different side to the Canaanites.

EXCAVATIONS AT UGARIT

For a long time, the Bible was the only source of information about the Canaanites and their religion, together with some material from ancient Greek writers. However, the excavations that began at Ugarit (on the coast of present-day Syria, north of Lattaqia) in 1929 considerably expanded this knowledge. In this area, during King Niqmad II's reign (*c.* 1360 BC), sacred texts were recorded on clay tablets at the king's request, using the cuneiform script invented by the Sumerians in the fourth century BC. Thirty-four deities were listed, beginning with the god residing in Tsafon, the sacred mountain. The deity of the cult of the dead came next, and thirdly El, the bull and source of creation, power, sagacity and virility. Dagan, a semitic god worshipped throughout the Near East, especially in the region of the middle Euphrates, was listed after that, then seven different Baals and the more minor deities. The rituals recorded on the tablets were all reserved to the king, or to the official priesthood who performed them in his presence. The Ugarit tablets also included texts concerned with oracles.

And they chopped down the altars of the Baals in his presence, and he cut down the incense altars that stood above them. And he broke in pieces the Asherim and the carved and the metal images, and he made dust of them and scattered it over the graves of those who had sacrificed to them.

Chronicles 2, 34:4

El was the paramount deity of the Canaanite religion. He was the father of gods and men and was benevolent and compassionate. He was also the source of creation.

The Canaanite fertility goddess Astarte. Astarte is equated with Ishtar of Babylonian and Assyrian belief and was also associated with the Egyptian Isis. The number of fertility gods worshipped by the Canaanites reflects their preoccupation with nature and the arid environment in which they lived.

FUNERARY FIGURINES

Up to the present, little direct evidence has been found for the daily practice of religion among the ordinary people of Canaan, despite the greatly increased knowledge made available by the excavations at Ugarit, which shared many customs with Canaan. However, a small insight into popular worship and rituals derives from the thousands of tiny bronze figurines which have been found in virtually all the excavations conducted in or around the area of ancient Canaan. These figurines were probably small representations of the great statues of gods and goddesses that were the subject of public worship in the temples. It is thought that they were votive offerings or offerings made to confirm or consecrate a vow. These figurines could be very beautiful, elaborate and expensive. One such, dating from around 1900 BC and measuring 235 mm (9 in) high, was worked in gold and silver foil. The clothing worn by the figurine was intricately decorated and showed the god wearing jewellery and a head-dress. By contrast, a limestone statue of the supreme Canaanite god El seated on a throne, excavated at Ugarit, and dating from the thirteenth century BC, was monolithic and less elaborate. El is depicted as an old man, with a grey beard and a sage, benign expression.

c. **7000–4000 BC**	Early Paleolithic (Old Stone Age) and Mesolithic settlements in the area of Canaan.
c. **3000–2000 BC**	Bronze Age settlers, including Semites, in Canaan
c. **2000–1500 BC**	Early recorded history of Canaan region
c. **1500–1200 BC**	Canaan dominated by Egypt
c. **1200 BC**	Israelites reach Canaan
c. **990 BC**	Final defeat of the Canaanites by Israelites
c. **950 BC**	Solomon, king of Israel, breaks Canaanite idols and altars

ANCIENT EGYPT

The Kingdoms of Egypt

Documented Egyptian history, from the unification of the country to the acceptance of Christianity as the official religion, lasted some 3,500 years. This huge expanse of time saw periods of confidence, prosperity and empire, separated by times of economic trouble and political fragmentation. But throughout, the fundamentals of Egyptian religion appear to have remained constant.

The pyramids at Giza are the most impressive testimony to Egyptian engineering and religious practice. The shape of the pyramid represents the rays of the sun and these tombs were designed to help the pharaoh achieve eternal life.

Egypt's Nubian Empire
The map shows Egypt's Nubian Empire. Nubia, on Egypt's southern frontier, was conquered and garrisoned by the pharaohs of the twelfth dynasty (1991–1783 BC) who built forts at strategic points. At the end of the Middle Kingdom control was lost, but the territory was reconquered by the eighteenth dynasty pharaohs (1552–1306 BC), who pushed it borders farther south. Nubia eventually broke away at the end of the New Kingdom.

EGYPT ENJOYED SEVERAL major periods of prosperity, with the state strongly centralized under the pharaoh who was regarded as a god-king. The first of these 'high points' was the Old Kingdom (Dynasties 3–6, *c.* 2650–2150 BC). At this time, the temples to the gods appear to have been rather small and the resources of the state were concentrated on the building of massive royal tombs in the form of pyramids. The pyramids were symbols of the sun, and of the primeval mound on which the sun first appeared. The pharaoh was the intermediary between the gods and people and was their provider. It was through the pharoahs that the aloof gods provided sustenance and justice to the people.

Troubled times followed the end of the Old Kingdom. There was no single ruling dynasty in control of the whole country and rival families competed for power. Egypt was reunited and enjoyed another period of prosperity under the Middle Kingdom (Dynasties 11–13 *c.* 2007 –1700 BC). During this period there were major developments in funerary practices and literature, both of which were no longer an exclusively royal preserve. Associated with this was an increased devotion to Osiris, the ruler of the underworld.

THE NEW KINGDOM

A second period of breakdown was followed by the reunification under the New Kingdom (Dynasties 18–20, *c.* 1539–1069 BC); this was also the time of Egypt's empire in western Asia and Nubia. The temples of the kings and gods now replaced pyramids as the focus of the state's building operations. The temples became vast structures serving as the theatre for elaborate festival processions. They were also the

storehouses for the wealth of the empire. At the height of Egypt's power came the one attempt to replace the many gods with worship of the sun alone. This phase, in the reign of Akhenaten (*c.* 1352–1336 BC) was short-lived, but had repercussions in the way people understood their relationship to the gods.

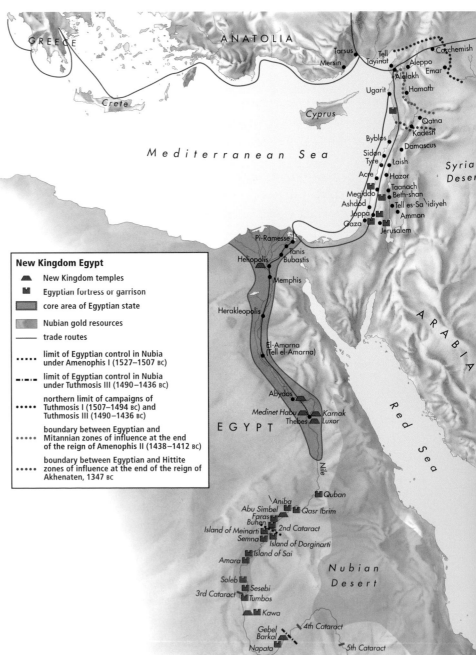

New Kingdom Egypt

- ◣ New Kingdom temples
- ⌂ Egyptian fortress or garrison
- ▬ core area of Egyptian state
- Nubian gold resources
- — trade routes
- ⋯⋯ limit of Egyptian control in Nubia under Amenophis I (1527–1507 BC)
- ▬·▬· limit of Egyptian control in Nubia under Tuthmosis III (1490–1436 BC)
- •••• northern limit of campaigns of Tuthmosis I (1507–1494 BC) and Tuthmosis III (1490–1436 BC)
- •••• boundary between Egyptian and Mitannian zones of influence at the end of the reign of Amenophis II (1438–1412 BC)
- •••• boundary between Egyptian and Hittite zones of influence at the end of the reign of Akhenaten, 1347 BC

THE LATE PERIOD

Following the end of the New Kingdom there was another period of fragmentation, and attempts by some rulers to regain Egypt's former power failed in the face of the Babylonian and Persian empires. Despite the loss of empire and periods of foreign rule, the Late Period (Dynasties 26–30, 664–323 BC) did see many huge temples constructed. This was also the time when the cults of sacred animals were most popular.

In 332 BC Alexander the Great of Macedon took Egypt from the Persians, and for the three centuries following his death the Ptolemaic Dynasty ruled the country. This period brought many Greek settlers to Egypt and saw the identification of Greek with Egyptian gods (so Re, the sun god, was identified with Helios, and the goddess Hathor with Aphrodite), and also the spread of some Egyptian cults around the Mediterranean. This process continued when Egypt fell under Roman rule, and the cult of Isis became one of the major religions of the Roman Empire. Christianity found a home in Egypt very early and monasticism flourished in the deserts. During the first centuries AD Christianity and the traditional Egyptian gods co-existed and there was certainly a strong influence from the old cults on many aspects of the worship and iconography of the newer religion.

EGYPTIAN DYNASTIES	
c. 5000–2900 BC	Predynastic
c. 2900–2650 BC	Early Dynastic Dynasties 1–2
c. 2650–2150 BC	Old Kingdom Dynasties 3–6
c. 2150–2007 BC	First Intermediate Period Dynasties 7–10
c. 2007–1700 BC	Middle Kingdom Dynasties 11–13
c. 1700–1539 BC	Second Intermediate Period Dynasties 13–17
c. 1539–1069 BC	New Kingdom Dynasties 18–20
c. 1069–656 BC	Third Intermediate Period Dynasties 21–25
664–332 BC	Late Period Dynasties 26–30
332–323 BC	Persian Empire under Alexander
323–30 BC	Ptolemaic Period
30 BC–AD 395	Roman Period

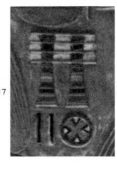

Painting from the tomb of the Horemheb, showing the pharaoh with Anubis, the jackal-headed god of the dead, holding his traditional symbol of an ankh. Anubis was believed to lead the souls of the dead into the Hall of Judgement. During part of the burial ritual, the priest would wear the mask of a jackal to simulate the god.

AKHENATEN: THE FIRST MONOTHEIST?

The most striking episode in Egypt's religious history is the 17-year reign of the pharaoh Akhenaten (c. 1352–36 BC) at the height of the New Kingdom. This is still one of the most controversial subjects in Egyptology. Ascending the throne as Amenhotep IV, the new pharaoh soon abandoned the major state cults, notably that of the god Amun, in favour of a solar cult emphasizing the visible disk of the sun, the Aten. At some point in the reign there was an iconoclastic phase when the images of gods, particularly Amun, were destroyed. The extraordinary style of art adopted at this time, allied with the poetry and content of the sun hymns, led early Egyptologists to present a false impression of the pharaoh as a true monotheist, and a pacifist. They also suggested that Akhenaten was the pharaoh who had befriended Joseph, and that his hymns to the sun were an influence on the biblical Psalms. Egyptologists now think that in many ways Akhenaten's religious ideas were reactionary,

attempting to reinstate the sun cult of the Old Kingdom pyramid builders, with its emphasis upon the pharaoh as the sole intermediary between the divine and human realms. The experiment proved unacceptable and following Akhenaten's death the traditional cults were rapidly restored.

Akhenaten offering a libation to the sun god Aten, after whom he named himself and his capital, Akhetaten. Akhenaten's cult was entirely based around worship of the sun, harking back to the days of the Old Kingdom.

The Egyptian Pantheon

Egyptian art presents us with hundreds of gods, many with animal or bird heads, some even more complex creatures combining a beetle's body, bird's wings and animal heads. Each of the different elements represented to the Egyptians a recognizable characteristic which encapsulated the nature of the god.

EGYPTIAN RELIGION developed in the long period known as the Predynastic Period (*c.* 5000–2900 BC) before the unification of Egypt into one kingdom. In the nineteenth century Egyptologists explained the many gods that characterize Egyptian religion as the product of this Predynastic Period. They thought that Egypt was divided into many small kingdoms or chiefdoms, each with its major centre and gods, a triad of creator god (usually male), consort and child. When Egypt was united these gods remained as the patrons of the different regions, and at a later stage there were attempts to rationalize and amalgamate gods with similar associations (such as solar gods). This interpretation served to explain the daunting number of gods in the Egyptian pantheon, but it is now regarded as simplistic. The Egyptians were polytheistic: they accepted the existence of numerous gods, some with very specific functions, and others who were only vaguely defined. They also created many new gods as occasion demanded. Some Egyptologists have claimed that – certainly by the later periods – all gods were aspects of one, and that Egyptian religion was moving towards monotheism. While a process of rationalization does appear to be a feature of the later periods, there was no attempt to abandon the polytheistic system.

DEPICTING THE GODS

One of the most striking features of Egyptian religious imagery is the way that animal and bird heads are combined with a human body. Gods can often be associated with more than one animal, representing different characteristics or phases of their existence. Some of the associations are obscure to us, but others are very obvious. The scarab beetle was a symbol of

Ivory carving showing the birth of the sun god Horus in the lotus blossom, protected by gods. Like Osiris and Isis, his father and mother, Horus was worshipped throughout Egypt, often as a divine infant.

Pyramids and Temples of the Old Kingdom
During the period of the Old Kingdom (*c.* 1539–1069 BC) the main focus of Egyptian religious practice was pyramid building, rather than temple construction. The pharaoh was thought to be the intermediary between humanity and the gods; the pyramids were representations of this power as well as conduits to the underworld and eternal life.

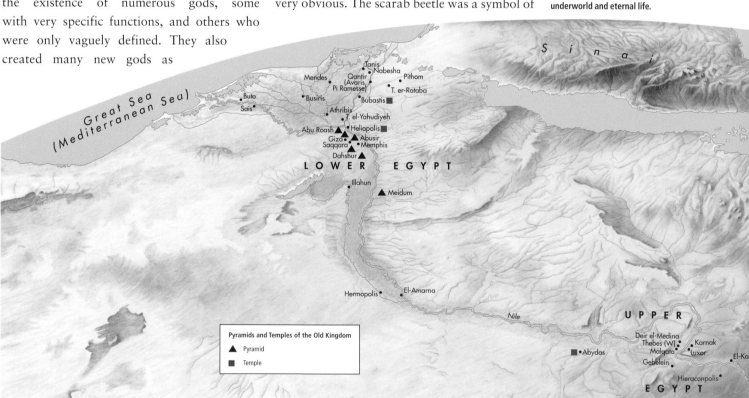

Pyramids and Temples of the Old Kingdom
▲ Pyramid
■ Temple

the creator god Khepri because it lays its eggs in a ball of dung. The scarab rolling the ball of dung was associated with the sun god pushing the sun disk across the sky; but more important, the small scarabs emerged from the dung as if they had created themselves. Emerging as the new-born sun, Khepri rose into the sky and was transformed into the falcon-headed god at the sun's zenith. After sunset he assumed the head of a ram to travel through the night towards his rebirth next dawn.

Many of the goddesses had an ambivalent nature, so Hathor could appear as the wild cow of the Delta marshes which had to be calmed, and in doing so became the domestic cow. Although calmed, such goddesses always had the potential to become violent again. This appeasing of violent aspects of the world is at the heart of Egyptian cult practices.

MINOR DEITIES

There were numerous minor deities who had specific functions in relation to the underworld, or protection in this life. The major deities tended to be rather less specific, although many appeared as creator or solar gods. Falcon-headed gods were common, and associated with sky. Many of the goddesses could appear as both vulture and as the rearing cobra, the *uraeus*, which spits fire at the pharaoh's enemies. Nekhbet, and other goddesses such as Isis, were thought of as the mother of the pharaoh, therefore they could assume vulture form and queens wore a headdress in the form of a vulture with extended wings; they could also be shown with vulture wings enfolding their bodies. In Egyptian hieroglyphic the word 'mother' uses the symbol for a vulture.

A palette showing a stylized head of Hathor the cow, dating from the Predynastic period. The protector of women, Hathor and was worshipped as the goddess of joy and love and she was thought to nourish humans with her milk.

Homage to thee, Osiris, Lord of eternity, King of gods, whose names are manifold, whose forms are holy, thou being of hidden form in the temples, whose Ka is holy.... Thou art the Great Chief, the first among thy brethren, the Prince of Company of the Gods, the stabiliser of Right and Truth throughout the World, the Son who was set on the great throne of his father Keb. Thou art beloved of thy mother Nut, the mighty one of valour....

Hymn to Osiris, from the Book of the Dead

OSIRIS AND THE AFTERLIFE

The Egyptians believed that it was the pharaoh who ensured the afterlife of the ordinary people: he cared and provided for them in the afterlife as he had on earth. Even so, during the Predynastic period, the dead were buried with food and other equipment to assist them. Towards the end of the Old Kingdom, with a decline in royal power, there was a change, and everyone expected to enjoy the afterlife. The cult of Osiris developed at the same time and rose to ever-greater prominence in the Middle and New Kingdoms. Osiris was a mythical pharaoh murdered by his brother, who cut his body into pieces and scattered them across the globe. These pieces were collected by his sister-wife Isis and mummified by Anubis, the dog- or jackal-headed god of the cemeteries, who invented embalming. Briefly restored to life he was able to father Horus (the pharaoh) before becoming ruler of the underworld. Every Egyptian could look forward to becoming 'an Osiris'. To this end elaborate preparations were made: mummification to preserve the body so that the soul (the *ba*) could return to it (the *ba* is shown as a human-headed bird, and is thought of as leaving the tomb and flying around), and a tomb and grave goods. Complex religious texts (the Book of the Dead) aided the passage of the soul through the gates of the underworld, to the judgement hall of Osiris, where the heart was weighed in the balance against 'truth'. It was only after vindication that the deceased could go on to enjoy the afterlife.

A papyrus from the Book of the Dead showing the deceased before Osiris, the Supreme Judge of humankind in the underworld. The complex rituals surrounding death and burial, including mummification, were all intended to assist the deceased to become an embodiment of Osiris.

Temples and Worship

In Egypt the priests performed rituals in the temples on behalf of the pharaoh, to ensure the preservation of the cosmos. Personal intercessions could be made in the home, in the major temples or village shrines, using intermediary statues or images carved on the walls, or when the god's statue was brought out in a festival procession.

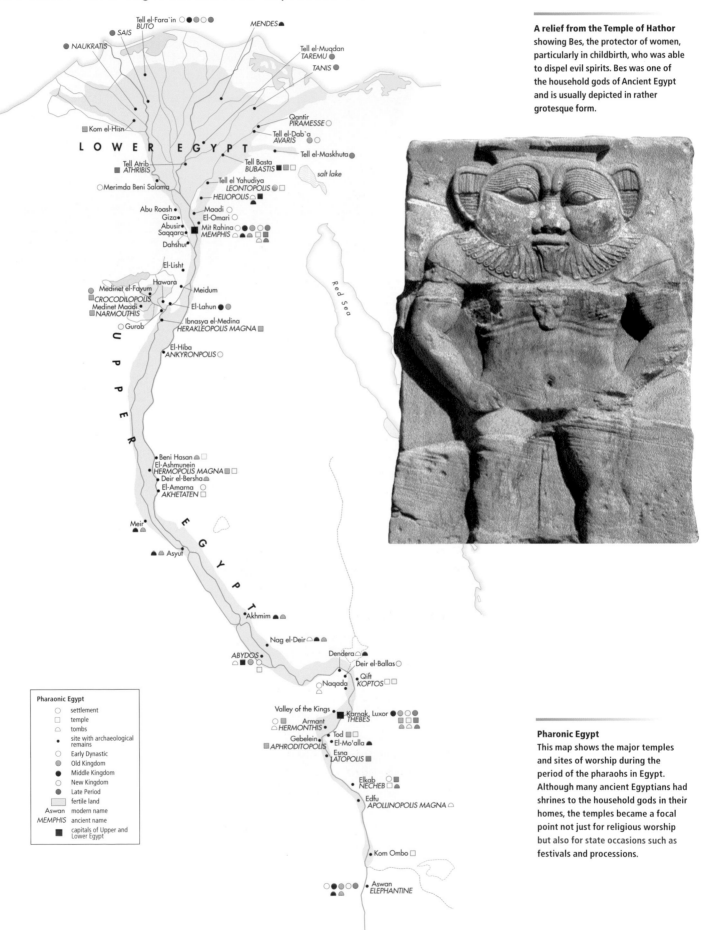

A relief from the Temple of Hathor showing Bes, the protector of women, particularly in childbirth, who was able to dispel evil spirits. Bes was one of the household gods of Ancient Egypt and is usually depicted in rather grotesque form.

Pharonic Egypt
This map shows the major temples and sites of worship during the period of the pharaohs in Egypt. Although many ancient Egyptians had shrines to the household gods in their homes, the temples became a focal point not just for religious worship but also for state occasions such as festivals and processions.

Pharaonic Egypt

- ○ settlement
- □ temple
- △ tombs
- • site with archaeological remains
- ○ Early Dynastic
- ○ Old Kingdom
- ● Middle Kingdom
- ○ New Kingdom
- ● Late Period
- ▨ fertile land
- Aswan   modern name
- *MEMPHIS*   ancient name
- ■ capitals of Upper and Lower Egypt

EGYPTIAN TEMPLES were a significant part of the state machine. Few temples from the early periods survive, and those that do are quite small. The major focus of state building in the Old Kingdom was the pyramid and its associated temple, emphasizing the role of the pharaoh as god on earth. In the New Kingdom (c.1539–1069 BC) temples were major land-holders and employers throughout the country. The temples became the repositories of the wealth of Egypt's empire, and they were the focus of the largest state building operations. This accounts for the vast scale of temples like that of Amun at Karnak, still one of the largest surviving religious complexes. However, the temples and the priesthood remained under the direct authority of the pharaoh: there was no division between Church and State.

In the New Kingdom festival processions became an important feature of religion, and this, too, played its part in the development of temples and the religious landscape of the cities. The gods now travelled between temples, along the river, canals or sphinx-lined avenues. Carried in the sacred barks (portable boats with a shrine for the statue of the god), the veiled images were still invisible to the ordinary people, but their presence was indicated by the head of the god which adorned the prow and stern of the bark.

GODS AND THE INDIVIDUAL

The Egyptians made offerings to their household gods, and perhaps to their ancestors, at shrines in the main rooms of their homes. These gods protected against the hazards of daily life, such as snakes and scorpions, illness and disease, and during the dangerous times of pregnancy and childbirth. The gods were often rather fearsome in appearance, and armed with sharp knives. Among the most popular of these gods was Bes, a dwarf with a lion skin around his face, who stuck out his tongue to ward off evil. Bes frequently accompanied another popular deity, Taweret, who was a pregnant hippopotamus with lion's paws and a crocodile tail: she also protected women during childbirth.

One significant development in Egyptian religious thought during the New Kingdom was that of the direct relationship of the individual to the major gods. These became more approachable, and a large number of inscriptions record prayers to the gods for help, or recording the afflictions (usually described as 'blindness') caused by 'sin' or taking the name of the god in vain. People could go to the state temples to pray, adore and present offerings to the gods. Access was limited to certain areas, such as the great forecourt, or a shrine at the back of the temple. The statues of pharaohs and officials set up in these outer parts functioned as intermediaries and passed on the prayers to the gods inside.

THE TOMB

The other major focus of religious activity was the tomb. Egyptian tombs were family vaults, focussed on a decorated tomb chapel built by the leading member. Here, at certain times of the year, families would gather to celebrate rituals of renewal with their ancestors, bringing the statues out from the chapel to receive the rays of the rising sun. Here they would gather to enact the elaborate burial rituals to ensure the journey of the soul into the afterlife.

Figures of the gods carved into the impressive exterior of the Temple at Edfu, one of the best preserved temples in Egypt. Temples of the Old and Middle Kingdoms were usually small, as these were the periods of the great pyramids, but during the New Kingdom, temples began to increase in significance and purpose.

THE HOUSE OF GOD

In form, the Egyptian temple combined the attributes of a house, with an image of the moment of creation. Protected by high towers (a pylon), the entrance led into a public open court, where people could come to make their offerings and prayers to the gods. Beyond this court, access was increasingly restricted. One or more columned offering halls, flanked with rooms for the storage of cult objects, led to the sanctuary, where only the highest priests could go. This sanctuary represented the world at the moment of creation and here the god's image resided in a shrine, the focus of the daily ritual. The temple precinct included other chapels, a sacred lake that supplied water for the temple rituals, houses for the priests when on duty, storage areas and workshops, and 'hospitals' in which the ill were treated, combining medicines and 'magic'. The roof of the temple was used for observations of the stars, and for the New Year festival when the statue of the god was taken to receive the rays of the rising sun.

GREECE AND ROME

Classical Origins

The civilization established by the ancient Greeks and subsequently built upon by Rome would in time be regarded as the foundation for 2,000 years of western history, though no-one could have forseen this imposing legacy. While the great states of Mesopotamia and Egypt flourished, stone-age farmers in what we now know as Greece were still scratching at the soil, eking out the sparsest possible of livings from year to year. The story of classical religion, like that of classical culture more generally, is one of local practices and traditions being brought gradually to coherence through the evolution of ever more far-reaching states and empires.

A Minoan vase. Motifs on Minoan pottery evolved from abstract forms such as spirals and circles, to more naturalistic depictions, such as the octopus shown above.

Mycenaean Greece
The Mycenaeans took control of the Aegean after the Minoan civilization had disappeared. They were apparently a warlike people, as proved by the impressive fortified citadels that have been discovered, as well as implements of war. Their great palaces and citadels testify to their major preoccupation: trade. The map shows sites of key buildings of the Mycenaean culture.

ALTHOUGH THERE ARE known to have been people in Greece from as long ago as Neanderthal times, the first distinctively 'Greek' culture is thought to have been imported by a wave of immigrants pushing westward from Anatolia some 4,500 years ago. With them they brought bronze-age metalworking skills unknown to the Neolithic farmers among whom they settled. Down the centuries many important cultural influences would come to the eastern Mediterranean across the Aegean and around the coastal fringes of Thrace. Much speculation surrounds the religious beliefs of the early Greeks, as there are few religious artefacts and little written evidence to indicate what they were. One theory is that they honoured their own ancestors as guiding spirits and worshipped the deities of local springs, the weather and other life-sustaining forces.

CRETAN CONTRADICTIONS

The first significant civilization in the area seems to have evolved not in mainland Greece itself, but on the isle of Crete where what is known as the Minoan civilization had its capital at Knossos around 2000 BC. As revealed to the modern world by the nineteenth-century archeologist Sir Arthur Evans, Minoan culture

(its name derived from that of its great mythical ruler King Minos) was a peace-loving culture of artistic accomplishment and nature-worship. Though later Greeks, envious of the Minoan achievement, might have told of the bull-headed monster held in the labyrinth beneath Minos's

palace, the reality was altogether gentler. For Evans, the Minoans' elevation of femininity over brute masculinity was symbolized by the image of graceful girl-gymnasts vaulting over the back of a charging bull. Finds from impressive arsenals of weaponry to evidence of human sacrifice (and possibly even cannibalism) have called Evans's idealized picture increasingly into question, yet he seems to have been correct in his view that the Minoans were subject to a matriarchy. Evidence has mounted that the king was a mere figurehead beside the high priestess who really ruled. Likewise, the great goddess Potnia far outranked the male deity who was at once her consort and son.

Ultimately, the issue of masculinity versus femininity misses the point of a religion whose main function may have had less to do with spiritual than economic life. The most vital role of the Minoan priesthood seems to have been in maintaining a highly centralized mercantile economy with contacts throughout the eastern Mediterranean: to this, all more obviously sacred roles may well have been secondary. Inscriptions found at Knossos, dating from the fourteenth century BC, appear to have been written in the hands of up to 70 different scribes, recording agricultural output in the city's hinterland in great detail. Meanwhile, the priests seem to have supervised a large number of craftsmen working in the palace precincts. Pots, jewels and other luxuries from Knossos have been discovered throughout Asia Minor and Southeast Europe, while Egyptian tomb-paintings attest to the visits of Minoan merchants.

THE MYCENAEANS AND AFTER

Records of Minoan culture disappear around 1400 BC, supplanted – if not actually destroyed – by the might of Mycenae, then emerging on the mainland. Apparently as austerely

masculine a culture as the Minoans were feminine and pleasure-loving, the Mycenaeans left an archeological legacy of heavy bronze swords and helmets, and warlike fortifications. Yet here too, appearances may deceive: the Mycenaeans' most important force may well have been their army of priestly scribes, for they were even more meticulous than the Minoans in their administration of what was clearly first and foremost a trading empire. Yet their reign was brief: by about 1200 BC Mycenean power itself was declining. The reasons for this remain obscure: historians have suggested that political instability further east left Mycenae cut off from its trading partners, economically stranded. Those same troubles, meanwhile, had their demographic impact too, setting off large-scale movements of peoples throughout western Asia. From the coastal settlements of what is now Turkey, it is thought, came the 'Sea Peoples', who ravaged much of the eastern Mediterranean with their raids. Meanwhile, the Dorians – warlike nomads from the western steppe – poured overland into northern Greece, the precursors of later hordes like the Huns and Mongols. By the beginning of the first millennium BC, the Mycenaeans had disappeared: Greece had little apparently to show for more than 3,000 years of history.

The famous gate of the Lionesses from Mycenae, Greece. The gate belongs to the late period of Mycenean culture and was built around 1250 BC. The carvings cover the triangle, a technique devised to even out the weight of the upper walls.

Fresco of a bull-fight found in the Palace of Knossos, Crete, dating from the sixteenth century BC. Excavations by Sir Arthur Evans here, the major city of the Minoan culture, uncovered a series of buildings, all lavishly decorated and revealing much about the Minoans, forerunners of the ancient Greeks.

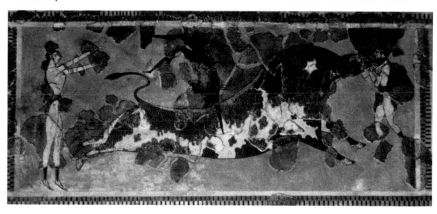

BLOOD RITES

Digging at Anemospilia, Crete, in 1981, Greek researchers Yannis and Efi Sakellarakis made a remarkable find after opening up what appeared to have been a basement room in an ancient temple that was believed to have been destroyed by an earthquake in about 1700 BC. There they found the skeletal remains of a boy, trussed up like a sacrificial bull, with a priest and priestess beside him poised to cut his throat with a knife and catch his blood in a cup. Speculation that the sacrificial victim was the son of one or both of his would-be dispatchers has never been confirmed, but there

can be no doubt that they were caught in the act of human sacrifice. The seismic disaster they were apparently seeking to stave off seems to have struck too suddenly for them to complete the ritual: buried beneath tons of fallen masonry, the tableau would remain frozen in mid-moment, lying undisturbed for 37 centuries. If the scene the Sakellarakises exposed amounts to an archeological snapshot of a pivotal point in the great Cretan civilization's agonising collapse, their discovery also spelled a severe fall in the Minoans' modern reputation for gracious humanity.

Homeric Gods and Heroes

The 'Dark Age' that followed the fall of Mycenae was not, perhaps, as black as it has since been painted, although there was no great civilization to chronicle its history or give it cultural coherence. Although cast by history in the role of wild invaders, the incoming peoples brought with them a spirit of cultural ambition and enterprise. Their knowledge of ironworking filled the breach that the now lost bronze technology had once filled, and a slow re-urbanization of the country began. From this early urban culture emerged the epic poems of Homer; chronicles of the distant Mycenean past and a defining work of future Greek cultural, religious and political consciousness.

THE IMPOSITION upon a culture of subsistence farming of a civilization that raised its eyes to the heavens can be seen represented symbolically in the story of the war between the Titans and Olympians. As recorded by Hesiod's *Theogony* (*c.* 700 BC), the world was once ruled by the Titans, the children of Gaia, the earth, and Uranus (Heaven), her son and husband. To this point, the antique order corresponded with the sort of matriarchy imagined by the Minoans, with their goddess Potnia, but events took a different turn in the developing Greek tradition. The story tells how Kronos, Gaia's youngest son, castrated his father and usurped his throne; he then married his sister Rhea, but in order to secure his position, he swallowed all their children as they were born. One alone escaped: the infant Zeus was smuggled to safety in Crete, where he grew to manhood plotting revenge against his unnatural sire. The god of open sky and mountain-top, Zeus was armed with flashing thunderbolts, and established his seat on the summit of Greece's highest peak, Mount Olympus, from where he led his own family in war against the Titans (now regurgitated so as to be able to help in their father's defence). The final victory of Zeus and his Olympians marked not only the end of the region's pre-Greek period, but also a significant break with a past in which mother earth had been at the spiritual centre of things.

WARS OF GODS AND MEN

The epics of Homer (eighth century BC) did more than anything else to forge a common Greek identity. His tale of the battle for Troy, the warlike *Iliad*, and his account of the long and difficult homecoming of the trickster Odysseus, the *Odyssey*, may differ significantly in tone and technique, but both hold up a set of Greek heroes for respect and emulation. These stories, and the values they enshrined, became part of the general Greek inheritance, uniting scattered communities which might otherwise have shared only mutual enmity.

THE OLYMPIAD

The Homeric poems also mark the unforgettable mythic debut of the Olympians as rulers of the heavens, the often all-too human divinities

A gold mask believed to represent Agamemnon, the legendary king of Argos and the man who instigated the Trojan Wars.

Pottery art showing a scene from the Trojan Wars. The prostrate figure at the bottom is Patroclus, a friend of the great Greek warrior Achilles. The death of Patroclus so enraged Achilles that he sought out the Trojan prince Hector, the two greatest heroes of the Trojan Wars engaging in a battle that ended with Hector's death.

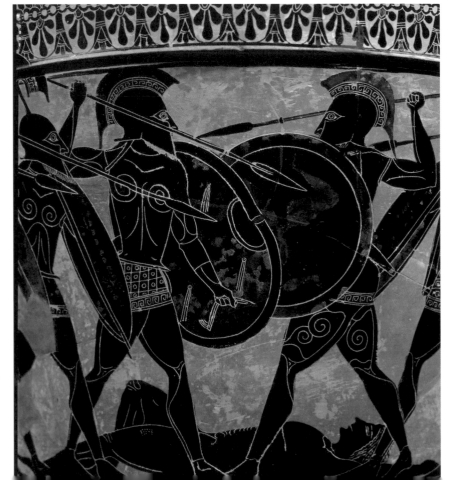

presiding over the fortunes – and misfortunes – of mortal men and women. Hence, outraged at the slight they have received in being placed behind Aphrodite in terms of beauty, Hera, Zeus's sister and queen, and his daughter Athene, the goddess of wisdom, both side with the Greeks in the hostilities that follow Paris's theft of Helen. While the goddess of beauty and love herself may stand loyally by her supporter's city, Aphrodite cannot finally prevail over the other goddesses, despite the assistance of her lover Ares, the god of war. Poseidon the earth-shaker, god of the sea, sets himself against Troy from the very start – although he also does his best to hinder Odysseus's subsequent homeward journey. Fortunately, the hero has help from Hermes, the messenger of the gods. Even Apollo, the radiant sun-god, is not above intervening to bring about the death of the apparently invincible Achilles, while his sister the virgin-huntress Artemis, goddess of the moon, also takes the part of Troy.

If the Greek gods as exhibited in Homer seem by today's standards more petty than divine, their foibles have the paradoxical effect of underlining the importance of human agency. A culture which saw so many mortal frailties in its deities was correspondingly quick to discern the potential for greatness in humankind: the result would be an age of unparalleled artistic and intellectual achievement. Long before the Parthenon or Plato, in the depths of a supposedly 'Dark Age', the ancient Greeks had set forth on the long road that would lead to modernity.

A fifth-century BC stone relief depicting Odysseus with his wife Penelope. The eponymous hero of Homer's *Odyssey* was known as a cunning and clever trickster. After the sacking of Troy Odysseus was drawn into many adventures, and the journey back to his native Ithaca took 10 years.

THE TROJAN WARS

Asked to judge which was the fairest goddess – Hera, Athene or Aphrodite – Paris, Prince of Troy, was offered various inducements to sway his decision. Hera, the consort of Zeus, offered him the gift of empire, while Athene promised him military might. Aphrodite, goddess of love, tempted him with the most beautiful woman in the world – and the young Paris could not resist.

This most beautiful woman was Helen, wife of Menelaus, the king of Sparta (and brother of Agamemnon, king of Argos). Paris eloped with Helen after being welcomed in Sparta as an honoured guest, and heroes from scores of Greek cities heeded Agamemnon's call to arms and lay siege to Troy in an effort to restore Helen to her cuckolded husband. The conflict that followed was a series of stentorian speeches and heroic single combats, with the warrior ethics of pride and honour. Thus we meet the courageous Ajax, the cunning Odysseus and the angry Achilles – all but indestructible since his mother dipped him in the Styx, the river of the underworld, when he was an infant. Only the heel by which she held him was left unprotected, and it was here that he would finally be caught by an arrow from Paris's bow, after the Greek had slaughtered Paris's brother, the noble Trojan general Hector. The famous tale of the Wooden Horse – the 'gift' within which Odysseus and his troops contrived to make their way into the city – does not in fact figure in Homer's *Iliad*, though it is referred to incidentally in the *Odyssey*.

Civilization and Religion

By the seventh century BC, Greece was shaking off the cultural slumber of the Dark Age, its scattered settlements cohering into larger city-states. No longer isolated, inward-looking agricultural communities, such cities had their own trading colonies in the world beyond: Greek merchants plied the seas from Italy and Egypt to the southern Ukraine. As the importance of such contacts grew, so the influence of the productive middle classes increased at the expense of the old aristocracies: the trend was inevitably towards more participatory forms of government. The Athens of the fourth century BC would become the timeless paradigm for democratic rule, but to a greater or lesser extent, all Greece shared in the great experiment.

R ELIGION IN THE Greek city state, or *polis*, was an inseparable part of civic life, its role more than anything the celebration of the community's collective achievements. The temple, in these circumstances, was not so much a secret shrine for an initiated priesthood as a prestigious public building, proclaiming the pride and values of the state as a whole. The great constructions raised by the Athenian statesman Pericles on the city's Acropolis from 449 BC were only the most conspicuous, concrete examples of this tendency: the Parthenon has endured as the

Statuette of a Greek youth. Warriors by nature, the ancient Greeks held the first Olympic Games in 776 BC. The Games were held to honour the Olympic Gods and comprised a series of tests of physical skill and agility.

Greek Colonization in the Mediterranean World
With the establishment of the city-states in the seventh century BC, Greece began to colonize the Mediterranean world. This map shows the location of the Greek colonies between 750 and 550 BC.

Greek Colonization in the Mediterranean World
- Greek heartland in 750 BC
- Greek parent community
- Greek oracular shrine
- 8th-century Greek colony
- 7th-century Greek colony
- 6th-century Greek colony
- Phoenician or Punic settlement
- Etruscan city
- Philistine city

ultimate symbol of 'classical' perfection. Its lines assert the triumph of human skill and ingenuity, a disdainful reproach to the rough untidiness of nature. A temple to Athene, the Parthenon enshrines for ever the co-opting of an Olympian goddess as tutelary deity to a single city.

FESTIVALS

The festival calendar in classical Greece likewise placed a premium on mortal, rather than divine, accomplishment: so it was, for example, with the original Olympic Games. First held in 776 BC in the shadow of Mount Olympus, this gathering brought the youth of Greece together to compete in running, wrestling and other tests of speed, strength and skill. Although the athletes' achievements were offered up to Zeus (there were games in the name of Apollo and Athena elsewhere), such tournaments were first and foremost a showcase for the grace and strength of the human body. The importance of Dionysos, god of revelry, cannot be overestimated: there were seven Dionysiac festivals a year in Athens alone. The whole city processed to the theatre, where music and dancing set the scene for programmes of drama from farce to tragedy.

A VENEER OF CIVILIZATION?

Yet if a city like Athens had much to celebrate, individual people still feared sickness and death, while states knew they were never entirely safe from the possibility of crop failure, plague or military defeat. The construction of a second fine classical temple to Athene on the Acropolis (the Erechtheion, around the much older shrine of Erechtheus, mythical king and archaic earth-god) underlines how reluctant the Athenians were to let go entirely of their older ancestral ways. In various of its aspects the cult of Apollo – and still more that of his son the serpent-god Asklepios, master of healing – hark back to pre-Olympian religious cults. As for the wild trances entered into by the more determined adherents of Dionysos, they suggest the sort of shamanism now associated with indigenous religions of the most 'basic' sort.

The remains of the Parthenon on the Acropolis in Athens. The Acropolis is the greatest relic of the ancient Greek city-states. The Parthenon is a temple to the goddess Athene and encapsulates the classical ideals of beauty and proportion.

DEATH OF THE YEAR

The tradition that Kore, the daughter of Demeter, goddess of the harvest, had been abducted by Hades, the ruler of the underworld, was commemorated by Athenian youths in an annual autumn pilgrimage to the scene of the crime at Eleusis, on the coast north-west of Athens. Enraged at her loss, the goddess of the harvest had struck down the crops where they were growing in the fields – they would not bear fruit again, she warned, until she once more had her daughter. Concerned that their human subjects would soon starve, the gods sent Hermes down into the earth to bring Kore back – if she had eaten nothing in her time below she would be free forever. Hades had tempted her to take a few pomegranate seeds, however, and she was thus deemed to have sealed her marriage with the infernal king. Although restored once more to her mother, Kore was from that time obliged to return to her husband's home for one season in every four. During that time Demeter's bitterness is marked by biting frosts and barren soil. The tradition of Kore's descent to the underworld each winter and her subsequent resurrection for the spring, clearly reflects an age-old concern with the continuation of the agricultural cycle (presided over, not by male Zeus, but by a female deity), as well as a more modern theological preoccupation with the question of life after death.

This relief from the fourth century BC includes depictions of Zeus, Apollo and Artemis. These three deities were part of the Olympiad, of which Zeus was the supreme god, and were seen as rulers of the earth and heavens. The Olympiad was believed to dwell on Mount Olympus, and it was beneath this sacred mountain that the first Games were held in 776 BC.

The Gods in Imperial Rome

The origins of Rome were obscure and unpromising: through the earlier centuries of the first millennium BC another civilization dominated what is now central Italy – the Etruscans. The lively culture of the Etruscans is best remembered for its elaborately decorated complexes of tombs, but they were also responsible for the drainage scheme which allowed the reclamation of the land on which Rome would be built. Expanding downward from the surrounding hilltops, under the auspices of Etruscan rule, the settlement established by Latin shepherds in the mid-eighth century was slowly evolving and as it grew, so did its confidence and self-belief: by 509 BC, Rome had succeeded in expelling its Etruscan overlords; as a republic, it would bring all Italy under its control. By the second century AD Rome's dominions spanned the known world, from Scotland to Syria, yet the civilization propagated there was recognizably Greek in origin.

A Roman silver coin from 235 BC depicting the double-headed Janus, one of the Roman gods not derived from the Greek pantheon. Janus was the god of new beginnings; his name has remained in the month January, where he was seen as looking back at the old year and forward to the new one.

The Peoples of Italy
The Etruscans were the dominant civilization in Italy throughout the early first millennium BC, but there were settlements of other peoples across the country as well. None were to pose a serious challenge to the Etruscans until the rising Roman republic finally drove them out. From this point, the Romans began extending the boundaries of their empire beyond their homeland and at its height, the Roman Empire ruled much of the known world.

A S MIGHT BE expected with so pragmatic a people, the Romans took over the Greek gods along with much else, adapting more or less the entire Olympian pantheon to their own purposes. Thus father Zeus became thundering Jupiter, his wife Hera the imperious Roman Juno, while Aphrodite became the love goddess Venus and chaste Artemis Diana. Athene passed her wisdom on to Minerva, the messenger Hermes was reinvented as Mercury. Yet such apparently straightforward transformations may mask rather more complex origins: the most famous Roman god of all, for example, was the war-god Mars. Although in time he assumed the attributes of the Greek Ares, he had in fact started life among the early Latins as an agricultural deity. Only as Rome's *raison d'etre* shifted down the generations from the farming to the military front did Mars by slow degrees take on his more warlike nature.

A BORROWED PANTHEON

There was in fact no shortage of gods and goddesses, but most found their identities merged with, and their functions assumed by, members of this new and Greek-derived pantheon. One uniquely Roman deity who did survive, however, was the double-faced Janus, god of gateways, entrances and exits, new ventures and fresh beginnings. Associated not only with daybreak but with the world's

creation, he was honoured on the first day of every month, as well as throughout Januarius, the first month of every year. Besides the great gods so far mentioned, the Romans held

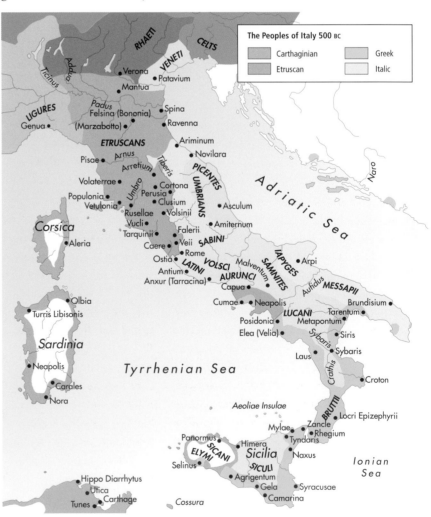

The Peoples of Italy 500 BC

Carthaginian	Greek
Etruscan	Italic

innumerable other minor deities in awe: the Lares (household spirits) and Penates (guardians of the pantry) were only the best known of these. If Janus presided over doorways, there were separate spirits responsible for hinges, thresholds and the doors themselves. For the pious Roman any action, from pruning a vine to embarking on an overseas voyage, might require the performance of precise rituals, special prayers and propitiatory offerings.

AUGUSTUS, EMPEROR AND GOD

As time went on, and power in what had once been a republic became concentrated more and more in the hands of individual leaders, Rome saw the development of what modern states would come to know

as the 'cult of personality'. The adulation accorded to generals such as Julius Caesar led to their elevation to effective dictatorship, a role merely ratified when, in 27 BC, Octavian, Caesar's great-nephew and adoptive son, and final victor in the long years of faction-fighting that had followed the dictator's assassination in 44 BC, enthroned himself as 'Imperator' or Emperor Augustus (the name simply means 'splendid'). In Egypt and the Asiatic provinces, where kings had long been venerated as gods, he was soon popularly regarded as a living divinity. After his death in AD 14, this became the official policy of Rome itself, and subsequent emperors were automatically promoted to the ranks of deities. So accepted a part of Roman life did such deifications become that, when the emperor Hadrian's young lover Antinous drowned during a visit to Egypt in AD 130, the emperor had the youth enrolled among the gods and worshipped at shrines throughout the Empire.

A statue of Athene. This is actually a Roman copy of an original statue of the Greek goddess. While the Romans had many of their own gods, as Roman civilization subsumed that of Greece, so too did they subsume their pantheon. The gods took on different names, but their functions remained essentially the same. The Greek Athene became Roman Minerva.

An altar to the Lares, spirits of the household, found in the Italian city of Pompeii. The Lares were often depicted, as here, carrying drinking horns, and small shrines were set up to them at the boundaries of farmlands.

GREEK GODS AND THEIR ROMAN COUNTERPARTS	
Greek	**Roman**
Zeus	Jupiter
Hero	Juno
Aphrodite	Venus
Artemis	Diana
Athene	Minerva
Hermes	Mercury
Ares	Mars

CYBELE: ASIATIC SAVIOUR

Although the Romans borrowed most of their pantheon wholesale from the Greeks, they were not too proud to take assistance wherever it was offered – especially in times of trouble. Their greatest fear in the early days of empire was the Punici, or Phoenicians, of Carthage. The region's foremost mercantile and naval power, Carthage effectively ruled the coasts – and thus the commerce – of the entire Mediterranean. If Rome was to expand its influence further, it would have to find a way of capturing Carthage. Conversely, Carthage knew it had to see off this threat to its own dominance. In a series of Punic Wars fought from 264 BC, the advantage shifted back and forth between the two rival empires, at one point threatening to see Roman power extinguished completely. In the years after 218 BC, the Carthaginian general Hannibal ranged relatively unhindered through Italy for several years, almost reaching the gates of

Rome before the general Scipio turned the tables. By 206 BC the Carthaginians, ousted from Italy itself, had suffered a serious defeat in Spain. The following year, however, a prodigious meteorite-shower fell upon the city, an apparent omen which sent the Romans into a fever of consternation. An oracle urged them to invoke the aid of the Phrygian mother-goddess Cybele, whose sacred throne was a massive black boulder fallen from the skies: she, the prophecy promised, would rid Rome of the Carthaginian menace once and for all. Envoys sent to Asia Minor to the Phrygian king returned bearing Cybele's throne: three years later, at Zama, Hannibal was finally vanquished.

A detail from a Roman shield, showing the goddess Cybele in a chariot drawn by lions. In their hour of need during the Punic Wars against Carthage, the Romans called upon this Phrygian deity to aid them in their campaign. She apparently answered their call and Carthage was eventually defeated.

Religion and Philosophy

The institutions of Greek and Roman religion are now a matter of strictly historical interest and the beliefs involved no more than an unusually rich and colourful mythology. But the philosophies first conceived in classical Athens and further developed in ancient Rome have remained in important respects as vital as ever. Religious and secular thought have been equally indebted to the work of these ancient pioneers. Without the ideas they set in motion the entire intellectual history of the western world would be very different.

PHILOSOPHY BEGAN in the open air, around the city square, or *agora*, of Athens, where experienced thinkers or 'sophists' gave lessons in logic and rhetoric – the art of persuasion – to the sons of more affluent citizens. This was the context in which the ideas first formulated by Socrates took shape, in the dialogues he had with his students at the end of the fourth century BC. He was compelled to commit suicide in 399 BC, charged with 'impiety' and the corruption of Athenian youth – the tradition of intellectuals upsetting those in power was established very early. Although Socrates left no writings, his teachings were recorded by his pupil Plato, whose own philosophical contribution cannot clearly be distinguished from his master's. It has, however, become conventional to attribute to Plato the distinction between material things and the ideas to which they give imperfect reflection, and in the case of humanity the difference between the body and the immortal soul. Plato's student Aristotle took the more down-to-earth view that we could really only know what we could perceive for ourselves through our physical senses: the tension between these two opposing philosophies would prove the main intellectual armature of western thought through more than 2,000 years.

THE SCHOOL OF ATHENS

The colonnaded walks, or *stoas*, of central Athens were a favourite haunt of philosophers, hence the name given to the body of thought first propounded by Zeno of Citium around the end of the third century BC. 'Stoicism', as it came to be called, involved the submission of the individual self to the providential workings of the universe at large, the quiet acceptance of adversity and good fortune alike. As modified by later Greek thinkers like Epictetus and by Romans such as Seneca, Stoicism became the pre-eminent intellectual movement of the ancient world. What may sound

The Greek philosopher Aristotle. Aristotle's work combined religion, philosophy and science and proved a lasting influence on later studies in these fields. His practical applications and belief in what the eye could see rather than the mind devise was a progression from the beliefs of his older contemporaries Socrates and Plato.

A Roman mosaic showing the Greek school of philosophy founded by Plato. Such schools consisted of philosophical masters teaching pupils in the open squares of cities such as Athens.

like a doctrine of passivity in fact involved the most strenuous efforts of discipline and self-control: in AD 65, after falling foul of his headstrong pupil Emperor Nero, Seneca took his own life in perfect calm – the ultimate stoic.

THE SCEPTIC

Sceptics such as Pyrrhon (*c.* 365–270 BC) and his followers took the 'small-s' scepticism of Aristotle to extremes, asking how far we could really know anything – even what our senses told us. Their solution, 'suspending judgement', may seem a defeatist one, but to the true sceptic, it was argued, it brought contentment and peace of mind. Pyrrhon's Roman successor, Sextus Empiricus, gave his name to the sceptical doctrine of empiricism, the belief that sense-experience was the essential – albeit insufficient – basis of all knowledge.

TRUE BELIEVERS?

How far did the ancients actually believe their own mythology? Did their tales constitute a religious scripture? And did they take what we would call a 'fundamentalist' view of their traditions' literal truth? From as early as the sixth century BC, in fact, the mythic conventions co-existed with a spirit of genuine scientific enquiry – however extravagant some of its findings may seem in retrospect. Pythagoras (b. *c.* 580 BC) formulated rules of geometry which hold today – as well as his idiosyncratic philosophy of reincarnation. By his doctrine of the 'transmigration of the soul', the spirit slips from one physical form to another in successive lives, with the potential for progressive purification through abstinence and virtuous living. One hundred years later Heraclitus suggested that the entire cosmos was in a state of perpetual flux; its governing principle, reason, was manifested physically in fire. Anticipating the findings of modern science, Democritus (*c.* 460–370 BC) proposed that all matter was made up of minute atoms assembled in different combinations; the philosophy of Epicurus followed from this strictly materialistic view. Since there could be no gods or life after death there could be no higher goal than the avoidance of suffering in the here and now – a serious argument only caricatured by later depictions of the Epicureans as a crowd of decadent pleasure-seekers.

A bust of Pythagoras, the Greek mathematician, who proposed the idea of reincarnation. He believed that the spirit moved from one life to another, in a different physical form each time.

Religions Under Rome

At its height in the second century AD the Roman Empire covered some five million sq km (2 million sq miles), occupying lands which now belong to over 30 different sovereign states. Around 100 million Roman subjects were drawn together into a single political entity, despite the enormous variety of their linguistic and cultural backgrounds. Yet, while their temporal authority was absolute, the Romans were much more relaxed about matters spiritual: under their iron rule a remarkable religious diversity was free to thrive.

DETERMINED STANDARDIZERS, the conquering Romans created an air of uniformity wherever they went in everything from law to architecture, from entertainment to roadbuilding, from fashion to city planning. It was precisely these profound rigidities, and the cultural confidence they gave, that enabled the expanding empire to display comparative tolerance towards local religious beliefs and ritual practices. In fact, the Romans were able to make such open-mindedness an instrument of pacification in newly conquered territories, native deities

being recruited to the Roman side. Rather as the old gods had been subsumed into the official Roman pantheon, indigenous cults were spliced together with Roman traditions by a process of 'syncretism'.

AN ECUMENICAL EMPIRE

In parts of Gaul the Roman war god was linked to a local god of light: Mars Loucetus, as he became known, was widely worshipped. At Bath the British spring goddess Sulis was associated so closely with the Roman Minerva that they became to all intents and purposes different

The Roman Empire by the Second Century AD
In the second century BC the area under Roman rule covered only Italy and its islands, and the small coastal area of Dalmatia to the east. Three hundred years later the empire's boundaries stretched as far north as the Scottish border in the British Isles, modern-day France and Spain, the coastal areas of North Africa and eastwards to the Black Sea. Some gods and goddesses in subject lands succeeded in maintaining their independent existence, and in some cases exerted a strong influence on the Roman people (e.g. Isis and Mithras). They became known as mystery religions.

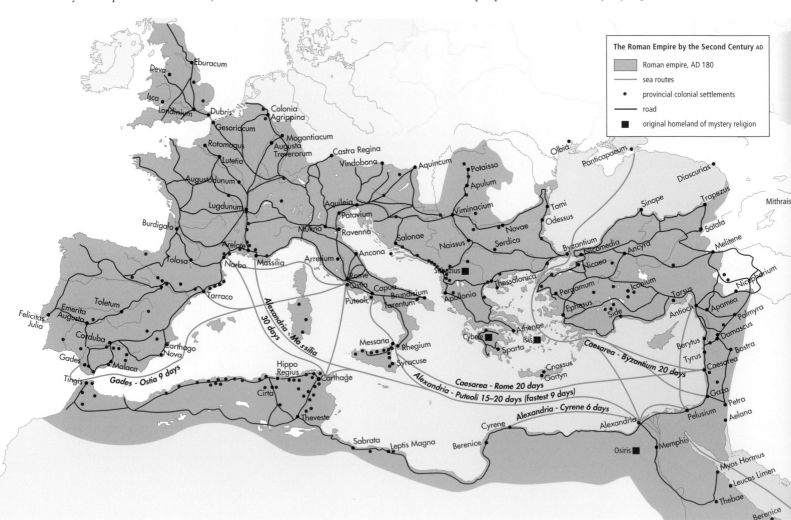

The Roman Empire by the Second Century AD

- Roman empire, AD 180
- sea routes
- • provincial colonial settlements
- ■ road
- ■ original homeland of mystery religion

facets of a single Romano-British deity. In North Africa, meanwhile, characteristics of the old Phoenician fertility god Baal-Hammon, renewer of all energies, were effectively grafted on to those of Jupiter, to produce a recognizably Roman deity, Jupiter-Ammon, whose particular characteristics were nevertheless appropriate to the traditions of a region on whose arid soils agricultural life had always been that much more precarious than they had ever been in Italy.

MITHRAS

Some gods and goddesses in subject lands succeeded in maintaining their independent existence: the Egyptian Isis, and her husband Osiris, for example. The latter's death each year clearly symbolized the death of the crops in the Nile Valley; the tears of the widow who restored him to life were the annual floods. At first an underground cult, confined to slaves, the worship of Isis had won a degree of official backing, and by the first century AD she had a prestigious temple in the heart of imperial Rome. By that time Mithras, the Persian god of light and truth, had won a wide unofficial following in the Roman army: a male-only cult, with tough initiation rites, it naturally

appealed to battle-hardened legionaries. Wherever the legions went, Mithras went too, the soldiers' guardian and guide: signs of his worship have been found in the very shadow of Hadrian's Wall.

The fort at Carrawburgh, Northumberland is one of five Mithraic shrines to have been found in Britain, and one of the best sources yet discovered of archeological insights into the workings of this secret devotion. Some 20 adherents seem to have gathered here at any one time, wearing masks to mark the level of initiation they had reached – those grades we know of are Raven, Lion, Soldier, Bride and Father. The ordeals endured by postulants hoping to progress from one grade to the next included everything from the binding of the hands with chicken intestines to the branding of the body with red-hot irons and even burial alive.

A second-century AD statue of Mithras sacrificing the bull. Mithras is one example of the influence of other civilizations on Roman gods and worship; he was originally a Persian god but the Roman army took him for their own and he became their mascot and their guardian.

RENDER UNTO CAESAR...

Roman tolerance was not, of course, unlimited: wherever native religions showed the potential for destabilization they were ruthlessly crushed, as the Druids were, for instance, in parts of Gaul. Denounced by later critics as a 'slave morality', Christianity's values of peace and forgiveness should have made it easy enough for the Roman Empire to absorb. This does seem to be the case: it was Jesus's misfortune that his mission on earth happened to coincide with a period of violent resistance in the province of Judaea. The chronicler Josephus, the only Roman author specifically to deal with Christ in his work, shows much more interest in the armed independence-struggle (and mass-crucifixion) of the Jewish Maccabees. Even afterwards, when Christ's followers did indeed suffer savage persecution, it was in the first instance a matter of political opportunism, the Emperor Nero needing to find a scapegoat for the disastrous fire that

destroyed much of his capital in AD 64. Only very slowly in the centuries that followed would Christianity's gospel of love come to be regarded as a serious threat to the mighty Roman Empire.

In 60 AD the Romans massacred the Druids of Anglesey, North Wales; peoples of many native religions were dealt with in this manner if the Romans thought they would undermine their authority.

NORTHERN EUROPE

Religion of the Landscape

Indigenous religion in northern Europe was based upon the activities of everyday life. The climate and landscape gave it its character, hunting and farming its deities and festivals. Focused on local cults and shrines, it was eventually overwhelmed by the better-organized Christian church.

Northern European Peoples

Offerings were cast into lakes and springs at certain times of year in thanksgiving or propitiation. Holy trees were protected by fences, and decked with garlands and ribbons. Sacred signs, images of gods and animals were carved on rocky outcrops; stopping-places along tracks and roads were marked by shrines to local gods as places of devotion for travellers.

Other holy places with no particular natural features have been marked by posts, images and temples. Cairns were generally erected where a sacrifice was made, or where a person had died. It was a sacred

Left: Northern European Peoples
With the decline of the Roman Empire the way was opened for expansion of the native northern Europeans. Germanic peoples spread northwards to Sweden and Norway and westwards into France. Later the marauding Viking Norsemen took this influence still further, expanding into Iceland and the British Isles and even on into the Mediterranean.

Loen Lake in Brigadal, *Norway*. Lakes were important sacred places in many pagan religions, and sometimes the site of sacrifices.

NORTHERN EUROPEAN religion is essentially polytheistic. Northern religion acknowledges spirit guardians of fields and flocks, earth spirits, water and tree sprites, spiritual protectors of travellers and seafarers, personifications of disease and death, and demons who bring bad luck. These are the innate spiritual qualities of places, expressed as guardian spirits or deities.

A SACRED LANDSCAPE

Religion in northern Europe is inextricably bound up with landscape, climate and the cycle of the seasons. The same features of landscape are sacred in the Celtic, Germanic, Slavic and Baltic traditions into which the main elements of northern European religion may conveniently be divided. They include hills and mountains, springs, rivers and lakes, special rocks and trees. Each have their particular marks of veneration. Mountains were ritually ascended on the holy days of the sky gods.

act to place a stone upon it with a prayer. From around the ninth century, labyrinths made of turf or stones were used in spring rites, weather-magic and ceremonies of the dead. Early Christian churches were built on such sacred places when the old religion was destroyed. There are 134 places in Brittany alone where Christian churches are built upon places of ancient worship.

Particular mountains were recognized as holy. Among the most notable are Mont Ventoux in Provence, the Celtic holy mountain of the winds; Helgafell in Iceland; Ríp in Bohemia, the place of the Czech ancestors; Horselberg, Wurmberg and Brocken in Germany; and the Polish holy mountains of Góra Kosciuszki, Lysa Góra, Radunia and Sobótka. Mountains dedicated to St Michael all over Europe were often formerly places of solar veneration.

RECORDS

Certain ancient texts, most notably the Irish *Dindsenchas* preserve landscape myths that date from pre-Christian times. The best record of landscape religion comes from Iceland. During the ninth and tenth centuries, the uninhabited island of Iceland was colonized by settlers from Norway and the Western Isles of Scotland. Their religious response to the landscape is recorded in *Landnámabók*. These settlers were acutely aware of the spiritual nature of places. Certain areas were not settled, being reserved for the *landvaettir* ('land wights') or spirits of place. Ceremonies were performed in honour of the *landvaettir*, and offerings left for them. More generally, prayers were directed towards Helgafell, the Icelandic holy mountain. Before praying, devotees first washed their faces out of respect.

The harbour at Heimaey, Iceland. The two volcanoes Eldfell and Helgafell, believed to be sacred to the Norse gods, can be seen in the background.

Heathendom is ... that they worship heathen gods, and the sun or moon, fire or rivers, water-wells or stones, or forest trees of any kind...

The Dooms of Canute, king of Denmark and England (1020–23).

SEASONAL FESTIVALS

Throughout northern Europe, religious festivals are linked with the seasons. The midwinter solstice, celebrating the increasing light after the longest night, is the major festival of the year. Celebrated with feasting and fires, disguise and games, it was the old Norse Yule, Slavic Kracun, and the Lithuanian Kucios and Kaledos. Most midwinter rites and ceremonies of the old religion were absorbed into Christmas.

In eastern Europe, the day on which the first thunder of the year was heard was sacred to the god Perun. Because hens begin to lay when days become longer than the nights, eggs are symbols of springtime. The oldest extant spring egg is from Wolin, Poland. Covered with marbled patterns, it dates from the tenth century. The Christian festival of Easter is named after the Germanic goddess of springtime, Eostre.

In Celtic religion, Beltane fires, sacred to the god of fire and light, Belenos, were kindled on May Day, and maypoles were erected. Midsummer was also commemorated by erecting poles and lighting fires. Harvest-time was the Anglo-Saxon festival of Lammas, the Celtic Lá Lúnasa celebrating the god Lugus. The ancestral dead were remembered in early November with festivals including the Celtic La Samhna and the Lithuanian Velines.

Celtic Religion

The Celts emerged as a powerful force in central Europe, later expanding to occupy the north-west. Acknowledging the divine in all things, their religion was influenced by Roman practices. The Druids are the best-remembered ancient priesthood of northern Europe, although they suffered persecution first by the Romans, then by the Christian Church.

DEFINED BY THEIR material culture, the Celts emerged as a recognizable group around the seventh century BC in Austria: the Hallstatt Culture. From the fifth century BC, the Greeks gave the name 'Keltoi' to the tribes of central Europe who raided their cities. During the late fifth century BC Celtic influences expanded westwards into what is now France and Spain, northwards to Britain and Ireland and eastwards through the Balkans into Asia Minor.

Early Celtic religion was aniconic (without images) and atectonic (without architectural settings). Celtic oral culture has left no ancient texts, and any information we have comes from contemporary Greek and Roman authors, in addition to archeology and later writings that put oral traditions in writing.

HOLY GROVES AND TEMENOI

Celtic holy groves (*nemetona*) were held in awe and approached only by members of the priesthood. The modern place-name element *nemet* or *nympton* denotes the former site of a holy grove. The goddesses Nemetona and Rigonemetis are named as protectors of groves. The *temenos* was the central place of collective worship for the continental Celts; it was an enclosure, defined by ditches, in which ceremonial gatherings took place and was generally square or rectangular. In central Europe the enclosures known as *viereckschanze* ('four-cornered fort') are Celtic *temenoi*, The *temenoi* contained aniconic or iconic images, sacred stones, ceremonial fireplaces, a tree or pole, wells and shafts for ritual offerings. Compressed earth at such places attests to ceremonial perambulation or dances around the central point.

IMAGES OF THE GODS

From the late sixth century BC, the Celts began to make anthropomorphic images from stone which were set up on burial mounds. Under the influence of Mediterranean culture, the Celts in

The Celts were head-hunters and, while human images are rare in Celtic art, the cult of the head had a special significance. They believed that the heads of those they had captured retained the spirit of the human and were seen as a source of wisdom.

the areas of present-day France, Germany and Switzerland adopted human form for their deities. Sacred buildings were introduced as the result of the influence of Roman religion and some 70 Celtic deities are named in surviving inscriptions from the Roman period.

Celtic Europe By 200 BC
The extent of the Celtic inhabitation of Europe is best identified through evidence of their material culture such as artefacts, burial sites, hillforts and settlements. The map shows their area of influence by 200 BC.

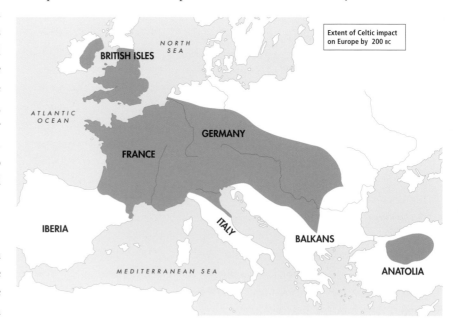

Extent of Celtic impact on Europe by 200 BC

NORTH SEA
BRITISH ISLES
ATLANTIC OCEAN
GERMANY
FRANCE
IBERIA
ITALY
BALKANS
ANATOLIA
MEDITERRANEAN SEA

A detail from the famous Gundestrup Cauldron, one of the finest Celtic relics to have been recovered in Europe. The detail shows the head of the god Cernunnos, whose name means 'the horned one'. Cernunnos was one of the lords of nature, animals and agriculture.

Julius Caesar stated that the Gauls considered Dis Pater, the lord of the underworld, to be their divine ancestor. In Ireland, the goddess Dana was the ancestress of certain tribes. The Celtic kings in Britain counted their descent from the divine couple Beli and Anna. Lugus, or Lugh, was the supreme god of the western Celts.

In Celtic regions under Roman rule, images and altars to Celtic deities bore inscriptions that reflected the *interpretatio Romana*. According to this, Lugus is equated with Mercury, Taranis, the Celtic god of thunder, with Jupiter, and Teutates, god of the tribe, with Mars. Gods of war, also assimilated with the Roman Mars, include Belutacadros, Cocidius, Corotiacus, Loucetius and Rigisamus. Ogmios, god of strength and eloquence, was equated with Hercules. Poeninus, god of mountain ranges, was also equated with Jupiter.

In common with other European traditions, the Celts acknowledged various gods of trades and crafts. Seafarers worshipped the sea-god called Manannan or Manawydden. Smiths had a god with a name close to the Irish Gobniu, Sucellos was god of vineyards and Rosmerta goddess of fruitfulness and financial gain.

A mythological representation of a Druid, one strata of the Celtic priesthood. Druidism was found only in Ireland, Britain and Gaul and these priests were responsible for the performance of religious ceremonies and ritual. Priests held the highest positions in Celtic society.

CELTIC PRIESTHOOD

The Celtic priesthood comprised the Bards, Vates and Druids, all of whom were restricted to Ireland, Gaul and Britain. The Bards were the genealogists, keepers of myth and song. Vates performed sacred divinations, whilst the Druids performed religious rites. The Roman author Lucan, in his *Pharsalia*, mentions the Gaulish Druids who lived in deep groves and remote woodlands. 'They worship the gods in the woods without using temples,' noted his commentator.

According to classical writers, the Druids, whose name meant 'men of the oak tree', were keepers of astronomical knowledge and regulators of the calendar. A first-century BC bronze calendar from Coligny in France, inscribed with Greek characters, is the only surviving example. Divided into 62 consecutive lunar months, it shows the main religious festivals of the Gallic year, with auspicious and inauspicious months. According to classical sources, the Druids taught the doctrine of transmigration of souls. In this belief, human souls at death enter into trees, rocks or animals, or newborn humans. Outside the Druidic order, each holy place had its own guardian, certain members of the family who owned the land. The office of dewar, keeper of sacred things, continued in Scotland and Ireland in a Christian context until the twentieth century.

Germanic Religion

Germanic religion was relatively uninfluenced by Rome. Spread to England in the sixth century AD, it was soon replaced by Christianity. In mainland Europe, it succumbed to the crusades of Charlemagne. It survived longer in Scandinavia, from whence it was re-exported to the British Isles by the Vikings, who also took it to Iceland and Greenland.

THE POLYTHEISTIC RELIGION of the Germanic peoples was centred upon the cult of the divine ancestor. In early times, the king's ancestor was also the tribal god, and this principle was maintained until well into Christian times. Seven out of eight Anglo-Saxon royal genealogies begin with Woden, as does the Swedish royal line. Folk meetings were held on moot hills, the burial mounds of ancestors, whose help was invoked in decision-making. Seeresess accompanied early Germanic rulers; they contacted the spirits of the ancestors by various divinatory techniques. From the fourth century AD, they used the runes – an alphabet derived from the Etruscans with religious significance, used in divination and sacred inscriptions – which were believed to come from Woden.

THE GERMANIC GODS

Germanic religion continued in Scandinavia until the tenth century AD, long after it had died out in England and Germany. The conversion of England began in AD 597, when the first Christian missionaries arrived in Kent and in AD 716 Boniface made his first trip to Germany. It was re-imported to parts of Britain (northern Scotland and eastern England) and to central Ireland by Viking and Danish settlers, although Christianity seemed to have survived the Viking raids, albeit with interruptions in Christian

A rune stone. Runes were used as written records by Germanic and Scandinavian peoples between the second and eleventh century AD, and were also believed to possess magical powers.

Settlements of the Germanic Peoples The Germanic peoples are classed as those peoples descended from the speakers of Proto-Germanic – the ancestor of German, as well as Dutch and Scandinavian. Germanic peoples shared a common culture and religion, which spread with them as they migrated.

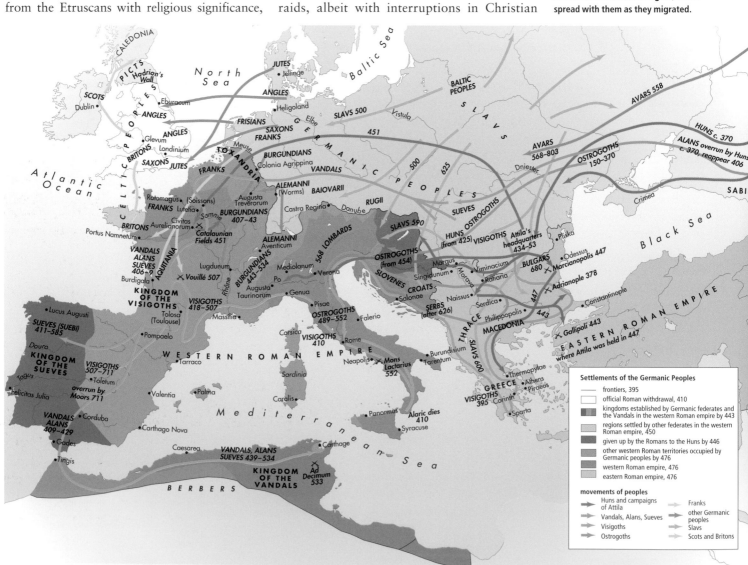

Settlements of the Germanic Peoples

- frontiers, 395
- official Roman withdrawal, 410
- kingdoms established by Germanic federates and the Vandals in the western Roman empire by 443
- regions settled by other federates in the western Roman empire, 450
- given up by the Romans to the Huns by 446
- other western Roman territories occupied by Germanic peoples by 476
- western Roman empire, 476
- eastern Roman empire, 476

movements of peoples
- Huns and campaigns of Attila
- Vandals, Alans, Sueves
- Visigoths
- Ostrogoths
- Franks
- other Germanic peoples
- Slavs
- Scots and Britons

NORDIC PRIESTHOOD AND TEMPLES

The office of Godi originated in the priest of a tribe or clan who held a certain sacred place in common. Godar were never full-time officials, but were rather horeditary landowners who had the duty to maintain ancestral holy places. In Iceland, the Godi in charge of the temple at Kialarnes, the direct descendent of the first settler, Ingulf Amarson, bore the title Alsherjargodi, or High Priest. In accordance with ancient tradition Iceland was divided into four quarters, each containing three jurisdictions, further subdivided into three Godord, each with its ruling Godi. The Icelandic law-making assembly (Lögrétta) was originally composed largely of Godar.

Norse temples were the personal property of the hereditary keeper of the land on which they stood. In Iceland, the *Höfud-hof* or public temples were sometimes owned by women. During the settlement period (ninth to tenth centuries AD), whole temples were shipped to Iceland. *Erbyggja Saga* tells of the Norwegian Godi Thórolf Mostrarskegg transporting his timber temple of Thor, complete with the sacred earth on which it stood. Some Norse shrines were dedicated to particular gods, such as the temple of the Black Thor at Dublin. Others housed many deities.

A Norwegian stave church dating from AD 1150. Churches such as these are believed to have been modelled on pagan temples, such those that were shipped from Norway to Iceland during the ninth and tenth centuries AD.

practice. In earlier times, the sky god Tîwaz was considered the chief deity. There is also evidence of an older, pre-agricultural pantheon, including the god Frey and the goddess Freyja, known in Scandinavia as the Vanir. In Anglo-Saxon England, Woden and Thunor were the major gods, whilst in Saxony, their counterparts, Wotan and Donar were venerated. Later, in Viking times, Odin (Woden) became pre-eminent, with the title Allfather. Thor (Thunor), god of the peasantry, was relegated to the status of son of Odin.

HOLY PLACES

The Germanic religious landscape was filled with sacred places. The Anglo-Saxon *Wih* was a holy image standing in the open. In Scandinavian practice, unsheltered images were protected by a fence of Hazel posts and ropes (the *Vébond*). More substantial was a shrine covered with a pavilion, the *Traef* or *Hørgr*. In Scandinavia and Scandinavian colonies, communal worship took place in the *Hof*, a hall-form farmhouse with a special extension, the *afhús*, where sacred objects and images were kept. Here, regular festivals were observed to mark the passing of the seasons.

There was a shrine in Saxony with a huge post called *Irminsul*, the 'universal pillar', which was destroyed by Charlemagne in AD 772. The shrines of the god Fosite, on the holy island of Heligoland, were destroyed in AD 785. In the Viking age, important temples of the Nordic gods stood at Jellinge in Denmark, Sigtuna and Gamla Uppsala in Sweden, Mæri, Lade, Skiringssal, Trondenes and Vatnsdal in Norway, Kialarnes in Iceland and Dublin in Ireland. Many Nordic temples contained images of more than one god, though some were dedicated to a single deity. At Gamla Uppsala, the Swedish royal centre, which emerged as the most important temple, there were images of Thor, Odin and Frey – the three chief gods.

Odin is called Allfather, for he is the father of the gods. He is also called Father of the Slain, for all who fall in battle are his adoptive sons. He gives them places in Valhalla...

Gylfagynning, Snorri Sturluson

Thor's hammer. In Norse religion Thor was one of the major gods in the pantheon, god of thunder and a protector of man and other gods. By Viking times Thor's position as a chief god had been usurped by Odin. Relics such as this have been found all over northern Europe and the hammer of Thor appears on protective amulets.

Slavic and Baltic Peoples

Slavic and Baltic religion followed the general pattern of the Celtic and Germanic traditions. Worship was conducted first in holy groves, and later in wooden temples served by priests and priestesses. In Lithuania, a state religion emerged in the thirteenth century whose remnants were still evident 300 years later.

THE SLAVS CAME into existence as a recognized ethnic group formed of the amalgamation of various tribes who came to occupy their territory in the sixth century AD. Their polytheistic religion continued long after the Christian church had taken over western and south-eastern Europe. In early times, the head of the family or clan officiated at religious ceremonies. From the eighth to ninth centuries onwards, a Slavic priesthood emerged. Rites formerly performed in open-air enclosures or groves were transferred to newly built temples. In Pomerania, there were three grades of priest. Central or provincial temples were officiated over by a high priest.

THE SLAVIC GODS

Byzantine chronicles of the sixth century AD mention the Slavic god Svarog, a god of fire and light, equating him with the Greek Hephaistos. His son, Dazbog, was paralleled with the sun-god Helios. Dazbog was brought into the pantheon of Kiev by Duke Vladimir in AD 980. As Svarozic (son of Svarog) the god Dazbog

was worshipped by the Elbe Slavs. In 1008 Bruno von Querfurt described his cult centre at Retra. Inside a castle with nine towers was a timber temple adorned with *aurochs* – horns bedecked with gold and jewels. Among others, the main image was of Svarozic, dressed in armour, with weapons. The temple was destroyed in 1068.

THE CULT OF PERUN

The thunder god Perun (Lithuanian Perkunas) was venerated throughout the Slavic and Baltic lands, in association with the weather- and wind-gods Erisvorsh, Varpulis and Dogoda. Perun is first mentioned in the seventh-century AD *Life of St Demetrios of Salonika*. In AD 980, an image of Perun with a silver head and a golden beard was set up by the side of the River Volchov at Kiev. At Perynj, near Novgorod, an eternal fire of oak branches was maintained in honour of Perun. Oak trees were sacred to Perun. In Poland, a holy oak was venerated at Czestochowa. In the tenth century, Russian devotees sacrificed chickens, made offerings of meat and bread,

Slavic farmyards had their own spirits; some were protective, some mischievous. This illustration depicts the *dvorovoi*, protector of people and animals on a farm. The dvorovoi was envisaged as an old man covered in hair; his realm was outside, and other spirits protected the hearth.

and shot arrows in honour of the god at a sacred oak on the holy island of Chortice in the river Dnieper.

LITHUANIAN STATE RELIGION

Lithuanian religion was formulated by Sventaragis in the sixth century AD, when the cult of Perkunas was established. All over Lithuania, on tracts of land called *alkos* sacred to the god, eternal fires were maintained by priestesses known as *vaidilutes*. Sventaragis established an ancestral centre in an oak grove at Vilnius, where the ancestors of the ruling dynasty were venerated.

During the early thirteenth century, in response to external threats, a polytheistic state religion was established by King Mindaugas. It amalgamated local cults, emphasized the worship of national heroes, practised cremation of the dead, and taught the doctrine of reincarnation. Until the early fifteenth century, Lithuanian royalty and noblemen were cremated in full regalia accompanied by their horses, dogs and falcons. As late as 1583, Jesuit monks visiting Lithuania reported that Perkunas was being worshipped at oak trees.

In addition to the Vilnius shrine, there was another important centre at Romuva (now in the Kaliningrad enclave of Russia), where, Peter von Duisburg records in 1326, a high priest, Kriviu Krivaitis, officiated. Whilst Perkunas was the major god, the Lithuanian pantheon contained many other deities, including the goddesses Zemyna (earth), Saule (sun), Gabija (fire), and Laima, goddess of individual destinies.

The oak was a tree sacred to Perun, the Slavic god of thunder, lightning and war. Perun was later re-embodied as Perkunas, an important Lithuanian deity. He, like Perun, was also worshipped at oak trees.

TEMPLES IN POMERANIA

Until 1123, when it was destroyed by Bishop Otto of Bamberg, a temple of Gerovit stood at Wolgast, a fortified holy island at the junction of three rivers in Pomerania. Until the same time, temples of Triglav existed at Wolin, Sezezin and the place that retains his name today, Trzyglów. The holy island of Rügen in the Baltic, settled by the Wends in the seventh century AD, contained two main temple enclosures, at Garz and Arkona. At Garz, an oaken image of the god Rugievit had seven heads and seven swords. A hereditary high priest who was the head of the ruling family officiated at the temple of Svantevit (Svarog) at Arkona. Svantevit was depicted in a multiple-headed image holding a horn. Comparable tenth-century images have been found in Poland in the Riavinski forest and the River Zbruc. The Rügen temples were destroyed in 1169 by Danish crusaders after fierce resistance from the men-at-arms dedicated to defend them.

In Vilnius ... Skirtnantas, the Lithuanian ruler, ordered vestals and priests to make offerings in honour of the gods and to the Great God Perkunas, who rules fire, thunder and lightning. Day and night, they were to feed the eternal flame with oak wood. If the fire ever went out, it was re-lit from sparks made with a great boulder.

The Lithuanian and Samogytian Chronicle

CENTRAL AND SOUTH AMERICA

The Maya

In what is now Mexico, the Maya dominated the lowland peninsula of the Yucatan highlands, Chiapas and most of Guatemala. There was never one unified theocracy but a number of aggressive city-states. The Maya favoured the arts and learning and pushed knowledge of astronomy and mathematics much further than any previous civilization in the Americas. They recorded much of their knowledge and beliefs by means of glyphs which, since their decipherment, have enabled us to know much more about their religion.

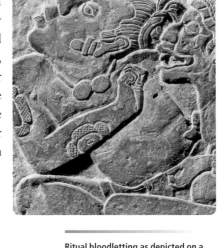

The Chacs appear in many forms in the Mayan area. This is a late classic mask at Chichen Itza.

The effects on the Mayan people of their huge pantheon of supernatural forces – deities, spiritual beings and essences, could in part be discerned or predicted by the use of their Calendars. The Tzolkin or divinatory calendar, consisted of a 260-day sacred round. Found exclusively in Mesoamerica, the calendar consisted of 13 numbers linked to 20 day names, each of which was a divine force: the first, Imix was linked to the earth monster.

All gods were endowed with a calendrical presence, some more directly than others: the Pahuatuns or wind deities (Ik in the calendar); the Chicchans, a giant snake (Chicchan); and the four Balams, jaguars who protected the cultivated fields (Ix). Also important were Exchel, the moon and the four Chacs or rain gods. (See also pages 84–85 on The Highland Maya Today.)

Ritual bloodletting as depicted on a relief at Palenque. Note the glyph on the arm of the figure to the left of the picture.

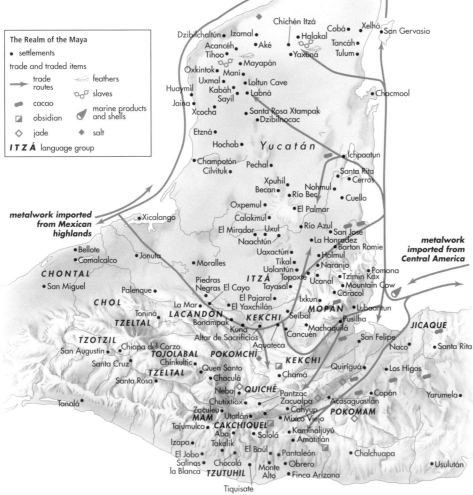

The Realm of the Maya
- • settlements

trade and traded items

→ trade routes	✐ feathers
◗ cacao	⚭ slaves
☑ obsidian	✦ marine products and shells
◇ jade	◆ salt

ITZÁ language group

Left: The Realm of the Maya
Like their neighbours, the Aztec, the Maya thrived on trade. This map shows the realm of the Maya, their settlements, their language groups and the items that they traded.

Right: A jade serpent recovered from a sacred well (or *cenote*) at Chichen Itza.

TIME LINE	
Olmecs	150–750 BC
Zapotecs	AD 300–600
Classic Maya	AD 300–900

MAYA COSMOLOGY

In Maya cosmology, seven layers extended above the earth ruled by the 13 deities of the Heavens: six marked the sun's ascent, six its descent and one its position at midday. Below the earth was Xibalba, the realm of the dead, consisting of four layers and ruled by the nine deities of the underworld, an unpleasant place of putrefaction and strong smells from which illnesses came. Each night, the sun passed through the underworld in the guise of a jaguar, descending through four layers before midnight, to ascend again (through four) to rise in the east. The underworld was linked to the heavens by a huge tree, the ceiba, which is still considered to be sacred in Mayan communities today. The tree marked the centre of the earth, distinguishing where the sun rose (our east and linked to the colour red) from where the sun set (west and linked to black). The north and south (or up and down) were simply known as sides of heaven and associated with white and yellow respectively.

The other, 365-day calendar was important for determining the dates of ritual. It consisted of 18 named months linked to 20 numbers (360) and a month of five days known as the Uayeb, whose days were considered particularly unpropitious. The 365-day calendar was based on astronomical calculations and intermeshed with the 260-day divinatory calendar. With the two calendars combined, an identically named day only occurred every 52 years, after which a new cycle began.

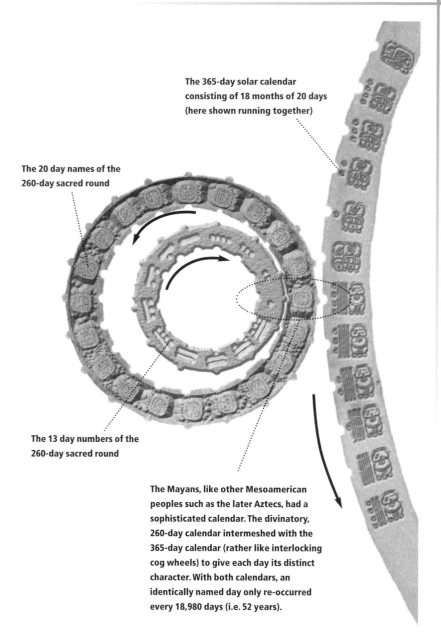

The 365-day solar calendar consisting of 18 months of 20 days (here shown running together)

The 20 day names of the 260-day sacred round

The 13 day numbers of the 260-day sacred round

The Mayans, like other Mesoamerican peoples such as the later Aztecs, had a sophisticated calendar. The divinatory, 260-day calendar intermeshed with the 365-day calendar (rather like interlocking cog wheels) to give each day its distinct character. With both calendars, an identically named day only re-occurred every 18,980 days (i.e. 52 years).

RECOVERING MAYA BELIEFS

It is the *Chilam Balam* and the *Popul Vue*, documents written after the Spanish Conquest, which began in 1517, plus the numerous depictions on pottery and sculpture, which tell us much of what we know about the Maya's beliefs, mythology and practices: such as those of the mythical hero-twins, Xbalanque and Hunapahu, sons of Hun Hunapahu (god of corn), who were monster slayers and ballplayers. More recently the decipherment of the Mayan hieroglyphic script has added detail which previously could only be guessed at.

Rituals were huge affairs, preceded by fasting, abstinence and ceremonial steam baths, accompanied by music, dancing and incense and attended by many. Autosacrifice was an important means of contacting the deities. By drawing a cord or piece of grass through the penis or the nose, and letting blood, visions could be induced, personified by the Vision Serpent. This was performed particularly by the king and his wife. Human sacrifice did occur, especially of war captives and occasionally of children, but not on a scale comparable to the Aztecs. Animals and birds were also offered, such as armadillos and parrots, and plants or plant products: copal, flowers, cacao, honey and the rubbery like *chichle*, from which chewing gum is made.

Deities varied from community to community as did the details of the calendars themselves. Both calendars are still to be found in use today, however, in many Mayan communities in the highlands of Guatemala, for divinatory purposes and to give shape to the ritual year.

The Aztecs

The Aztecs were an itinerant people who settled in the Valley of Mexico between AD 1200 and 1300. From humble beginnings they rose to become the dominant political force in Central America by the time of the Spanish arrival in 1519. Daily life was dominated by the sun, Tonatiuh, who by the time of the Aztecs (1350–1525) was often equated with Huitzilopochtli, their principal deity and also a god of war. He demanded to be fed by blood in order to keep rising, necessitating human sacrifice.

Above: Coatlicue, or 'She of the Serpent Skirt', was a terrifying female goddess with command over the earth, life and death.

W HAT WE KNOW of Aztec religion is primarily due to the accounts of those Spanish friars who, after the Aztec defeat, became interested in the beliefs and practices they were attempting to stamp out. The Aztec codices, folding screens books made from deer skin, give us details in a pictorial language while the sculptural forms can tell us what their deities looked like.

THE RISE OF THE LAST SUN

The Aztecs were the last of a number of different cultures that occupied the Central Mexican plateau and the most belligerent, although their expansionist empire lasted only a century. Huitzilopochtli owed his pre-eminence to the Chichimeca-Mexica tribal peoples whose deity he was. They had made Tenochtitlan (today Mexico City) their home in around AD 1325, after a long journey south from Aztlan during the fifth and final Sun, which was to bring earthquakes and famine.

THE COSMOS

According to myth, there had already been four previous Suns, each of which had been destroyed. But the last was a Sun of movement, such that some of the gods had even sacrificed themselves in order to keep it in motion. The world was believed to consist of a disc surrounded by water with 13 layers above and nine layers below. In the highest lived Ometeotl, the omnipotent supreme being, deity of duality both masculine and feminine, but who also lived in Mictlan, the underworld and peopled all the other layers. Ometeotl had four sons, the four Tezcatlipocas, (a name usually translated as 'Smoking Mirror') two of whom

The Aztec Empire to 1519
The Aztec relied heavily on trade and tributes for their livelihood. The map shows the major sites, settlements and trading routes of the Aztec Empire to 1519. The expansion of the Empire was also driven by the need to acquire captives for use as human sacrifices.

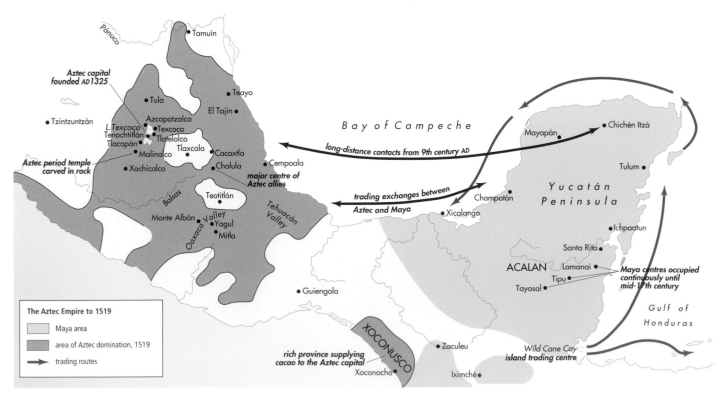

are sometimes known as Quetzalcoatl ('Plumed Serpent') and Huitzilopochtli ('Hummingbird on the Left').

Associated with the four early Suns, they were responsible for creating fire, a half sun and moon, water, other divine beings and the calendar. But it was the fifth Sun that completed the cosmos.

THE FESTIVALS

The Aztecs had two calendars, the Haab and the Tonalpohualli, but most of the large monthly religious festivals were related to the former, the 365-day cycle. Many were for agricultural matters and dedicated to Tlaloc and the Tlaloque (the deities of water and fertility), while others propitiated Huitzilopochtli, Tezcatlipoca or Xiuhtecuhtli (deity of fire), or female deities, such as the goddess of love, Xochiquetzal ('Precious Flower') or Coatlicue ('She of the Serpent Skirt').

These were lavish and costly affairs, at least in Tenochtitlan which was a large and sophisticated city, with 30 distinct classes of priests and priestesses, education for women, and slaves. The ceremonies were held in the open air and were attended by thousands, including the common people. During the preparatory days, the priests fasted (one meal per day) and observed prohibitions (on bathing and sex). An all-night vigil preceded the festival itself, which was usually of several days duration. Shrines were embowered and decorated with flowers, and offerings of food, clothing and rubber-spattered papers were made, accompanied by burning incense and libations. Through-out the festivities sacred songs were sung, music played and there was dancing.

Festivities in the countryside were simpler, more benign and often dedicated to local and feminine deities (such as Tonantzin, who represented the power of the earth). For although the Aztecs conquered a huge area and brought all the foreign deities into their pantheon in Tenochtitlan, they were unable to obliterate local customs.

Most pre-Christian practices were eradicated, with time, by the Spaniards but there are today groups in Mexico City who are disaffected with their lives and with globalization. Calling themselves the Mexica, they are attempting to reinvent Aztec religiosity.

Below left: The Aztecs were obsessive about pollution. Here, in a sixteenth-century codex, a baby is depicted as it is about to be immersed in water soon after the birth. The Spaniards assumed this rite was equivalent to baptism.

QUETZALCOATL

Although still part of the Aztec pantheon, Quetzalcoatl (as the plumed serpent) was of less significance than at the time of the earlier city-state of Teotihuacan (150 BC–AD 750 – see Time Line below), where he was revered as a feathered celestial dragon. For the later Toltecs (AD 900–1200), he became the patron of warriors and associated with the morning star.

Above: A stone bust showing Quetzalcoatl's head emerging in human form from the plumed coils of his serpent body.

THE SACRIFICES

Each festival had one or more processions which included those to be sacrificed, sometimes dressed up as deities (*ixiptla*), whom they impersonated for a day or two, living in luxury, before their hearts were cut out with an obsidian knife and offered up in ceremonial vessels and their flayed skins worn by male dancers. These were theatrical occasions with dramatic appeal

and a compelling political message: that the Aztecs were the servants of their deities. Often thousands of men and women were sacrificed, captives from neighbouring groups, their bodies allowed to fall down the steps from the top of the ceremonial pyramids, after which their heads were placed on the skull rack and their flesh cooked.

TIME LINE	
Teotihuacan	150 BC–AD 750
Toltecs	AD 900–1200
Aztecs	AD 1350–1525

The Incas

The Incas were originally a mountain culture, brought to the Cuzco Valley by legendary leader Manco Capac in 1200. They gradually established their dominance over other valley cultures, until at their height they incorporated much of Peru and Bolivia, and sections of Chile, Argentina and Ecuador. At the head of the empire was a divine monarch, who demanded a loyalty akin to slavery, but provided for all the needs of the people in return. Religion was organized in a similar fashion, with Viracocha, the supreme immanent deity, responsible for all the others. The most important religious ceremonies took place in Cuzco, the centre of the empire, for the Sun (Inti), his consort the Moon (Mama Qiya) and Ilyap'a (the thunder and weather deity).

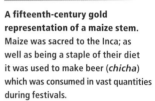

A fifteenth-century gold representation of a maize stem. Maize was sacred to the Inca; as well as being a staple of their diet it was used to make beer (*chicha*) which was consumed in vast quantities during festivals.

T HE CONSOLIDATION of the Inca empire had occurred (*c.* 1400) only a little over a century before its conquest by the Spanish in 1532, and covered parts of present-day Peru, Bolivia, Ecuador and Chile. Although Viracocha was considered to be omnipresent, this name was just one of the many attributions given to the deity before the arrival of the Spaniards.

THE INCA COSMOS

At the beginning of the cosmic cycle, Viracocha was associated with Lake Titicaca, out of which the sun, moon and stars emerged and ascended as gods. The numerous lesser deities were believed to have emanated from the caves, hills, springs and mountains, many taking animal (zoomorphic) or bird (avian) forms. The Quechua-speaking indigenous people today still associate their deities with these sacred locations known as *huacas*. Considered to be animate, they are imbued with supernatural power and mythic significance, and are usually marked by stones. Some are the tombs of ancestors, which contained their mummies during the time of the Inca empire. It was to the *huacas* that sacrifices of alpacas and llamas and sometimes children were made, linked to divination by ritual specialists. Mostly of regional significance, nonetheless travellers made and still make offerings of coca, *chicha* (beer), pieces of clothing or an additional stone, particularly during pilgrimages. The earth itself, known as Pachamama (the earth mother) has not only to be consulted, but also assuaged.

SACRED GEOGRAPHY

Conceptually, the Inca cosmos was divided into spheres linked together by Viracocha (as the cosmic river). This earth (*kaypacha*) was seen as an almost vertical domain, probably because of the immense physical diversity that characterizes the region – rising from sea level to high mountains in a very short distance.

Only east and west were named, where the sun rose and set while the country was seen to consist of four unequal ritual quarters, as was Cuzco itself. Radiating out from the Coricancha (the temple of the Sun in Cuzco) were *ceques* –

An Inca sacrifices a child at one of the sacred places known as a *huaca* and probably to Pachacamac, the male earth deity.

a series of some 41 conceptual lines along which still lie some 328 *huacas*.

The various parts of the empire were linked together by a network of roads along which messengers ran carrying *quipu*, bundled cords, from which hung dyed knotted strings. These were coding devices that could communicate information at a distance: the Incas lacked a written language which means that all of our information on their religious practices is post-conquest.

INCA HISTORY AND RITUAL

The first Inca (king) was Manco Capac, who was also seen as an androgynous founder ancestor. All subsequent Incas and their wives, (the Coyas) were also considered to be of divine descent: the Inca, the son of the sun; the Coya, the daughter of the moon. Their festivals were ordered according to a calendar based on the moon and stars and consisting of 12 months. They gave particular importance to the Milky Way, two of whose constellations were named as a baby and an adult llama. The Pleiades,

DIVINATION

As all illness was believed to be due to supernatural causes, divination was important for curing when amulets, plants, guinea-pig fat and parts of other animals were administered. For really serious illnesses or for taking important decisions, an oracle would be consulted such as at the Apurima *huaca*, where a tree trunk, had a 'gold band the thickness of one hand ...wrapped around it; this band had a pair of solid gold breasts on it' and was dressed in women's clothing 'of very fine gold and many ...large pins'. '...this post was covered in blood from the sacrifices that were made there.'

known as Qolqa ('the granary'), were particularly important for prognostication of agricultural fertility and many of the bigger ceremonies centred around the growth cycle.

Important rituals were held also at solstices. During the festival of Qapaq Raymi in December, as held in Cuzco, boys of royal descent were initiated and llamas sacrificed to the sun. The llama was sacred to the royal lineage. So, for the Ayriwa celebrations, in April, a perfect white llama was dressed in red with gold ear ornaments and taught to ingest coca and *chicha* and allowed to live. For other festivals, the llamas were less lucky and were usually sacrificed, sometimes in large numbers and usually accompanied by prayer, music, dancing and drinking.

By the time of Pachacutec, anthropomorphic statues had been made, such as that of Viracocha fashioned from gold and representing a young boy. Viracocha was also believed to be a culture hero and to travel throughout his dominions and according to myth disappeared across the ocean to the north-west.

Tiahuanaco: Gateway of the Sun. This solar deity has 19 ray-like projections coming from its head and it is holding two staffs which become condor heads at their bases. On either side are winged attendants with either avian or human heads.

Inca Empire
The Inca empire expanded rapidly in the fifteenth century. From Cuzco, the Inca emperor exerted rigid control over this extensive territory by means of a highly trained bureaucracy, a state religion, a powerful army and an advanced communications network. The final expansion under Huayna Capac put the Inca world under great strain, however, and by the arrival of the Spanish conqueror Pizarro, in 1533, civil war had split the empire in two.

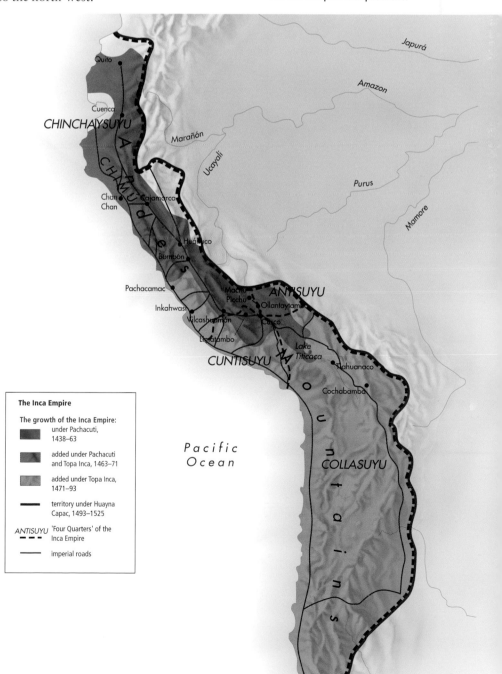

The Inca Empire

The growth of the Inca Empire:
- under Pachacuti, 1438–63
- added under Pachacuti and Topa Inca, 1463–71
- added under Topa Inca, 1471–93
- territory under Huayna Capac, 1493–1525
- *ANTISUYU* 'Four Quarters' of the Inca Empire
- imperial roads

Indigenous Religions

SHAMANISM

Shamanism

Shamanism is recognized as the world's oldest religious tradition, evolving before the Neolithic period (*c.* 8000–3000 BC) and the Bronze Age (2000–500 BC). It was originally practised among hunting and gathering societies of Siberia and Central Asia.

THE WORD *SAMAN* is derived from the Tungus people of Siberia, becoming *shaman* in Russian, and has been interpreted to mean 'he who knows' or 'one who is excited, moved, raised.' References to these figures include medicine men, sorcerers, magicians, necromancers, ascetics, healers, ecstatics, acrobats and Brahmans, but essentially the shaman is an indigenous practitioner whose expertise lies in entering a trance which enables his or her soul to travel to the upper and lower worlds of the spirits and demons. Alternatively, in mastering the spirits, the shaman will invite the spirits into him or herself. The shaman's journey through this altered state of consciousness is conducted in order to pass into the world of the spirits as a mediator for his tribe or people.

Shamanism is believed to have been present in most parts of the world, but it is known to have originated in Siberia. There is contention over whether seeds of shamanism arose naturally or were disseminated by means of trade routes, migration or oral traditions. It is plausible that most religions and cultures have acquired it or incorporated it through an innate human desire or inherent social need to communicate with the otherworld.

Shamans come into their roles for a variety of reasons. Often it is a question of inheritance, or they are something of a social misfit, or else they undergo an alteration in character. They may appear possessed and experience remarkable behavioural changes and neurosis. This is referred to as the Initiation Crisis. Generally, once initiated, these symptoms disappear and the shaman abandons his or her former life in submission to a new path. Women are as likely as men to be shamans. Essentially the shamans are in possession of a supernatural gift that is received from the spirit realm and the donor becomes the spiritual guide or spiritual 'spouse'. Shamans know initiation when they have an apparition of their guide, who will seemingly steal the soul and travel to another realm of the cosmos where the soul will perish, only to be reproduced and, in a sense, reborn into a new vocation.

THE ROOTS OF SHAMANISM

Siberia is the homeland of the shaman, where they have been an integral part of the culture of such peoples as the Tungus, the Mongols, the Samoyedes, the Inuits and the Altaians – from whom the term and definition 'shaman'

A pottery jar from the Mochica culture (located along the desert coast of Peru), representing a shaman; the image holds a wooden stick which was used to prepare the coca ball.

A shaman's soul catcher, from British Columbia. Once the shaman has gone into a trance he or she will journey to the spirit world and will there bargain for the return of lost human souls.

has originated. Siberian shamans have clearly distinguished between the realms of the cosmos, according it upper, middle and lower realms. Shamans can rescue souls from the lower realm of the cosmos, whilst attaining council from those in the heavens. Siberians also distinguish shamans as being 'black shamans' or 'white shamans'. The black shaman calls upon a wicked deity and the wicked spirit whilst shamanizing, whereas the white shaman applies to a benevolent deity and to good spirits.

SOUTH AMERICA

South American shamans are distinguishable by attaining mastery over the auxiliary spirits, through whom the shaman acquires poems, music, songs and chants. This music and verse is of prime importance to their power and their ability to shamanize. Some

SHAMANIC RITUAL AND PROPS

Shamanic rituals differ in all traditions, yet all share certain characteristics. These are associated with the trance-like state attained by the shaman in order to journey to the outer realms or to submit to possession by the otherworldly spirits. To coax the shaman into trance certain props are used. The most common of these is the shaman's costume which, when examined, reveals the core beliefs of shamanism, as any doctrine or myth might. The Siberian costume consisted of a caftan adorned with mythical animals and iron discs, used for protection whilst in combat with the spirits. A mask is a very common feature sported by the shaman. Often grotesque and extraordinary, with extravagant colour and awesome designs, it allows the shamans to be transported, disguising them from their peers. Often the shaman is blindfolded and so journeys by an inner light, isolated from the outer reality. Animal skin, fur, feathers, bones, bells, a staff, a crown or cap and staves make up the shaman's regalia. During the ritual, the shaman will induce violent breathing, may shake or sweat furiously, and may dance in a wild, frenetic manner, aided always by the constant and climactic beating of the drum.

South American shamans are also known to use hallucinogens, psychotropic plants and tobacco whilst shamanizing.

In Peru and Native Amazonia, shamans acquired their powers from nature spirits of plants and animals, or from deceased shamans or mestizo, aided by periods of isolation and starvation. During the initiation period, psychotropic plants are ingested at specific times, whilst a strict diet and celibacy are observed. The plants are alleged to teach the shamans how to overcome the evil spirits of the earth, waters and air, and how to journey within the cosmos.

No one enters uninitiated into the sea of mysteries. It is necessary that his spiritual senses be attuned, that they may grasp the spiritual tones and spiritual forms and colours.

Ph. Kontuglou

Shaman in Nepal dressed in full shamanic regalia entering a trance aided by the sound of the flutes. The shaman will frequently wear a mask to aid the inner journey and will dance wildly to the beat of a drum.

OCEANIA

Death, Ghosts and the Soul

The collection of islands in the Pacific Ocean and East Indies known as Oceania was colonized by hunters from Southeast Asia around 30,000 years ago. From this time a belief system developed that is still practised today. The belief in ghosts, as a projection of the life-force of a person, is central to spiritual thought throughout Oceania and has in fact become fused with Christianity rather than pushed away by it. The acceptance of Christian religion has not caused the demise of two of the important aspects of Oceanic traditional religion: ghosts and sorcery.

THE SPIRITUAL RESIDUE of a person after life has departed the body takes the form of a ghost – a *masalai* in the New Guinea Tokpisin language. These ghosts share the same life space with the community of living persons and constantly intrude, usually undesirably, in the affairs of the living. Men (it is only men who deal with ghosts in most of Melanesia) attempt both to placate the ghosts and to appropriate their special powers – to find lost objects; to foretell the future, to interpret dreams – for their own purposes.

THE FOI

The Foi inhabit the Mubi River Valley in the Southern Highlands Province, a long and somewhat narrow valley which runs from northwest to southeast. The Mubi River and all its smaller tributaries flow in this direction. The

Foi do not speak of 'west' or 'east', but rather 'upstream' and 'downstream' as their main cardinal axis. The other dimensions they refer to are 'above', for places higher in altitude, and 'below', for places lower in altitude.

The afterworld in Foi is a place called *haisureri*, sometimes translated by the Foi as 'white sand'. It is conceived as a beautiful region with fine sandy banks that lies far downstream, beyond the valley and beyond the places that the Foi traditionally knew of in pre-colonial times. They believe that when people die their souls travel downstream until they reach this place, and in *haisureri* they continue to live, eat the special ghosts' food that grows only there, and carry on in a caricature of living society.

Upstream, by contrast, is the source of all water and the source of all life – they sometimes refer to the distant west as *me ga kore*, (the 'place-

The Foi and the Daribi
The Foi inhabit the Mubi River Valley in the Southern Highlands Province of Papua New Guinea, and the Daribi inhabit the southern part of the Simbu Province around Mount Karimui.

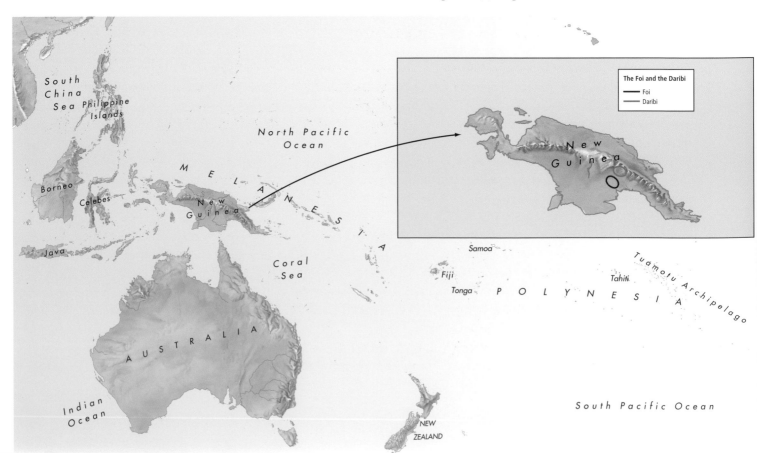

It is not just the flow of water and digestion that are modelled by these macrocosmic orientations, but also the moral direction of the flow of social energy. By stipulating that men and women should inhabit distinct spatial zones, a visible flow – of food, sexual fluids, children – is set up between them. Pearl shells, which are given by men to other men in exchange for women as brides, govern the marital destinies of women and men, and thus also flow in similar mythical directions.

Left: The Foi people of the Mubi River Valley believe that the afterlife is enjoyed in an idyllic region known as *haisureri*. For the Foi this is a physical place that exists just beyond the realms of the lands they knew and inhabited in ancient times.

source-upstream'), and it is the direction from which pearl shells are thought to have originated, as well as certain brightly coloured shrubs and flowers associated with pearl-shell magic.

THE DARIBI

The Daribi inhabit the southern part of Simbu Province around Mount Karimui. Their macrocosm is similarly oriented by the flow of the Tua River, only in this case it flows from east to west, thus paralleling the movement of the sun. It is interesting to note that in the cases of the Foi and Daribi it is the movement of water that is the primary orienting movement, and movement of the sun, by contrast, is interpreted accordingly. Thus, for the Foi, the sunset is associated with the origin and source of water and has connotations of vitality and life. The red of a flamboyant sunset reminds them of the red paint that young men and women wear at dances, a time when flirtation, sexual play and marriage proposals are approved of. It also, of course, reminds them of the red colour of pearl shells.

A modern Oceanic festival in traditional dress. For the Daribi peoples, festivals and ceremonies such as these become a form of mating ritual and flirting where sexual interaction between men and women is encouraged.

THE DARIBI LONGHOUSE

The Daribi longhouse is oriented with the front of it facing east so that the rising sun may shine through the front door. This is considered the 'face' of the house, and is the only end provided with a ladder for entrance – all coming and going is through the front door. The back door, by contrast, is used to throw rubbish and food remains out, and is also used as a latrine by the men and women.

Thus, the Daribi longhouse is a miniature or microcosmic version of the more encompassing world space or macrocosm. The analogy of the longhouse is that of the human digestive tract, in which food and other materials enter from one end and excretion takes place out the other. Men live in the direction of the sunrise while women live in the direction of the sunset, the place where water and ghosts go. For the Daribi the sunset means just the opposite to that of the Foi: it is associated with death and the place the ghosts go, for ghosts follow the direction of water in both the Foi and Daribi traditions.

Unlike the Foi, both Daribi men and women live in the longhouse, which is divided into male and female areas: men live in the 'east' or 'front' section, while women live in the 'rear' or 'west' section. East also means 'higher' in Daribi, as 'west' means 'lower' or below; some Daribi longhouses are constructed of two stories, in which case the men sleep in the upper half.

The Mythic Chieftainship

Unlike most interior New Guinea societies, in island Melanesia, as in Polynesia, the institution of chieftainship is a central social and cultural institution. The chief has certain religious and ritual responsibilities and partakes of a certain divinity himself. He is the incarnation of certain deities, as in Hawai'i, or of the totem, as in New Caledonia.

POLYNESIAN SOCIETIES IN general are hierarchical, usually with a chiefly ruling class, commoners, and a lower or slave class. As well as the king being of divine origin, the head of a family also mediated the divine realm. This function was increasingly taken over by a class of priests. There is much variation in the region as to how separate were the roles of chief and priest and the kinds of secular power they exerted.

CHIEFLY POWER

The primary concern of religion was protection of the people – individual and group – from divine malevolence. Strict adherence to laws and procedures was necessary to keep the divine and physical worlds in harmony. The main functions of priests were the foretelling of events through divine intercession, and leading ceremonies to ensure the conventional stability of society.

A statue of the Avatea of Rurutu, the original eastern Polynesian creator God. Eastern Polynesia shared many beliefs and practices with South America, including many of their gods, fertility rites and the practice of human sacrifice.

The death of Captain James Cook at Kealakekua Bay, Hawaii, as depicted by John Cleveley the Younger (1747–86). On his arrival in Hawaii, the inhabitants venerated Cook as an incarnation of their fertility god, Lono. Cook had arrived at the end of the Makahiki festival, and circled the island in a clockwise direction, just as local legend predicted that Lono would. He ushered in the period of Lono's ascendancy on leaving the island, by departing in the correct anti-clockwise direction. However, on his return he inadvertently snubbed Hawaiian cosmic protocol by arriving in the wrong direction, angering the islanders and causing his death.

All chiefly power in Polynesia is made possible by divine power. In the Marquesas, the birth of a firstborn is referred to as the epiphany of a god, according to the anthropologist Douglas Oliver. It has also been reported that Marquesans believed that the firstborn was sired by an ancestral divinity.

THE SACRED KING

In Tonga, the sacred king is known as the Tu'i Tonga. He was the main mediator between the realm of the human and that of the divine, and is said to have descended from the sky. In the myth, the first Tu'i Tonga was Aho'eitu. He was the son of the earth-mother Ilaheva, who was made pregnant by Eitumatupu'a, the sky god, who then went back to his heavenly realm. As a small boy the son goes to heaven to find his father. When the god sees his son, he falls to the ground, so overwhelmed is he by his son's beauty. Later, Aho'eitu defeats his older brothers, who in revenge, kill him and eat his body. The god father, however, forces them to regurgitate the body, which he god then brings back to life and sends to earth to be the first Tu'i Tonga.

Stone petrolgyphs in Hawai'i were important ritual anchors between the surface world and the divine sky realm. Hawai'ian shrines, called *heiau*, were often built upon a sacred foundation of stones. One such place is Kukaniloko. When Kukaniloko was used as an ancient birthing place, there was a large stone that presumably held the mother up in a sitting position. A chief was required to stand before each woman. The child born would be called 'a chief divine; a burning fire'. The name Kukaniloko itself means 'an inland area from which great events are heralded'.

A statue of the Hawai'ian war god **Lu**, which would once have adorned a temple on the island. Wood carvings such as this was the most common form of representation in mythology and religion of the area.

HAWAI'IAN GODS

Humans and gods would compete over the power to reproduce themselves. La'ila'i is the older sister of both god and human and is also the firstborn. Her brothers, sometimes described as twins, are Ki'i (a man) and Kane (a god). She weds both of them, giving birth to both the line of humans and of gods, though the children of Kane are senior to those of Ki'i. As the generations succeed each other, the line of men repeatedly marry back into the line of gods, according to the Kumulipo chant.

In Hawai'i, the time of the god Lono begins with the winter rainy season, the period when all things planted bear fruit. Lono is the god of regeneration and fertility, while Ku is the god of war and sacrifice. This generative power is maintained at the expense of its opposite, the power of war, which is the province of the god Ku, whose temple rituals are suspended during this period. After Lono departs, the king had to re-sanctify the temples of Ku by means of human sacrifices.

It is said that Lono, as part of the general fertility he brings, descends from heaven to mate with a beautiful woman. Thus, when Captain Cook arrived, from the proper direction, at Hawai'i at the time of Lono, it was thought he was the god. The Hawai'ian women paddled out to meet him and his crew, eager to mate with the gods in the hope of bearing a sacred child who would be chief.

Millenarian Movements

Cargo cult is the label given to a series of millenarian and apocalyptic movements that arose in many South Pacific islands following European colonization. What these cults have in common is a perception of the magical source of western material wealth and the Pacific islanders' attempt to recreate that magical procedure so as to attain the wealth themselves.

THE CARGO CULT in Melanesia was in many respects an 'inverted anthropology' – it was the attempt by Melanesian people to analyze the source and substance of the western material world in terms of their own magical and spiritual cosmos, and efforts were expended to obtain access to this world by means of their own 'magical technology'. They saw acceptance of Christianity as the Europeans' ritual means of obtaining the cargo. This approach still remains fundamental to many Melanesians' responses to governance and economic issues of today, although the cargo cults as such have become institutionalized and 'routinized' to a large extent.

THE VAILALA MADNESS

In 1919, on the south coast of Papua New Guinea, one of the most dramatic of the Melanesian cargo cults started. The ancestral spirits communicated to certain men that western 'cargo' or material goods would be arriving by aeroplane. People abandoned their gardens and engaged in frenzied acts of spirit possession. This was called 'The Vailala Madness' by the anthropologist F. E. Williams. For the next 10 years the British colonial administration imprisoned all men who took leadership roles in inciting hallucinatory activity and by 1931, the cult had died out.

Left and right: Illustrations showing a wooden temple relief carving and dance masks from Melanesia. Sculptures and masks were decorated to intensify their spiritual power, and were often in the image of an ancestral spirit.

New Oceanic Cults
The twentieth century witnessed the rise of many new religious cults in areas of Oceania. The extreme and sometimes bizarre nature of some of these movements had led to them being given the label 'cargo cults', although this is now seen as a derogatory term. Most proved to be short-lived. The map shows the areas in which these new cults arose, alongside the traditional tribal settlements of the area.

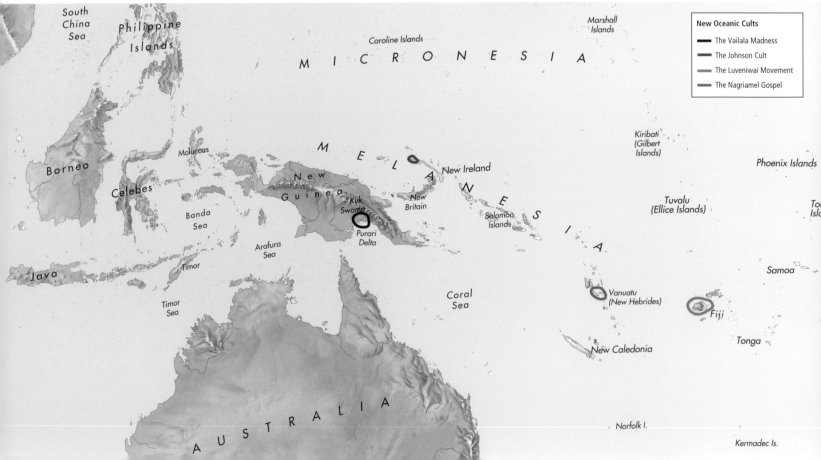

New Oceanic Cults
— The Vailala Madness
— The Johnson Cult
— The Luveniwai Movement
— The Nagriamel Gospel

THE NAGRIAMEL GOSPEL

In the New Hebrides (now Vanuatu) in 1966, Jimmy Stephens became a prophet and called his reform movement Nagriamel – which was a symbol for the restoration of traditional custom. On the island of Espiritu Santo, Stephens and his followers spread the Nagriamel gospel, which aimed to recover land that had been appropriated by the Europeans. He continued to be an important political presence well after the independence of Vanuatu, but was eventually imprisoned.

THE LUVENIWAI MOVEMENT

In Fiji, a secret society arose towards the end of the nineteenth century. The movement focused on the class of indigenous spirit beings called *luveniwai* ('children of the water'). These were small elves or dwarfs that lived in areas of waterfalls and dense jungle. Many people believed they were spirits of abandoned infants. The Luveniwai Movement attested that each person could have a personal guardian spirit of the forest – they met in secret clearings in the forest, drank kava and performed ceremonies. The movement eventually attracted the attention of the colonial government when people involved refused to work and ordained it illegal.

THE JOHNSON CULT

One of the most bizarre of the cults was the so-called Johnson Cult of New Hanover in Papua New Guinea. In 1933, the people of the island petitioned for independence, demanding repatriation of foreign-owned plantations. In 1964, when the first elections were held in Papua New Guinea, the people of New Hanover became persuaded that the then US president, Lyndon Johnson, would be the person to lead them to a better government. They collected a large amount of money in shilling coins and gave this to the local Catholic missionary with instructions to send the money to President Johnson to cover his travelling costs to New Hanover. The money was returned to them, but their desire to install President Johnson as their leader continued for some time after that.

NEW MEN

In the Purari Delta of Papua New Guinea's south coast, there arose after the Second World War the movement of 'New Men' led by Tommy Kabu. Like Yali of Madang District, Tommy Kabu served in New Guinea during the war and saw something of Australia during the war years. When he returned to the Purari Delta, he started a movement that advocated destruction of traditional religion, the wholesale adoption of Christianity, and the reformulation of local society on a business cooperative basis. He and his followers also rejected the colonial administration of their area, preferring to form their own police force and build their own jails. Tommy Kabu himself was impressed with the administrative detail of western life; he built his own 'office' which he littered with printed papers of all kinds, including copies of articles from Reader's Digest, to create the impression of official administrative functioning. The New Men were to embark on western-style business ventures, to market sago and copra to Port Moresby. However, because of their lack of understanding of real business fundamentals, and the formidable resistance of the social system to western-style individualism, these ventures failed. By the mid-1950s, although the first steps had been taken, the people of the Purari River Delta had only succeeded in introducing destructive influences into their traditional cult life.

AUSTRALIAN ABORIGINALS

The Dreaming

The most distinctive concept of Australian Aboriginal religion is that of the 'dreaming' or, as it used to be called, the 'dreamtime'. This refers to a primordial creative period when ancestor beings roamed the land, in various human and animal forms, creating the landscape and the species of the earth as humans find them in the present day.

I N THE CENTRE of Australia and the Great Victoria Desert, the term for the creative period when the earth and all its contents were first made by the ancestors, is *djugurba*. Not only was it the initial form-creating period of the world, but its creative powers exist to the present day. The ancestors continue to exert their form-making powers, and it is up to humans to detect this power and tap into it for their own purposes. The word 'dream' is highlighted, as many Aboriginal people say that ancestors and ancestral power often reveal themselves in dreams. There is much less discontinuity between the waking life and the dream life in terms of everyday meaning and significance for Aboriginal persons, although of course Aboriginal people know the difference between the real world and the dream world.

CREATION MYTHS

Most of the major Australian creation myths detail the wanderings of mythical beings. They moved from place to place, creating waterholes, rocks, creatures, landscape features, and also giving these things their names. The pathway of a single creator being or a single route of travel is

A female figure, which can represent different sacred beings in different aboriginal tribes. In aboriginal religion and mythology many creatures can be either male or female, such as the rainbow serpent.

Aboriginal Australia
When Europeans first began to settle in Australia towards the end of the eighteenth century there were already 300,000 people on the continent. As the frontier was pushed forward, the competition for land and water became fierce. The native population began to decline almost immediately. Since the 1970s, however, large tracts of land have been returned to the aboriginals and the aboriginal population is now estimated at around 350,000.

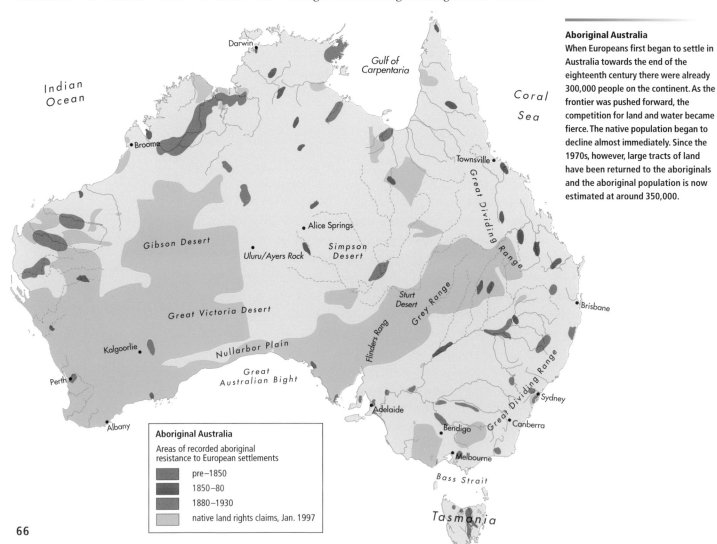

Darwin
Gulf of Carpentaria
Indian Ocean
Coral Sea
Broome
Townsville
Great Dividing Range
Alice Springs
Gibson Desert
Simpson Desert
Uluru/Ayers Rock
Great Victoria Desert
Sturt Desert
Grey Range
Flinders Rang
Brisbane
Kalgoorlie
Nullarbor Plain
Great Australian Bight
Great Dividing Range
Perth
Sydney
Adelaide
Canberra
Albany
Bendigo
Melbourne
Bass Strait
Tasmania

Aboriginal Australia
Areas of recorded aboriginal resistance to European settlements

- pre–1850
- 1850–80
- 1880–1930
- native land rights claims, Jan. 1997

called a dreaming track. These can be very long and can connect dozens of groups literally across the breadth of the continent. The tracks criss-cross Australia and thus provide a network for religious and social communication between groups at very great distances from one another.

The dreaming track is a single thing and can be said to have a beginning and an end. But because different Aboriginal groups occupy only restricted portions of the route, they only 'own' part of the myth and its associated ritual. This creates the condition under which different groups come together to perform their own special segments of the total myth, although because of the length of the tracks, it could never

be performed as a complete ritual performance. Thus, in a certain important sense, traditional Aboriginal groups of Australia were only parts of a larger mythological whole which they could infer but the extent of which they did not know.

SUPREME BEINGS

In south-east Australia, there is the widespread belief in a supreme being, a male 'All-Father'. He is called Ngurunderi among the Ngarrindjeri of the Lower Murray, South Australia, Baiami among the Wiradjuri of New South Wales and Victoria, and the Kamilaroi of New South Wales and Queensland. In the Lower Murray, Ngurunderi travelled along the south coast, creating the contours of the coastline and the mouth of the Murray River. Pursuing his two wives who had fled, he caught up with them around Cape Willoughby and caused the sea to rise, drowning them. They turned into the Pages Islands there.

The Rainbow Serpent is also a widespread figure across Aboriginal Australia. It is always associated with rain or water and is often said to inhabit deep water holes. Around Ayers Rock (Uluru) it is called *wanambi* and is regarded as very dangerous and is treated with great circumspection by local Aboriginal people.

FERTILITY

Bolung among the Dalabon of the Northern Territory refers explicitly to the rainbow. The Dalabon believe that if a woman is to conceive, she must be entered by a rainbow snake, and that after death the performance of the proper ceremonies will transform a person's spirit back into its rainbow-snake form. *Bolung* as an adjective, however, means anything that had creative, transformative power in the Dreaming period.

In Western Australia, a similar idea is contained in the notion of *ungud*. *Ungud*, is a property of the *wandjina* paintings found in caves of Western Australia. These paintings show beings with no mouths and often no bodies. The *wandjina* are the creative spirits that made the land and its features. *Ungud* is the creative power that made the *wandjina*

powerful. The *wandjina* have the power to make babies and ensure the coming of the wet season and the flourishing of edible plants and animals.

In the Pilbara region of Western Australia, south of Kimberly, early reporters mentioned the concept of *tarlow* – a pile of stones or a single stone set apart to mark some spot of particular fertile power, the power to make things increase and multiply. Among the Karadjieri of Western Australia, there are centres of ritual that belong to all-important plant and animal species, upon which increase rites are performed. The performance of these rites thus keeps Dreaming power alive in the present.

A painting of a *wandjina* found in a cave in Western Australia. *Wandjina* are clan spirit beings, named creator figures, each of whom is responsible for forming a part of the landscape. It is believed that when a *wandjina's* work was completed, he or she would enter a cave, lie down and die. Cave paintings such as this are believed to be the literal incarnation of these ancestral beings.

Initiation

The initiation of boys was and still is one of the central ritual events of the community, especially in central Australia. Both circumcision and sub-incision of the male genitalia were practised over a considerable area of interior Australia. As well as this, the focus was on the training of boys in the sacred mythology and ritual of their group.

I N THE WESTERN desert, there are four main stages to initiation. First, the initiate is taken from the care of his female kinsmen. He is then painted with older men's blood and then with red ochre. After this, he is isolated with the other initiates for up to a year. In the second stage, fire is thrown over the heads of the novices. Older men take blood from their arms and use it to fasten bird feathers down in the shape of sacred totemic designs. In the third stage, the circumcision of the novices is performed and they are taken back into the seclusion camp to heal and to be shown the sacred bullroarers (oblong pieces of wood inscribed with sacred designs; the noise they make when swung over the head is believed to be the voice of the ancestor). Later on they are returned to the camp where their arrival is celebrated by their relatives. The novices are taken on to their country and instructed in their territorial mythology. After this, the novices may be sub-incised, a process whereby an incision is made in the underside of the urethra. In the last stage, the novices receive their cicatrizations – scars made on the initiate's back which leave a permanent raised weal of flesh on the body. At this point the young men are considered fully initiated and may participate in a range of rituals and ceremonies performed by men.

A carved aboriginal ancestor board. The cult of the ancestor features large in aboriginal religion. Native Australians believe that the bodies of ancestral creator beings become detached from the spirit and fixed in the landscape.

An Australian aboriginal elder. Human first settled in Australia when the land was joined to what is now Indonesia and Papua New Guinea probably around 40,000 years ago. Australian religious traditions have been passed down through the generations and survive today in areas of native settlement.

CIRCUMCISION AND SCARIFICATION

In eastern Arnhem Land, the boys who are being prepared for circumcision are told that the mythical python Yurlunggor has smelled their foreskins and is coming to swallow them, as he swallowed the mythical Wawilak sisters in the myth. The novices are also smeared with ochre during the *djunggawon* initiation cycle, which stands for the blood of the Wawilak sisters in the myth. In the Kunapipi (Gunabibi) initiation, men let blood from their arms fall upon the sacred trench dug in the ground – again, this is supposed to represent the Wawilak sisters' blood.

Sub-incision is practised in the Great Victoria Desert, northern South Australia and central Australia. In these areas, the wound is subsequently opened up in certain ritual contexts, so that blood may flow from the man's genitals on to his legs during dancing.

Scarification of the body was also practised extensively throughout Australia, particularly in Queensland. Parallel scars were made on the chests of initiated men among the Butchulla and Kabi Kabi of the Wide Bay Coast of central Queensland as late as the twentieth century. Among the Dieri of Northern Australia cicatrizations are common.

Aboriginal women body painting in Alice Springs, Northern Territory. Body art is said to convey a religious status upon the wearer, and is part of the tradition for reciting the dreamtime mythology through the use of iconographic symbols.

THE WAWILAK MYTH

The Wawilak myth is central to the Australian Creation. At the beginning of time, it is said, the Wawilak sisters travelled north from their home in central Australia towards the sea. As they travelled they named places, animals and plants, and dug holes in the ground from which water sprang. On their journey they stopped near a waterhole in which Yurlunggor, the great python, lived. It was here that one of the sisters (the eldest) polluted the waterhole with her menstrual blood. Yurlunggor was angry and emerged from the waterhole, commanding a great flood and heavy rains. The water covered the whole earth and everything on it. The flood receded as Yurlunggor descended back into the waterhole.

MAORI

Maori Religion

Maori are the indigenous people of Aotearoa (New Zealand). They name themselves *tangata whenua* ('people of the land' or 'locals'). Maori often say that they are very spiritual people. Although many Maori identify themselves as Christians, Baha'is, Rastafarians or as members of other religions, there is a sense in which these religions are added to an omnipresent and traditional Maori spirituality that informs much of contemporary Maori culture.

MAORI SPIRITUALITY IS centrally concerned with relationships between people, and between them and the land. It is about genealogy, family and neighbourliness, and it is about the importance of particular locations and what takes place there. These concerns underlie the highly respected arts of oratory and carving that are especially evident in Maori gatherings of various sorts. Such arts and encounters engage the dynamics of *mana* and *tapu*, and involve a wide community of human and other-than-human persons. All of this (and much more) comes together when Maori meet guests on *marae* (sacred spaces) and their associated buildings: *wharenui* (meeting-houses), and *wharekai* (dining-halls).

MANA

Traditionally, when a child is born its placenta is buried in the family's land, and establishes the child's rights in that place, its *turangawaewae* ('standing place'). Throughout life each person is encouraged to exercise their rights not only in living in a place, but also in acts that unfold inherent potential and increase the prestige of the family and place. Everything and everyone is understood to have an essence, *mauri*. As people develop their abilities and realise their potential, they increase in *mana* (charisma or the authoritative prestige of gifted people). Some people, places or things have more *mana* than others – they are more gifted, valued or powerful. Encounters between different strengths or kinds of *mana* are potentially fraught, if not dangerous: whose prestige is greater? How will one strength affect the other? Should one skilful ability come into contact with another? Especially difficult are encounters between different tribes, or between Maori and other peoples. These encounters are therefore controlled by social restrictions, *tapu*, a word widely known in its wider Polynesian form *tabu*. Sometimes *tapu* involves keeping *mana*-full things or people separate, establishing a place and clear boundaries for every activity. However, when it is necessary to bring two *mana* together there are careful protocols and procedures that negotiate the boundaries and establish new relationships.

The religion of native New Zealanders – Maori – is complex. While ancient traditions and mythologies have been passed down through generations, today many Maori regard themselves as Christians, Baha'is or Rastafarians.

The carvings on the inside of the meeting house depict the ancestors of Ngapuhi tribe, Hineamaru and Rahiri and the wall carvings tell ancestral stories.

MARAE

When hosts receive visitors they typically do so on the *marae*, an open space in which potential becomes apparent as different *mana* encounter one another. The local hosts greet visitors, recognize their *mana* and that of their ancestors (who are ever-present with the current generation), but also insist on the pre-eminent *mana*, prestige, of local ancestors and community. By various ceremonies the visitors are brought into the *marae* space and their potential friendship is established rather than their potential hostility. The gifts of oratory are demonstrated in speeches made and received by hosts and guests. These refer to aspects of traditional knowledge (*korero tahito*) that demonstrate respect to both parties. Local ancestors are also present in the form of more-or-less elaborately carved meeting houses (*wharenui*): their arms outstretched in welcome of visitors, their spine supporting the roof that shelters those currently alive and making space for further talking and decision-making.

Illustrations from 1847 depicting Maori chiefs Te Heuheu and Hiwikaw Yaupo Te Kawaw in traditional dress.

MAORI TRIBES

Maori identify themselves not only as the indigenous people of the land, but also as members of particular tribes, *iwi*, which are further sub-divided into clans, *hapu*, and families, *whanau*. Around 1,000 years ago Maori migrated from elsewhere in the Pacific in a fleet (or series of fleets) of large canoes, *waka*. Each *iwi* descends from a common ancestor who captained one of those canoes and first settled a particular area in the new land, Aotearoa, Land of the Long White Cloud (or Long Twilight). Within each *iwi*, families trace their descent from more recent but also highly honoured ancestors. Thus *whanau* refers not just to a relationship between parents and their children, but includes the ancestors, all those alive today, and those yet to be born. Each family community has strong ties to particular places where ancestors lived and are buried, where each generation is born, works, socializes and gives birth to the next generation. In speech-making, *korero*, people introduce themselves by referring to place and genealogy. Thus, someone from Ruatoria might begin with:

Ko Hikurangi te maunga,
ko Waiapu te awa,
ko Ngati Porou te iwi.

Hikurangi is the mountain,
Waiapu is the river,
Ngati Porou is the tribe.

Maori Traditional Knowledge

Maori oratory is rooted in traditional narratives that should not be mistaken for primitive, childish or erroneous 'myths'. If orators refer to the rain as the tears of Father Sky, sad at his separation from Mother Earth, they are not confused about the nature of the cosmos, but reinforcing a point by referring to ubiquitous signs of relationship, desire, disappointment and so on.

THE FOLLOWING SUMMARY of a traditional Maori theme is not principally about 'how the world got to be as it is' but might establish a point about the constraints imposed by over-close relationships. It continues to demonstrate that space is needed if people are going to grow towards the fulfilment of their potential.

Some time ago in the evolution of all things, Father Sky and Mother Earth were so intimately devoted to one another that there was no space between them. The children born of their passion had neither light nor space in which to

grow. The overwhelming closeness of the parents caused a division in the affections of the children. Eventually, with considerable effort, Tanemahuta pushed his father up and away from his mother. With space and light to grow, the children took on the responsibilities of furthering the great unfolding of life's potential.

These acts engendered not only growth, but also further acts both of conflict and community. Tanemahuta's act is partly replicated every time someone skilfully makes space for life and potential. It is clear in the tall forest trees (Tanemahuta's domain), but also in the lifting of roofs above floors in *wharenui* and all other *whare* (houses). It does not encourage disrespect to parents, partly because it was only justified by the extreme conditions endured before the separation, and partly because traditional knowledge also speaks of the priority of peace despite the occasional necessity of conflict.

MAUI

It is not only gods who contribute to the creative unfolding of potential; humanity is also implicated in the choices and constraints that arise in life. Maui, ancestor of all Maori, achieved many things that made life better for his relatives and descendants – and, indeed, for all humanity. Maui considered the day too brief to be useful. So, with the help of his brothers, he trapped the sun in a large net, and forced it to travel across the sky slowly enough to provide sufficient time and light to achieve great things. On another occasion Maui is said to have used New Zealand's South Island as a canoe from which to fish up the North Island out of the depths. However, in the end, Maui failed. Or maybe it is simply that he tried to go too far, and his failure must be counted a benefit to all. Had his attempt to gain immortality for humanity succeeded, there would be absolutely no room left on earth by now. In brief, an orator might

A wooden carving from Rotorua in New Zealand. Life-like figures are known as Tekoteko, and are a dominant feature ore typically carved with the head larger than the body, owl-likw eyes, a protruding tongue and tattoed or incised bodies.

A Maori animal totem. One of the fundamental beliefs of Maori traditional religion is the need for space, to grow and fulfil potential. This is encapsulated in the myth of Father Sky and Mother Earth.

draw out the following traditional knowledge to support a particular argument about restraint.

Maui hoped that immortality might be found by entering the body of the divine-ancestress. Transforming himself into a lizard, he warns his companions not to laugh. But the sight of Maui entering head-first into the vagina of the sleeping Hine-nui-te-po was far too funny. The twittering laughter woke the sleeper, who closed her legs and crushed Maui to death.

Over the last 30 years there has been a renaissance of Maori culture. Traditional knowledge has been found to be rich and resonant and, importantly, well able to speak to contemporary concerns and issues. Even in an era when most Maori live in cities rather than small villages, when they participate in global forums like the internet and trade, and even when many are unemployed or impoverished, the knowledge of divine and ancestral deeds is increasingly valued. Maori cultural centres have been established in the cities, children are introduced to Maori language via traditional stories and elders again explore the wisdom handed down in powerful and evocative oratory. What may seem like myths of strange and miraculous events are

rediscovered as resources for facing ordinary life and its concerns, whether everyday or overwhelming. Central to Maori knowledge and culture is the creation and maintenance of more respectful relationships and lifestyles.

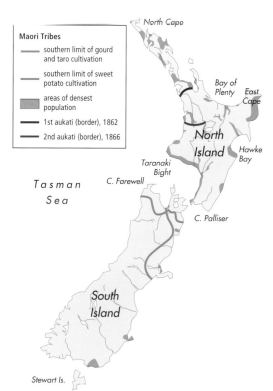

Carved corner of a Maori meeting house. Meeting houses are a significant part of Maori culture. The apex of the roof is the head of the ancestor, the ridgepole his backbone and the rafters inside the house symbolise his ribs.

Maori Tribes

There are more than 40 different Maori tribes. The map shows the main areas of Maori settlement in New Zealand before European contact in 1769. Although most food was obtained through hunting and gathering, the Maori also cultivated the land. The limits of this cultivation are shown on the map. In the 1860s the Maori fought bloody campaigns against the British in defence of their lands. Aukati was a border proclaimed by the Maori king to limit European penetration from the south.

NATIVE NORTH AMERICA

North American First Nations

When, from the end of the fifteenth century, Europeans began to explore North America, they found a large and culturally diverse population. However, epidemics and frequent warfare – coupled with the loss of land and resources to an increasing flood of immigrants – decimated the scattered populations. It was only in the 1960s that a resurgence began.

OVER MANY THOUSANDS of years successive migrations of peoples had filled every inhabitable region of North America, from the Arctic tundra, to the interior plains, and from the sea coasts to the desert plateaux of the arid south-west. Speaking over 300 distinct languages, each tribal group had developed its own distinctive culture, mythology and rituals, specific to living in harmony within their local environment. Scholarly estimates, based upon both oral tradition and archeological evidence, suggest that the population of the Americas prior to the arrival of Christopher Columbus in 1492 exceeded 100 million.

POPULATION DECLINE

The native population had no immunity to European diseases such as influenza, diphtheria or smallpox and by 1600 some 20 epidemics had swept through the Americas, decimating the population until less than one-tenth of the original number remained.

As increasing numbers of European settlers arrived they came into conflict with the native peoples. Genocide obliterated some first nations that, together with their unique languages, cultures, oral histories and cosmologies, disappeared for ever.

Treaties were negotiated between native nations and European representatives from Britain or France, but these were routinely

Ruins of a Native American village from the Pueblo period (1050–1300) in the Mesa Verde National Park, Arizona. The adobe houses are built in the recess of a cliff. In addition to the dwelling houses, villages such as this often had *kivas*, or ceremonial chambers, which were distinguishable by their circular shape.

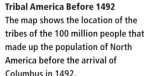

Tribal America Before 1492 The map shows the location of the tribes of the 100 million people that made up the population of North America before the arrival of Columbus in 1492.

Tribal America Before 1492
- Arctic
- Sub-Arctic
- Northwest Coast
- Plateau
- Great Basin
- California
- Southwest
- Great Plains
- Northeast
- Southeast

ignored by the newly arriving, land-hungry settlers. Many natives were killed in skirmishes with settlers, or in concerted attacks by armed forces, such as the massacre of the Lakota people at Wounded Knee in 1890.

Successive waves of immigrants surged westwards and flowed over traditional native gardens and hunting grounds. European encroachment and annexation of 'Indian Lands' forced native peoples on to diminishing areas of 'reservation' lands, which were generally of marginal productivity. Without a viable economic base, the majority were condemned to poverty.

The immigrants viewed the remnants of the native nations as just one more obstacle in their way. In 1830 President Jackson ordered the mass relocation of all 'Indians' living east of the Mississippi. Although Cherokee elders fought this policy in the courts, the people were still forced to migrate from their ancestral lands and to relocate far to the west. Herded by federal soldiers, sick, exhausted and starving, many died along the 'Trail of Tears', which is only now beginning to be mourned and commemorated in art, literature and song. Land loss or relocation also entailed spiritual bankruptcy, for relationship to the spiritual world is mediated through the land.

DISINHERITANCE

Both American and Canadian governments assumed that total assimilation of their native populations was inevitable. From the late nineteenth century right up until the 1980s many thousands of native children were forcibly taken from their families to residential schools or removed for adoption into 'white' families. The use of indigenous languages was forbidden. Almost all traditional religious

RE-ESTABLISHING TRADITION

Gradually the old religious traditions and ceremonies are returning. Often elders can still remember how sacred dances and rituals were conducted. Museums and public art galleries have been ordered to repatriate sacred artefacts, dance masks, etc. to the tribes to which they belong and to return ancestral bones for re-burial. Native languages and spirituality now form established courses in many universities, while Aboriginal elders work as chaplains in many hospitals, universities and prisons.

ceremonies were declared illegal (despite charters in both countries proclaiming freedom of religion). West-coast Potlatches, sun dances, sweat lodges and sweetgrass ceremonies were all banned. Only on the large reservations of the Pueblo peoples in the arid south-western USA did the traditional cycles of religious rituals and ceremonies continue undisturbed.

Some left the reserves for urban centres. Many still remain on isolated and resource-poor reservation lands, where poverty, unemployment, illness, alcoholism, domestic violence, child abuse, despair and soaring suicide rates are endemic.

By the 1960s there were government proposals for 'extinguishment' (in the USA) and 'termination' (in Canada). These proposals would have effectively ended all treaty rights and treaty status of native peoples.

RESURGENCE

In the mid 1960s, however, a series of conferences convened by native peoples began to publicise their plight and awaken public outrage. The glorious pioneering history recounted in text books was challenged by native communities who had experienced their own history as a continuous tragedy of injustice, broken treaties, persecution, violence, plunder and suppression.

There followed a series of very public and televised events: the occupation of the abandoned prison island of Alcatraz (1969), native militant youth holding out against USA marshals for 71 days at Wounded Knee (1973), or Canadian Mohawk people defending their tribal lands against encroachment at Kanehsatake (1990).

In the USA the Indian Self-Determination Act was passed in 1975. Each recognized tribe is entitled to receive assistance in establishing its own government, court system, police and schools. Each may operate as an independent nation, developing their land as they wish. This development already includes everything from resorts and casinos, to industrial developments and toxic and nuclear waste dumps. In Canada the movement towards complete self-government is progressing more slowly.

An Indian reserve for the Blackfoot tribe. The Native Americans were driven further and further west as European settlers claimed native lands. Eventually reservations such as this were established by the United States' government, under the guise of providing places where the natives could live free of harassment. In reality they were little more than enclosures through which the natives could be controlled.

Since the 1960s native ceremonies and rituals have experienced a resurgence and celebrations such as this, a pow wow ceremony competition of the Navajo tribe, are helping to reestablish the native way of life.

Spirituality

The recent resurgence of native spirituality provides the self-respect and cultural identity essential to the ongoing struggle to regain treaty lands and achieve political independence. Despite wide variations in mythologies, ceremonies and rituals, it is possible to generalize. Native spirituality expresses the close relationship between people, nature and the spirit world. Its re-introduction sometimes causes friction with older tribal members who have become devout Christians, but is of increasing appeal to the young and to the wider North American public.

NATIVE TRIBAL CULTURE and self-image are based upon the continuous habitation of place. People and place together form a social, cultural and spiritual unit. Prominent landscape elements are the sacred sites – places where the spiritual world is manifest. They may mark the place of the emergence of a people from the underworld, or of its creation by mythological spirit powers. Here the ancestral bones rest.

Oral histories, stories of origin and of ancient mythological creatures vary across the continent, but all serve the function of culturally bonding a people together. They all stress the interaction between people and the natural and spiritual world. Story-telling, chanting, dancing and role-playing wearing elaborate dance masks enable people to actively participate in addressing issues of ultimate concern, and expressing the unity and spiritual origin of all things.

HIEROPHANIC NATURE

Nature is experienced as hierophanic, that is, manifesting the spiritual. It is said that nature itself is the cathedral, the site where the spiritual may be encountered. For each tribal group, certain specific places (a high mountain or a spring, for example) and specific creatures will assume special significance, and can and do become vehicles for revelation. A bear, a buffalo, a raven, and so on will, on occasion become, or body forth, the power of the spirit world to protect, teach, warn or heal tribal members.

The focus upon spatiality may be expressed in the medicine wheel, a circular form, frequently marked out in rock patterns on the land. The medicine wheel is a symbol of inclusiveness, of the four directions (north, south, east and west), of the whole people (children, youth, adult and elderly), of the circle of the teepee, inside the circle of the tribe, inside the circle of the world. Prayers can be addressed to and blessings sought from the four directions.

RESPECT FOR ANIMALS

Spirituality is pervasive throughout all life and, therefore, all animals are part of the sacred creation. They contain a spiritual essence no less significant than our own and so must be treated with respect. It is often possible to be in spiritual communication with an animal spirit. A hunter may 'call' animals towards himself. On killing an animal for food, the hunter should make a reciprocal

A headdress in the shape of the Thunderbird, from the British Columbia coastal region, is an important figure in Native American religion. The Thunderbird was believed to cause thunder when it flapped its wings and lightning when it flashed its eyes.

A rattle in the shape of a raven from the north-east coast of America. The link between spirituality and nature was implicit in Native American religion, and animals were considered to have a spiritual nature in the same way as humans. Animals and birds, in particular the raven, were thought to contain the power of the spirit world and used to help humans.

offering, possibly of tobacco, offered to the animal spirit and to the Creator in thanksgiving, respect and acknowledgement of the hunter's reliance upon the animal for survival.

SHAMANISM

Shamanism is found throughout Native North America. The shaman (usually a tribal elder or holy man) has, by fasting and prayer, established a close relationship with his specific guardian animal spirit. He undertakes journeys into the spirit world where he may be given wisdom to prophesy, to give warnings to his people, or inform people why certain animals are scarce and where they should hunt. He has extensive knowledge of herbal remedies and may be called upon (instead of, or in addition to, modern medical facilities) to provide both physical and spiritual healing.

Shamans, with their healing powers, are highly respected. Their activities they carry out are extremely diverse, ranging from knowing the movements of Arctic fish, to healing with sand paintings and traditional chants in the south-western deserts. Today, some undertake work as counsellors, advisors or chaplains in hospitals and colleges. Their clients increasingly include non-native followers.

A Native American medicine man in costume. This medicine man is wearing a wolf skin and carries a drum and spear. Medicine men perform many of the same functions as shaman, but do not possess full magical powers.

NATIVE NORTH-AMERICAN ART

There is an amazing variety of works of great artistic merit created, not primarily for decoration, but as an expression of the spiritual manifest in all things. Art is not a separate category but rather a symbolic representation of a spiritual reality. Each pattern and decoration, each shape and colour, each rattle and feather, is symbolic and carries a specific meaning. Often these symbols are highly stylized. Art is used to decorate both sacred objects (e.g. dance masks) and everyday items of clothing, housing, and implements of daily life such as canoe paddles, pottery, baskets etc. Art honours the object by affording it meaning. It is an expression of the role of the object in the sacredness and interacting unity of life, and the great circle of being.

A sand drawing of the Pueblo people, from the Mesa Verde National Park in Arizona. Native American art is complex and carefully thought out. Shapes, colours and subject all have symbolic meanings and as such art is widespread, appearing not only on spiritual objects but also everyday items.

Ceremonies and Rituals

Across North America there is not only a wide variation in the type and purpose of ceremonies but also in their continuity. The Pueblo peoples of south-western USA, were never subjected to military conquest and, having rejected the early Spanish missionaries, maintained their traditional ritual cycles without interruption, preserving much of their culture and mythology intact. In contrast, Canadian First Nations are reinstating traditional ceremonies and dances that were prohibited by law for many years. In other communities, especially those of the south-eastern USA, where people were displaced from their lands, and many of the ancient traditions and ceremonies were irretrievably lost.

CEREMONIES AND rituals reinforce a reciprocal relationship between people, nature and the spirit world. Spiritual power or Orenda (Iroquois), Manitou (Algonquin), Wakan-Tanka (Sioux) or Kachina (Hopi), ensures the abundance of nature, and people play an essential role in this by offering gifts, rituals and gratitude.

Before most ceremonies a sweat lodge is built for purification from sin, addiction and brokenness. Constructed of saplings bent together to form a half sphere, with the entrance facing east, it is covered with cedar boughs and tarpaulins to ensure darkness. Very hot rocks are placed in the central fire-pit and, accompanied by prayer and chanting, cold water is sprinkled on them. The lodge combines earth, air, water and fire. Aromatic herbs, drums and rattles may also be used.

VISION SEEKING

Another widespread tradition is that of vision seeking. After receiving instruction from a shaman, and after making offerings and receiving purification in a sweat lodge, the vision seeker goes to a wilderness location to spend several days in solitude, fasting and prayer. The seeker may have dreams and see beyond the physical world into the spiritual. Many receive a visit from an animal who will reveal itself as being the person's spiritual guardian.

CEREMONIES OF SOUTH-WESTERN USA

Pueblo traditions are based upon a cosmology of the emergence of people from underground worlds. The stonewalled, underground *kiva* chambers symbolize emergence from the womb

of the earth up a vertical axis. Located in the centre of the village, the *kiva* is the domain of the men and is where the Kachina masks and costumes are stored.

The annual ritual cycle follows the seasonal cycle of nature: cultivation of crops in the summer and harvest in the fall being followed by the dance and ceremonial cycles, generally lasting from the winter to the summer solstice. For the complex cycle of masked dances and ceremonies, the sacred masks are brought out of storage in the *kivas* and may be repainted and decorated. The dances form a liturgical cycle in which both mask and dancer become the embodiment of the spirit power that is represented. Dolls are made for the children as small replicas of the Kachinas, so that they can learn to recognize each of the masks and associated spirit powers.

CEREMONIES OF THE CENTRAL PLAINS – THE SUN DANCE

For so long declared illegal, it is only since the 1970s that a slow revival of the Sun Dance has been possible. It is held annually by an

A Hopi Kachina doll representing a divine ancestral spirit. The Kachina is the spiritual power towards which the Hopi offer their worship. Dolls such as this form part of sacred ceremonies and are made for the children of the tribe.

Sweat lodge rituals are still carried out by Plains indians. The pole frame-works shown here, which traditionally would have been covered with buffalo hides, are covered with cedar boughs and tarpaulins, and the circular depressions on the ground are the fire pits. During the ritual the men of the tribe sprinkle water onto hot rocks to create a vapour which is believed to bring on spiritual purification.

increasing number of bands. A dance arena is selected and surrounded by an arbour of poles and evergreen branches. A central pole is erected, representing the axial centre of existence, linking dancers to both the circle of earth and the celestial circle of the spirit world.

Following weeks of preparation, the dancers begin each day with a sweat lodge, and fast throughout the four or more days of the ceremony. They circle the arena continuously during daylight hours, accompanied by groups of drummers who maintain a steady rhythm, like the heartbeat of the earth. It is also a test of endurance and bravery. Some of the young men choose to have skewers placed through their back or chest muscles, attached by ropes to heavy buffalo skulls. They compete to drag the skulls the furthest, and can win prestigious awards.

CEREMONIES OF THE NORTH-WEST COAST – THE POTLATCH

The nations of the Pacific north-west acknowledge the profound spiritual relationship that exists between people and nature, by carving the story of the family relationship with both real and mythological creatures into house posts, mortuary poles and totem (or family crest) poles.

The most important ceremony is the potlatch (prohibited from 1884 until 1951). In large and wonderfully carved assembly halls, feasting is followed by elaborate dances in which the dancers wear huge, fabulously carved masks to depict ancestral legends honouring a particular chief or clan. Dancing is followed by a lavish 'give-away', in which the giver of the potlatch gains status by his generosity. Potlatches may be held to celebrate any major event such as a birth, wedding, anniversary or appointment of a new chief.

A nineteenth-century hide painting showing the Sun Dance. This celebration thanked the Sun for past favours and ensured continued protection.

CONFLICT OF INTEREST

While the last few decades have seen an extraordinary resurgence in Native religion in North America, accompanied by rapid educational improvements and political changes, many thousands of native people, especially those on the more remote and resource-poor reserves, remain in poverty and are seriously marginalized with few prospects for a better future.

As the destructiveness of the modern North American way of life has become increasingly apparent, native spiritual teaching has become increasingly appealing to many in 'mainstream' society. There is a certain irony that the native integrated worldview of a sacred earth, where people, nature and land are interdependent and hierophanic, is in absolute contrast to the economic aspirations of many band councils (the local community organisation responsible for First Nation affairs) to develop casinos, resorts, mines, industries, in fact anything that will catapult band members into the materialist, consumer mainstream.

THE POWWOW CIRCUIT

The recent resurgence in national pride and culture has led almost every tribal group and reservation to hold a regular summer celebration (homecoming), during which powwow dances form an essential part of the celebration. The powwow is a series of dances in which participants circle the dance arena to the rhythm of different drum groups. It may last anywhere from a few hours to several days. There are different categories of dancing; some for men, or for women, or children, and some open for everyone present to join in. There are different categories of the very elaborate types of dance costume. Prizes may be awarded for dancing and for costumes. Notable performers, a skilled hoop dancer, for example, may be invited to come a considerable distance to give a solo performance. Many younger band members spend their summer months on the powwow trail, moving from one celebration to another. They carry with them not only costumes and drums, but also new cultural, political and economic ideas and cement friendship bonds between Native peoples of many different cultures.

CENTRAL AND SOUTH AMERICA

The Amazonians

Not only is the longhouse the centre of the everyday lives of the Amazonian people but, during ritual, their house becomes the cosmos. With the assistance of the shaman, space and time become one as the participants experience the invisible world which is essential to their continuing wellbeing.

A Makuna shaman takes snuff. The inhaling of hallucinogenic snuffs helps induce visions, which put men in touch with the spirit world.

THE PEOPLES WHO inhabit the Amazonian forest, located predominantly in Brazil but also Venezuela, Colombia and Peru, live by shifting agriculture; hunting, fishing and gathering.

For them the cosmos is animate. According to their cosmologies, the universe has three layers, each peopled by different beings. In the underworld live aquatic creatures, the most important of which are the anaconda or caiman. In the sky live the birds, of which the vulture or harpy eagle are the most significant for myth and beliefs generally. On the earth live people and forest-dwelling creatures, of which the jaguar is the most powerful. All creatures are believed to be controlled by the 'master of animals' who is sometimes the group's shaman.

SHAMANISM

The shaman is often the only individual with a specialized role in the community. Able to see the invisible world, which co-exists with the visible, shamans communicate with it and are responsible, for example, for releasing game animals for which the souls of new-born babies have to be exchanged. They can also travel to the

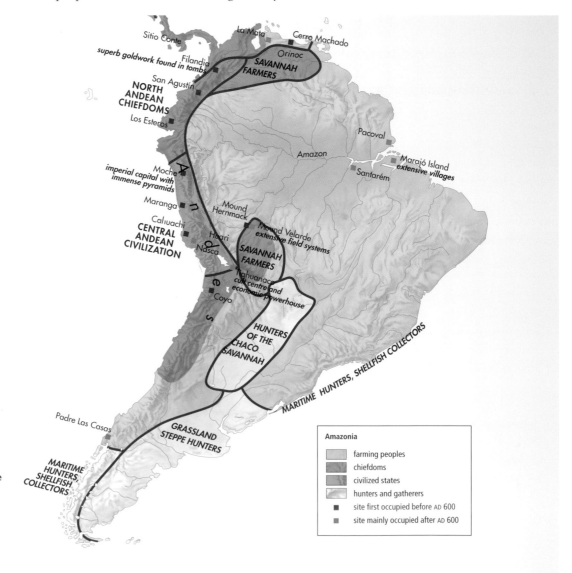

Amazonia
The map shows the settlement of the peoples of the Amazon and South America from 300 BC to AD 1300.

Sitio Conte
La Mata
Cerro Machado
superb goldwork found in tombs
Filandia
Orinoc
SAVANNAH FARMERS
San Agustin
NORTH ANDEAN CHIEFDOMS
Los Esteros
Pacoval
Amazon
Marajó Island
extensive villages
Moche
imperial capital with immense pyramids
Santarém
Maranga
Mound Hernmack
Caluachi
CENTRAL ANDEAN CIVILIZATION
Mound Velarde
extensive field systems
Huari
Nasca
SAVANNAH FARMERS
Tiahuanaco
cult centre and economic powerhouse
Coyo
HUNTERS OF THE CHACO SAVANNAH
MARITIME HUNTERS, SHELLFISH COLLECTORS
Padre Las Casas
GRASSLAND STEPPE HUNTERS
MARITIME HUNTERS, SHELLFISH COLLECTORS

Amazonia

	farming peoples
	chiefdoms
	civilized states
	hunters and gatherers
■	site first occupied before AD 600
■	site mainly occupied after AD 600

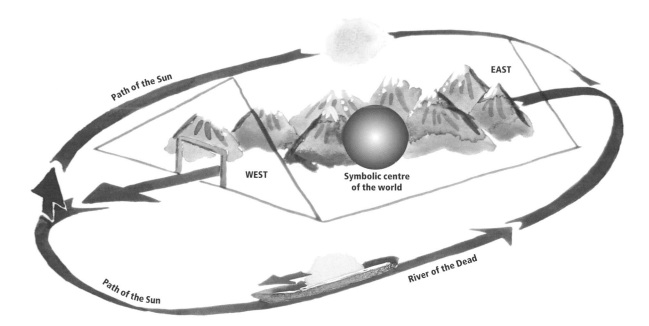

Path of the Sun

EAST

WEST

Symbolic centre
of the world

Path of the Sun

River of the Dead

different layers of the cosmos or send others there in trance or by means of hallucinogenic drugs. In many groups, the son of a shaman is apprenticed to his father, but in others, men become shamans by means of a severe illness, by revelation or simply ambition.

The latter pay for their initiation and accumulate power in the forest through direct experience. It is a hard training involving sexual abstinence, fasting, vomiting and other dietary prohibitions. The shaman enters into a relationship with one or more ancestral spirits, and is given his spirit weapons. Potency lies in the invisible world which is viewed with ambiguity (as is the self-made shaman). All shamans have access to considerable power which they can use for good or evil: the most powerful can turn themselves into jaguars. Mostly, however, a shaman does good in his own community but wards off mystical attacks sent by shamans from elsewhere.

CURING

Shamans can cure both physiological illness and social disorder; they may blow tobacco smoke over the patient, suck out spirit weapons or go into a trance to fight the spirits causing the problem. More powerful is water throwing carried out in the

midday sun. For this water scented with aromatic leaves is thrown over the patient's body which is thought to 'trawl' through it removing 'spines, bundles of fur or feathers which the shaman throws away amid much blowing, clapping of hands and flicking of fingers'. The shaman makes a performance out of such rituals: for he has to not only know all the myths, rites and other esoteric knowledge (of plants, animals and the stars) but also to add something of himself to become highly respected.

THE HE OR YURUPARY CULT

For the Barasana, who live in the upper Vaupes region in Colombia, the anaconda is the first ancestor and associated with the sacred *He* flutes and trumpets which are kept under water and represent its bones. *He* refers to a timeless generating force, known also as Yurupary. In myth, Yurupary was the culture hero who established order in nature and taught the first men rules and ritual conduct. These instruments must never be seen by women and girls, and only by boys who have been initiated. During ritual, as those involved dance and chant, ancestral time is recreated; the house is seen to become the cosmos.

The house becomes one with the universe and the spirit world which it represents. An imaginary river seen as flowing through the middle of the house is the underworld river of the dead, who travel in their burial canoes. The sun's canoe travels in the opposite direction so that it can rise once again in the east.

A shaman distributing coca during a Baransa chanting ceremony. The chants recite the journeys of the first ancestors, or He people, from their original home to the place where their descendants dwell. During such chants, the specialist chanter recreates the mythical journeys, by making his soul leave his body.

THE BARANSA HOUSE AS COSMOS

During ritual, the floor of the house is conceptualized as the earth, the roof becomes the sky supported by the house posts which become the mountains. The horizontal roof beams represent the sun's path. Any grave under the house is seen as being in the underworld, and the ritual ornaments hanging from the ceiling beams, collectively known as 'macaw feathers', act as the mediator between

the earth and the sky. The cassava griddle used by the women is like the cosmos, and said to be the one dropped by the female maker of the world (Roumi Kumu), when there were only sky people and the Primal Sun. She was the originator of domestic fire, and it was her sacred beeswax gourd that gave men their shamanic power.

The Huichol

The Huichol believe that their ancestors gave them the task of looking after not only their community but the whole cosmos. Every year they perform rituals for the earth led by their shamans. But these can only be performed after they have made a pilgrimage to the sacred land of Wiricuta, the birth place of the sun.

Men dressed up for a festival. Their clothing is heavily embroidered with symbols showing the close relationship between the Huichol and nature.

THE HUICHOL LIVE high up in the inaccessible Sierra mountains in the state of Sinaloa, Mexico, where they grow the staples of maize and beans. They number around 20 000, and today have only a small amount of land, the terrain in the immediate vicinity was once all theirs and they were predominantly hunters rather than agriculturalists. Today, much of that land has become the property of ranchers and peasant farmers. Despite the proximity of mainstream Mexican society, the Huichol's sacred beliefs and practices have remained comparatively unchallenged, and there are only a few traces of Catholicism, such as the mention of Jesucristo in their prayers.

HUICHOL DEITIES

All aspects of their cosmos are imbued with supernatural significance. The most important deity is Tatawarei (Grandfather Fire), made manifest long ago by the Animal People (specifically Deer Person and Ant Person), while Tayaupa (Our Father Sun) was subsequently created when a Huichol boy was thrown into the water to become the sun. He travelled down through five levels to the underworld and eventually emerged in the east in a burst of volcanic activity. The Huichol feel ambivalent about Tayaupa: he is potent and can be dangerous. The pilgrimage into the desert to Wiricuta, 480 km (300 miles) away, is partly to make offerings to him but it is also to hunt for peyote, a hallucinogenic cactus, which today has close associations with corn: both considered to be aspects of Tateima (Our Mothers or Mother Earth).

THE PILGRIMAGE TO WIRICUTA

In spring, before the start of the ceremonies to bring rain, up to 12 men and women make the pilgrimage led by their *mara'akame* (or shaman who is also priest, healer and community leader, and can be either male of female). The shaman wears deer antlers attached to his hat and becomes Tatewari accompanied by the mythical Kauyumari (the sacred Deer Person and culture hero). This is a tough journey requiring abstinence from salt, sex, washing, full meals and sufficient sleep for its duration, not just for those who go but for those who stay behind too. Peyote is believed to have been given to them by the deer and is 'hunted' until it reveals its whereabouts. Once gathered, it is treated with the greatest respect and carefully brought back.

Tatewari, having guided their quest, is equally important on their return: the Huichol circle the fire to thank him for their successful quest. Before any ritual, Tatewari prepares them. They 'confess' their misdoings to the fire which cleanses them and Tatewarei is fed a small

The Huichol
The Huichol live high up in the Sierra mountains of Sinaloa, Mexico (see map).

The Huichol
— area of inhabitation

A shaman during ritual wearing his feathered hat (his assistant on the left is playing a drum).

portion of all food and drink. Collected also in Wiricuta is a yellow root whose sap is used to decorate the faces of the entire community with designs showing their respect for Tayaupa.

THE CEREMONIAL CYCLE

The main rituals are to Tateima and Nakawe (Grandmother Growth) whom they believe they must nurture before the rains will come and the corn ripen, accompanied by music, song, prayers and chants. Amidst many candles and flowers decorated with ribbons, a cow is sacrificed (in the past this would have been a deer, but today the Huichoi do not hunt much). The blood not only feeds Tateima but unites everyone and everything, as each in turn has a little daubed on his or her forehead and on all their possessions.

Rain is believed to come from the sea and so, to ensure its continuance, the Huichol also make pilgrimages, not to the nearest ocean (the Pacific) but to the Atlantic. Entire families travel with their children, who are blindfolded as they approach. After keeping vigil on the beach all night, the children are ritually presented to the sea at dawn.

A depiction of Tatewari; much of Huichol imagery is inspired by their use of peyote.

PEYOTE

During the dry season, the Huichols use peyote for many of their rituals, thereby increasing their knowledge of their cosmology. Children are introduced to it little by little when still quite young. During one whole day, they are taken on a metaphorical journey to Wiricuta by the shaman, by means of chants and songs accompanied by drumming. When initiated, they stay up all night to dance and sing with everyone else and experience the full sensory complexity of their cosmos. It is not unusual for Huichols not to sleep for three to four nights in a row; a female shaman, sitting in her sacred chair in the *tuki* (sacred house), has been known to chant for up to 36 hours non-stop. However, only the shaman reveals to others what he or she has learnt from peyote.

The Highland Maya Today

The indigenous peoples of Mexico and Guatemala although apparently Roman Catholics, have their own cosmologies. Some of their rituals occur in the church, where they venerate their saints, but in their everyday lives, the sun and the moon are more important.

THE TZELTAL, who live in the highlands of Chiapas, Mexico are just one of many Maya groups with rather similar oral traditions. An egalitarian people, they grow corn and beans for their own consumption, on the land surrounding their scattered homesteads. Each house has an altar, consisting of a simple cross placed on the dirt floor, an incense burner and candles, framed by pine boughs. In each parish, crosses mark natural features which are considered to be sacred, such as springs or limestone shafts, generically known as *metik-* or *tatik-anjel*. At these, prayers are offered daily, addressed to *ch'ultatik* (the sun), *ch'ulme'tik* (the moon) and to *kaxeltik* (the earth). The sun is responsible for giving men their vital heat (*k'ahk*), while the moon, the mother of the sun, is concerned with the welfare and fertility of women. She is also responsible for rain and associated with water holes and lakes (*metik-anjel*). But it is *kaxeltik* (also feminine) who is the protector and sustainer and to whom prayers are said for both planting and the harvest: she is the greatest threat to people, bringing both life and death.

THE FESTIVALS

The Tzeltal, in common with many other highland indigenous peoples in both Mexico, Guatemala, Bolivia and Peru, had imposed on them, by the Spaniards in the sixteenth century, what are known as cargo systems or civil-religious hierarchies. Today, cargo holders – eight couples for each saint – continue to organize the main festivals for a year, which centre on the church in the small town in each community. Each of the 11 or so festivals is marked by a period of communal living, very different from their normal isolation. Special foods are prepared to be consumed by all, after their saint's clothing has been ritually changed and washed on one day, and their saint has been taken out in procession around the town on the next. During these five days, there is constant activity, either in the cargo holders houses or in the church, where music is played and toasts drunk to the saints and to each other.

THE SAINT-GODS

In Tenejapa, the images of the indigenous saints in the church are different from those venerated by the Roman Catholic *mestizos*. There *ch'ultatik* (the sun of the parish) becomes Kahkanantik (or burning protector), the principal male deity, but known to the *mestizos* as San Alonso (Saint Alphonsus). He is the patron saint of the community for both Catholics and indigenes. The moon becomes *halame'tik* (a synonym for *ch'ulme'tik* – Dear Mother) but is known as Santa Maria (the Virgin Mary) to the

Carnival is the only festival that occurs in the countryside. For its duration, men dress as women and drink, play, dance and make music at various sacred sites.

The Tzeltal
The Tzeltal live in the highlands of Chiapas, Mexico near the border of Guatemala (see map).

The Tzeltal
— area of inhabitation

mestizos. Other figures include Tatik Mamal (Old Father), the brother of Kahkanantik, while Santa Luca, or San Ciako (Santiago or Saint James) have names closer to Catholic usage. Rather than calling these images saints, they can best be referred to as saint-gods, as they incorporate a measure of Catholicism which is underpinned by the Mayan pre-Colombian beliefs and practices of the countryside. The range of saint-gods varies from community to community, and as each community sees itself as the 'true people' distinct and better than its neighbours, there is only occasional contact between them during pilgrimages.

Today an increasing number of people are being attracted to various faiths, such as Jehovah's Witnesses, the Adventists and the Baptists, in part to avoid the financial responsibility of caring for the saint-gods. But it is not yet clear that these new affiliations will last and whether the Maya peoples will revert to the beliefs and practices they had before.

The sacred effects of a saint-god are honoured during ritual. Here the women have been washing the old coins that hang from the neck decorations.

A parish healer making a cross for the altar of a house under construction. He will be invited to pray when there is illness, family difficulties or other problems.

THE CHURCH

Nominally Roman Catholic, the church is shared by the *mestizos* and the indigenes, although the *mestizos'* Catholic services never overlap with the indigenous use of the church. On a Sunday during a festival, for example, the space of the church will be used all morning by the indigenes who come to pray and hold ceremonies for their saint-gods accompanied by music and ritual drinking. Then after midday, *mestizo* women descend with brooms to sweep it out, clean it up and replace the pews, readying it for their Catholic service taken by the local priest later in the day.

AFRICAN TRADITIONAL RELIGION

Religion in Africa

Africa has a rich cultural and spiritual heritage, expressed in complex and historically diverse religious traditions. Amidst the tremendous diversity there are a number of common features: above all, a concern for community and the expression of common humanity (the word used in many Bantu languages is *Ubuntu*). Community involves not only the living, but also those not yet born and those who have died: the 'living dead', in the famous phrase of the Kenyan theologian and thinker, John Mbiti. Religion is an orientation of the present community towards the spirit world. The spirit world lies parallel and beyond the world of sense perceptions.

Shango (or Chango), the god of thunder, fire and, in modern times, guns, from the Dahomey culture of what is now Benin, East Africa.

IN *AFRICANS: The History of a Continent* (1995, p. 1), John Iliffe writes: 'The central themes of African history are the peopling of the continent, the achievement of human coexistence with nature, the building of enduring societies, and their defence against aggression from more favoured regions. As a Malawian proverb says, "It is people who make the world; the bush has wounds and scars." ... Until the later twentieth century ... Africa was an underpopulated continent. Its societies were specialised to maximise numbers and colonise land. Agricultural systems were mobile, adapting to the environment rather than transforming it, concerned to avert extinction by crop-failure. Ideologies focused on fertility and the defence of civilization against nature.'

THE CELEBRATION OF LIFE

African traditional religion is thus centrally concerned with the establishment and building up of human society, with human flourishing and the celebration of life. But it is also intensely aware of the fragility of life. Existence and wellbeing are constantly threatened. Much of African religious practice is devoted to coping with the eruption of evil and its persistence in the world.

African approaches to religion may be characterized as the glorification of everyday life, imagined and enacted through ritual. Religion is not enshrined in books, in scriptures or written liturgies, but in customs and ritual performance, in folk tales and proverbs, creation myths, prayer and invocation, music and dance. The spirit world

is mediated through sacred sites and persons: priests and diviners, kings and elders, musical performers and official 'remembrancers'. They function as guardians and transmitters of that corporate sense of community; they define a society's place in the natural world and its relation to the spiritual world.

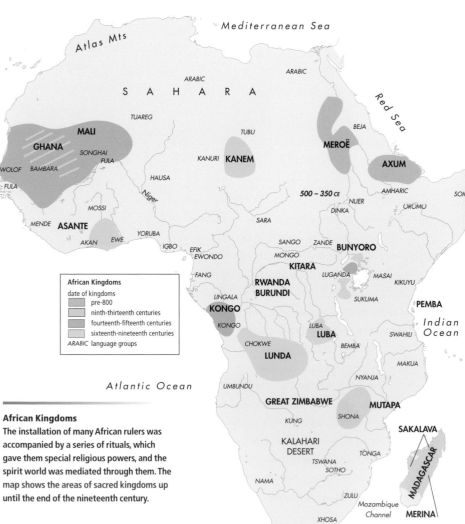

African Kingdoms

date of kingdoms
- pre-800
- ninth-thirteenth centuries
- fourteenth-fifteenth centuries
- sixteenth-nineteenth centuries
ARABIC language groups

African Kingdoms
The installation of many African rulers was accompanied by a series of rituals, which gave them special religious powers, and the spirit world was mediated through them. The map shows the areas of sacred kingdoms up until the end of the nineteenth century.

RELIGIOUS DIVERSITY

Religion in Africa is bound up with the whole structure of society and its communal self-understanding. Yet it would be wrong to regard religion in Africa as fragmented and ethnocentric – the term 'tribal religions', so often used in the Western discourse, is unfortunate. Africa does indeed contain a wide diversity of particular ethnic groups. But there has always been an immense amount of interaction between peoples. The fact that different language groups live in close proximity means that many Africans are multi-lingual, speaking a variety of vernacular languages, as well as a lingua franca such as Swahili or Hausa, in addition to proficiency in a world language such as Arabic, French or English. In religion there is an equal diffusion of concepts, forms and practices over wide areas. For example, the name for God (or divinity) may have wide currency over large areas. Spirit-possession or witch-eradication cults transcend ethnic boundaries. Nor is such interaction confined to ethnically similar people. There is much interaction, for example, between Bantu speakers and Luo in eastern Africa; between Khoi and San (the pastoralists and hunters of southern Africa) and their Xhosa and Tswana neighbours. African traditional religions do not operate in timeless non-historical contexts. There is much evidence of the interchange and development of practice and ideas over time. 'Traditional' does not mean that African religions exist primarily as backward looking, quaint survivals. They are responsive to new situations, not least to the forces of modernity and globalization.

CHRISTIANITY AND ISLAM

In different ways, both Christianity and Islam have been the means by which modernity has penetrated Africa. Yet both these religions have a long history on the African continent, and have a long 'pre-modern' encounter with Africa in the form of Coptic and Ethiopian Christianity and North African Islam. Both religions have incorporated dimensions of traditional African religion into their own systems. Even when they denounce many aspects of African religion as 'pagan', they still cannot avoid expressing the spiritual aspirations of African religion. Nevertheless Islam and Christianity are seen as different in kind from the African spiritual sensibility – in East Africa, Islam and Christianity are called *dini* (from the Arabic word). *Dini* implies a religious body which can be distinguished from and stand over against other institutions in a society, which a person joins. African traditional religions do not function in this way. Rather, they are constituted by the totality of being and practice in a community. Islam and Christianity may strive for a total transformation of a society, but they recognize a disjunction between present ideal and reality.

Left: **Khoisan rock art in Namibia.** The Khoisan (a modern term for the ancient Khoi and San peoples) are believed to be one of Africa's first peoples. Their paintings are believed to be the work of shamans, depicting trance visions, symbols of supernatural potency, rain-making and healing rituals, combining geometric forms with images of humans and animals.

A village of the Dogon people in Mali. The Dogon have achieved some notoriety among fringe historians for their seeming knowledge of the binary nature of the star Sirius, an important part of their religion.

African Cosmologies, Gods and Ancestors

African societies are concerned with the enhancement of life: the health of human beings and of livestock, the fertility of the land and the prosperity of the whole community. Ancestors (the 'living dead'), nature spirits and gods are guardians of the community. These beings are refractions of spirit, the High God, the dynamic principle of life. African cosmologies attempt to explain the loss of immediacy between the two worlds and to account for the fragility and disharmony of existence.

A painted wooden and straw mask, probably used for ritual purposes, from the Kuba people of the Congo, central Africa.

CREATION STORY (MORU, SUDAN)

When God created the world, Heaven and earth were close together, connected by a leather ladder. People were constantly moving to and fro. They loved to attend the dances and feasts of heaven, and returned to earth rejuvenated. One day a girl was grinding some sorghum (sorghum is a grain used for food and to make beer). She delayed and was late for the dance. In her haste she started to climb the ladder without washing her hands. The trail of sorghum on the ladder attracted the hyena. He began licking the ladder. That set him to gnawing at the leather, until the ladder broke. So the communication between earth and Heaven has been broken. People cannot be rejuvenated and death has come into the world.

ORIGIN OF DEATH (ZULU)

The chameleon was entrusted with a message to take to earth – immortality for humankind. But he loitered on the way and was beaten to earth by the lizard. The lizard also had a message – death for humankind. Thus death came into the world.

GODS AND ANCESTORS

The African cosmos is populated by spirits who occupy a realm which is outside normal reality, but which impinges at many points on human society. There are nature spirits who typically inhabit the uncultivated places and wilderness which stand over against the abode of people. Such spirits are by their nature fickle and best avoided; their potential for harm to human society is great. The ancestors are more directly involved in the life of the community; they are also more benign, though they can be offended. In many African societies the dead are buried near the homestead, and the ancestors of the family have a tangible presence. In some societies, there is a class of ancestors who assume wider significance, as heroic figures, who achieve divinity, and whose cults spread far and wide.

The Dogon of Mali have a complex cosmology, symbolically mirrored in the architecture of village and homestead and of the human body itself.

THE YORUBA PANTHEON

The Yoruba of Nigeria have developed a rich urban culture of historical depth. Each city state has an *orisha* or divinity, with its own

Eguguns (resurrected ancestors) return to their descendants at a festival in Porto Nuevo, Benin.

priesthood and cult and method of divination. Above all the *orisha* is Olorun, the Lord and owner of the Sky. Olorun is also know as Olodumare, the Creator, the 'owner of the spirit of life' and the one in charge of the destiny of human beings. Olorun apportioned oversight of the world to the orisha divinities. The *orisha* are representations of the divine, and mediate between God and human society. They include Esu, a trickster god, of a type familiar in other parts of Africa (for example among the Bushmen of the Kalahari). Ogun is the god of iron and war. Sango, the deified fourth king of the ancient Yoruba kingdom of Oyo, is a particularly popular *orisha* much depicted in sculpture. In life regarded as a tyrant who committed suicide, in his heavenly guise he is the god of thunder. Sango is noted for his capricious behaviour in both giving and destroying life. He is the object of a major cult of possession.

AN AFRICAN MONOTHEISM?

One of the most vigorous debates among students of African religion and anthropologists has been the role and importance of a 'high god', a 'great spirit'. Christian missionaries often attempted to discover such a concept, so that they could use his name for the God they proclaimed. At the same time they tended to disparage the African conception of deity as *deus otiosus*, a god who had departed from direct concern with the world and humanity. Anthropologists have sometimes been sceptical of the antiquity of most concepts of high gods, seeing this as an alien discourse in which outsiders have imposed their views. There was a growth of what has been called 'ethical monotheism' in many societies in the nineteenth century, relating to the enlargement of scale resulting from Africa's incorporation into a global economy, requiring attention to a divinity who is above and beyond the particular concerns of the local community. This accounts for some of the attraction of Islam and Christianity, but it also helps to explain the rise of universalist traits within African religions themselves.

THE CASE OF BUGANDA

Like neighbouring societies Buganda (south of what is now Uganda) in the nineteenth century had a strong awareness of ancestral spirits (*mizimu*) and the nature spirits (*misambwa*) who inhabited the swamps, forest and wilderness. However, as a strong, centralized state, with a monarch (the Kabaka), Buganda also had a series of national gods: the *balubaale* (singular *lubaale*). These were of two kinds. The 'gods of the mainland' were mainly personifications of natural forces: Ggulu (the sky), Walumbe (death), Kiwanuka (thunder) and Kawumpuli (the plague). The 'gods of the lake' were heroic figures originating from the Ssese islands of Lake Victoria (Lake Nalubaale). *Mukasa* was the god of the lake – his symbol was a paddle – and he was regarded as overwhelmingly beneficent, particularly to pregnant women and never demanded human sacrifice. In contrast, his brother Kibuuka was the god of war, associated with the long struggle between Buganda and its neighbour Bunyoro. On the lakeside, shrines (*masabo*) dedicated to Mukasa, with their distinctive paddle insignia, are still common. The name of one *lubaale*, Katonda ('Creator'), has been adopted by Muslims and Christians to describe the supreme God.

In many parts of Africa, kings were accorded a divine status. This was not so in Buganda, at least during the lifetime of the Kabaka, whose power was seen as distinct from that of the *balubaale*. On the king's death, the jawbone was separated from the body and buried separately. Both burial sites became the focus of a cult, distinct from the *balubaale* themselves. In Buganda, there was a deep ambiguity about the spirit world, sometimes expressed in proverbs of surprisingly modern scepticism: 'You are wasting your time begging health from a jawbone: if it could give health, why did its owner die?' Islam and Christianity dealt a severe blow to the public expression of traditional religion. But its ethos and spirituality survived in the covert construction of shrines, consultation of diviners and a reverence for the Kabaka as a symbol of national identity.

A figure of male twins from the Yoruba of Nigeria. In African traditional religion twins are often seen as having a special connection with the spirit world, and were often either venerated or killed at birth.

The Celebration of Life and Cults of Affliction

African traditional religion is concerned with the enhancement of life. It celebrates community, health and prosperity, fertility and procreation. Africans are also acutely aware that these values are fragile. Harmony with the spirit world is necessary for human flourishing; but, if mishandled, the spirit world can also exercise malign power in ways which diminish and negate life.

RITES OF PASSAGE are important stages for the affirmation of life. They are liminal experiences when people stand on the threshold of the spirit world, times of celebration but also of danger.

Fertility and procreation are celebrated, but they are surrounded by danger. The birth of twins illustrates the combination of vitality and danger. In some parts of Africa, twins are regarded as an anomaly: by mischance the spirit counterpart of the child has also been born, an offence to the spirits and a danger for all. In parts of East Africa, by contrast, twins are regarded as a special blessing, a sign of the super abundance of the spirit world. Special twin names are given not only to the children, but to those who are born after them, and to the parents themselves. Such names are held in great honour.

A fertility statuette showing a mother and child from the Baoule culture of the Ivory Coast. The breasts and reproductive features are often exaggerated on fertility sculptures to emphasize their importance. The navel is also depicted as large and sticking out, as a symbol of continuity of life.

Naming is of great importance and often has strong religious connotations. Children are given the names of divinities. If the birth has been difficult, or occurs after a history of trouble within the family, the name might have a somewhat derogatory implication, in the hope that the vengeful spirit may overlook the rejoicing and not inflict further punishment.

INITIATION

The most important communal rites are often at adolescence when boys are initiated through circumcision. They are sent away from normal human society and for a time live beyond its rules. In the circumcision camp, on the boundary between civilization and wilderness, humanity and the spirits, initiates learn important new skills appropriate to the adult world, gender and sexual roles, the history and ethics of the group as transmitted from one generation to the next. Not all African societies perform circumcision. The Zulu are said to have abandoned circumcision during the time of Shaka, when it would have compromised the fighting effectiveness of the *impi*. Female 'circumcision' is less common than male circumcision. But where it does occur it is meant to have the same socializing role. Missionaries strongly condemned female circumcision in the 1920s and were in turn attacked for wanting to destroy African culture. More recently human rights and women's groups have renewed the opposition to the practice, insisting that it is, in effect, female genital mutilation.

MASKS AND MASQUERADES

The great communal celebrations of rites of passage or harvest festivals, as well as initiation into healing or status cults, are often

A rain festival is held at Nok in Nigeria. Rain festivals are often held annually or seasonally, rather than merely at times of drought.

AFRICAN NOVELISTS

Modern African novelists have tackled many themes associated with traditional religions sensitively and powerfully. *The Mourned One* (1975) by Stanlake Samkange, a Shona from Zimbabwe, is concerned with the plight of a woman who gives birth to twins. The Kenyan writer, Ngugi wa Thiong'o in *The River Between* (1965), explores the dilemmas of a young Kikuyu girl torn between the desire to undergo the rite of initiation into full womanhood, and the opposition of her parents, Christian converts. Chinua Achebe's *Things Fall Apart* (1958) is the classic account of the onslaught of western colonialism on African cultural and religious values.

accompanied by pageants and masquerades, dramatic performances, song and dance in which the relationship between the spirit world and human society are enacted and re-enacted. In donning a mask the performer loses his own individuality and entirely becomes the entry point for communication with the realm of spirit.

SICKNESS AND MISFORTUNE

Africa has always been a harsh place in which to live, environmentally and politically. Infant mortality has always been high; more recently, the AIDS pandemic has affected especially the strong and economically productive sections of society. Yet, only the death of the very old can easily be accepted as part of the natural flow of events. The death of younger people needs explanation, as does illness and bad luck, particularly if they are recurrent. There may be proximate explanations – a specific symptom or event – but what is the enduring, determining cause? The problem may be located in a failure to respect ancestors or other spirits, or the accidental or deliberate failure to comply with certain norms. It may be caused by jealousy on the part of kinsfolk or neighbours, or be due to the malice of witchcraft.

A number of religious professionals can be consulted. There are healers who are skilled in herbal medicines. Diviners use a variety of paraphernalia – bones, cowry shells, animal sacrifice – to discover the reasons. Mediums are possessed by spirits and act as their mouthpiece in diagnosing the problem and offering solutions. Witches and sorcerers also have access to spiritual powers. They do not admit freely to such deeply anti-social activity. The covertness of their activity is itself the cause of alarm and anxiety. The problem is that spiritual powers can be used for both good and evil.

SPIRIT POSSESSION

The search for relief and therapy is often embodied in 'cults of affliction'. In Bantu-speaking areas these often go under the general name of Ngoma ('drum': referring to the music and dance which may be part and parcel of membership of the group). Such groups have a public existence and (unlike witchcraft activities) have respect from society. But initiates enter into a secret world, which may involve learning an arcane language and the symbolic performance of acts normally taboo. Women are often the majority. They may begin their involvement by consulting a diviner for some particular problem during pregnancy and be gradually drawn into membership. By becoming adept at healing or divination, women have opportunities to gain a status otherwise denied them.

A boy of the Samburu tribe of Kenya prepares for his circumcision. Many African tribes see circumcision, which often takes place at puberty, as an initiation into manhood.

African Religion, Politics and the Challenge of Modernity

Because African traditional religion was so closely integrated into society, it has often been regarded as lacking the critical distance from the centres of power effectively to challenge authority: it served rather to sacralize political and cultural institutions. For example, a territorial cult like that of Mbona in the Shire and Zambesi valleys of Malawi and Mozambique may have begun in opposition to local power, but it soon became co-opted into those structures. Yet there are a few examples of religious opposition to the status quo.

AN EARLIER AFRICAN opposition to colonial rule is associated with the young Xhosa girl Nongqawuse. The Xhosa had suffered intense pressure on land and resources emanating from Afrikaner and British farmers for half a century. Nongqawuse had a vision in which the ancestors promised to rise from the dead and, with the help of the Russians (who had just fought the British in the Crimea), to drive out the British and renew the land. To realise this the Xhosa should refrain from planting crops and kill all their cattle. The prophecies deeply divided the Xhosa people, but the overall result was famine, death, the exodus of young men to work as landless labourers on European farms, and a further erosion of Xhosa culture. Nongqawuse's message, with its adoption of Christian elements (such as resurrection of the dead) into a Xhosa cultural framework, shows the cultural adaptability of African religious sensibilities, even though in this case to negative effect.

A mask originating from the Congo. African gods are believed to have a dual nature, which is both creative and destructive, and which is often conveyed through the use of masks.

The Reaction Against European Imperialism
Growing dissatisfaction with colonial rule resulted in revolt throughout Africa from the late nineteenth century onwards.

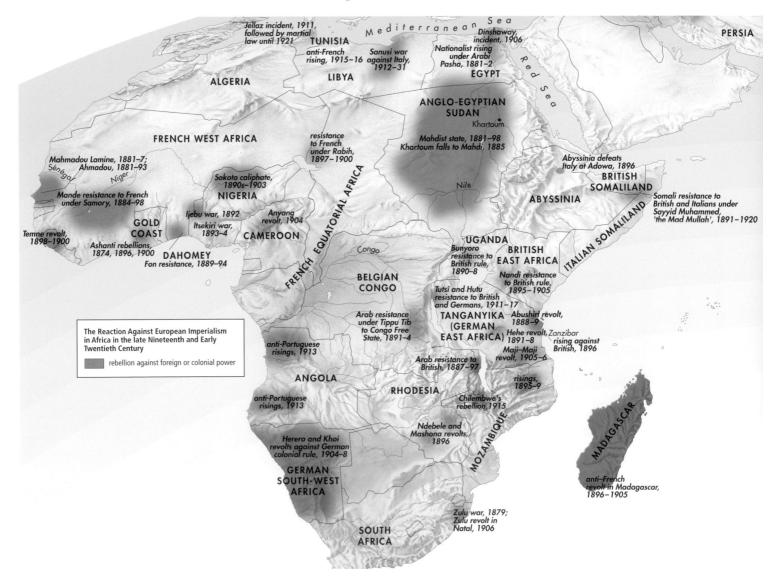

The Reaction Against European Imperialism in Africa in the late Nineteenth and Early Twentieth Century

▮ rebellion against foreign or colonial power

Such responses of distress have been repeated at critical periods in Africa's confrontation with external forces. The Maji Maji revolt against German rule in East Africa between 1905 and 1907 dispensed a sacred water to make people immune from the guns of the aggressor. In the aftermath of military defeat in Northern Uganda after 1986, Alice Lakwena, possessed by 'the holy spirit' and other spirits of the Acholi people, waged a spiritual battle. She promised immunity from bullets, and looked the spirits to restore purity and dignity to the polluted land.

PRIVATIZATION OF RELIGION

One of the startling changes of modern African life is the increasing privatization of aspects of the traditional African religious vocabulary and repertoire. Islam and Christianity have become major players in public life at a whole variety of levels – the institution of a traditional ruler, the rites of passage: particularly of birth and death. Traditional rituals are becoming secularized, divorced from the religious concepts which formerly gave them coherence. A religious element is often sought from the local priest, pastor or imam.

In the search for health, however, African traditional understandings continue to flourish, not least in urban settings. Politicians, business men and women, civil servants and teachers, not to mention the army of workers and job seekers, all have reason to consult traditional diviners and healers both as a remedy for sickness (in situations where public health provision declines) and for success in work or love. Students look for success in exams.

Such consultation may be conducted in secret and with a certain amount of shame. It may also involve the use of anti-social forms of the manipulation of the spirit world. Beliefs in witchcraft have a long history in Africa. The reluctance of colonialists and missionaries to recognize the reality of witchcraft and their willingness to punish those who made accusations as much as the actual witches offended African distinctions. It has not reduced the fears of witchcraft. The insecurities of modern life have if anything led to increased manipulation of objects for a harmful purposes. In the 1990s the disintegration of states such as Liberia and Sierra Leone was accompanied by an increased fear of the harmful effects of witchcraft in political power struggles and as a resource for undisciplined boy soldiers.

Carvings at the sacred shrines of Oshogbo, Nigeria. Today Oshogbo is a centre of Nigerian art, and many of the Oshogbo artists, often deriving their styles from the old traditions, have become internationally renowned.

ISLAM AND CHRISTIANITY

In North Africa the process of incorporating African religious values into Islam has gone far. Sufi brotherhoods have historically been at the forefront of this movement. In Morocco the Gnawa cult emphasizes healing rituals, with music playing an important role. Its origins are traced to the black slaves who came to Morocco from sub-Saharan Africa, and the sensibilities of a spirit-possession cult of affliction seem evident.

Christianity has always been more wary about bringing these two worlds together, though African Instituted Churches, such as Aladura churches in Nigeria and Zionists in Southern Africa, have often emphazised healing and prayer. Modern Pentecostalism, however, is loud in its denunciation of the traditional spirits, all of whom are demonized. Yet they do address the issues of healing on a similar conceptual footing to traditional understandings, and this may be one reason for the rapid expansion of this type of Christianity in late twentieth-century Africa.

NEO-TRADITIONAL MOVEMENTS

There have been attempts to reinvent African religion as a 'religion' like Christianity or Islam. In Gabon, Bwiti freely incorporates Christian elements. Outside Africa, Candomblé in Brazil mixes local Catholicism and Yoruba orisha.

These movements are interesting, but they are not the major way in which African traditional religion survives. For most Africans this is more likely to be through the articulation of an authentic African spirituality within Islam and Christianity and in the wider social, political and ecological concerns of African life.

A wooden figure of an unknown god from the Yoruba pantheon of Nigeria.

SHINTO

The History of Shinto

Shinto – the traditional belief system of Japan – has no fundamental creeds or written teachings, and is n
particularly evangelical. However it resonates with a veneration for Japanese tradition and the invisible
presence of innumerable spiritual powers, or *kami*. Thus the spiritual insights attributed to Japan's ancie
inhabitants are regarded as just as valid now as throughout all the vicissitudes of history. Shinto is
essentially a body of ritual to relate with *kami* in a way that is respectful, warm, open, positive and vibrant
Local festivals (*matsuri*) have become so much part of social life and enshrine so much traditional
Japanese morality and social behaviour that participation seems natural common-sense, good
neighbourliness and part of being Japanese. Shinto has thus become a vehicle for many themes, and nee
not operate merely on the basis of conscious 'belief'.

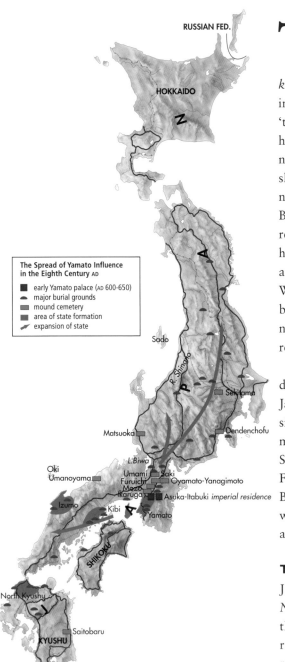

The Spread of Yamato Influence
in the Eighth Century AD
- ■ early Yamato palace (AD 600-650)
- ⌒ major burial grounds
- ▬ mound cemetery
- ▬ area of state formation
- ↗ expansion of state

T HE NAME 'Shinto' combines the
Chinese characters for *kami* and way,
(implying the way to/from and of the
kami). It was originally chosen by government
in the seventh century to distinguish
'traditional' worship from Buddhism. Shinto,
however, is clearly not simply an indigenous
native cult but reflects much of the ancient
shamanic traditions common to its Asian
neighbours. Historians can also pinpoint how
Buddhist, Taoist, Confucian and, more
recently, Christian philosophy and customs
have been adopted because of the attractions
and challenges of Chinese, Korean and
Western civilization. At times Shinto has also
been used by the Japanese State to unify the
nation under the Emperor, as a national
religion, against foreign enemies.

This background of political and academic
debate however has usually been alien to most
Japanese people, who have always spoken
simply of 'the *kami*', (never 'Shinto') and
moreover practise a mixture of Buddhism and
Shinto, without any sense of contradiction.
Furthermore, few Japanese would refer to either
Buddhism or Shinto as 'religion', or *shukyou*,
which is usually equated with pushy evangelism
and quibbling over dogma.

THE KAMI

Japan's earliest histories, the *Kojiki* and
Nihonshoki, were compiled on the orders of
the imperial family in AD 712 and AD 720
respectively, for the purpose of justifying the
royal lineage, and describe many of the most

Shinto festivals (*matsuri*) are very
much a part of the fabric of life in
Japan. Pictured here are participants in
the Maple Festival, a traditional Shinto
seasonal ritual for which people dress
in ancient costume.

**Left: The Spread of Yamato
Influence in the Eighth Century AD**
In the eighth century AD Shinto became
a political entity when Yamato writers
ascribed divine origins to the imperial
family, and so claimed legitimacy for
rule. Shinto thus became an essential
weapon for Yamato expansion. The map
shows the directions of this expansion.

important *kami*. Although there was an obvious political aim to unite all the regional and clan deities under the authority of the imperial, Yamato, clan-deity Amaterasu O-mikami, the *kami* of the sun, these legends provide an explanation for most Shinto rituals and the starting point for any official, Shinto 'theology'.

Some basic concepts that emerge are:

- *Kami* are not necessarily the same as 'gods'. They can die, and decompose like mortals. Some are human. There is no easy divide between what is animate and inanimate, cultural and natural, human and divine. Rather, all creation is the expression of spiritual powers. All things are bound together in a kind of spiritual family, and it is natural therefore to try and relate with the world emotionally, as well as materially and scientifically. Spiritual power is not spread equally, but can be recognized as especially powerful in particular phenomena and these are the *kami*.

- The *kami* are invisible and countless. Shinto focuses upon those that reveal their importance to people. Particular *kami* are identified with the kitchen, safety on the roads, education etc. Others are identified with places, especially forests, mountains or waterfalls, that seem especially numinous, or natural phenomena that are especially awesome, such as winds and thunder. Individuals too, who seem possessed of a special charisma or just very successful, might be called *kami*. Other, less important, spiritual forces are recognized, such as

mischievous elements like fox-spirits, *kitsune*, or tree spirits, *tengu*. These may be called on to communicate with us through mediums, to explain their behaviour. On special occasions, the *kami* may also possess a medium to send an important message.

- Individuals should venerate and entertain the *kami* most important to them, not only because their good will is required but also because they appreciate that individual's concern. They are not all-knowing, and want to be informed about significant events. They love most to see individuals enjoying themselves in a happy community.
- There is no teaching about the original creation of the universe, or about any future end or final judgement. Likewise, there is no clear description of any after-life. After a person dies, they simply merge with their ancestral *kami* and have no individual soul such as is taught in Christianity or Buddhism. Primary identity thus reflects membership in a community and social roles.
- Purity is essential to a right relationship with the *kami* and the avoidance of failure or disease. Many rituals feature the exorcism of sins in order to be restored to original purity. Cleanliness, sincerity (*makoto*) and politeness in particular signify freedom from bad external influences, and reliability. The *kami* are especially repelled by blood and by death. Traditionally, women were banned from shrine events during menstruation; those who worked with dead bodies, such as tanners, were not tolerated and soldiers required special purification after battle.

Every Shinto shrine has its own local deity. The Grand Shrine of Ise is dedicated to the sun goddess Amaterasu, one of many thousands of deities in the Japanese Pantheon, shown in this 1860 woodblock print by Utagawa Kumisada (1786–1865) re-emerging from her cave, lured by a sacred mirror.

A young woman at a Shinto shrine. Worshippers visit shrines for many reasons: for purification rites, to pray to the *kami* for good health or for luck.

Shinto Shrines (*jinja*)

Shinto shrines and ritual very carefully mark entry into a special world. Even in a bustling city, shrines express a different atmosphere. Surrounded by evergreen trees, and approached on a noisy gravel path, they still everyday conversation. There is a special silence, broken only by ritual hand-claps, or the sound of crows and seasonal insects. Shinto ritual, including music (*gakaku*) and dance (*kagura*), is characterized by a special slow, measured pace, appropriate to the timeless *kami* and quite different from daily life outside. On special occasions (*matsuri*) a mass of local people will be crowded together in noisy festivity, letting themselves go in front of the *kami* in ways they would never dream of doing outside the shrine.

I T IS IMPORTANT that the shrines blend into the environment chosen by the *kami*. Traditionally built from wood and generally left untreated, they need regular repair or rebuilding, and the work of the local community is thus bound to the life of the local shrine. This is still the tradition of Japan's most celebrated shrine, the Grand Shrine of Ise, dedicated to Amaterasu and reconstructed in ancient style every generation. Worship is done primarily in the open air, and the key buildings enshrine the tokens that are the focus of veneration.

THE KAMI

The *kami* do not 'live' in the shrines, and must be summoned politely. The approach to each shrine is marked by one or several great gateways, or *torii*, and there will be a basin to rinse hands and mouth. A shrine is usually dedicated to one particular *kami*, but may host any number of smaller shrines, representing other *kami* that local people should also venerate. Sacred points, such as entrances or particular trees and rocks, will be marked off by ropes of elaborately plaited straw, or streamers of plain paper.

Heinin-Jingu Shrine in Kyoto, founded in AD 792, is a major centre of Shinto worship. Powerful aristocratic families commissioned and supported many of the shrines in Kyoto, and the tradition of representing family honour through the shrines is reflected in the grand scale and elaborate architecture of the shrine complexes.

Prayers, for everything from getting a job to recovering from a serious illness, are often written down, or brought ready printed, and pinned up at Shinto shrines, such as this one in Osaka, Japan.

The *kami* are usually summoned by pulling a bell-rope outside the shrine, making a small (money) offering followed by two hand-claps, a short silent prayer, and two bows, but variation is tolerated and this procedure is longer at the most important shrines. The primary audience is always the *kami*. *Matsuri*, for example, seem great fun but always begin with an invitation by priests facing away from the people, towards the *kami*, and inviting them to attend, and end with priestly farewells on their departure.

Traditionally, the professional priesthood was limited to the great shrines, and local people took it in turns to be the priest. But recently the professional priesthood has grown to about 20,000, including 2,000 women priests. All except the smallest shrines will be the responsibility of a team of priests (*guji*) of various ranks, assisted by a team of local (unmarried) girls (*miko*) who perform ceremonial dances (*kagura*) and other services. Most new priests are now university graduates, usually from Shinto universities, and are often from priestly families. There is no equivalent to a Pope or leader of Shinto, and each shrine is independent. But most shrines are linked together through the national shrine organization (*jinja honcho*) which provides information and administrative services, and helps represent Shinto overseas.

Shinto Today

There are four major seasonal events: New Year, Rice-Planting (spring), O-Bon (a visit by the ancestors in mid-July or August) and Harvest Thanksgiving (autumn). In addition there will be the festival days of the local *kami*. There will also be special events to mark rites of passage, such as presenting a new-born baby to be recognized and protected by the *kami*, followed by further presentations during childhood (boys aged five, girls aged three and seven), then a coming-of-age ceremony when 20. Within the last 100 years, marriage has also begun to be celebrated at the local shrine. Funerals are left to Buddhist priests, since shrines must avoid pollution.

Left: A contemporary Shinto ceremonial procession in Kyushu, Japan. In modern-day Shinto, there is no formulaic system of belief, and it is characterized by the observance of festivals and ceremonies, rather than doctrine.

MOST TRADITIONAL FAMILY homes feature a *kamidana* or shelf on which amulets and tokens of the *kami* are displayed. Particular rooms associated with pollution or danger, such as the toilet and kitchen, may also feature amulets.

THE ROLE OF THE EMPEROR

The failure of Japan's brutal adventure into mainland Asia from 1894 to 1945, in the name of the emperor, has complicated his place in Shinto. The emperor has been promoted as Shinto's high priest, Japan's primary link with the most important *kami* – notably Amaterasu O-mikami – since the very foundation of the Japanese state by the Yamato clan around the early sixth century. Between 1868 and 1945, this tradition was interpreted to make him head of state, and State Shinto was promulgated as the chief arm of government, but the emperor was not given any clear mandate to rule.

Since 1945, the Japanese constitution forbids any formal link between members of government and religious activism. The Shinto ceremony when the crown prince formally becomes an

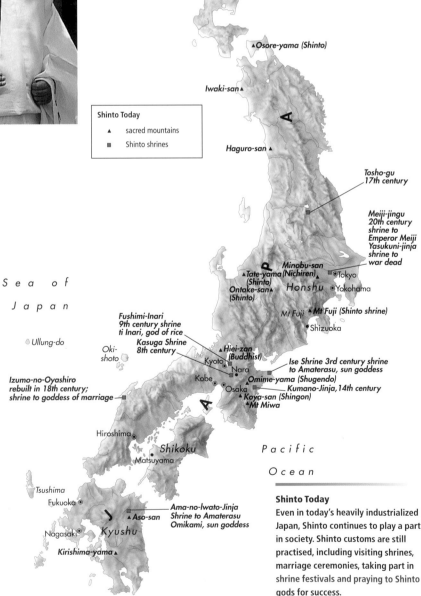

Shinto Today
▲ sacred mountains
■ Shinto shrines

Shinto Today
Even in today's heavily industrialized Japan, Shinto continues to play a part in society. Shinto customs are still practised, including visiting shrines, marriage ceremonies, taking part in shrine festivals and praying to Shinto gods for success.

emperor in theory makes his body the host of a *kami*, but in Japanese law the Emperor is now merely the symbol of the Japanese nation and not a religious figure. He still has a busy schedule of rituals to perform, such as offering the first fruits after harvest to (other) *kami*.

The myth that all Japanese are 'children of the *kami*', especially Amaterasu O-mikami, through the emperor, has made it easy to generate a proud nation unified on the basis of a common ethnic origin. It fails, however, to respect the rights of those whose roots do not lie in the Yamato tradition, such as the Ainu or Okinawans, or immigrants, and claim the right to be different.

NEW SHINTO SECTS

Since around the middle of the nineteenth century, as Japan faced up to all sorts of crises due to foreign imperialism and internal change, a variety of local Shinto cults appeared. Typically, they introduced new, hitherto unknown *kami*, who could help the people and meet the new challenges. Often they assumed an international character, unlike traditional Shinto, and sought to compete with Christianity as evangelical, saviour religions.

Insofar as they played down the significance of the emperor, they were suppressed until 1945. Since then, some such as Tenri-kyo, Sekai Kyusei Kyo and Mahikari have enjoyed spectacular success for example in Southeast Asia or South America, where similar spirit-based cults are indigenous.

Shinto priests perform part of a fire ceremony in Osaka. Fire is an important part of many Shinto ceremonies, and is seen, like water, as a purifying force.

World Religions

BUDDHISM

The Buddha

The Buddha was born, lived and died a human being. He is not a god. The special thing about him was that he realized the state of sublime wisdom and compassion called Nirvana. He discovered the causes of all suffering, and the way by which all beings could reach the same state.

G AUTAMA SIDDHARTHA, the historical Buddha, was born in the year 566 BC, the son of the king of the Sakya people in present-day Nepal. At his birth it was prophesied that he would either become a world ruler or a great sage. His father wanted the former, so he arranged for his son to be brought up without seeing the troubles of the world. Gautama grew up to be a handsome youth, who excelled in all kinds of activities. He lived a happy and contented life within the walls of the palace, and married a princess, Yasodhara, who bore him a son, Rahula.

ENLIGHTENMENT

One day, Gautama persuaded his groom to take him outside the city walls. There he encountered four things which changed his life. First he saw an old man, then a sick man, and a corpse. Gautama was shocked, and asked for an explanation. The groom told him that these conditions were normal, and happened to everyone. Gautama then met a wandering holy man, who had given up everything to practise the religious life and seek the answer to suffering. He radiated a sense of serenity which Gautama knew he had to find.

Soon afterwards, Gautama shaved his head, and slipped out of the palace. He wandered far and wide, begging for his food, and subjecting himself to all kinds of austerities. Eventually, almost dying with hunger, he decided such practices would not achieve his goal. He resolved to practise a middle way between

The temple of the Golden Buddha at Wat Traimit, Bangkok, Thailand, is famous for its five and a half ton Buddha statue of solid gold, rediscovered in the 1950s after being hidden to protect it from invaders.

Buddhism
Buddha was born in the year 566 BC in Nepal. At his birth it was prophesied that he would either become a great ruler or a great sage. Today, 360 million Buddhists account for almost six percent of the world's population across 92 countries. The map shows the distribution of Buddhists throughout the world.

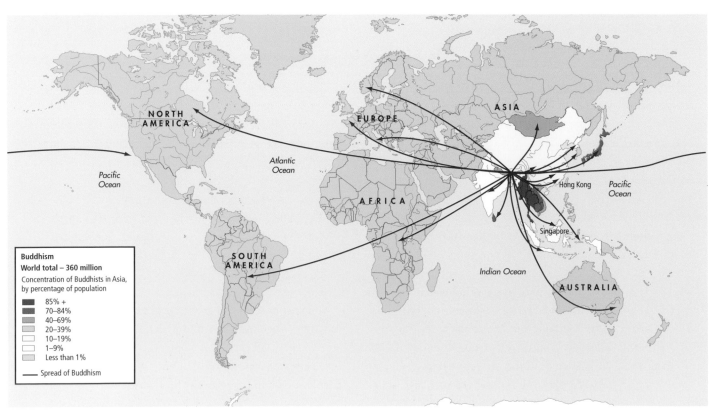

Buddhism
World total – 360 million
Concentration of Buddhists in Asia, by percentage of population

- 85% +
- 70–84%
- 40–69%
- 20–39%
- 10–19%
- 1–9%
- Less than 1%
- —— Spread of Buddhism

austerity and luxury. He took a little food, and sat beneath a tree at a place called Bodh Gaya in present-day Bihar, vowing not to move until he had achieved his goal.

At the age of 35, on the night of the full moon in May, he realized Nirvana, (awakening, enlightenment) entering into deep meditation and becoming the Buddha, the Enlightened One. The Buddha would never explain Nirvana, saying that it is essentially beyond words and thoughts, and so Buddhists also refrain from speculating about it.

HIS MESSAGE

At first, the new Buddha was reluctant to instruct others, feeling that they would not understand. However, the god Brahma appeared to him, and begged him to teach 'for the sake of those with but little dust in their eyes'. He agreed, and delivered his first sermon on the Four Noble Truths in the Deer Park near Varanasi, India. In his lifetime, the Buddha taught all who wanted to listen, men and women, rich and poor. We are also told that he taught animals and spiritual beings of various kinds.

His message was always the same: 'suffering, the causes of suffering and the way out of suffering'. He did not talk about God or the soul, or encourage speculation in matters that could not be proved. Rather, he specifically told people to believe and practise only those things which were helpful and led to freedom and peace of mind. It was a combination of profound wisdom and deep compassion, and a practical way which could be followed by those who wished. This teaching he called the Dharma. Many of his disciples chose to follow the Buddha into the homeless life, and thus was born the Sangha, or community.

Eventually, the Buddha's life came to an end, and he passed away aged 80 at Kusinara, India. His followers were grief-stricken, but the Buddha's final words to them were, 'All conditioned things are impermanent. Strive on!'

A 14-m (46-ft) long reclining Buddha at Vihara in Sri Lanka. Reclining Buddhas represent the death of the historical Buddha, with the accompanying extinction of desire and attainment of Nirvana.

THE HISTORICAL BUDDHA*

566 BC	Buddha born
550 BC	Marries Yasodhara
535 BC	Son Rahula born
536 BC	Leaves home
528 BC	Achieves Nirvana and preaches first sermon
526 BC	Founds Sangha
c. **523 BC**	Order of nuns founded
c. **522 BC**	King Bimbisara donates bamboo grove at Magadha
483 BC	Achieved Parinirvana (dies)

* The dates are traditional, but not universally recognized.

THE FOUR NOBLE TRUTHS

The Four Noble Truths are the heart of the Buddha's teaching. They are:

- The fact of suffering;
- The cause of suffering;
- The fact that there is a way out of suffering;
- The way itself.

The Buddha observed that all beings suffered. The cause of this suffering is selfish desire, and a misunderstanding of the nature of 'self', which is not the fixed, separate and enduring entity that it appears to be. What we call 'self' is actually a collection of *skandhas* (heaps or particles) which are constantly changing. These are form, feelings, perception, mind-contents and consciousness. The relationship of these constitutes our 'self' at any moment, and creates *karma* (action and reaction) which influences our birth, life and rebirth. One of the *skandhas* is form, so rebirth is always in some form, which need not be human.

Having discovered for himself that there is a way out of suffering, the Buddha proceeded to outline it. This is the final Truth, The Noble Eightfold Path of the way out of suffering:

- Right view (understanding, attitude);
- Right aim (intention, resolve, motive or thought);
- Right speech (not lying, slandering or gossiping);
- Right action (or conduct);
- Right livelihood (means of living);
- Right effort;
- Right mindfulness (awareness of things as they are);
- Right concentration (contemplation, meditation).

The Buddha summed up this path as: 'Cease to do evil; learn to do good, and purify your heart.'

Early Buddhism

Following the death of the Buddha in 483 BC, the concept of the Sangha, or community, of monks grew ever more important. The Buddha had ordained monks in his lifetime, calling them to follow the homeless life and practise the Dharma, and their number continued to grow after his passing.

T HE FIRST MONKS were considered to be *arahats*, beings enlightened by the Buddha's teaching. There was no formal ordination ceremony. The Buddha taught them the Dharma, and invited them to leave home and family. They in turn ordained others. The Buddha had charged his followers to 'travel for the welfare and happiness of people, and out of compassion for the world', and this they did. Some 200 years after the Buddha's death the movement had spread throughout India. They depended on lay people for food and other necessities, and the relationship grew whereby the monks were fed in return for teaching.

Much of Buddhism's early success was due to the patronage of higher class members of society such as King Bimbisara of Magadha and many of his court. The king gave the Buddha a bamboo grove where the monks could stay. It was considered an action of high merit to give to monks, so they were well supported in their work of spreading the Dharma. However, the Buddha's teaching also embraced the lowest classes, as he rejected the caste system and taught that all could attain enlightenment.

ORGANIZATION

Soon after the Buddha's death (in approximately 483 BC), the First Great Council of 500 senior

monks was held. These monks were all *arahats* who had known the Buddha. They met to recite the teaching as they remembered it, and to agree a definitive version. However, there were some who did not agree that the Council had preserved the pure teaching of the Buddha.

The teaching was preserved in oral tradition, and it was not until many years later that it was written down. It was grouped into three *pitakas* or baskets. Vinaya consisted of the rules for monks (*bhikkhus*) and nuns (*bhikkhunis*). These not only provide guidelines for the

Giant Buddha at Kandy, Sri Lanka; the Buddha ordained monks and nuns in order that his word might be spread amongst the laity. This continues to this day, with many monks relying on donations of food and essentials in return for their teaching and wisdom.

The Spread of Buddhism by AD 500 Despite humble beginnings the message of Buddhism soon spread. This map shows the diffusion of Buddhism throughout the near and far east by AD 500.

The Spread of Buddhism by AD 500

→ spread of Buddhism

---- first area of Buddhist missionary activity

-·-·- area of rise of Mahayana Buddhism

● Buddhist sites

monastic life, but allow for settling of disputes and imposing discipline. Sutta is the collection of the Buddha's sermons, while *abhidamma* (higher Dharma) consists largely of philosophical analysis of the Buddha's teachings. It was the differing interpretations in this section which caused most of the disputes between the various emerging schools.

THE TWO TRADITIONS

A second Great Council took place around 383 BC. By this time, several schools had come into existence. Part of the controversy was over whether Buddhists should only try to gain their own enlightenment (*arahats*) or whether they should seek the freedom from suffering of all beings (*bodhisattvas*). In fact, as compassion is an essential aspect of Buddhist practice, this is largely a question of semantics. Today, there are two main traditions, the Theravada or Teaching of the Elders, and the Mahayana or Greater Vehicle, which contains a number of different traditions such as Zen, Vajrayana and Pure Land.

While the various schools differed in many ways, they were united by the Dharma, and by the *vinaya*, the rules of monastic life, even though interpretations differed.

As time went by, Buddhism tended to lose its distinctive character due to the influence of various Hindu teachings, and so virtually disappeared from India as a separate religion.

A Buddhist monk standing outside the temples at Angkor Wat, Cambodia. These huge temples date from the eleventh to the thirteenth centuries AD.

THE SANGHA

The original meaning of Sangha is the community of monks. Today, different traditions place different emphases on what constitutes Sangha. In the Theravada and some Mahayana traditions, the Sangha is limited to those who have 'embraced the homeless life' – even though they may live in monasteries. The Buddha himself laid down rules for the monastic Sangha. At the First Council, 227 rules were recited, and these became the basis for the Sangha. Monks (and nuns) are celibate and keep other *vinaya* rules, such as the times they may eat.

In other Mahayana traditions, such as Zen and Pure Land, the term Sangha is used for all 'Disciples of the Buddha' whether lay or monastic. In these traditions, priests can be married and the temple may be a family affair.

Nuns have extra rules to follow, including being subservient to monks. Originally, the Buddha was reluctant to ordain nuns, and only did so after much persuasion. This was mainly because of the attitude to women prevailing in his time. In some schools the order of nuns died out, and today efforts are being made to restore it from traditions where it survived.

Buddhism has not been free from the patriachal attitudes associated with other religions: the Buddha was reluctant to ordain women as well as men, and nuns have never enjoyed the same status and support as monks. Pictured are nuns praying at Anuradhapura, a holy place in Sri Lanka.

Theravada Buddhism

Theravada – the Way of the Elders – is the oldest form of Buddhism, being largely unchanged from the third century BC. It is found throughout Southeast Asia. Its teachings come from the Pali Scriptures, interpreted in a conservative manner which gives prime importance to the Sangha of ordained monks and the liberation of the individual.

PALI IS AN Indian language which is similar to the one which the Buddha spoke. It is one of the two languages of the earliest Buddhist writings, the other being Sanskrit. It is possible that Pali was the language in which the oral tradition was preserved, and it was certainly the one in which the first written scriptures were produced, in Sri Lanka in the first century BC.

The written scriptures adhere faithfully to the pattern of oral tradition established by the great Buddhist Councils, namely, *vinaya*, *sutta* and *abhidamma*. They show the Buddha as a human being – albeit a unique one – who realized Nirvana through his own efforts, and they give his teaching of the way to attain a happy, peaceful and contented life. The Pali Canon mentions few miraculous events, but emphasizes the life and teaching of the Buddha as the great miracle.

A young monk says prayers at the Wat Patoom Wanaram temple in Bangkok, Thailand, kneeling before statues of the Buddhas. Thai Buddhists tend to follow the Theraveda school of Buddhism, and traditionally young men have been expected to perform a period of religious service as a monk.

THE WAY OF THE ELDERS

The essence of the Theravadin way is based on the monastic life. This is the way to attain Nirvana, and, for most lay people, the goal is to be reborn in a life where they can become a monk or nun. Many laymen become monks for a few months, either in their teens or after their families have been cared for.

Theravada Buddhism
The map shows the main areas of Theravada Buddhism in Southeast Asia today.

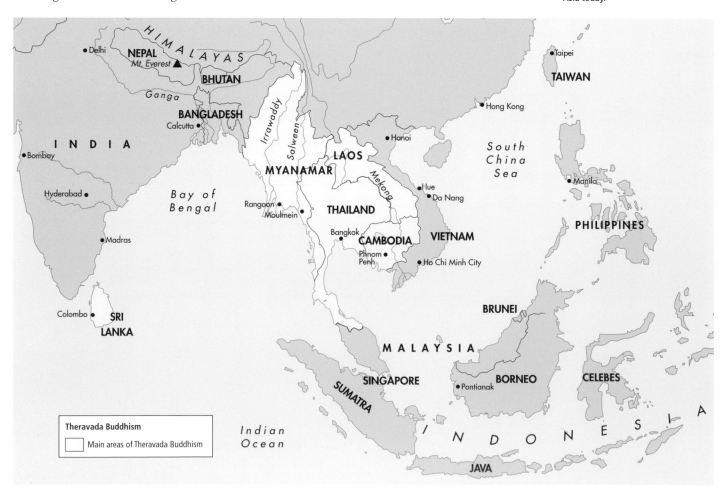

Theravada Buddhism
☐ Main areas of Theravada Buddhism

The Sangha is supported by lay people, and monks are not allowed to work or handle money. Their main activities are meditation, study and teaching the Dharma. Their only possessions are their robes, and a few articles for daily use such as a toothbrush and begging bowl.

The Theravadin Sangha claims unbroken succession from the Buddha, as each ordination has to be conducted by a number of fully ordained monks.

TEACHINGS AND PRACTICE

The teachings of the Theravada are the basic ones of Buddhism. They are the Signs of Being, (*dukkha*, that life is essentially unsatisfactory, *annica*, that all things are impermanent or constantly changing, and *anatta*, that we do not have a permanent unchanging self); the Four Noble Truths and the Noble Eightfold Path. The practise of morality is very important, based on the Precepts or rule of life. The five basic precepts are:

- Not to kill or harm living beings;
- Not to take what is not freely given;
- Not to indulge in sexual impropriety;
- Not to use slanderous or lying speech;
- Not to become intoxicated by using substances which cloud the mind.

Monks and nuns follow these and a lot more.

People become Buddhists by announcing, usually before a monk, that they, 'Take refuge in the Buddha, Dharma and Sangha', and by agreeing to follow these five precepts.

Theravadin Buddhist practice has little in the way of ceremony, though devotees will attend a temple for a *puja*, or recitation of portions of the Pali scriptures. Important times in a person's life will also be marked by chanting.

An important practice is meditation, which is the way the Buddha achieved his goal. There are many kinds of meditation, and the basic forms practised in Theravada Buddhism are also found in other traditions.

The upper terrace at Borobodur, Java, at dawn; inside each of the domes is a statue of the Buddha. Built between 750 AD and 850 AD Borobudor represents a Buddhist vision of the cosmos, peaking with Nirvana at its centre.

Buddha image within the Shwedagon Paya complex, Yangon, Myanmar.

MEDITATION

Meditation is one step on the Eightfold Path, and one practice through which Buddhists aim to become free of suffering. Four main types are practised within Theravada Buddhism.

- *Samatha* or concentration is the peaceful calming of the mind through concentration. It is usually practised by watching the breath, and being aware of it without trying to change anything.
- Mindfulness consists of being aware of the activities of body and mind in whatever we might be doing, and watching the mind's reaction.
- *Metta* or loving kindness is the practise of suffusing all beings with thoughts of wellbeing and loving kindness. 'May all beings be well and happy' is the traditional phrase. 'All beings' include those we love, those we like and those we dislike, beings other than human, and ourselves.

- *Vipassana* or insight meditation enables us to be aware of the ever-changing nature of the self, and its relationship with the world around us. In it, there is direct observation of the physical and mental components that make up what we call our 'self'.

It is preferable to learn meditation from a teacher, and in the Theravada this is usually – though not always – a member of the Sangha.

Mahayana Buddhism

Mahayana is the form of Buddhism found in Tibet, China, Mongolia, Vietnam, Korea and Japan. It recognizes the Theravadin scriptures, and adds many more, some of which were composed after the historical Buddha's lifetime. Some were based on remembered teaching, others are mythological, and some are said to have been recorded and hidden until the time was ripe to reveal them.

IN MAHAYANA BUDDHISM, Buddha is not limited to the historical Gautama. There are other Buddhas recognized who are not historical figures, but who represent different aspects of his enlightenment. Two of the principle ones are Amitabha (the Buddha of Infinite Light) and Bhaisajya (The Medicine Buddha), but there are many more. Their lives and teachings were revealed by Shakyamuni Buddha, and are recorded in the Mahayana scriptures to help disciples understand various practices.

There are also *bodhisattvas* such as the Chinese Guan Yin or the Tibetan Tara, who represent the personification of active compassion, and Manjusri, the manifestation of wisdom. Bodhisattvas are often spiritualized beings who were disiples of the historical Buddha, but who delayed their own enlightenment, choosing to remain on earth, until all beings are freed from suffering. Their power can help practitioners who know the correct way of invoking it.

A gilt-bronze sculpture of Amitayus, the Buddha of Infinite Life, from Tibet. He is meditating upon a vase, symbolizing longevity.

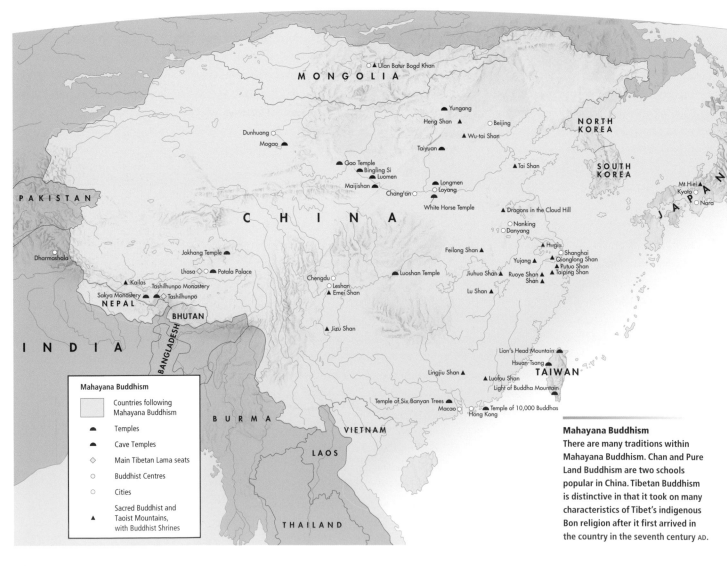

Mahayana Buddhism

There are many traditions within Mahayana Buddhism. Chan and Pure Land Buddhism are two schools popular in China. Tibetan Buddhism is distinctive in that it took on many characteristics of Tibet's indigenous Bon religion after it first arrived in the country in the seventh century AD.

BUDDHA NATURE

Another important aspect of Buddha in the Mahayana is Buddha Nature, which is latent in all, and which the various practices reveal. In the earlier Buddhism, enlightenment was something that could only be achieved by the few, after many lifetimes, and then only by those who were ordained. The Mahayana emphasizes that Buddhahood is not limited, but is the Real Nature of living beings, with them from the very beginning, and only needing to be revealed.

The essence of Buddha Nature is emptiness, in that it is still not a 'self', but is something that is beyond the ability of words to describe. It is sometimes referred to as 'the Unborn' or 'Mind' (capitalized) and said to be the perfect balance of wisdom and compassion. It is hidden by the defilements or hindrances of greed, anger and ignorance, and the various practices of the Mahayana are taught because they have been found to remove these hindrances, and allow the Buddha Nature to shine forth.

PRACTICES

Mahayana practices include all the forms of meditation previously mentioned, as well as the practise of morality. However, it also includes a number of other practices not found in the Theravada.

One of these is the Bodhisattva Vow, through which practitioners dedicate their practice to the release of all beings from suffering, and vow to master all the teachings and practices of the Buddha Way. Further, they vow not to attain their own enlightenment until all beings are freed from suffering. For Mahayana practitioners, it is the removal of suffering from the world that is more important than personal release.

In general, Mahayana Buddhism is more ritualistic, although the ritual is seen as being a form of conscious yoga in which there is visualization of spiritual beings and an acceptance of the power of their help. This power is a living reality for Mahayana Buddhists, and can help relieve suffering in this world and the next. For example, within the Pure Land tradition, Amitabha vowed to help ordinary beings to attain enlightenment, even if they have not mastered their own defilements.

Left: Caves in China and Tibet are often used to house Buddhist shrines and statues, such as this twelfth-century sculpture of the Buddha entering Nirvana at Daoding Hill, China.

TIBETAN BUDDHISM

Tibetan Buddhism, with its mysterious practices and colourful art, is becoming better known in the West, partly due to the influence of His Holiness the Dalai Lama. The Tibetan tradition is subdivided into a number of different schools which contain the whole range of Buddhist practices.

The principle teaching is the Lam Rim or graduated path, the first part of which consists of taking refuge in the Triple Jewel (Buddha, Dharma and Sangha), the practice of ethical behaviour and basic meditation. The second stage empowers meditations which help to overcome the limitations of greed, anger and ignorance, and an understanding of the interdependence of all existing things. The final stage is the Bodhisattva Path, in which the practitioner seeks full enlightenment for the benefit of all beings, through the development of Great Compassion and Perfect Wisdom. The Vajrayana or Diamond Way is the highest practice, which aims at achieving Buddhahood in this lifetime.

The Tibetan tradition encourages the use of grand ceremonies, music, dancing, chanting, and colourful paintings of various deities, the production of which is itself a spiritual practice. Many of its foremost lamas or teachers are *rimpoches*, or rebirths of famous lamas of the past, the discovery of whom is rigorously tested.

Tibetan Buddhism also has a tradition of silent meditation without symbols called Dzogchen, which is in many ways close to Japanese Zen.

Stone Mandarins stand guard over the entrance to the tomb of Emperor Tu Doc in Vietnam, one of the finest of Hue's royal tombs of the Nguyen Dynasty (1802–1945).

Zen Buddhism

Zen is the Japanese form of the Chinese Chan, which is the phonetic pronunciation of the Sanskrit *dhyana* or meditation. The practice of meditation – sitting or moving – is the basis for Zen activity of all kinds, whether in the temple, tea-room, the home or the martial arts practice hall.

I T IS SAID that Zen started one day when the Buddha silently twirled a flower instead of speaking. None of his disciples understood, except Mahakasyapa, who smiled. The Buddha then explained that the essential truth of his teaching is beyond words, and that he had given it to Mahakasyapa.

The tradition passed down through a number of Indian patriarchs to Bodhidharma, who brought it to China in the early sixth century AD. He was summoned by the emperor, who asked what merit building temples and translating scriptures had gained him. 'No merit at all', answered Bodhidharma, who then retired to a cave to meditate for nine years. Huike, the first Chinese patriarch, came to Bodhidharma seeking peace of mind. 'Bring me your mind and I will pacify it', said Bodhidharma. 'I cannot find my mind', Huike answered. 'There! I have pacified it', exclaimed Bodhidharma.

From such beginnings, Zen extended throughout China in ways that were often similarly unintelligible to the reasoning mind, and spread to Japan, Korea and Vietnam.

JAPAN

When Zen reached Japan, it became at the same time more organized and more iconoclastic. Phrases such as 'If you meet the Buddha, kill him' sought to drive Zen practitioners beyond the confines of organized religion. Three major streams emerged, as well as many charismatic figures who were outstanding in their own right.

- Soto Zen was founded by Dogen (1200–53). It emphasized *zazen* or sitting meditation, through which the sitter's Buddha Nature is revealed. Enlightenment is seen as a gradual process, revealed in the process of sitting.
- Rinzai Zen was founded by Eisai (1141–1215). It emphasizes meditation on *koans*, riddles that have no logical answer. This creates a 'great ball of doubt', the shattering of which brings about sudden *satori* or enlightenment.

- Obaku Zen, the smallest of the schools, was founded in China, and maintained Chinese traditions in its chanting, ceremonies and other practices, retaining aspects such as the Pure Land teaching.

In addition to meditation, all traditions include in their training work such as cooking or sweeping, and religious ceremonies with bowing and chanting.

ZEN ORIGINALS

One of the greatest Zen originals was Bankei (1622–93). Although he trained in orthodox Zen, he taught that all beings had what he called 'the Unborn Buddha Mind', and the only thing necessary was to remember this at all times. Formal meditation and religious practices were not necessary. Though he left no official successors, many were said to have become enlightened just through hearing him speak.

Towards the end of the seventeenth century, Rinzai Zen became stagnated and declined. Hakuin Zenji (1686–1768) reformed the monastic orders, systematizing *koan*

A monumental seated stone Buddha from the thirteenth century at Kamakura, Japan. Gigantic Buddha statues are common in China and Japan, and the largest in the world is on top of a mountain in Hong Kong.

practice, and insisting on the value of *zazen*. He also had many lay disciples who he taught according to their needs. He left many enlightened successors.

Ryokan (1758–1831) is one of the best-loved poets in Japan. A Soto monk and hermit, he lived alone practising meditation, writing poems and playing with the local children. His simplicity and childlike nature impressed all who knew him, and is clearly obvious in his poetry.

ZEN BUDDHISM	
*c.*500 BC	Founded by the Historical Buddha as the Dhyana (meditation) tradition
c. AD 470	Bodhidarma 28th Indian Patriarch born
AD 530	Bodhidharma creates the Chan tradition in China
AD 543	Bodhidharma dies
AD 638	Hui Neng (6th Chinese Patriarch who established Chan in China) born
AD 713	Hui Neng dies
c. AD 786	Lin-Chi (Rinzai) born in China
AD 866	Rinzai dies.
1141	Eisai (who took the Rinzai tradition to Japan) born
1215	Eisai dies
1200	Dogen Zenji (founder of the Japanese Soto tradition) born
1253	Dogen dies.

ZEN AND THE ARTS

Zen had an impact on all aspects of Japanese life. Millions of people who never practised religious Zen were influenced by it through arts such as calligraphy, painting, tea ceremony, flower arranging and music.

One of the most typically Zen arts is calligraphy, which varies from formal characters to a free style that is hardly readable by ordinary Japanese. It was valued so much that it often replaced the Buddha image in temple and family shrines. Most of the celebrated Zen *roshis* – a word literally meaning 'old boy' but signifying master – were famous for their calligraphy and poetry, being pestered by disciples to 'write something' for the home, or even for mundane uses such as shop signs.

This background of meditation was also true of the so-called martial arts. In judo, karate, kendo (sword-fighting) and archery, meditation, both sitting and moving, is a part of the traditional training. The essence of these arts is not to hurt the opponent, but to resolve the conflict in the most harmonious way possible, which often leads to one party backing down without a blow being struck.

In all arts, the Zen way of teaching includes mindfulness, which is a form of meditation. The potter pauses before putting the clay on the wheel, the musician practises 'Blowing Zen' as he plays his bamboo flute. The Zen influence on the tea ceremony emphasizes being in the moment, and caring for the guests. It has evolved it into a religious ritual, a moving meditation of hospitality. And, above all, the Zen ideal of the natural garden inspires visitors the world over with its peace and tranquillity.

The tea ceremony, invented in the seventeenth century, is practised as an art form in Japan. Although not specifically religious, its meditative and reflective spirit draws great inspiration from Zen Buddhism.

A Zen garden in Kyoto, Japan. Zen gardens are designed to facilitate quiet reflection, and mirror the whole cosmos in miniature.

Living Buddhism

In spite of persecution – most notably in the last 70 years – Buddhism is still one of the world's major religions. It has a significant presence in most countries in the East – even where governments have been hostile – and is growing in the West. Practices vary considerably, as do the forms of Sangha and the style of temples and monastic buildings.

IT IS SAID that the Buddha taught 84,000 different ways to enlightenment. Meditation is the traditional practice to this end, but other forms of Buddhism have evolved to meet the needs of suffering beings today, and have become ever more popular.

In the Pali Canon, the Buddha refrained from commenting on what happens after death. However, in some Mahayana scriptures, he told of Buddha-lands created by the enlightenment of other Buddhas, into which we might be reborn. The basic practice for this is simply chanting the name of the Buddha concerned, such as Amitabha or Guan Yin. This practice became widespread in all Far Eastern Buddhist countries, and it has become one of the most popular of all Buddhist traditions.

Other forms of Buddhism also use chanting as a practice, principally those based on the Lotus Sutra, such as the Tendai and Nichiren schools. The Lotus Sutra is considered to be the synthesis of all the Buddha's teaching, and chanting its title is one of the most suitable ways to enlightenment in this contemporary age.

ENGAGED BUDDHISM

Another phenomenon of Buddhism has evolved in the form of what is called 'Engaged Buddhism'. Traditionally, Buddhism was concerned with the removal of the causes of suffering through the individual. Today, some Buddhists are concerned with working to bring about changes in society, improving the welfare

The symbol of the Buddha's eyes, shown here on the wall of the Swayambhunath temple in Kathmandu, Nepal. The eyes are a striking reminder to Buddhists that they are being watched by the Buddha, and in Nepal are a common feature of everyday life, appearing on religious buildings, and even on T-shirts.

110

of those who suffer. They see their work as the engagement of compassion in the suffering world, and use the term 'Engaged Buddhism' to explain their motivation.

Because non-violence is one of the Buddhist precepts, it is consistent for Buddhists to have concerns for peace, and to work actively in this field. Today, there are many other aspects of engaged Buddhism, such as a hospice for AIDS sufferers in San Francisco, and a scheme for feeding homeless people in London. Buddhist monks in Thailand have 'ordained trees' by wrapping them in Buddhist robes to stop illegal logging operations, and something similar has been done in Nepal. Buddhists also actively campaign for animal welfare and refugee work, particularly with Tibetan refugees. They have also worked with the 'untouchables' in India, and with re-building Cambodia after the genocide there.

FESTIVALS AND CELEBRATIONS

One major feast, Vesak, is celebrated by Buddhists the world over. It brings together Buddhists from Theravadin and the various Mahayana schools. This is the Buddha's birthday, which is celebrated on the day of the full moon in May. Theravadin Buddhists also celebrate the Buddha's enlightenment and death on the same day. Others celebrate his Nirvana in December and his death in February.

Special ceremonies are used to celebrate the Buddha's birthday. In Chinese and Japanese

Three monks take tea together at a monastery in Bangkok. Many Thai men enter a monastery for one or two years at some stage in their lives.

traditions, a statue of the baby Buddha is bathed with sweet tea by all present, and there are street processions with elaborate floats commemorating events from the Buddha's life.

Another festival that is celebrated by Buddhists everywhere is that of the New Year, although the date varies from country to country. New Year celebrations are often mixed up with local traditions providing lavish festivities with music and dancing in which everybody can join. The Sangha are invited to bring a blessing to the New Year by chanting and making offerings to the Buddha. It is also a time when individual Buddhists will seek to forgive those who may have harmed them, and make reparation to those they have injured in any way.

RITES OF PASSAGE

Rites of passage also differ from country to country. They are as important for Buddhists as for any other religion, as they are seen as emphasizing the Buddha's teaching of change, and bringing it home to those concerned. It is also important for people to be able to celebrate them, and invoke the Buddha's blessing on the occasion.

Births, marriages, naming ceremonies and funerals are all commemorated in ways that follow national customs and legal requirements. The Buddhist element usually consists of chanting from members of the Sangha, probably in the local temple of those most concerned. There may also be rites such as giving new Buddhist names, the exchanging of tokens and sprinkling of water as a sign of purity.

As in other religions, the religious ceremonies are usually followed with a feast or party, sometimes with music and dancing, and often with special food.

Four young Buddhist monks at the Bodnath Stupa, Kathmandu valley, Nepal. Buddhist novices often enter a temple at a very young age, but do not necessarily take lifelong vows.

CHRISTIANITY

The Life and Teaching of Jesus

Jesus of Nazareth, c. 6 BC–AD 32, is the most important person in the Christian religion. While his teaching followed the traditional Jewish style of religious debate it is who he was that is central for Christians. They believe Jesus was the Son of God, that he was born on earth, lived the life of a human being, was crucified, died and then rose from the dead. His dying and rising revealed God's love for the world and offered all people the possibility of eternal life.

FOR CHRISTIANS the most important event in history has been, and will always be, the birth, life, death and resurrection of Jesus.

Historically nothing of his life is known outside the four gospels contained in the Christian Bible. These, however, are not primarily historical accounts; rather they give an interpretation of what the life of Jesus meant. Consequently there are some events and stories that appear in two or three of the gospels and some that are distinctive to one. There is, however, a core to Jesus's teaching; the Kingdom of God is now present, God has sent prophets in the past but now Jesus's coming opens up the possibility for all people to enter that Kingdom. Jesus is the fulfillment of God's promises to the people of Israel, that they would be his people, he would give them a land (Israel) and he would be their God.

At the time of Jesus's birth (now considered to be between 6–4 BC) the Romans ruled over the land of Israel. They were the major force in the Mediterranean world. The Jews, and Jesus was a Jew, were allowed certain 'freedoms' in order to practise

their religion but were aware of the presence and pressure of their Roman overlords.

THE JEWISH CONTEXT

There were various Jewish groups jostling for position at the time of Jesus's teaching life. The

Jesus Christ is the central figure of Christianity; the symbol of the cross on which he was crucified is synonymous with the Christian faith.

Jesus's Palestine
Jesus was born in Palestine during the reign of Herod the Great (37–4 BC). Herod was a client king of the Romans and he left his kingdom to his three sons, Herod Antipas (Galilee and Peraea), Philip the Tetrach (northern Transjordan) and Archelaeus (Judaea, Samaria and Idumaea). In AD 6 the Roman government took control of Archelaus's territories which were later ruled by Pontius Pilate.

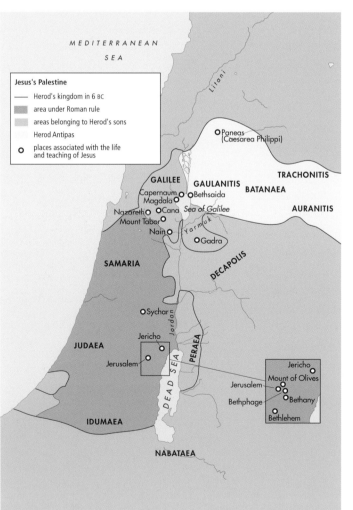

Jesus's Palestine
— Herod's kingdom in 6 BC
area under Roman rule
areas belonging to Herod's sons
Herod Antipas
o places associated with the life and teaching of Jesus

MEDITERRANEAN SEA

Litani

Paneas (Caesarea Philippi)

GALILEE GAULANITIS BATANAEA TRACHONITIS
Capernaum Bethsaida
Magdala
Nazareth Cana Sea of Galilee AURANITIS
Mount Tabor Yarmuk
Nain
Gadra

SAMARIA DECAPOLIS

Sychar

Jericho
JUDAEA Jordan PERAEA
Jerusalem DEAD SEA

Jericho
Mount of Olives
Jerusalem
Bethphage Bethany
Bethlehem

IDUMAEA

NABATAEA

Pharisees are shown in the Gospels to be Jesus's enemies because he challenged many of their ideas and attitudes, although they were concerned to maintain the essential qualities of Jewish life and religion. Disputation, debate and interpretation were part and parcel of their method of teaching. The Sadducees, another group, reflected the interests of more traditional Jews. There were other groups, like the Zealots who were more 'Messianic' in flavour. They were expecting the arrival of the 'Anointed One' (Messiah, in Greek 'Christ') who would release them from Roman domination.

JESUS'S LIFE

The Gospels of Matthew and Luke say that Jesus was born in Bethlehem and grew up with Joseph, his father, and Mary, his mother, in Nazareth, in Northern Galilee. Joseph is traditionally believed to have been a carpenter and would probably have taught the growing Jesus something of his trade.

It is likely that Jesus's ministry began when he was about 30 years old. He probably taught for three years after being baptized in the River Jordan by John the Baptist (his cousin). Christians believe John was the forerunner of Jesus, preparing the way for him. Jesus travelled throughout Israel, teaching and healing. He gathered many men and women around him; key amongst them were 12 men called disciples. Jesus became involved in conflict with the religious authorities in Jerusalem. He was arrested, tried and nailed to a cross, crucified and died. Christians believe, and the Gospels recount, Jesus rose from the dead. He met his followers and ate with them. After a few weeks he was taken up into heaven promising to return at the end of the world. Jesus's followers believed he was the Messiah who had brought about the Kingdom of God. This was a dangerous idea to the Romans who thought this might mean a challenge to their power and equally disturbing to the Jewish authorities.

Jesus taught in synagogues. The main concern of many Jews, however, was that he appeared to claim to forgive sins and only God could do that. Jesus was therefore claiming to be divine and that was not acceptable to the Jewish religious authorities.

In this thirteenth-century stained glass window Jesus is depicted teaching in a synagogue. Although he was a Jew, the Jewish authorities did not welcome him forgiving peoples' sins, something they believed only God could do.

For God so loved the world, that he gave his only son, that whoever believes in him should not perish but have eternal life.

John, 3:16

A service at an American Pentecostal church. Pentecostal churches take their name from Pentecost, when the Holy Spirit descended upon the Apostles and gave them the gift of tongues, the ability to speak in any language they pleased.

THE PARABLES

Jesus used parables and healings to help people understand his teaching. He taught that the Kingdom of God (an acceptance of God as Ruler and King) had arrived and it was possible for everyone to enter that Kingdom. What was necessary was to see what Jesus did and hear and understand his teaching. Some of his parables, including *The Sower* (Mark 4:3–20), *The Good Samaritan* (Luke 10:30–37) and *The Lost Son* (Luke 15:11–32), are very well known and are stories in themselves; others like *The Lost Coin* (Luke 15: 8–10) and *The Lost Sheep* (Luke 15:3–7) are short and easily remembered. Jesus, like all great teachers, took examples from everyday life with which his hearers would be familiar. Everyone knows the joy of finding something that was lost or re-uniting relationships.

His healings and miracles taught about God's power and authority. Jesus could do these things because he was carrying out God's will. He did remarkable things to challenge those around and to help people be more aware of the will of God and the nearness of God's Kingdom.

For Christians the greatest miracles were his birth, death and resurrection (rising to defeat death). It was a demonstration of the love, authority and power of God.

The Early Church

At Pentecost the disciples of Jesus received the power of the Holy Spirit.
They went out to teach and preach across the known world. St Paul,
who as Saul, had not been one of Jesus's followers, was tireless in his
preaching of the Gospel and travelled throughout the Mediterranean.
As time passed and numbers grew, the small groups of Christians began
to organize themselves. They also suffered persecution.

A 6th-7th century fresco depicting
Jesus, from the monastery of Saint
Jeremiah in Saqqurah, Egypt.
Christianity has a long tradition in
Egypt, with the founding of the church
attributed to St Mark, between 48 AD
and 61 AD.

FTER THE EVENTS of Jesus's life,
death and resurrection had been
completed, his followers gathered to
celebrate the Jewish festival of Pentecost. In the
Acts of the Apostles, the coming of the Holy
Spirit is recorded. The Holy Spirit of God
arrived in the upper room of a house where the
disciples were gathered with the sound of a
mighty wind (the Hebrew and Greek words for
'spirit' can mean 'breath') and looked as if each
of the disciples had a tongue of flame on his
head. This powerful event gave the disciples
power and courage to go out to preach in many
different languages.

The disciples became known as 'apostles' –
from a Greek word meaning 'sent as messengers'.
They went out to preach the good news (the
Gospel) of the risen Christ.

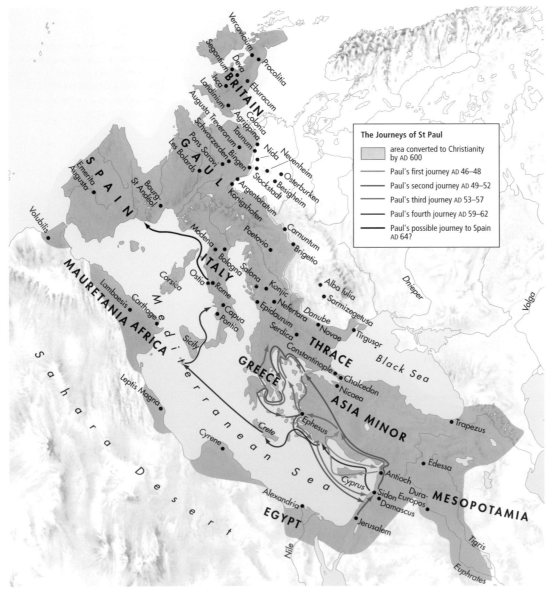

The Journeys of St Paul

	area converted to Christianity by AD 600
	Paul's first journey AD 46–48
	Paul's second journey AD 49–52
	Paul's third journey AD 53–57
	Paul's fourth journey AD 59–62
	Paul's possible journey to Spain AD 64?

The Journeys of St Paul
Paul was deeply committed to taking
the message of Jesus Christ to the non-
Jewish (Gentile) world. The map shows
his missionary journeys, details of
which are known from his surviving
letters and the Acts of the Apostles.

There are many stories of where they went and what they said but Peter, who is considered to be the leading disciple, ended up in Rome, the centre of the Roman world. It is believed he was crucified there after he had founded a Church. He was the first Bishop of Rome.

PAUL AND THE EARLY YEARS

The most significant apostle was not in the upper room at Pentecost. He is St Paul who, before his own conversion, when he was known as Saul, had persecuted the followers of Jesus. At his conversion on the road to Damascus he had a vision of Jesus that changed his life. He took the name Paul to show the change he had experienced and after a few years' quiet reflection set out to take the message of Jesus across the Mediterranean world.

Paul wrote a number of letters contained in the Christian Bible. These were written before the Gospels and tell us a lot about Paul himself as well as about the growing groups of Christians. He was passionate, strong-willed and strong-minded and deeply committed to taking the message of Jesus Christ to the non-Jewish (Gentile) world. He probably died in Rome at about the same time as Peter, i.e. AD 60–65.

AS TIME WENT BY

The early followers of Jesus believed the end of the world would come very soon with everyone living under God's rule. As the apostles died and the years passed the end did not arrive and each Christian group began to organize itself. Bishops, elders and deacons took a role in the organization and administration of the church with the bishops taking responsibility for the care of people within a larger area. The bishops of Rome, Jerusalem, Constantinople, Alexandria and Antioch became the most influential.

Christians soon changed their day of worship from the Jewish Sabbath to the first day of the week, Sunday. This marked a move away from their Jewish origins and recognition that Jesus's resurrection was the most important event. Easter and Pentecost were important festivals but Christmas does not appear to have been celebrated at all.

Persecution of the Christians in the Roman Empire largely finished when Constantine was Emperor in AD 312 although there were outbreaks during the next two centuries. During the fourth century Christianity became much more formalized, church building took place and by AD 381 Christianity was the official religion of the Roman Empire. In its turn it was not averse to persecuting others now that it had the support of the Empire.

Above: The apostles taught that Jesus's mother Mary had a visitation, known as the Annunciation, from God's messenger, the archangel Gabriel, telling her she was to bear the son of God.

It is their habit, on a fixed day, to assemble before daylight and to recite by turns a form of words to Christ as God.

Pliny the Younger, early second century

Left: As the Christian faith became more widespread and established, permanent places in which to worship God were built, such as this church dating from AD 500 in the Taurus mountains in Turkey.

AD 48–60	Paul's missionary journeys
AD c. 100	First reference to Christians
AD c. 110	First accounts of Christian martyrs (e.g. Polycarp)
AD 175	First reference to the four Gospels
AD 200	Christians symbols in Roman catacombs
AD 312	Constantine becomes Emperor
AD 313	Christians granted freedom of worship
AD 381	Council of Constantinople: Christianity becomes the official religion of the Roman Empire

JEWISH ROOTS

The early Christians were Jews and, although Christian teaching spread rapidly to the non-Jewish world, they continued to attend synagogues and follow the traditional Jewish way of life. The followers of Jesus were regarded as a new Jewish sect, rather like the first century BC Jewish group of Essenes who lived by the Dead Sea. As they developed, however, the Christians were influenced by Greek ideas and symbols. Some of the early representations of Jesus (200 years after his death) show him in the Graeco-Roman style of a shepherd carrying the lost lamb, or as a sower scattering seed for future harvest. In the artwork of the time Jesus was depicted in much the same way as other gods or kings.

Christianity was called 'The Way' for several decades after Jesus's death and the religion developed as a secret society. In the third and fourth centuries there were influential bishops and thinkers some of whom became saints and martyrs. But in the first centuries there were no agreed guidelines and the 'Christian Church' was a collection of small communities. There were no church buildings.

The symbol of the fish became common for early Christians. Fish figure in the Gospels; some of the disciples were fishermen and the Greek word for 'fish' has five letters standing for the initial letters in the Greek phrase 'Jesus Christ God's Son Saviour'. It was a secret code to help Christians communicate with each other without the state realizing.

The Christian Bible

The Christian Bible took nearly 400 years to reach its final form. It consists of two 'testaments' or 'promises'. The Old Testament is almost entirely made up of the Jewish scriptures and is written in Hebrew. The New Testament is written in Greek and tells of the new 'testament' made by God through the life, death and resurrection of Jesus.

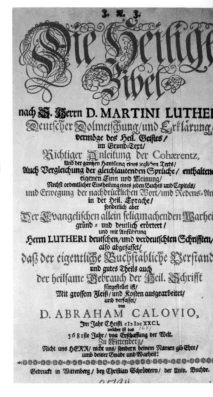

Until the sixteenth century, when Martin Luther translated it into his native German, the Bible was only available in Hebrew, Greek or Latin. Since then, it has been translated into almost every existing language: the entire Bible is available in 330 languages and the New Testament in a further 700.

THE NEW TESTAMENT was probably written by a variety of authors between AD 48–95. Christians believe the Old Testament shows how God had promised the coming of Jesus, the Messiah, to the Jews for centuries. Jesus fulfilled those prophecies and writings so the Gospels and Epistles (letters) relate the story of a new promise – 'a new testament'.

EPISTLES

The Epistles (the Greek word for 'letters') are the earliest known Christian writings. Paul wrote some of the epistles within 20 years of Jesus's death. He pays little attention to the detail of Jesus's life concentrating much more on what his life meant. There are other letters, some attributed to the apostles, written over a period of 50 years or so but little is known of most of their authors.

GOSPELS

There are four Gospels (the word means 'good news'), Matthew, Mark, Luke and John. These are the only records of events in the life of Jesus but he wrote none of them. They all give a slightly different view of the meaning of Jesus's life and have different accounts of his death and resurrection. They were probably written between 30 to 70 years after Jesus's death.

The final collection of books in the Christian Bible was finally agreed at a Council in Carthage in AD 397. Even today however, there is no complete agreement as the Roman Catholic Bible includes a group of Jewish writings called the Apocrypha not normally found in other churches' Bibles.

USING THE BIBLE

The Bible is used in nearly every Christian service. Some Christians believe it to be literally true; others believe it uses symbols, metaphors and stories to express a truth. All Christians believe that in some way the Bible is inspired by God and it should be studied. It provides knowledge about God and the meaning of Jesus's life, who Jesus was and what he taught, and is the basis and major source of the churches' teachings.

For some churches, particularly the Protestant and Pentecostal Churches, the Bible is a direct point of reference when seeking guidance from God. There is less emphasis on the importance of a priest or minister to interpret what the Bible says and this 'direct revelation' has played a powerful part in the development of Protestantism.

This belief was also a driving force in the translation of the Bible from the Latin to the vernacular. Martin Luther's translation of the Bible into German, in the sixteenth century, combined with the development of the printing press (and subsequent rise in literacy), made the Bible more widely available in his native Germany. However, it was not until the formation of the Bible societies, such as Canestein Bible Society, from the eighteenth century onwards that Bibles became available on a mass scale. These societies were formed with the sole purpose of translating and distributing the Bible worldwide, and have been responsible for translating the Bible into hundreds of languages. The most well-known of the contemporary Bible societies is probably the Gideons, who place Bibles in hotels for the use of commercial travellers, across the globe.

PERSONAL AND PUBLIC RESPONSES

Virtually every Christian reads the Bible regularly; some study it daily using a guide to encourage reflection. Many will have favourite passages, often learned by heart, which they will re-read at special times.

The cycle of readings in some churches ensures the key aspects of Jesus's life are linked to the Old Testament and the Epistles. The aim is not only to give encouragement to the congregation but also to demonstrate the 'wholeness' of the Bible.

You shall love the Lord your God with all your soul and with all your strength and with all your mind, and your neighbour as yourself.

Luke, 10:27

So now, faith, hope and love abide, these three; but the greatest of these is love.

1 Corinthians, 13:13

The strength of the Bible for Christians is that it reveals God's continuing part in creation: the gradual unfolding of sacred history. There are many different writers, writing hundreds of years apart, yet Christians see in the Bible a collection of insights, understandings and revelations about God and God's purpose for the world. This ultimate revelation is found in the person of Jesus and Christians read about Jesus in the Christian Bible in order to understand more clearly what God's purpose is for the world and how Jesus's life reveals God's love.

THE WORD OF GOD

Christians believe the Bible shows how God created the world and has remained concerned with the world. They believe the Old Testament can only be fully understood by accepting that Jesus is the Son of God. The life of Jesus is the fulfillment of what is prophesied in the Old Testament.

All the New Testament writers have their own interpretations of Jesus's life. Among the Gospel writers, Matthew writes to show how Jesus brings in the Kingdom of God, which is open to all people; Mark tells of the 'immediacy' of Jesus's mission; Luke has an interest in the poor, the outcast and the place of women in society. John's Gospel is very different from the other three gospels – it places great emphasis on the importance of faith and belief.

The Bible is treated with great reverence, read with devotion, studied intently and used constantly by Christians as a resource for life.

An intricately decorated page from St Luke's Gospel of the Lindisfarne Gospels dating from *c.* AD 698. The Gospels in the Bible contain Jesus's life story and details of his teachings, as interpreted by four of his followers.

Central Beliefs

Christianity is a religion of salvation. Human beings have become separated from God through disobedience. Jesus's life and death renewed that relationship giving an opportunity to enter into a special relationship with God. How this salvation occurs leads to the main beliefs of Christianity: the Trinity, the Incarnation and the Atonement.

THERE ARE OVER 22,000 Christian groups and denominations and they all have different views about the person of Jesus. Most Christians believe, however, that Jesus was the Messiah (the Anointed, the Christ) and the Son of God. He died for all people as the Old Testament had prophesied; he rose from the dead, also as prophesied. This triumph over death was witnessed as true by his followers. Jesus's story is why Christians often say Jesus is alive now and lives in each person.

CREEDS

The first followers of Jesus could rest their faith on what they knew and had seen. Quite soon, however, as other people came to the 'Way' they would be baptized, as Jesus was, into the faith of the Way. Statements of belief or 'creeds' arose as people came to join Jesus's followers and wanted to make a declaration of belief and be baptised. In doing so they put away their previous beliefs, were 'washed clean' and became Christians.

Two of the creeds, the Apostles' Creed and the Nicene Creed (325 AD), are probably used most frequently today. They developed from the early creeds used at baptism and were intended to act as a safeguard against wrong beliefs.

THE TRINITY

The most mysterious and least understood of all Christian beliefs is the Trinity. Christians believe there is, and always has been, only one God. Christians do, however, refer to God in three ways: as Father, the Creator; as Son, Jesus Christ; and as Holy Spirit, the power of God which people feel and experience in their lives. Thus God is expressed as Father, Son and Holy Spirit.

While Christians believe that God is Father, Son and Holy Spirit, the words used to describe this belief never fully capture the experience. Human language falls short when trying to express the nature of God. What the Trinity expresses is the personal nature of God and therefore the personal relationship that exists between God and creation.

New members of an Adventist church are baptized in Port-au-Prince, Haiti. Like many evangelical denominations, the Adventists practise full-immersion adult baptism in indoor pools and, occasionally, natural sources of water, as opposed to the infant baptism from a font practised by, amongst others, Anglicans and Catholics.

An eighteenth-century, Spanish depiction of the Virgin Mary surrounded by the Holy Trinity. Christians believe in the threefold nature of God and that He has manifested Himself in three ways: as Father, Son and Holy Spirit.

becoming a human being God revealed the extent of love He felt for creation; to be born and live as a complete human being was the only way to save all people.

SALVATION AND ATONEMENT

What were people to be saved from? Christians believe that sin is what separates people from God. It is not simply wrong-doing but a misuse of the free will given to humans by God. The sin of Adam in the Garden of Eden was disobedience – a failure to do God's will. They were given responsibilities in the garden but disobeyed God by eating from the forbidden tree. The cycle of sin could only be broken by God's son, Jesus, being born on earth and, through his life, death and resurrection, removing the stain of sin.

Jesus, therefore, atones for the sins of the world and recreates at-one-ment, the bringing together of God and human beings. At the heart of Christian belief is Jesus Christ who brought victory over evil and death.

THE INCARNATION

Virtually every Christian believes that, in some mysterious way, Jesus was fully God and fully human and by becoming fully human, God is willing to share our pains and difficulties. Jesus knew pain and humiliation, was frightened, cried, and shared human experience. In

A Christ figure from an Easter passion play in Sri Lanka. The Passion of Christ is the term traditionally used to refer to his trial, crucifixion, death and resurrection; passion plays re-enact, often with great emotional force and dramatic skill, these events.

PERSONAL RELATIONSHIPS

The story of Adam and Eve in the Garden of Eden has been interpreted in many different ways by Christians. Some continue to believe its literal truth, although there is some evidence to suggest that Christians have never been fully in agreement about its historicity. Most Christians regard it as a powerful story illustrating an inherent tendency in humans to fail, to be less than perfect. What greater failure than to fail to follow their Creator God's words and commands? The story is a metaphor of what life could be like if humans accepted God's rule. The disobedience and deceit had to be healed and redeemed in some way, but humans could not do it alone, they needed God's help to heal the separation.

Belief in Jesus as God's Son and Saviour means, for Christians, that all sins are forgiven and each person can enter into a special relationship with God. Christians believe that by believing in Jesus's life and teaching the original disobedience of Adam and Eve is healed. The outward sign of this is baptism, which symbolically 'washes away sin'.

The belief in the Trinity affirms there is one God, but Christians use three ways to express that oneness – Father, Son and Holy Spirit. It is a statement of the relationship between the persons of the Trinity, reflecting the personal relationship between God and creation.

For most Christians the mysterious nature of these beliefs is irrelevant. For them the experience of forgiveness, of being reconciled to God and feeling the presence of the Holy Spirit is more than enough. The doctrines of the Church are important but personal experience is much more significant.

I believe in one God, the Father Almighty....
And in one Lord Jesus Christ, the only begotten Son of God
And I believe in the Holy Spirit, the Lord, the Giver of Life, The forgiveness of sins....

Extract from the 'Nicene Creed'

Rites and Practices

Christians practise their faith through worship and prayer, public and private, and by reading and studying the Bible. There are, however, two major rites, Baptism and Holy Communion (given different names in different churches), which are almost universal within Christianity. The Gospels record Jesus's baptism by John the Baptist and tell the story of the Last Supper with his disciples.

THERE ARE TWO major practices in which most Christians participate. These are: baptism, universally agreed as the way in which one becomes a Christian; and celebrating Holy Communion (the Mass, the Eucharist or whatever name churches give to the way in which Jesus's last meal with his disciples is commemorated). Generally only the Religious Society of Friends and the Salvation Army do not commemorate Jesus's Last Supper with a re-enactment of the event.

BAPTISM

Most Christians regard baptism as a means of re-birth. It washes away their old life and starts a new life following Jesus Christ. Jesus's baptism at the hands of John the Baptist in the River Jordan acts as a model for Christians.

Churches vary in their practice. Baptists believe that only believers can be baptized so they don't baptize babies since infants are not old enough to make a personal commitment to Christ. Baptists, like many Protestant churches, baptize by total immersion and in warmer countries this will take place outside in a river or pool.

Other churches, such as the Roman Catholic, Orthodox and Anglican Churches, baptize children when they are still babies. The Russian Orthodox Church traditionally baptizes babies when they are eight days old, immersing the babies completely in water. Other churches may sprinkle the baby with blessed water from the font and anoint them with *chrism* (oil). In these churches the godparents, adults chosen by the baby's parents, make promises to help the child grow up in the Christian faith.

HOLY COMMUNION

Churches use a variety of names for the ceremony recalling Jesus's Last Supper with his disciples the night before his death. They shared bread and wine with Jesus, who asked his disciples to remember him in the breaking of bread and the drinking of wine. The churches also have different beliefs about how to remember the meal. Roman Catholic churches celebrate Mass daily as do some Anglican churches. Others celebrate less frequently, with United Reformed and Baptist Churches perhaps once a month.

Orthodox and Roman Catholics believe that the bread and wine fully become the body and blood of Jesus when the Thanksgiving prayer is offered to God. Jesus is physically present so worshippers can share in his sacrifice.

Most Protestants do not believe this change takes place. For them the service is a memorial where Jesus is symbolically present.

There are other rites of passage: marriage and funeral rites, and, in some churches, confirmation where the promises made at Baptism are confirmed by a bishop laying hands on the person being confirmed. All churches find ways to express how the Christian faith affects the lives of each believer.

A Catholic bishop gives communion to his congregation. Communion, the ritual recreation of the Last Supper and a symbolic consumption of the body and blood of Christ, is the most important element of Christian worship. In some Christian traditions, most notably Catholicism, it is believed that an actual transformation takes place, and the bread and wine actually become the body and blood of Christ. This process is known as transubstantiation.

A baby being baptized at a font.
The act of baptism symbolizes the washing away of original sin inherited from Adam and Eve, and signifies the start of a new life as a member of the Christian church.

For as often as you eat this bread and drink the cup, you proclaim the Lord's death until he comes.

1 Corinthians, 11:26

As the body is buried under water and rises again so shall the bodies of the faithful be raised by the power of Christ.

From a Baptist baptism service

I baptize you in the name of the Father, and of the Son, and of the Holy Spirit.

Universal words at Baptism

SACRAMENTS: OUTWARD SIGNS OF INNER BLESSINGS

Some churches are 'sacramental'. These churches usually accept the authority of a bishop, and the Mass of Holy Communion has a central place in their worship. Certain rites, called sacraments, are performed to mark special occasions in the life of the Christian.

At confirmation, a candidate kneels before a bishop who 'confirms' the promises made at baptism by laying hands upon the person's head. By being confirmed the person confirms their belief in and commitment to the Christian faith.

Couples who get married in church express their love for each other before God and the Christian congregation. They make their promises to each other and are guided through the service by the priest who sends them out into their life together with God's blessing.

Some Christians will become priests, the sacrament of taking holy orders. After a period of training they will be received, or ordained, into the priesthood by a bishop. Others will become monks or nuns following in the great monastic tradition of people such as St Benedict, St Francis or St Clare. After a period of training, they will make vows or promises of poverty, chastity and obedience when they enter the Order they have chosen.

The sacrament of confession or reconciliation is also available in these churches. The believer goes to the priest to confess their wrongdoings in private and in confidence. The priest absolves the person's sins in the name of Jesus Christ through their spiritual authority as a priest. The priest suggests acts of penance that will depend on the person and the sins, but it normally includes prayers of penitence.

A priest who anoints the sick person with oil and prays for healing carries out the sacrament of anointing the sick. The last rites, or extreme unction, are given to people who are near to death. The purpose is to give them peace as they face God in the knowledge that their sins are forgiven and they are safe in God's hands.

A Christian bride has her wedding photograph taken in a studio in Shanghai, China. The Christian wedding ritual has become a worldwide Western one, and in Japan, for example, couples will often undergo a Christian-style marriage alongside a traditional Japanese Shinto ritual.

Festival and Celebration

Christian festivals can be grouped under three sections. The most important group surrounds Easter and follows the cycle of the moon so Lent, Easter, Ascension Day and Pentecost fall on different days each year. Christmas follows the solar calendar so the dates connected with the birth of Jesus occur on the same day each year. The third group is the celebration of the lives of individual saints and martyrs; these occur on the same day each year.

EASTER RATHER than Christmas is the major Christian festival. It is the time when the central belief of Christians – that Jesus died and rose again – is celebrated. Easter Day, the day of resurrection, is always a Sunday in March to May; the Friday before, when Christians remember Jesus's death, is called 'Good Friday'. 'Good' because of the good deed Jesus performed – taking all the sins of the world on himself and enabling people to enter into eternal life.

Christians prepare for Easter Day, a time of delight and exhilaration, by undertaking a period of discipline and self-denial. This season of Lent lasts for 40 days. 'Lent' comes from an old word for spring because Easter is a springtime festival in the northern hemisphere. It used to be a time when prospective Christians were prepared for baptism but now it usually commemorates Jesus's 40 days in the wilderness. Lent is heralded by Ash Wednesday when some Christians have a cross of ash placed on their forehead as a sign of sorrow for their sins. In some Orthodox churches Lent is called the Great Fast and many Christians of all denominations fast or go without favourite foods as well as preparing themselves for the coming events of Easter. Some churches remove or cover images or icons during Lent and do not decorate the building with flowers; other churches do not hold marriages.

HOLY WEEK

The week before Easter (Holy Week) re-enacts the last week of Jesus's life. Palm Sunday is the first day of Holy Week and commemorates the entry of Jesus into Jerusalem when people welcomed him by waving palms. As the week continues the end of the penitential period draws near. In Seville, Spain, penitents dress in black with their faces covered and parade to show sorrow for their sins. On Maundy Thursday, the day before Good Friday, many church leaders re-enact the occasion of Jesus's

washing his disciples feet by washing the feet of ordinary people. It is a reminder that at their last meal together Jesus commanded his followers to serve others before eating bread and drinking wine.

Good Friday is the most solemn day of the Christian year. Some Christians walk through the streets carrying a cross and in Jerusalem pilgrims carry the cross along the traditional route of Jesus's walk to his crucifixion.

Easter Day, by contrast, is a joyous time celebrating the resurrection of Jesus from the dead. In Orthodox churches 'new fire' is brought out from the altar and carried into the church. Jesus is often referred to as the light of the world and the darkness of death is banished by new light.

The Easter cycle continues with the festival of the Ascension where Christians remember Jesus being taken up into heaven watched by his followers; and is completed at Pentecost when,

Members of a Catholic church in London re-enact the Stations of the Cross, the traditional divisions of Jesus's trial and Crucifixion, at Easter. While still common worldwide, particularly in South America, such performances are becoming less frequent among Catholics in Britain and North America.

Christians believe, the Holy Spirit settled upon the apostles giving them power to go out and preach the Gospel to the world.

CHRISTMAS

The second cycle of festivals surround Christmas and celebrate the birth of Jesus. As with Easter, there is a period of preparation, Advent (coming), when Christians remember their sins and prepare for the 'gift' of Jesus's birth. Today Christmas in most Christian traditions is celebrated on 25 December. Some Orthodox churches celebrate it on 6 or 7 January (the difference is caused by changes to the calendar system). The date of Christmas was decided upon by the Emperor Constantine during the third century AD who chose the date of a Roman sun festival and by doing so he changed a non-Christian celebration into a Christian one.

Epiphany – the 'showing forth' of Jesus to the world – comes 12 days after Christmas. The festival marks the arrival of the Magi (wise men or astrologers who had 'seen' news of this birth in the stars) from the East. The Christmas cycle finishes with Candlemas (2 February) when Christians remember Jesus's presentation by his parents in the temple giving thanks to God for the safe birth of their son.

THE SAINTS

Saints are individuals believed to have possessed miraculous powers, and have lead exemplary lives. Not all churches uphold the importance of saints but the Roman Catholic Church, Anglican and the Orthodox Churches continue to recognize the unique contribution of some Christians (St Nicholas on 6 December providing gifts for children).

For a saint to be recognized as such, they must be canonized by the church. This involves proof that they performed miracles, and of their virtuos life. Beatification requires proof of two miracles and preceeds canonization. Proof of further miracles is required for Canonization, and until 1983 the prospective saint's life was put on trial by the church, with their reputation questioned by a Advocatus Diaboli, or Devil's Advocate. Many have a special day on which thanks is given for their lives and Mary, the mother of Jesus, has a number of days devoted to events in her life. One of these days, the Annunciation, remembers the obedience and acceptance of Mary receiving the news from the angel Gabriel that she was to bear the child Jesus (25 March).

Roman Catholics also believe that it is possible to ask the saints to pray on their behalf, a process that is known as intercession. Certain saints are believed to have special affiliations with particular trades, or solving certain problems, and it is to these Patron Saints that people will turn when making a specific request.

This beautiful sixteenth-century German wooden alterpiece shows the Adoration of the Magi. After Jesus's birth three wise men, or Magi, came to visit him, the first non-Jews to do so; this visit is now celebrated by Christians as the festival of Epiphany. The Magi are thought to have been members of the priestly caste of Persia, and brought prophetic gifts for the young Jesus. Gold represented kingship, frankincense symbolized the spirtual path of his life and myrrh, being an ointment which was used to anoint the dead and wounded, indicated the suffering that he would have to endure.

Mary, holding Jesus, the Son of God. The portrayal of mother and child as shown here is one of the most enduring images of Christmas.

THE CHRISTMAS STORY

The Christmas story is taken from the Gospels of Matthew and Luke. The versions are very different from each other with each writer presenting Jesus as the Messiah but using distinctive symbols and illustrations. They agree, however, that Mary was a virgin and Jesus is God's son. Matthew reveals Jesus as the King and Lord before whom all people, including the Magi (non-Jews) come to pay homage. The importance of his birth is told in the heavens, has been prophesied, and heralded across the world. Joseph is the receiver of dreams in which God tells him what to expect and what to do. The brutality of Herod is underlined in his effort to kill the newborn 'king' and the family of Jesus has to flee into Egypt for safety, returning only after Herod's death.

Luke, on the other hand, places supreme importance on Mary, the mother of Jesus, and on God's concern for the world. Mary is obedient, chosen as the woman worthy to be the mother of God. Jesus's birth is a difficult time for his parents. He is born where the animals are kept and it is the shepherds who are given the privilege of being first to receive the news. For Luke, Jesus has come into the world to help the poor and under-privileged and it is to them that God's son is first revealed.

The Catholic Church Worldwide

About half the Christians in the world are Catholic (approximately one billion people), and nearly half of these live in Latin America. The Pope, who lives in the Vatican City, Rome, is the head of the Catholic Church and is elected by a college of senior clerics called cardinals. The Church is strongly sacramental. It places great importance on rites and ceremonies marking the life of each Catholic.

THE CATHOLIC CHURCH traces its origins back to Peter, one of the original disciples, who died in approximately 64 AD. The Gospel of Matthew records Jesus telling Peter, his leading disciple, that he would have the Keys of the Kingdom of Heaven – in other words, to life after death. Peter is also referred to as the 'rock' on which Jesus would build his Church.

Peter is believed to have been the first Bishop of Rome, a title held today by the Pope, the leader of 1 billion Catholics. No other Christian leader claims such authority directly from Jesus himself. The word 'Catholic' means 'universal' and reflects a worldwide church.

THE SACRAMENTS

The Catholic Church, along with other Christian denominations, is a sacramental church, that is it has rites and practices that are visible signs of God's power. Through sacraments the Church provides all Roman Catholics with a firm and supportive structure by which to order their lives. Babies are baptized, then at about seven years of age children receive their First Communion where they share in the sacrament of the Mass. Young people are able to make their own commitment in their early teens when they confirm their faith and a bishop lays hands on them.

The seven sacraments provide a life journey for the Catholic: baptism; first communion; confirmation; marriage; confession; healing; ordination. In the marriage service bride and groom make promises to each other before God. The church does not recognize divorce. Death, although a sad time for those left, is a celebration of the dead person being called home to be in God's presence.

A nun praying in convent. Like priests, nuns devote their lives to God, and spend a great deal of their time working for the benefit of the community in which they live, including caring for the sick and elderly, running orphanages or teaching.

The Catholic Church
Between 1464 and 1514, successive popes issued a series of edicts to the Spanish and Portuguese crowns, giving them the task of converting the 'heathen peoples' to Catholicism which exploration was bringing under their control. Today there are over one billion Catholics living across 202 countries.

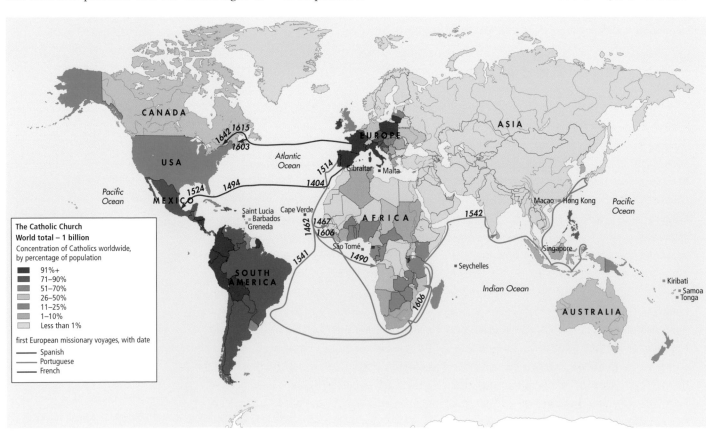

The Catholic Church
World total – 1 billion
Concentration of Catholics worldwide, by percentage of population

- 91%+
- 71–90%
- 51–70%
- 26–50%
- 11–25%
- 1–10%
- Less than 1%

first European missionary voyages, with date
- Spanish
- Portuguese
- French

THE PRIESTHOOD

The Church is hierarchical, with the Pope at the top of the pyramid. Then there are cardinals, archbishops, bishops and so on. The priesthood is male and celibate for they are 'married' to the Church and are thus able to commit themselves fully to the welfare of the Church and its people. A bishop (or archbishop) is a church leader who has responsibility for the church in his area called a diocese. Often one archbishop will be the leading church representative of his country and many have the title cardinal. It is from the cardinals that the Pope is elected.

All priests have to complete a period of training before they are ordained. The length of time can vary but it may take more than four years before the bishop lays his hands on the head of the would-be priest. The laying on of hands is a sign of God's help passed down through the priesthood from the first Bishop of Rome.

CHANGE AND STABILITY

The Catholic Church offers stability, authority and comfort to its adherents in a changing world. There have, however, been changes in the last 50 years: the Mass is no longer conducted in Latin but in the language of the country; many monks and nuns wear ordinary clothes rather than the traditional habits; and there are changes in the attitude of the Catholic Church to other Christian churches. The Church can be seen as authoritarian but in practice there is scope for debate and argument on every ethical and theological issue. The breadth of the Church allows, even encourages, discussion and only occasional fragmentation.

Left: A Catholic bishop in Haiti. After centuries of sending primarily European clergy and missionaries to Asia, Africa and South America, the Catholic Church has, in the last hundred years, instead recruited from the indigenous population.

THE CATHOLIC NETWORK

The strength of the Catholic Church lies in its worldwide structure. It has a network stretching across the whole world and, in addition to the priesthood, there are large groups of monks and nuns committed to teaching, preaching and social work. The Church has the ability to recognize difference within unity. Thus there can be very different approaches to religious ideas and practices, for example, Catholics in Latin America compared with more traditional Catholics in Rome. It is comparatively rare for a person to be asked to leave the Church (excommunicated).

The Catholic tradition should be present in every aspect of life. The Church creates a 'cradle to grave' lifestyle in which the importance of the sacraments is always present. There has always been a strong commitment to education within the Church and children are taught the basic principles of Catholicism from an early age. Its worldwide outreach makes it very influential religiously and politically. Catholics can move easily from country to country knowing they will be well received and being familiar with the services and rituals of the Church. The organization of the male-only priesthood ensures that family duties and family life do not impinge on the commitment of the priest to his work for God and for the Church.

Jesus depicted healing a leper. Among Jesus's teachings was the concept of caring for everyone, even those such as lepers, who were regarded by the society of the time as outcasts. This tradition is still followed by those who devote themselves to the service of the Catholic church today.

The Orthodox Churches

The Orthodox churches each have their own distinctive history but are a group of churches based on an historic tradition. This tradition arose in the East and the churches of Constantinople, Antioch, Alexandria and Jerusalem grew at the same time as the Western Church expanded in Rome. The leaders of the churches are called patriarchs and they work together ecumenically. At the heart of all Orthodox churches lies the Divine Liturgy, the worship of God, continually celebrated regardless of social environment and political pressure.

ALTHOUGH THERE are different Orthodox churches, usually based on historic and ethnic tradition i.e. the Greek Orthodox, Russian Orthodox, Serbian Orthodox, they all share the same living tradition of worship.

The word 'orthodox' means 'right' or 'true worship' and the Orthodox churches trace their origins back to the very beginning of the early Christian church. Rome was then the capital of the Roman Empire but the four eastern churches of Jerusalem, Constantinople, Alexandria and Antioch remained in a strong relationship with each other. The authority of the Bishop of Rome was a growing problem for the bishops in the Orthodox churches who believed Church government should lie within an ecumenical group of bishops, not be focused on one.

TOGETHER BUT AS INDIVIDUALS

The Orthodox East and the Roman West slowly moved apart from each other during the first 1,000 years of Christianity until a definitive separation occurred in 1054. The Orthodox churches became the established religion in countries like Russia, Bulgaria and Greece and have continued to survive in spite of attacks in the twentieth century during periods of communist and other authoritarian governments. The organization of the Orthodox churches allows each country to develop its own language and customs within the context of sharing the same worshipping tradition.

WORSHIP

Worship within the Orthodox Church brings all the senses together. The building is often lit only with candles and there is a strong smell of incense. Most Orthodox churches do not have seats, worshippers stand and move about during services. The floor represents the world and heaven the ceiling, so large icons of Jesus often

First World War Russian Orthodox soldiers kiss an icon before going into battle. While they share many of the same elements of beliefs and worship, the different Orthodox churches have all developed their own unique traditions.

The Orthodox Church
After the split of the Orthodox East and the Roman West in 1054, the Orthodox churches became the established religion in countries like Russia, Bulgaria and Greece. They have continued to survive in spite of attacks in the twentieth century by communist governments (the collapse of the Soviet Union has led to a revival of Orthodoxy). The map shows the various religious divisions within Eastern Europe.

The Orthodox Church
majority religion
- Orthodox*
- Catholic
- Lutheran
- Muslim
- Other States

* Ukraine has a strong Uniate minority

look down upon the worshippers. At the opposite end of the church from the entrance is the sanctuary where the altar stands. The sanctuary is separated from the main body of the church by a screen called an *iconostasis*. On it are painted events from the life of Jesus, the Gospel writers and/or Orthodox saints. Only the priests, acting on behalf of the people, may open the screens' doors and pass into the Holy Sanctuary.

DIVINE LITURGY

The most important service in the Orthodox churches is the Divine Liturgy. This is the name given to the re-enactment of Jesus's life, death and resurrection. The bread and wine become transformed into the body and blood of Jesus. Only Orthodox worshippers receive the bread and wine, on a long spoon, but during the service bread is blessed by the priest and shared by all the people after the service. This is called an *agape* (a Greek word meaning something like 'unconditional love') and is symbolic of the sharing of love between Christians.

THE FIVE PATRIARCHS

One important aspect of the Orthodox churches is their firm commitment to the concept of the Church as a 'pentarchy'. That is the five patriarchs of Rome, Constantinople, Antioch, Jerusalem and Alexandria preserve the true faith. Theodore in the ninth century refers to 'the five-headed body of the Church' meaning those five patriarchs working together. None was superior to another – a very different concept from the Catholic Church in Rome. Tradition is the key to truth for the Orthodox and this inbred familiarity with the tradition is the key to the spread and survival of the Orthodox churches into the Middle East, India and beyond. New practices would mean that the rites and beliefs handed down from the apostles would be altered. So it was no surprise when the gradual drift of the Eastern churches from the West was recognized in 1054.

The emphasis on tradition has meant that the Orthodox churches have acted as a stable influence during changes across the centuries. In the nineteenth and twentieth centuries the churches kept the spirits of the nation alive in countries like Russia, Romania and Bulgaria.

PRIESTHOOD

Orthodox priests are very distinctive people in the community with their beards, black hats and long black robes. The senior archbishops are called patriarchs or 'great fathers' and are usually monks. As with priests in other churches the priest is the representative of the people and through him the worshippers reach out to God; and through the priest God responds. The priest is the mediator between God and the people.

Greek Orthodox clergy worshipping, surrounded by icons. Icons are a point of revereance in the Orthodox religion, believed to intensify religious focus, so that the supplicant becomes closer to God. During the Iconoclast Controversy in Asia Minor (AD 726–843), however, opponents claimed that the focus on icons was akin to idolatry, which resulted in the banning of icons, and the destruction of many early examples. The Byzantine empress Irene (AD 750–803) spent her reign restoring the icons, and the controversy finally ended during the reign of Michael III (AD 836–867).

A Greek Orthodox priest in his church in Rhodes. Priests are highly revered in their communities as mediators between God and the people.

The Anglican Communion

The 'Anglican Communion' is the name given to the collection of Anglican churches worldwide. They all derive from the Church of England but each has their own system of government with their own archbishops and bishops. They may have very different views from each other; some ordain women priests and bishops, others have women priests but no women bishops and some have neither. The Anglican Communion regards itself as being both Catholic and Reformed (Protestant).

THE COLLECTION of worldwide Anglican churches is usually referred to as the Anglican Communion. There are Anglican churches in many countries of the world with their own structure of archbishops, bishops, priests, and so on. The leaders meet regularly to confer.

There are differences of view in different parts of the Anglican Communion and while the Church of England may have an influential voice, individual churches will go their own way. In recent times the clearest examples of this have been the ordination of women as priests in some parts of the Anglican Communion and not others and the appointment of women bishops in some parts of the Anglican Communion.

Although such different points of view might put strains on relationships inside the Anglican Communion the very nature of Anglicanism is to strive for balance in all things. The Anglican Communion is neither Roman Catholic nor Protestant, though, in its variety, it has elements of both. It is understood by Anglicans to be a bridge born out of an historical situation that continues to be a link between two of the great divisions within Christianity.

ORIGINS

The English Reformation in the sixteenth century was perhaps the most uncertain of any in Europe, arising almost by accident. When Henry VIII declared himself Supreme Head of the Church of England and challenged the authority of the Pope (in the 1530s), there was

Salisbury Cathedral, England. English cathedrals, such as Salisbury, are part of the Church of England, which is essentially a synthesis of the Catholic and Protestant traditions.

The Anglican Communion
The collection of Anglican churches is usually referred to as the Anglican Communion. Today there are believed to be more than 70 million Anglicans worldwide.

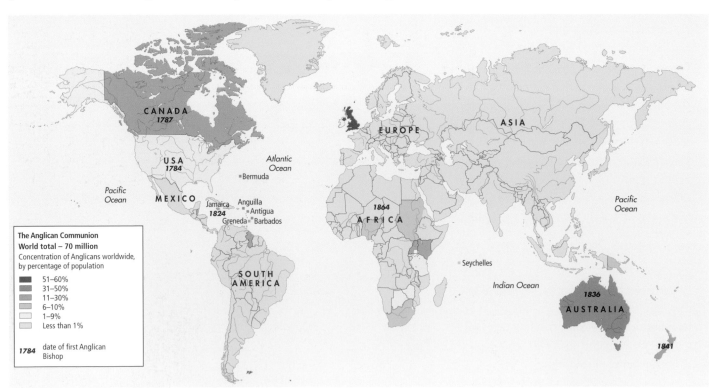

The Anglican Communion
World total – 70 million
Concentration of Anglicans worldwide, by percentage of population

- 51–60%
- 31–50%
- 11–30%
- 6–10%
- 1–9%
- Less than 1%

1784 date of first Anglican Bishop

CANADA 1787
USA 1784
Bermuda
MEXICO
Jamaica 1824 Anguilla
Antigua
Greneda Barbados
Pacific Ocean
Atlantic Ocean
SOUTH AMERICA
EUROPE
ASIA
AFRICA 1864
Seychelles
Indian Ocean
Pacific Ocean
AUSTRALIA 1836
1841

little actual change in church services. Henry wanted no real change with the past, he only wanted the Pope to agree to his divorce from his first wife, Catherine, but he closed monasteries and persecuted Protestants and Catholics alike. Slowly, however, over the next twenty years, the Mass was abolished (though it continued under another name) and the emergence of an English prayer book moved the Church of England away from Rome.

If there was a key figure in the English Reformation, after Henry, it was Archbishop Thomas Cranmer. He moved the emerging church towards Protestantism emphasizing the Bible as the living word of God, laying the foundation of the Church of England as a Bible-reading church. Mary, Henry's daughter, had him executed when she tried to restore Catholicism.

In the Elizabethan era the shift to a national church continued, still a feature of Anglicanism today. Later, in the seventeenth century, the Church of England was given form and order through the publication of the Authorized Version of the Bible in 1611 and the new Prayer Book of 1662. The unresolved doctrinal differences between Catholicism and Protestantism continue to cause discord, to a lesser degree, in the Anglican church today.

ANGLICANISM TODAY

The Archbishop of Canterbury is often regarded as the leader of the Anglican Communion but he does not hold the same position of authority as the Pope in the Roman Catholic Church. What is distinctive about the Church of England is that it remains an established church. The British Parliament begins its sessions each day with prayers, bishops are appointed on the recommendation of the Prime Minister and the monarch remains the Supreme Governor of the Church of England. But things might change...

The choir of Winchester Cathedral, England, singing during a service. Music has long been central to Christian worship, and a large number of the West's most important works were composed for liturgical use. Although the style may vary between the various churches of the Anglican Communion, the music used during worship will usually include hymns and singing by a choir, with congregational participation.

An Anglican bishop in the USA. The Anglican Communion has members worldwide, most particularly in those areas where the British Empire either colonized or traded.

RITES AND PRACTICES

One unique feature of the Church of England is to be seen at the coronation of the monarch. At her coronation in 1953 Elizabeth II received the title 'Supreme Governor of the Church of England', being anointed by the Archbishop of Canterbury. This reveals the 'established' links between the throne and the Anglican altar, between the landed powers and the Anglican religion.

In doctrine, Anglicans use scripture, tradition and reason as God-given ways to understand revelation; reason being the way to interpret scripture and tradition. At parish level there is a combination of individual and parochial freedom under the authority and guidance of a bishop.

Some parish churches, by tradition, will be more Catholic in their worship, using incense, emphasizing the sacraments and placing importance on Holy Communion (often called 'Mass' in some churches). Other churches will be plain, have no statues, will not use incense and place greater emphasis on preaching, reflecting a more Protestant ideal. Such tensions extend into attitudes towards church government, social concerns and ethical issues.

Luther, Calvin and the Reformation

During the early fifteenth century there was a re-birth, or Renaissance, in learning in Europe, in which many scholars returned to the study of Classical literature. Theologians such as Erasmus (1466–1536) began to question the disparity between the practices of the Catholic church and the teachings of the early Christians. The worldliness and extreme wealth of the church were criticized and a movement for reform began, which crystallized with the actions of Martin Luther in 1517.

Sixteenth-century altarfront
illustrating Martin Luther preaching to the faithful. Luther's individuality and vision resulted in him gaining a strong following from those disillusioned by the Catholic Church.

I f Martin Luther (1483–1546) was the father of the Reformation, Jean Calvin (1509–64) ensured that it would continue and develop. Of the many discontented thinkers pushing against the ills of the Catholic Church, these two men were the foundation upon which much would be built. Luther's frustration with the Church may have kindled revolution but Calvin created the political vision of the 'City of God'. The Reformation represented the shift of power from the aristocracy to the middle classes.

Martin Luther defined the ideology of early Protestantism. There had been rumblings of discontent with the practices of the Catholic Church for very many years but Luther's individuality coincided with a set of favourable political and social circumstances. The other great reformer, Jean Calvin, was strongly influenced by Luther but, as someone who liked order, he was a very practical person who applied his thinking directly to political issues.

The Reformation
Although Luther and Calvin were arguably the main protagonists of the Reformation, the Anabaptists, the Anglicans and the Hussites all had a major part to play. The map shows the Reformation in Europe in the mid-sixteenth century.

The Reformation

☐ Roman Catholic	☐ Lutheran
☐ Orthodox	☐ Calvinist
☐ Islam	☐ Anabaptist
☐ Hussite	☐ Anglican

borders, 1572
Dots indicate a mixture of faiths
Light = small minority
Heavy = larger minority

LUTHER'S STATEMENT

It was on 31 October 1517 that Luther pinned his '95 Theses' to the north door of the Castle Church in Wittenberg. The document, which would be read by worshippers coming to church on 1 November (All Saints' Day), attacked the Church policy on indulgences (the Church sold indulgences to the people to take away their sins). Luther believed this practice was not present in the Bible and that is encouraged people to turn their mind away from Jesus Christ and God's forgiveness.

'PROTESTANTS'

Luther, a monk and professor of Biblical Studies at Wittenberg, was finally excommunicated on 3 January 1521 and outlawed later in the year. He continued to write, however, in powerful, readable German. In 1529 the emperor, Charles V, attempted to move against him but some of the German princes stood up in 'Protest'. Luther had touched the nerve of German nationalism but other groups who stood in opposition to the Pope were ready to use his name. There was an aspect to Luther's vision that attracted the kings and princes of other nations and Lutheranism spread rapidly into the Baltic States. The power and authority of the Pope was broken by the advent of Lutheranism.

JEAN CALVIN

If Luther was charismatic, Jean Calvin created Protestantism as a credible alternative to Catholicism. Often referred to as the 'Reformer of Geneva,' Calvin was French. In his book *Institutes* (1536) he produced a clear defence of Reformation beliefs and ideas. In his later edition (1559) he argued forcefully how Protestant beliefs can sustain (and undermine) the state. He wove a fabric of Protestant ideas into the political, social and economic framework of the state. Calvin created a virtual theocracy (a society ruled by God) in Geneva.

Calvin taught that knowledge of God could only be found in the Word of God, that only God could pardon and save and only baptism and communion were sacraments. He gave great importance to the external organization of the Church, with the Church in Geneva being, in effect, a theocracy, a church and state ruled by God as interpreted by Calvin. Calvin argued that if God is all-knowing and all-powerful then God knows who will be saved and who won't. This doctrine, called predestination, became a feature of the reformed churches that followed Calvin's teaching. It was his way of teaching that humans are saved by God's power alone; it has nothing to do with good works or good behaviour.

DIFFERENT CHARACTERS

Luther was a Catholic monk who later married because he came to believe there was no difference between priests and the laity. Calvin was a humanist attracted by the application of Protestantism to the organization of Church and State. They were different characters, coming from different backgrounds. Luther may not have wanted, initially, to leave the Catholic Church, but Calvin was never part of it. Luther was to influence Calvin but Calvin was to move off down a different road from Luther. He was far more politically concerned than Luther, whose ideas were used by others for their own purposes.

The French reformer Jean Calvin was responsible for turning Protestantism into a way of life rather than a set of ideals. He argued that the Protestant Church should be highly disciplined if it was to survive.

German caricature of Martin Luther as a seven-headed monster. In medieval art such images were often used to depict the antichrist, whom Catholic writers identified with Luther.

LUTHER VERSUS CALVIN

Luther's main emphasis in his teaching was on 'justification by faith'. This meant that God saves sinners through them believing in, and having knowledge of, Jesus Christ. All the benefits of Christian living flow from this. Like all the Reformers, he believed in the authority of the Bible as understood by those who read it. Salvation did not come, as the Catholic Church taught, through sacraments.

Luther, Calvin and the other Reformers were not always in agreement. Luther taught that, in some sense, Christ's body was a 'real presence' in the bread blessed at Holy Communion. Calvin and his followers rejected this; Christ's body was in heaven and not on an altar; Christ meets his followers at the Communion table in their hearts not in a piece of bread.

Sieben Köpffe Martini Luthers
Vom Hochwürdigen Sacrament des Altars / Durch Doctor Jo. Cocleus.

Whereas Luther retained much of the ceremony of the Catholic Church, other Reformers wanted worship to be as simple as possible, reflecting scriptural practices. Luther believed the Church was an earthly creation and could never be perfect and encouraged strong church–state links. Calvin had two distinguishing features of the Church: gospel and sacraments, but 'discipline', later to become essential, would be important if the Church were not to fragment.

For all Reformers the first priority was to put the Gospel into the hands of Christians in the form of a Bible in their own language.

The Protestant Churches

The variety within Protestantism is an illustration of how strongly individualism has grown during the last 500 years. Many protestant groups were persecuted; some fled to the New World, while others divided and sub-divided. At the heart of each movement was the individual's search for God and acceptance of the Lordship of God. This was to be found in scripture and in teaching, preaching and study.

ONE OF MARTIN LUTHER'S key beliefs was that of the importance of the indiviudal within the church, a belief that remains prominent within all of the protestant churches today. It is the responsibility of each person in the community of the Church to work towards their own salvation guided by scripture.

THE PRESBYTERIAN CHURCH

The Presbyterian Church arose out of the Calvinist side of the Reformation. Calvin taught that the Church was to be a right-living fellowship of men and women. Elders were chosen who had every day jobs and could offer spiritual leadership in governing the Church. This could include disciplining those who transgressed. So the church was a place where people were made Christian and kept Christian. The main belief of this Church is that God is Lord and Sovereign of all in the lives of men and women. Another belief was in predestination – that God predestined (intended) some people to be saved and others to be damned.

The most influential Presbyterian in the English-speaking world was John Knox (1513–73). The national Church of Scotland is Presbyterian and was formed by him in the sixteenth century.

METHODISM

Methodism began as a society within the Church of England and John Wesley (1703–91) and his brother Charles (1707–88) tried to keep it there. John was a powerful preacher of deep piety and with his brother wrote many hymns still sung today. An influence on John Wesley was the Moravian church, founded in the eighteenth century, with its emphasis on Christian living and God's forgiving love. In 1738 Wesley wrote: 'I felt I did trust in Christ, in Christ alone for my salvation; and an assurance was given me, that he had taken away my sins, even mine, and saved me from the law of sin and death.'

Methodism attracted social groups who felt excluded from the Church of England. Wesley and his followers had great success in growing industrial areas like South Wales and South Yorkshire, but the countryside too was a fertile field.

Wesley provided people with a sense of purpose, hope and worthiness founded upon Biblical teaching, the power of prayer and hymn singing allied to his own deep love of God.

After John Wesley's death the Methodists broke from the Church of England and then broke again into other smaller churches. The most famous is probably the Salvation Army founded by William Booth in 1861. Methodism is strongest today in North America and today there are more than 50 million Methodists worldwide.

John Wesley, here pictured preaching to followers, founded the Methodist church in the eighteenth century. Methodist worship is free of much of the ritual associated with the Anglican church, and through music and scripture, encourages people to find their own salvation.

A Quaker meeting. Quakers believe that salvation comes from within, and that traditional worship with its elaborate ceremonies detract from a person's ability to concentrate on communicating with God

THE RELIGIOUS SOCIETY OF FRIENDS

The Religious Society of Friends (called 'Quakers' because a judge trying George Fox, the founder of the movement, was told to 'quake at the voice of the Lord') is traditionally considered to have begun on Pentecost 1652 when Fox preached to an enormous crowd. He criticized the Church for stressing outward things and not inner meanings. When Fox died in 1691 there were meetings of Friends all over Britain and America. There are approximately 300,000 Quakers worldwide today, and they are a non-violent, non-sacramental people who worship largely in silence with no fixed order of service. There are no priests and no celebration of Communion. It was, and is, a constant search for truth.

The practice of Christian baptism stems from Jesus's baptism by John in the River Jordan. In some churches, children are baptized while infants; the Baptist church is different in that the ceremony of baptism is reserved only for adults who are ready to make a personal commitment to the Church.

BAPTISTS

In the seventeenth century groups of Baptists were emerging in England and Holland. They claimed freedom from state interference and practised 'believers baptism' (adult baptism for those who profess belief). At the heart of the Baptist movement was, and is, a desire to find and follow the pattern of the churches founded by the apostles who baptised adults. This has been the pattern for all succeeding generations.

Today the Baptist Church worldwide is thriving with an estimated 70 million members. This may be due to the strong Baptist conviction that their church is their personal responsibility. The organization of each congregation is democratic, although Deacons are appointed to help the day-to-day running of the Church. Some churches also appoint Elders. While the Bible is central there is no final agreement about how the Bible should be interpreted. Some believe it is literally the Word of God, others believe they should look behind the words to interpret them in a modern-day context.

In the USA the Baptists are the strongest Protestant tradition. Baptists have a strong history of missionary activity stretching back to the foundation of the Baptist Missionary Society in 1792. The enthusiasm of the missionaries in parts of Africa and India was not to be doubted but met with greater success in Africa than India. Today the strength of the Baptists in the USA means missionary activity can be well funded as it reaches out across the world.

1. *Doing no harm by avoiding evil.*

2. *Doing good of every possible sort and as far as possible to all men.*

3. *Attending to all public worship, especially the Lord's Supper and observing private prayer, Bible study and fasting.*

'Rules of the Society of the people called Methodists', John Wesley, 1 May 1743

The Pentecostal Movement

The Pentecostal movement takes its name from the account of the coming of the Holy Spirit to the disciples at Pentecost when they were gathered together after Jesus's ascension (Acts 2:1–4). The apostles experienced the power of the Holy Spirit's presence through wind and fire and received the gift of speaking in tongues – that is to speak in many languages. These two aspects lie at the heart of the Pentecostal movement. It is probably the fastest-growing of all the Christian churches.

THE PENTECOSTAL MOVEMENT is not a denomination or a sect. It really is a movement, which, while it has created new churches, has also found a home in the traditional churches. It began in the USA at the turn of the twentieth century partly as a reaction against very formal styles of worship and partly, as Pentecostalists would say, as a result of the actions of the Holy Spirit. This led to many churches being established, all involved with innovation, experimentation and a rejection of formal, ordered worship: Assemblies of God, Pilgrim Holiness Church, Church of the Nazarene are just some of the names, perhaps the best known being the Church of God in Christ. Although there is a link between the Pentecostal Churches they are all distinctive and separate. Organized very differently from the Catholic and Orthodox Churches, they rely upon the power of the Holy Spirit and the raw emotional appeal of the minister or pastor.

Services at Pentecostal churches are not organized like in traditional churches. Instead of a structured, more formal type of worship, the service relies on music and on the words spoken by the minister, who generally uses extremely direct and emotional language.

The Pentecostal Movement
The Pentecostal Movement began in the USA at the turn of the twentieth century as a reaction against very formal styles of worship. It is one of the fastest growing religions, with over 100 million followers worldwide.

The Pentecostal Movement
World total – 100 million
Concentration of Pentecostolists worldwide, by percentage of population

- 11–30%
- 6–10%
- 1–5%
- Less than 1%

BELIEFS

Pentecostalists believe in prophecy, speaking in tongues (a gift given to the disciples at Pentecost to speak so they can be understood by people regardless of which language they speak), visions and, like many other Christians, the power of healing. Their worship is informal and uses powerful preaching, rhythmic singing and chanting. Sin is often regarded as the cause of ill health, physical or mental, and to cure such illnesses is to release people from the evil power of the devil. The Devil is a real person who can and does influence and inhabit people. When possessed a person needs to be cleansed and have the Devil cast out so they can be healed. This is done in the name of Jesus and follows the example of Jesus casting out spirits in the Bible. Pentecostalists believe that Jesus Christ will return to this world, literally, in person and in the near future. There is a vivid understanding of the afterlife with, Heaven and Hell being real places of rewards and punishments usually depicted in stark word pictures. In the early days they drew their huge congregations from the poor and the outcast – often a mixture of black and white people – and while there are some very large black Pentecostal churches it is by no means a black religious phenomenon.

PENTECOSTALISM

An important feature of the Pentecostal movement has been the way in which some of its features have been incorporated into the worship of the more traditional and mainstream churches. The term usually used to describe the movement in this case is 'charismatic'. The word means 'gift' (of the Holy Spirit) and some charismatic mainstream Christian services have much the same power and force as the Pentecostal services. Pentecostalism touches the emotions, allows people to forget about their everyday life and lose themselves in the power of the Holy Spirit. The Devil can possess people to drive them away from the knowledge of Jesus or can cause illness and 'demonic possession'. In the Pentecostal movement the power of the Spirit lies very close to everyday life. The minister can exorcise the Devil and cure sickness by calling on the Devil (or devils) to leave the person – but always in the name of Jesus. In a world where people can suffer great poverty and oppression, the vigour, vitality and sheer force of communal expression creates a situation where people believe they can feel God's presence. For a time they are taken out of the ordinary world to live in God's world.

A female choir in a Harlem gospel church. The African-American evangelical churches of the United States place a heavy emphasis upon music as part of their services, thus creating the genre of 'gospel' music, sometimes used for secular as well as church purposes.

INFLUENCE

The influence of the Pentecostal movement over the last 100 years has been enormous. On the one hand there has been the rapid growth of Pentecostal churches and the huge congregations they draw. On the other hand, Pentecostalism has been incorporated into other more traditional churches. Even in Japan where the number of professing Christians is small, the Makaya Church mingles folk religion with Christian Pentecostal practice. In Russia and other countries dominated by Communist rule in the twentieth century Pentecostalists met in secret. In Brazil, where Catholicism has always ranged from local cults to the more coherent political theology of Liberation, there has been a massive expansion of Pentecostalism. What is 'on offer' is warmth, fellowship and the power of the Holy Spirit. The sheer energy, force and vigour of Pentecostalism can remove people from the worries and fears of everyday life. Worship transforms the person and the world in which they live. The lack of a formal structure allows each person to respond to the power of the Spirit in his or her own way. It is an individual communalism.

During worship, it can feel like heaven is descending to earth, the Holy Spirit seems to sweep us into the reality of the presence of Jesus.

Heidi Therese Fageraas in One Island, Many Faiths Rachel Morton

The Diversity of Christianity

Religions are not monolithic: rather the reverse is true. Some Christians are barely recognizable to other Christians because they dress, worship and even behave so differently. To move from attending an Easter procession in Latin America to the Easter Day service in a Methodist church in England is to move to another world – cultural and religious diversity is increasingly recognized as enrichment to understanding the life of Jesus Christ.

IT MAY BE more accurate to write about 'Christianities' rather than 'Christianity'. The diversity is remarkable and, in one sense, a great strength. For all Christians, Jesus Christ is 'a-cultural' – that is, he is not identified in any one cultural form. So Christians express their commitment to the person of Jesus in ways that reflect their culture. Some Christians worship in simple ways – churches are austere and so are the clothes worn by pastor and congregation; others celebrate their faith with rich flamboyance and varied ceremonial.

LATIN AMERICA

With the large number of Christians living in Latin America, it is of key importance to the future of the Catholic Church worldwide. The late twentieth century witnessed the development of what is called 'Liberation Theology'. The Church became the main home for the oppressed, offering freedom, spiritually and (often) politically, and championed their cause.

The strong devotion of the poor to Mary, the mother of Jesus, is a feature of liberation theology. In the Magnificat, in Luke's Gospel, she prays that 'the powerful will be cast down and the poor exalted'. In her 'appearances' to the faithful, Mary speaks in Indian languages identifying the traditional Catholic image with the revolutionary who reacts against the oppression of the state.

TENSIONS

Generally in Latin America Christianity has a rich vibrant expression. It is popular and fulfils human as well as religious aspirations. The Catholic Church does continually wrestle, however, with the cultural expression of people being drawn into Christianity that includes the remnants of indigenous tribal religion and African nuptial traditions.

In places like Guatemala the Catholic Church is viewed with suspicion by the authorities because of its liberationist approach. The poverty of the people fires their radical thinking. Society offers them nothing but oppression. The only way to give vent to their feelings is through the voice and action of the Church. The government prefers American-financed evangelical groups because they appear to offer individual salvation to each person with no political challenge to the order of the state.

CHANGES IN ATTITUDE

In the years following the Reformation, European Christianity spread inevitably becoming associated with imperialism as

Catholic nuns in London, England. Christianity is an extremely diverse religion encompassing a huge range of cultures, and Christians in different countries tend to worship in ways that suit their culture rather than according to a prescribed formula.

A Catholic church in Calcutta. In India there are many Christian communities, mainly the result of colonial missionary activity, though there are also older communities that claim to descend from the preaching of the Apostle Thomas, traditionally supposed to have travelled to India after Pentecost.

European states moved into the Americas, Africa and Asia. The armies of Europe brought with them a religion framed in a very different way from the indigenous religions in the countries they conquered. It was only in the later years of the twentieth century that the association of Christianity with white domination and rule began to erode. The strong conviction that God was on their side led the (white) missionaries, on occasions, to criticize the indigenous religion and patronize Christian converts. The development of 2,000 years of Christian thinking in the West made it hard to re-interpret Christian belief in the context of Chinese and Indian societies. Western thinking, based on Greek ideas from the first century onwards, had defined the Christian faith. It was not, and would not be, easy for western Christians to acknowledge deeper insights that would come from Africa, India and the Far East.

Generally there has been a decline in the numbers professing Christianity in the western churches, although churchgoing is still strong in the USA. An example of the changing pattern of Christian affiliation may be reflected in the fact that 40 per cent of Roman Catholic cardinals now come from the developing world where, in the main, Christianity, in its many forms, flourishes. There is a challenge to the churches as, in the West there is an interest in spiritual issues matched by a decline in the importance of traditional forms of Christianity.

'If your missionaries would step out their carriages and live with the poor and the outcast, Christianity would flourish,' Mahatma Gandhi.

GROWING ECUMENISM

The twentieth century witnessed the beginning of a recognition that the churches should work together; and a new era in the life of the Church was to be enriched by contributions from the East and, of course, Africa. The World Council of Churches has become a symbol itself of this willingness to grow together, though it still has its own problems of speaking with one voice. The ultra-conservative churches are often concerned lest they reduce the emphasis on the literal truth of scripture and are suspicious of the motives and pronouncements of the Roman Catholic Church which they interpret as claiming superiority over the other churches.

Christmas Mass being said in Chengdu, Sichuan province in China. In the twenty-first century, the Christian Church is keen to halt its decline in numbers by being much more open to input from worshippers from all over the world, so giving the faith a greater feeling of unity in which one group does not feel inferior to another.

FUNDAMENTALISM

In one sense all Christians are fundamentalists because they accept the fundamental truth revealed by God in Jesus Christ. The term, however, is normally associated with Protestant groups who believe that every word of the Bible is the Word of God. In the USA there is a growing fundamentalist body of nearly two million people who make up what is called the 'moral majority'. The moral majority take what they believe to be Biblical teaching as absolute on all occasions, particularly in relation to moral issues such as abortion, capital punishment, and so on. They hold solidly to a literal view of creation as found in the Book of Genesis. One of their attractions is that in a materialist world where traditional values are challenged there is a clear message and formula for belief and behaviour. Normally critical of the traditional mainstream churches they are increasingly successful in countries formerly under communist domination. Always patriarchal, they have been referred to as 'evangelicals who are angry'. Many fundamentalist churches are rich, direct, identify worldly success with God's blessing, and have a very strong appeal to the emotions. Some congregations run into tens of thousands.

42% of the USA populace agreed:

The Bible is the Word of God and is not mistaken in its statements and teachings.

Gallup Poll, USA, 1978

CONFUCIANISM

The Life and Teachings of Confucius

Confucius (551–479 BC) was a teacher and political reformer who lived in China at a time when the power of the Zhou Dynasty (c.1027–256 BC) was in decline, and the political system was undergoing change. The Zhou kings had become mere figureheads, ruling over a small enclave in the centre of their nominal domains, and real power was in the hands of the rulers of various principalities, which were in perpetual competition with each other, each trying to enrich itself at its neighbours' expense.

An early nineteenth-century Chinese illustration of the philosopher Confucius (551–479 BC). While Confucius believed in gods and spirits, his philosophy concentrated on the practical applications of ethics, loyalty and scholarship.

Confucianism in East Asia
The map shows the influences of Confucianism in East Asia. Confucius (551-479 BC) was a teacher and political reformer born at a time when the Zhou dynasty was in a state of decline. Mencius (371–289 BC), developed Confucianism further, became a travelling advisor to rulers and wrote the Book of Mencius. Zhu Xi (AD 1130–1200) distinguished Confucian realism from Buddhist idealism, and advocated meditation.

CONFUCIUS'S SURNAME was Kong and his personal name Qiu. In later life he came to be known as Kong Fuzi (Master Kong). This was Latinized in the sixteenth century by Jesuit missionaries as Confucius. Very little is known about Confucius's life, though legends abound. He was born and spent most of his life in Lu, which was one of the smaller states situated in present-day Shandong Province in East China. He belonged to a relatively small educated class of civil and military functionaries who were schooled in the Six Arts, which comprised ceremonies, music, archery, chariot driving, writing and arithmetic.

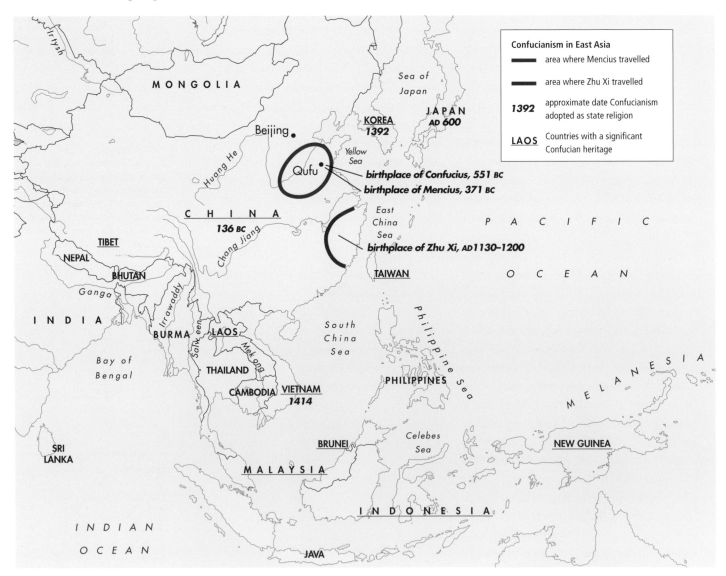

Confucianism in East Asia
— area where Mencius travelled
— area where Zhu Xi travelled
1392 approximate date Confucianism adopted as state religion
LAOS Countries with a significant Confucian heritage

He also became conversant with the ancient classical books on poetry, history and divination. Although he claimed that his best subjects were archery and chariot driving, his education and upbringing prepared him for public service, and this remained his ambition all his life.

MORAL PHILOSOPHY

Confucius deplored what he regarded as a decline in moral standards, not only in Lu but in all the states of the Zhou domains. His study of ancient books led him to believe that this decline had come about through a failure by the rulers of his time to maintain the standards of a supposed golden age of antiquity. In a bid to halt this decline he developed a system of moral philosophy for the guidance of his contemporaries. In 497 BC he was appointed Minister of Justice in Lu where he hoped to put his ideas into practice, but he soon fell out of favour and spent the next 13 years travelling from state to state attempting to find a ruler willing to accept his advice. In this endeavour he was unsuccessful and he finally returned to Lu where he spent his remaining days teaching.

CONFUCIUS THE TEACHER

Confucius had been a teacher most of his life. He believed that in education there should be no class distinctions and once said that he would teach anyone who came to him bearing the school fees of 10 pieces of dried meat and performed the entrance ceremony. When one of his followers was asked what sort of man Confucius was, he did not know how to reply. Confucius said: 'Tell him that Confucius is a man who is tireless in learning and tireless in teaching. When inspired, he even forgets to eat.' Confucius may well have had thousands of students during his lifetime, but he also had a small number of close followers, or disciples, of which we know the names of 25. Although a moralist he was not a fanatic and did not demand perfection from his students. He was delighted if they made an effort to understand his teachings and showed some progress in their studies.

The school of philosophy which Confucius founded is known in China as the Ru school, the word *ru* coming to mean scholars or moralists. He transmitted his ideas mainly through word of mouth to his students. His words were compiled by his followers not long after his death into a book entitled *Lun Yu*, or *The Analects of Confucius*, which became one of the most influential books of East Asia, including China, Japan, Korea and Vietnam.

A late nineteenth-century Chinese illustration of Confucius teaching his pupils. Confucianism places a strong emphasis upon schools and learning in order to pass the learning of one generation onto the next.

CONFUCIUS THE MAN

Although he was honoured in his lifetime, Confucius never made extravagant claims for himself. He was willing to learn from anyone. He said that in any group of three people there must be one from whom he could learn something. He was also modest about his attainments saying that in any hamlet of 10 houses there was sure to be someone as loyal and dependable as himself.

The human side of Confucius is illustrated by the following story: Once when he was with four of his students he asked them what they would wish to do if a prince recognized their qualities and gave them the freedom to do as they pleased. One said that he would like to take charge of a state surrounded by powerful enemies. Another said that he would like to be put in charge of a district of 500 square miles, which he would make prosperous within three years. The third student said he would like to be a minor official assisting at ceremonies at the royal ancestral temple. The fourth student said: 'In springtime I would like to take a group of adults and youths to bathe in the river Yi, and, after bathing, go to enjoy the breeze in the woods by the altars of Wu Yi, and then return home singing.' Confucius sighed and said: 'You are a man after my own heart'.

Confucius regarded himself more as a teacher and imparter of knowledge than anything else. During his lifetime, his students numbered in their thousands and benefitted from his tireless teachings. Here he is depicted on one of his many journeys through China with two of his followers.

CONFUCIUS THE MORAL PHILOSOPHER

Confucius thought of himself as a transmitter rather than an innovator and although he is reputed to have edited several of China's classics, he never wrote a book himself. He was nonetheless the originator of many of the basic ideas which have sustained Chinese civilization for well over 2,000 years.

Confucius admired the founders of the Zhou Dynasty, who had ordered the feudal hierarchy and devised the ritual and music which he considered of key importance in maintaining social harmony and stability. He had special praise for the Duke of Zhou, brother of King Wu of Zhou, founder of the Dynasty. He believed the Duke's rule embodied the qualities of humanity and moral order which were dear to him. He once said 'I am slipping. I have not dreamed of the Duke of Zhou for a long time.'

But in drawing lessons from the past, Confucius was primarily concerned with the society of his own time. For example, he extolled the virtues of the *junzi*, which originally meant 'prince' or 'ruler', and contrasted it with those of the *xiao ren*, meaning 'small men' or 'common people'. But he used these terms in a new sense, namely with reference to people who exhibited superior or inferior moral qualities regardless of which class they belonged to. The term *junzi* is sometimes translated into English as 'gentleman' or 'superior man'. Thus: 'The gentleman is calm and at ease, the small man is anxious and ill at ease.'

Above: An eighteenth-century wall painting shows an imaginary meeting between the founders of the three religions of China; Lao Zi, the founder of Taoism, is on the left and Confucius is on the right, holding the infant Buddha in his arms.

Left: Qilin, a mystical beast at Confucius's temple at Qufu. The Qilin was sent by Heaven to remind Confucius' family that, while they were the greatest family in China, they did not have the Mandate of Heaven so were not equal to the emperor. The emperor held his position by virtue of this Mandate, which represented the will of the Gods. Confucius asserted that the Emperor should govern in a fair and just manner, or risk losing the approval of the Gods. Loss of the Mandate of Heaven would result in cosmic and social disorder, and eventually in a change of dynasty.

c. 1027 BC	Establishment of the Zhou Dynasty whose founders were revered by Confucius
722–481 BC	Spring and Autumn period; rise of the principalities
551–479 BC	Life of Confucius
c. 479–381 BC	Life of Mo Zi, first opponent of Confucius
c. 450–221 BC	Period of the Hundred Schools, including Mohism, Taoism, Confucianism etc.
c. 371–289 BC	Life of Mencius
c. 298–238 BC	Life of Xun Xi
221–209 BC	China unified by the Qin Dynasty; Confucians persecuted
136 BC	Acceptance by Emperor Wudi of Dong Zhongshu's promotion of Confucianism
AD 2nd century	Buddhism spreads to China
11th century	Rise of Neo-Confucianism
1130–1200	Life of Zhu Xi

REN

According to Confucius, the supreme virtue of a gentleman was *ren*. This term, which has been variously translated as goodness, benevolence and human-heartedness, is the sum total of all virtues. Confucius said that fortitude, simplicity and reticence are all close to the meaning of *ren*. When one of his followers asked him how to practice *ren* Confucius said: 'Love people'. He believed that the sage rulers of antiquity were men of *ren*, but he denied that he himself had attained *ren*: 'How dare I say that I am a sage or a man of *ren*? But I delight in striving toward *ren* and never tire of teaching what I believe.

Ren is closely connected with *shu* (reciprocity), in that a man of *ren* judges others by the same standards that he sets for himself. Confucius said: 'Do not do to others what you do not wish to be done to you.' and 'The good man is one who, wishing to sustain himself, sustains others, and, wishing to develop himself, develops others. To be able to use one's own needs as an example for the treatment of others is the way to practice *ren*.'

Confucius also placed great emphasis on *yi* (righteousness). This meant doing what is morally right and proper in any situation, having regard for the five cardinal relationships upon which the family and society in general was said to be based: those between sovereign and subject, father and son, husband and wife, elder and younger brother, and friend and friend. While *ren* is the inner quality of goodness in the gentleman, *yi* is its outward manifestation in action, by which his character may be judged.

CONFUCIUS AND THE SPIRITS

Confucianism is sometimes classified as one of the three religions of China, but it differs from other religions in that it does not put the worship of a deity or deities at the centre of its doctrines or observances. Confucius avoided religious controversy, preferring to concentrate on the problems of humanity. This was because he wished to counter the popular superstitions which were rife in his time. To his disciple Zi Lu who asked about the worship of spirits he said: 'You still do not know how to serve men, how then can you serve spirits?' When Zi Lu asked him about the dead Confucius said: 'You still do not know how to serve the living, how then can you serve the dead?'

Confucius did not deny the existence of spirits and he approved of the ritual practices of the Zhou kings who were entitled to make sacrifices to the supreme spirit, Heaven (Tian). He believed that every citizen had a duty to pay regard to the will of Heaven. He also approved of the proper enactment of ancestral rites carried out by the population at large. But he considered that such rituals were important primarily to ensure the cohesion of the State and the family. He said that one should sacrifice to the spirits as though they were there, recognizing that even in those days not everyone believed in them.

A statue of a Confucian official erected in Qufu, where Confucius is buried. From the Han dynasty (c. 206 BC) to the mid-nineteenth century, Confucian teachings, with their espousal of the concept of selfless public office, were the cornerstone of the code of practice for the Imperial Civil Service.

After Confucius

Following the death of Confucius his disciples continued to expound his teaching and his message sprea
through the various states of what is now north and central China. The followers of Confucius, notably
Mencius and Xun Zi, expanded the scope of Confucius' teaching, touching on issues, such as human natu
which were contentious in their day.

MENCIUS (fourth century BC) considered that man was inherently good, and it behoved the ruler to liberate this goodness by setting a good example which the people would follow 'like water rushing downhill'. Xun Zi (third century BC), on the other hand, believed that man naturally tended toward evil and that this tendency had to be curbed through education. In spite of these differences both Mencius and Xun Zi believed that men had the potential to become sages, and both belonged to the Ru school of philosophy.

By the time of Mencius, other schools of thought had emerged in what became known as the period of the Hundred Schools. First the Mohist school, based on the teachings of the philosopher Mo Di (470–391 BC), who rejected Confucianism's emphasis on a hierarchical society and advocated universal love, and later Daoism, which rejected all moral systems and sought to harmonize the life of humanity with the forces of nature.

China was unified under the Qin in 221 BC (the dynasty from whose name the word China derives). Yet another school, the Legalists, who believed that loyalty to the emperor and the state was the highest virtue, then became dominant, and many Confucians were put to death and their writings, together with those of the other schools apart from the Legalists, were banned. But quite soon, the Qin was overthrown and the Legalists discredited. The Han Dynasty rulers, anxious to rebuild their bureaucracy on a firm ideological foundation, turned to Confucianism to provide it, and Confucianism became the orthodox school of thought supported by the majority of Chinese rulers for two thousand years.

The philosopher and politician Dong Zhongshu provided the theoretical basis for the ascendancy of Confucianism when he recommended to Emperor Wudi in 136 BC that Confucianism should be the means by which the rulers should effect general unification, and that

Residents of Qufu, in Shandong Province, China, celebrate the anniversary of Confucius's birth.

Confucianism Today
Although Confucianism lost its status as a state orthodoxy early in the twentieth century, it has continued to exert an influence on the minds and social mores of the Chinese and other East Asian peoples. The Chinese Diaspora has created communities in places such as the USA, Europe, Canada, South America and Australia where people are attracted to the Confucian concepts of loyalty and filial piety.

Confucianism Today
World total – 6 million
- Important centres of Confucianism
- Countries influenced by Confucianism
- Areas in which Confucianism plays a role in the Chinese Diaspora

'All not within the field of the Six Classics should be cut short and not allowed to progress further.' The Six Classics were the ancient books on which Confucius based his teaching. Dong Zhongshu's intention was to discourage all other schools and promote Confucianism as an ideological basis for the education of officials. At the same time a cult of Confucius was encouraged, Confucian temples were erected in all towns and for a while Confucius was widely regarded as a god, but from the first century onwards this period of glorification ended and in later ages, although still highly honoured, it was as a great teacher rather than a divine being.

The downfall of the Han Dynasty at the beginning of the third century AD was a great blow to Confucianism, since the system of government which nurtured it was in a state of collapse. During the following four centuries China was divided politically and the new religions of Buddhism and Taoism spread throughout China, adding a new religious dimension to Chinese life. Buddhism, in particular, became popular among all strata of society, right up to the imperial court. By the ninth century AD it was regarded as a menace to Confucian supremacy, as well as a drain on the exchequer, and severe measures were taken to restrict the number of Buddhist monasteries and temples.

NEO-CONFUCIANISM

In the eleventh century an intellectual movement within Confucianism sought to counter both Buddhism and Taoism. This movement is known in the West as Neo-Confucianism. There were several schools of Neo-Confucianism, but the most influential figure in the movement was Zhu Xi (1130–1200) also known as Zhu Zi (Master Zhu). Zhu Xi was a clear thinker who had wide knowledge and a voluminous literary output. His most important contribution was the commentaries he wrote for the Four Books of Confucianism: The Analects of Confucius, The Book of Mencius, The Doctrine of the Mean and The Great Learning. In 1313 the Emperor ordered that these four books should be the main texts used in the state examinations and that their official interpretation should follow Zhu Xi's commentaries.

Zhu Xi developed a theory which is known as Li Xue (The Doctrine of Li). According to this theory every object in the world, whether animate or inanimate, possesses an innate principle or *li*, which differentiates it from other things. For example, the *li* of a ship enables it to go on water

and the *li* of a cart enables it to go on land. Similarly human nature is the *li* of humankind, which the Neo-Confucians, like Mencius, thought to be inately good, though it could be tarnished by earthly passions. But not only animate and inanimate objects had their *li*, but also government and social institutions. Although it was not intended by Zhu Xi, this was taken by some to mean that current institutions were immutable. Generally speaking the imposition of Neo-Confucian orthodoxy during the Yuan, Ming and Qing dynasty had the effect of obstructing political and intellectual change from the fourteenth to the nineteenth centuries.

Because of its idealization of the past and espousal by those in society opposed to change, Confucianism lost its status as a state orthodoxy early in the twentieth century, though it continues to exert an influence on the minds and social mores of the Chinese and other East Asian peoples. The concepts of loyalty and filial piety, which Confucians have promoted through the centuries, are still very much alive.

The entrance to the forest site of Confucius's tomb in Qufu, his hometown, is known as the Dalin gate. It is guarded by two lion-dog statues; fierce mythological creatures that chase away intruders.

THE CONFUCIAN CLASSICS

Confucius based his teaching on six classic books: the *Yi* (Changes), *Shi* (Odes), *Shu* (History), *Li* (Rites), *Yue* (Music) and *Chun Qiu* (Springs and Autumns). In the second century BC these were reduced to five, the Book of Music having been lost. The first three of these books were dignified by the addition of the word *jing* (classic): *Yi Jing*, *Shi Jing* and *Shu Jing*.

The Analects of Confucius mentions both the Book of History and the Book of Odes, the former only twice but the latter twenty times. The Book of Odes contains 305 songs, including dynastic hymns sung at the early Zhou court and poems akin to folk songs, including some love songs, from the various states of the middle Zhou period. According to Confucian tradition they were collected and edited by Confucius himself, but this is doubtful. Confucius certainly loved

them, knew many of them by heart, and he could probably sing them. He recommended them to his students because it would teach them about the customs of other states, to live harmoniously with other people, and provide an outlet for their emotions.

The Book of Changes is a manual of divination which originated in the Zhou court and was later added to by Confucian scholars. The system it used was based on the manipulation of yarrow stalks to form 64 hexagrams corresponding to all the structures and changes of the universe.

The Book of History is an assorted collection of official documents dating from the early Zhou period, most of which were of little interest to Confucius. *Springs and Autumns* were the annals of Confucius' own state of Lu, in which the daily events of the period from 722 to 481 BC are recorded. Confucius is said to have compiled this book himself, though there is no evidence for this.

HINDUISM

Foundations of Hinduism

The word Hindu is derived from the name given to the people who settled on the banks of the river Sindhu (Indus in northern India). The name was corrupted to Hindu over the course of time, and so their system of beliefs was given the name Hinduism. Hinduism is regarded as the most ancient living world religion, being over 5,000 years old. It originated on the subcontinent of India but its uniqueness lies in the fact that it was not based upon or started by any one single individual, and its origins cannot be traced back to any particular historical period. Hinduism is regarded as a way of life, not just a religion. It leaves itself open to different interpretations and views which have led to the diverse cultural groups of Hindus that can be found around the world.

The Sanskrit text of the Sri Bhagavata Purana, which chronicles the ten avatars of the god Vishnu.

Foundations of Hinduism
Little is known for certain about the origins of Hinduism. It is believed to be linked to early cult practice, but it is known that it spread through India during the Vedic period. The spread of Vedic culture can be followed using the evidence of the discovery of ceramics in northern and central India. The religion was further developed during the Epic period when two of Hinduism's greatest epic poems, the *Mahabharata* and the *Ramayana*, were composed. These both contain references to locations throughout India which have since become places of pilgrimage.

HINDUISM HAS AN enormous collection of texts as its basis which were conceived many thousands of years ago in the Sanskrit language – the root of all modern Indian languages. These were not actually written down until relatively modern times but were passed down by learned *rishis* or sages who realized these teachings. There was no single author of these teachings and they were also compiled by various different *rishis*.

These Hindu scriptures contain systematic explanations on various subjects including science, religion, metaphysics (first principles), philosophy and spiritual knowledge. They are not limited to a few books because Hinduism is not confined to a single set of ideas and so

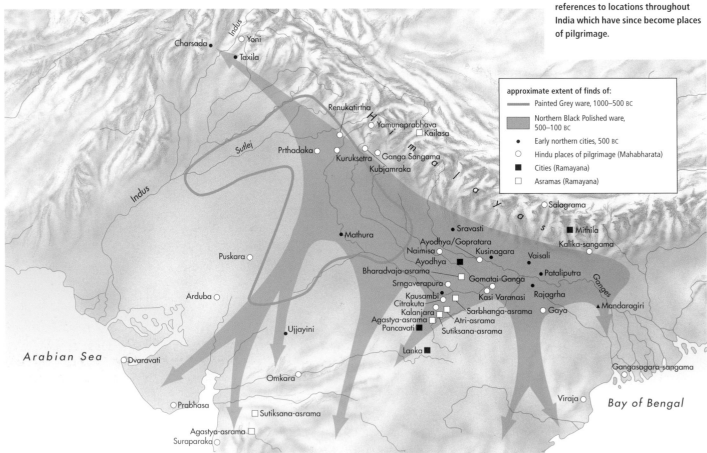

approximate extent of finds of:

— Painted Grey ware, 1000–500 BC

■ Northern Black Polished ware, 500–100 BC

• Early northern cities, 500 BC

○ Hindu places of pilgrimage (Mahabharata)

■ Cities (Ramayana)

□ Asramas (Ramayana)

the scriptures have become a home for many different schools of thought. They are the product of relentless investigations into the facts and truths of life carried out by the ancient sages of India. They are divided into two main categories: Shruti ('that which is heard') and Smriti ('that which is remembered').

THE SHRUTIS

These deal with the never-changing, eternal principles of Hinduism. Shrutis consist of the Vedas, which are the root of the Hindu religion and are possibly the oldest books in the world. There are four Vedas:

- **Rig Veda** – deals with general knowledge, and is the longest of the Vedas;
- **Sama Veda** – deals with knowledge of worship (*upasana*) and is also the originator of Indian Classical Music;
- **Yajur Veda** – deals with knowledge of action (*karma*)
- **Atharva Veda** – deals with knowledge of science, and other miscellaneous subjects

There are also the Upanishads, of which there are approximately 108. These are known as Vedanta ('the end of the Vedas') They were written to make understanding of the Vedas easier. They contain the essence of the Vedas and also conclusions from them (hence the name Vedanta). There are many dialogues between students and their gurus or teachers in the Upanishads and this obviously simplifies the principles which are laid down in the Vedas so that the student can understand.

THE ORIGINS OF HINDUISM

One popular theory suggests that Northern India was invaded by Aryans at around 2000 to 1500 BC, and their culture merged with that of the Dravidian tribes who were living there at the time, to form slowly into more modern Hinduism. However, this is contested by many scholars because scriptures such as the Vedas say that India was the immemorial home of the Aryans. Archeological evidence suggests that writing and silvercraft was being used in 7000 BC, thus implying that there was a greatly advanced civilization existing in India at this time.

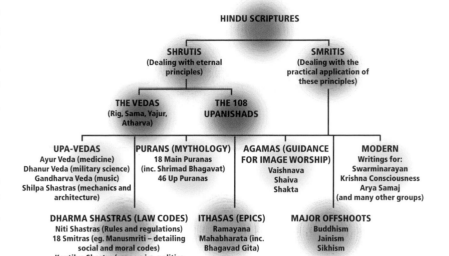

HINDU SCRIPTURES

SHRUTIS (Dealing with eternal principles)

SMRITIS (Dealing with the practical application of these principles)

THE VEDAS (Rig, Sama, Yajur, Atharva)

THE 108 UPANISHADS

UPA-VEDAS
Ayur Veda (medicine)
Dhanur Veda (military science)
Gandharva Veda (music)
Shilpa Shastras (mechanics and architecture)

PURANS (MYTHOLOGY)
18 Main Puranas (inc. Shrimad Bhagavat)
46 Up Puranas

AGAMAS (GUIDANCE FOR IMAGE WORSHIP)
Vaishnava
Shaiva
Shakta

MODERN
Writings for:
Swarminarayan
Krishna Consciousness
Arya Samaj
(and many other groups)

DHARMA SHASTRAS (LAW CODES)
Niti Shastras (Rules and regulations)
18 Smitras (eg. Manusmriti – detailing social and moral codes)
Kautilya Shastra (economics, politics and law)

ITHASAS (EPICS)
Ramayana
Mahabharata (inc. Bhagavad Gita)

MAJOR OFFSHOOTS
Buddhism
Jainism
Sikhism

THE SMRITIS

These explain the practical applications of the eternal principles described in the Shrutis. They detail social and moral codes in the 18 Smritis, the most famous of which was written by Manu which explains the four stages of life and the division of labour through a class system. Manu was a great *rishi* (*master*), who lived in an era preceding that of the *Ramayana* and *Mahabharata* as there are references to Manu in these scriptures.

There is also advice for rulers on policies, laws and codes of conduct (Niti Shastras and Kautilya Shastra). Medicinal science (Ayur Veda), military science (Dhanur Veda), musical science (Gandharva Veda) and mechanical science (Shilpa Shastra) are all explained in detail.

The Smritis also contain the Puranas, of which there are 18 major ones. These are a series of myths and legends, as well as the stories of great men which were designed to simplify religious teaching for the benefit of the people. However what is most famous about the Smritis is the two great epic poems, the *Ramayana* and the *Mahabharata*. The characters described in these epics give a set of ideals to which a person can aspire and so they display the perfect examples of kindness, nobility and faithfulness which are intended to inspire the reader.

The *Mahabharata* contains the famous section known as the Bhagavad Gita, which is the essence of the Vedas and the Upanishads, which have been beautifully condensed into 700 concise *shlokas* (verses). It is renowned as the jewel of ancient India's spiritual wisdom, and was spoken by Lord Krishna (an incarnation of Vishnu) on the great battlefield of the *Mahabharata*.

The most important and famous Hindu Scriptures. There are many more which have not been mentioned here but it is possible to see the large foundation which Hinduism has.

The god Vishnu, portrayed in his avatar, or incarnation, as Krishna. He prepares to catch the devout child Prahlada as his father, the evil king Hiranyakasipu, throws him from a cliff. Hiranyakasipu, a magician, believed himself to be the only god, and only the faith and stoic endurance of his young son converted him back to true religion.

Major Beliefs and Concepts of Hinduism

It is a commonly held belief that Hindus worship many Gods. However, God in Hinduism is thought of as Brahman – the Absolute. This is to say a being without form who pervades everything, is present everywhere, is all-knowing, is all-powerful and who transcends time and space. This is the Nirguna (attributeless) Brahman. There is another aspect of God, and this is Saguna (with attributes) Brahman.

THERE ARE DIFFERENT schools of thought about the nature of Brahman. Among these are three main ones. Shankara charya is the upholder of attributeless Brahman i.e. there is only one Brahman and the individual soul is also Brahman, with *maya* (the material world) being an illusion or a dreamworld of Brahman. This philosophy is termed absolute non-dualism. Ramanuja charya stood for Brahman as being full of attributes: He is the ocean of wisdom, bliss and grace. *Maya* is a power of Brahman and is a part of him. The individual soul is also a small part of Brahman, and when experiencing bliss can be said to be the same as Brahman. This is qualified non-dualism. Madhava charya said that in Brahman there are both aspects. He is attributeless as well as full of attributes. Also, the individual soul is limited and is under the influence of *maya*; while Brahman is all powerful, all pervading and all knowing, and *maya* is subject to Him. Therefore the individual soul should always try to seek God. This philosophy is termed dualism. There are all these different views, which may cause confusion, but the Upanishads also declare that self-realization is the supreme unity, and in it alone all differences are harmonized.

A preacher giving a sermon in a Hindu temple. He is seated in a chair dedicated to Ved Vyasa, composer of the Vedas and the writer of the *Mahabharata*; such a seat is found in many temples.

FUNDAMENTAL HINDU CONCEPTS

Life is a long journey back to the creator, 'interrupted' by death for the person's own good, to continue the journey in another body. This concept of rebirth is explained simply by Lord Krishna in the Bhagavad Gita as follows: 'As a man leaves an old garment and puts on one that is new, the spirit leaves his mortal body and then puts on one that is new.'

The law of *karma* is the concept that 'As you sow, so shall you reap.' Therefore action and reaction (on a physical, mental and spiritual level) are equal and opposite. *Karma* is what a person does, what a person thinks, and even what a person does not do. The results of one's actions in one life can also be carried over to the next, which can affect one's fortunes depending on the individual's past actions.

MOKSHA

Moksha is the goal of life for all Hindus. *Moksha* means total freedom from all pain and suffering. It is the mind which is said to be the cause of suffering, or freedom from suffering. If a state of mind is reached when one is able to transcend the pains and the pleasures of life, when one's will merges with the will of God, then that person has attained Moksha and is

Everything can be sacrificed for truth, but truth cannot be sacrificed for anything.

Swami Vivekananda (1863–1902)

free from the cycle of births and deaths. This joining oneself with God is called yoga.

This science of yoga, consisting of different paths, has been beautifully explained in the Bhagavad Gita: e.g. in Chapter 2.50 Shree Krishna says 'Yogah Karmashu Kaushalam', meaning 'devote yourself to yoga-divine union'. Skilfulness and excellence in action is yoga; all activities performed with God-consciousness is the supreme yoga. The subdivisions are as follows:

Karma Yoga (the Path of Action) is that if a person acts with his or her mind fixed on Brahman (God) he or she will become free and at peace. The results of one's actions should be offered up to God in order to become one with Him.

Jnana Yoga (the Way of Knowledge) is achieved through study, meditation and contemplation.

Bhakti Yoga (the Way of Devotion) is worshipping God through a particular image or form, and keeping one's mind constantly upon God by prayer and devotion.

Mantra Yoga uses chants of the all-pervading sound 'Aum' with the name of one's chosen deity.

Raja Yoga (the Path of Dedication) focuses on control of the mind, often through meditation, or *pranic* (life-force breathing), which allows one to commune with God.

Most seekers practise some or a combination of all these paths to succeed. However it is Hatha Yoga (physical postures and breathing exercises,

regarded as the first stage to reach God) which is practised with considerable interest in the West. This is not to be confused with the other forms of yoga, although good health is the first requirement if one is to attain *moksha*.

AUM

Just as an acorn seed has the potential of a huge oak tree, so does this symbol hide the potential to give us meaning and direction in life. The scriptures say 'In the beginning was the word'. This word is Aum. This sound is the music of the spheres in the galaxy. This short word is the primal sound and it is said to emanate from the right side of the brain, and pervade down the spine and through the whole body. The seeker tries to chant 'Aum' to perfection for full purification of the mind and subsequent realization. Yogis hear this sound when they are sitting in meditation totally at peace. The Katha Upanishads say 'The Goal which all the Vedas declare, which all the austerities aim at and which men desire when they lead a life of continence I will tell you briefly: IT IS AUM.' Nearly all chants or mantras have Aum in front of them. All seekers of truth try to tune in with the cosmic sound of Aum because it is the voice of God. It is declared in the Vedas to be the only support for reaching up to the Absolute.

Shabari, a devotee of Rama in the epic *Ramayana*, waited in her ashram for his arrival for many years, meditating all the time upon him. She is considered a perfect example of devotion to God the yogic tradition.

The Aum Symbol

Hindu Gods and Goddesses

Those who are beginning on a path of spiritualism cannot immediately embrace the concept of the Absolute or Brahman. It is much easier to contemplate a physical manifestation of God, and use that as a means to concentrate and focus one's mind.

The many manifestations of God give the different aspects of the Absolute through which He can be reached. The Absolute controls the universe through three major qualities, regarded as the Trinity or Trimurti of Hinduism:

- **Brahma** – The Creator
- **Vishnu** – The Preserver
- **Shiva** – The Destroyer

All three of these are inseparable and operate simultaneously. The function of Brahma is to create through the will of God. Vishnu in turn preserves what is created, and to that end he is said to have incarnated on earth during various stages of humanity's evolution to destroy evil and re-establish righteousness. Shiva is regarded as the destroyer, for he is believed to

periodically destroy the world when evil has prevailed, so that it might be recreated in its pure form. In temples he is worshipped in the phallic form of a Shiva *lingam* which represents the indefinable nature of the Absolute. His physical form is that of an ascetic (one who has given up the world and its pleasures); and his ash-covered body serves to remind all that the body eventually ends up as ash.

THE DIVINE MOTHER

The female aspect of God is a fundamental part of Hinduism and the all-compassionate form of the Divine Mother is very dear to all Hindus. There are many different female deities.

Saraswati, the consort of Brahma, represents the power of knowledge, best utilized to find God. The symbols used for gaining knowledge are rosary beads, books and music. Her white sari signifies purity of motive to gain knowledge.

The consort of Vishnu, Lakshmi, is the goddess of wealth. She is said to have accompanied Vishnu in his avatars (e.g. as Sita when he incarnated as Rama). She is seen standing on a lotus flower. The lotus grows in muddy waters yet is beautiful; similarly humanity needs to learn to live in this harsh world with detachment from its surroundings.

Parvati, the consort of Shiva, is more commonly worshipped as the destructive form of the Mother Goddess, called Durga or Kali. She is called upon to destroy evil in times of need and to give protection to good people. Her form, riding upon a tiger and holding symbols of power in her eight hands emphasizes this purpose.

THE AVATARS OF VISHNU

Vishnu is thought to have incarnated nine times already upon the earth, in various different forms, to save humanity from evil. His most

An image of Shiva from Madras, India. Shiva, one of the divine aspects of Saguna Brahman, is thought to represent destruction. He also is associated with asceticism and yoga, as well as being recognized as a god of fertility.

That only which we have within, can we see without. If we meet no Gods, it is because we harbour none.

Ralph Waldo Emerson, in Worship (1803–82)

Mother Parvati, pictured here, is Lord Shiva's consort. With her eight arms and ability to ride a tiger, she is revered by Hindus as a protector of good and a destroyer of evil.

famous incarnations for Hindus are as Rama and Krishna, the central characters in the epics *Ramayana* and *Mahabharata* respectively. They have a rich cultural significance and provide models for society. Therefore Vishnu is worshipped mainly through the forms of these incarnations.

However the Buddha, progenitor of Buddhism, and Mahavira, founder of Jainism, are also believed to be his incarnations who came at times when society needed rejuvenation.

There is a tenth Avatar of Vishnu called Kalki who will come at a future time to save mankind and to promote righteousness.

SANTS (SAINTS)

All Hindus look upon saints as a reflection of God. The saint would have many of the qualities that one would associate with God. India has produced many saints or masters who would fit this description. Among them are Guru Nanak, the founder of Sikhism, Ramakrishna Paramahansa, Sai Baba and Chaintanya Mahabrabhu. Shree Chaitanya Mahaprabhu was a great saint born in 1542. He propounded the message of devotion to Lord Krishna. According to him, glorifying the divine names and attributes of Lord Krishna through chanting is the supreme means of salvation.

Chanting the name of the Lord is the essence of all teachings and is the only means of salvation in this present age called Kali Yuga. Swami Prabhupada, the follower of Chaitanya Mahaprabhu and founder of the Hare Krishna movement (short for the term International Society for Krishna Consciousness, or ISKCON), brought these teachings to the West. It is a common site to see a group of devotees (many wearing saffron robes) on the streets chanting the famous Maha (Great) Mantra:

Hare Rama Hare Rama Rama Rama Hare Hare Hare Krishna Hare Krishna Krishna Krishna Hare Hare

Recently, Paramhansa Yogananda (author of *Autobiography of a Yogi*) has rekindled the teachings of Lord Krishna as Kriya Yoga (i.e. yoga of spiritual practices) in the West, and particularly in the United States.

The avatars of Vishnu represent his ten reincarnations on earth. Avatar means 'one who descends'; traditional Hindu belief is that God (Lord Vishnu in this case) becomes incarnate in order to restore goodness and save the world from evil.

THE LIFE OF LORD KRISHNA

The birth and early life of Lord Krishna is fully narrated in the Srimad Bhagavatam, written by Veda Vyasa, a great sage – regarded as the literary incarnation of God, as his ultimate spiritual fulfilment. An avatar of Vishnu, Lord Krishna was born in a prison but was moved overnight to safety to the village of Gokul. Hindus consider Lord Krishna as a full manifestation of God's consciousness. His *lila* ('cosmic play') in the first 12 years of his life is the most profound. In his company all the villagers experienced the love of God. Lord Krishna's life mission had to continue and he moved to Mathura, where he killed the evil king Kansa and released his parents from prison. Finally, in the great symbolic battle of Kurukshetra (narrated in the *Mahabharata*) between the forces of good and evil, Lord Krishna became the central character. The revelation of the Bhagavad Gita on the battlefield was a crucial part of the fulfilment of his mission on earth. The Vedas are too complex for the ordinary man and the Gita as its summary is beautifully given to Arjuna, the ideal disciple (the individual soul) by Lord Krishna (the spiritual Godhead) overflowing with compassion.

Hindu Life

Human life is considered a journey to meet with the creator, yet human desires need to be fulfilled along the way. The Hindu way of life combines both these needs in the four stages (ashrams) of life.

THE FIRST, or student, stage (Brahmacharya) is for good education, self discipline, learning about one's *dharma* (a person's rightful duty to self, family and society) and laying a good foundation to life for being physically and mentally strong for the future.

Entering the family life (Grihasta) is the second stage. Life is not complete without marriage and children. A loving caring family environment enables one to serve others, including the community and the nation. This stage of life allows the acquiring of material possessions for comfortable living and enjoyment of worldly happiness through the satisfaction of man's natural desires.

The third stage is retirement (Vanaprastha). Once the children are all settled one can start withdrawing oneself from worldly desires and attachments to devote more time to spiritual pursuits.

The final stage is Sanyasa (preparing for *moksha*) when one renounces all desires, possessions and needs, spending every moment in meditation. There are some who take up this stage from a young age, even before marriage, to spend the rest of their lives in pursuit of self-realization. It is the duty of the Grihasta to provide for the day-to-day needs of the *sanyasi*.

HINDU SAMSKARAS

Within the above-mentioned four stages (from birth to death) there are 16 Samskaras (sacraments). Apart from the funeral sacraments all the others are causes for celebration. Friends and relations are invited, fed and entertained with dance and music. While some of the 16 are rarely practised nowadays, the main ones are as follows:

- The birth ceremony. This simply consists of welcoming the child into the world by giving it a taste of honey and whispering the name of God into its ear. The naming ceremony is performed a few days later.
- The sacred thread ceremony. Some families still perform this ceremony, where the child is 'initiated' and given a sacred mantra or name of God to chant regularly.
- The Hindu marriage. This is a sacred step in one's spiritual growth as one enters the second stage of life. Puja is offered to Ganesha,

A marriage ceremony taking place in Kerala, India. Marriage is one of the most important rites of passage for Hindus as it signifies the beginning of the second stage of life.

Hinduism Worldwide
Hinduism and its associated way of life was once confined to India and the subcontinent. However, as migration of people and ideas became commonplace in the nineteenth and twentieth centuries, during the colonial and post-colonial eras, the religion spread throughout the world. The map shows the spread of Hinduism and the number of followers around the world.

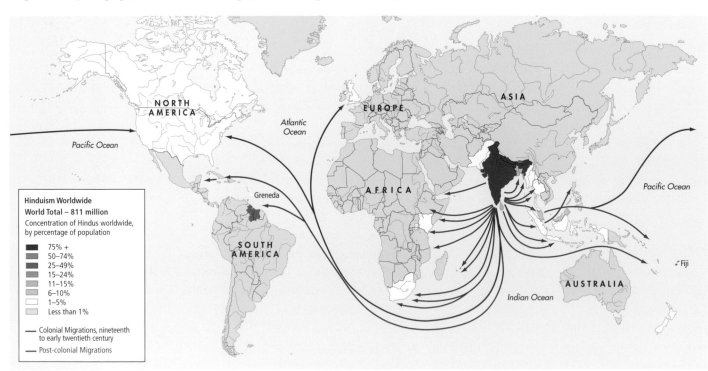

NORTH AMERICA
EUROPE
ASIA
Atlantic Ocean
Pacific Ocean
AFRICA
Pacific Ocean
Greneda
SOUTH AMERICA
AUSTRALIA
Fiji
Indian Ocean

Hinduism Worldwide
World Total – 811 million
Concentration of Hindus worldwide, by percentage of population

- 75% +
- 50–74%
- 25–49%
- 15–24%
- 11–15%
- 6–10%
- 1–5%
- Less than 1%

— Colonial Migrations, nineteenth to early twentieth century
— Post-colonial Migrations

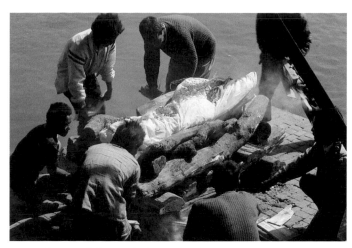

A body is prepared for cremation in Varanassi, India. Because of the Hindu belief in reincarnation, the physical body is believed to be of little significance compared to the immortal soul, and so bodies are normally cremated and the ashes scattered.

- **Brahmins**: those who took to learning and imparted knowledge and spiritual guidance to others;
- **Kshatriyas**: those who were to defend and protect society (as warriors and lawmakers);
- **Vaishyas**: those who provided for the material needs of the people, especially food;
- **Sudras**: those who served the community.

Vishnu and the God of Fire for their presence. The bride and groom meet under a decorated canopy (*mandap*) and garland each other. The vows are taken by going round a fire in the *mandap* in the presence of the guests, the priests and God. There are four (or in some regions, seven) vows taken as per the requirements of the second stage in life.

The bridegroom's parents bless the couple and offer gifts to the bride. All those assembled shower flowers and blessings on the couple, completing the marriage.

- The final Samskara is after death. Hindus believe that the *atman* (soul) never dies, only the body. The body is bathed, clothed and brought home. The last rites are performed symbolically, offering food and clothing for continuation of the onward journey. The body is usually cremated in the presence of a large gathering. Prayers for the peace of the departed are offered for 11 to 12 days before the final concluding rite. The ashes that are collected are dispersed in flowing waters.

MAIN PHILOSOPHIES OF WORSHIP

Hindus can worship the deity of their choice. In the path of devotion, those who see God as the Divine Mother and worship all the female forms as one, are called Shaktas. Those who worship Shiva as the all-pervading God are known as Saivas and those who worship Vishnu (usually as Lord Krishna) are Vaishnavas. The Agamas are the writings which deal with all aspects of these philosophies.

THE CASTE SYSTEM

Thousands of years ago a Varna, or class, system was introduced into Hindu society, in order to give it a strong infrastructure. Each person was put into one of the four classes according to the role in society they could best perform.

Originally all the classes were equal, but the system slowly became corrupt, as the class began to be determined by birth, or caste, rather than personal qualities. This caused discrimination and created divisions in society. However, in modern times, through the efforts of Mahatma Gandhi and many other enlightened Hindus, the system has been outlawed, and although its influence is still strong, Hindu society is being reoriented.

A statue of the god Ganesh from Sri Lanka. Ganesh was guarding the entrance to where his mother Parvati was bathing when his father, Lord Shiva, whom he had not yet met, returned home from a long journey. A fight ensued in which Ganesh was beheaded. When Shiva discovered Ganesh identity, he replaced his son's head with an elephant's, the first that could be found.

GANESH

Ganesh or Ganapati (meaning 'leader of men') is the son of Shiva and Parvati. He is the first one to be worshipped during any ritual as he is considered the remover of obstacles. The mystical form with the elephant head is very symbolic and signifies the qualities required for leadership which are big ears (be a good listener), and a long nose (be aware of what is going on around you). His broken tusk signifies knowledge and the whole tusk means faith. Only faith will reveal to one the mystery of the form (or Absolute God). Ganesh is very popular with Hindus and is on the front of all wedding invitations. The story of the losing of the original head and acquiring of the elephant head is narrated in detail in Ganesh Puran. Shree

Ganesh explains this event as his own *lila* ('cosmic play') with the dual purpose of inspiring man to have a growing compassion for the animal kingdom and to fulfil the wishes of the aggrieved mother, for Ganesh to be accepted by all as the first one to be always worshipped.

Hindu Places of Worship (*mandir*)

A *mandir* or temple is a Hindu place of worship. While most Hindus have a shrine in their own home to worship the deity of their choice, a (purpose-built) temple for the whole community has great importance. It serves as a centre where God is worshipped in the presence of a congregation. Many festivals, religious events and regular ceremonies are held with great enthusiasm, to create a religious atmosphere which encourages the mind to turn towards God for real peace.

WHILE THE TEMPLES in India are usually dedicated to one deity, those around the world (in the West) have evolved to keep all the major deities in one temple. This is so that a smaller community of devotees will all be able to find the deity of their choice to which they can offer their prayers while also being able to pay their respects to the other deities in the temple.

PUJA (WORSHIP)

The temple is meant to reflect the human body. It has an outer structure with shrines, inside which the deities reside. The human body is an outer casing inside which God resides, in the form of the *atman* or soul.

The deities in a temple are regarded as living entities after installation ceremonies, and the resident priest has to look after them as such (i.e. wake them, bathe them, put clothes on them, offer them food and put them to sleep). Some devotees visit the temple regularly, others when they have the time or on special occasions. They offer *puja* (worship) collectively with the priest during the daily service and also partly by themselves individually in a number of different ways:

- The devotee touches the floor as he enters the temple.
- Shoes are removed, as one is treading on holy ground.
- The bell in front of the shrine is rung to make him (the devotee) wake up to the fact that he is in the presence of God.
- The devotee stands with folded hands in front of the shrine as he says his prayers, or in some cases he may prostrate himself on the floor to display his total submission to God.

- He may offer fruits, flowers, dried fruit or milk by leaving it in front of the shrine as thanksgiving.
- The devotee continues his prayers as he circumnavigates the shrine in a clockwise direction. The shrines are built specifically to facilitate this. This ritual has a deep meaning. Just as the earth goes around the sun, its sustainer, the devotee reminds himself that God is his sustainer, and the centre of his life.

One of the numerous temples at Khajurah, Madhya Pradesh in India, Kadariya Mahadev is decorated with 872 carved figures which, like many others in the town, are depicted in erotic postures. The temple was constructed between 1025 and 1050.

Hindu Places of Worship
Pilgrimages to shrines or sacred sites are very important within the Hindu tradition. Ceremonies are held with great enthusiasm in order to create a religious atmosphere which encourages the mind to turn to God. The map shows various holy places within India.

Hindu Places of Worship
- ⊡ Places associated with Visnu
- ☐ Places associated with Shiva
- ▭ Sacred bathing sites

The offering of food to the deities is followed by a devotional song usually expressing the idea, 'O God, you have made everything, but please accept my humble offering to you.' At other times (usually two to three times a day) there is the *arti* ceremony. This is performed by the priest, who, using cotton wicks and clarified butter, lights five lamps in a plate – the *arti* plate. As everyone present sings a prayer the priest rotates the *arti* in a clockwise direction in front of each deity. When the prayer has been completed each person present places their right hand over the lamps and proffer it to their foreheads, thus receiving the light of God. All the offered food is now collected and distributed amongst the devotees as *prasad* (blessed food). The *prasad* is received by the devotees as a part of God's grace. Many Hindus offer *puja* and *arti* regularly, or at least light a *diva* (a small, sacred lamp) in the morning or at twilight.

PUJA ON SPECIAL OCCASIONS

Devotees come to offer *puja* with the help of the priest on occasions such as:

- A newly married couple who will come to the temple to seek God's blessing for the success of their marriage.
- A newly born baby (approximately one month old) will be brought to the temple as its first excursion out of the home, by the parents, accepting the baby as a gift of God.
- After successful completion of a fast for family protection and prosperity.
- To ask for the recovery from illness of a loved one, or for other similar occasions.

KALASHA

The *kalasha* consists of a clay or copper pot filled with water with its mouth surrounded by leaves and covered by a coconut. The pot itself symbolizes the physical human body, the water inside representing the 'water of life' or the individual soul.

On all auspicious occasions *puja* of the *kalasha* is performed first. Prayers are offered to Varuna, Lord of Water, that all the holy waters of the sacred rivers be present in the *kalasha*. Water (being the greatest purifier) is then sprinkled on all the devotees for their purification and protection. The water in the *kalasha* is usually from one of the sacred rivers in India.

When the *kalasha* is moved from one place to another it is always carried on top of the head, giving it the highest position in all respects. Inside temples it sits permanently on the highest spot above the dome of the main shrine.

The shrine of Radha and Krishna at one of the oldest temples in Europe, Shree Santan Mandir, Leicester, UK.

A Mandir is a centre for realising God.
A Mandir is where the mind becomes still.
A Mandir is a place of paramout peace.
A Mandir inspires a higher way of life.
A Mandir teaches us to respect one another.

Pujya Pramukh Swami Maharaj (b.1921)

Bottom left: The *puja* ceremony consists of offerings and prayers to ones own deity to bless a particular venture. The elephant-headed god Ganesh is often particularly invoked at the start of a new enterprise.

Below: The *arti*, a ceremony in which lamps, incense, and other auspicious items are offered to God, is normally performed by priests but, on special occasions such as the one shown here, is performed by ordinary devotees.

THE SACRED COW

The cow was perhaps the first animal to be domesticated by Hindus in India. It was a real blessing to the ancient rural community because it provided milk, from which many other common food products could be made. Cow dung would also be used as a fuel and could be mixed with mud for plastering walls and floors. On farms, bulls were used to plough the fields as well as being used for travel and transport of goods. It is hardly surprising that soon the cow occupied in the life of man the same position as a mother in the life of a child. It became unthinkable to kill and eat the flesh of one. In Vedic literature the cow is a symbol of the divine bounty of the earth and the scriptures prohibit the slaughter of cows. This is the reason for the Hindu reverence for cows, and why Hindus refrain from eating beef. This belief is also designed to encourage people not to harm or kill any creature, and so many Hindus are vegetarians.

Hindu Festivals

The Hindu Calendar is full of festivals, religious, cultural and social. Some of the Hindu festivals are multi-purpose e.g. Holi is a religious festival and also a festival welcoming the spring season. Everybody likes festivals because they give relief from the day-to-day routine of life. Festivals can raise new hopes and help people to make spiritual progress. The festivals are varied and colourful and temples get crowded at these time as people always come (for Darshan) to offer their prayers. Some of the most important festivals are Diwali, Navratri, Janmashtami (birth of Lord Krishna) and Holi.

D iwali truly reminds us of a rich and exciting tradition and heritage left by the great teachers of the past. It is a five-day festival. The first three days are dedicated to the female deities Mahalaxmi, Mahakali and Mahasaraswati, the goddesses of wealth, strength and knowledge (the word maha means 'the purest'). Prayers are offered to use these gifts for the highest good of humanity. The fourth day is the Hindu New Year's Day – a day of forgetting, forgiving and conveying good wishes to one and all for a happy and prosperous new year. The fifth day is a demonstration of love between the brother and the sister with partaking of food together and a sharing of gifts.

A popular story of Diwali comes from the *Ramayana*, where Lord Rama, the incarnation of Vishnu, goes into exile for 14 years, along with his brother and wife, Sita. She is kidnapped by the demon Ravana. However, with the help of the monkey-god Hanuman, his devoted servant, and the monkey army, Rama kills Ravana and rescues Sita. After the 14 years are over he returns to his capital city of Ayodhya, and the people welcome him by lining the streets with *divas*, as he returned in the middle of a moonless night.

This doorstep has been decorated with a rangoli pattern. Designs such as these, incorporating symbols like the swastika, are traditionally drawn during Diwali to welcome Lord Rama home to Ayodhya.

OTHER FESTIVALS

Navratri, or the 'Nine Nights', festival takes the form of celebrating by dancing to music around images of the Divine Mother. The devotees dance by clapping their hands (*garba*) or by using small sticks (*raas*). The festival takes place to celebrate the victory of the Divine Mother over the demon Mahishasur. The more devout devotees of the Divine Mother fast and devote as much time as possible during the nine days and nights to praying and receiving blessings.

Celebrating Navarati, London. Navaratri, the Festival of Nine Nights, is celebrated in honour of the goddesses Durga, Laksmi and Saraswati. The tenth day, Dussehra, commemorates the victory of Rama, hero of the epic *Ramayana*, over the demon Ravana.

The birthday of Lord Krishna during August is celebrated at midnight (Indian Time). Devotees come to do *darshan* and receive the privilege of rocking the cradle of baby Krishna.

HINDU VALUES THROUGH FESTIVALS

Guru Purnima is celebrated on the full moon day in around June or July. *Puja* is offered to Veda Vyasa first, the compiler of the Vedas and the writer of the *Mahabharata*. *Puja* is then offered to one's own guru or spiritual guide (or Lord Krishna if one does not have a guru.). This is the only day when the followers are allowed to give whatever they want to the guru, who usually accepts it. The concept of the guru being like God is very important in Hinduism and this festival is intended to encourage this ideal in students.

Raksha Bandhan occurs on the next full moon (during July or August). The sister ties a multicoloured string – *rakhi*, on the right wrist of the brother. This symbolizes the affection between the sister and brother who in return promises to protect her throughout the year.

The sacred river Ganges is one of the most important Hindu sites, and millions of devotees make pilgrimages to bathe in it each year.

A woman prays at first light in the river Ganges, india.

DIVA

The *diva* is very important to Hindus in the temple and particularly at Diwali or Deepavali (which means 'festival of lights'). The poet Rabindranath Tagore (Nobel prize winner) summarizes beautifully the depth of its significance for humanity:

> Who will take up my work?
> asks the setting sun.
> None has an answer,
> in the whole silent world,
> An earthen lamp says humbly
> from a corner
> I will my Lord,
> as best I can!

The sun here represents Brahman and the little lamp represents the individual soul. The message is that if the sun lights the whole world, then each individual soul should accept responsibility to light the four walls of his or her home, be he father, mother, son, daughter, etc. A caring, loving family unit is the building block to serve our human family with God as our father and mother.

PILGRIMAGE

India is thought of as the holy land of all Hindus. Temples, rivers, mountains, cities and other holy places are reminders of historical events from the scriptures or of saints and sages who lived up to the teachings of the scriptures. During pilgrimage whatever one's status, the simplest living and highest thinking are of the essence. Any difficulties encountered are considered as a test of one's strength of will for the success of the pilgrimage. Pilgrimage may be for the fulfilment of a vow or as a result of a birth or death in a family.

The River Ganges is revered as 'Mother Ganga' and the devotees have faith that bathing in the holy river will wash away their sins. The river's forceful and destructive flow from the heavens is believed to be halted through flowing first into the matted locks of Lord Shiva and then letting it flow more gently for the benefit of mankind. The Kumbha Mela, a gathering of all Hindus, at Allahabad on the banks of the Ganges is held every 12 years, and is the biggest gathering of people that takes place in the world. The most recent took place in January 2001.

ISLAM
Allah's Guidance

The core of Islamic belief is the 'Oneness' of the Divine Perfection of Existence. The Divine, who does not depend on any for existence, is constant, unchanging, reliable and thus, the only Reality. It is impossible for ephemeral, perishable creation to resemble the Creator on whom it depends for its very existence.

The word Allah written in Arabic, the name of the Almighty Creator, the very essence of Divinity, in whom all creation finds its every bounty.

Every manufacturer of complex equipment understands the need to provide guidance on how optimum operational efficiency is to be achieved. It therefore needs little imagination to understand why the Creator needs to provide guidance for the successful existence of humanity. For, in addition to being responsible for their own lives, human beings are responsible for care of the environment upon which their, and all other life depends. The Creator's guidance is thus all-embracing.

ALLAH

Whilst the word 'Creator' describes one Divine attribute, the Arabic name Allah represents the totality of the attributes of the Divine Perfection of Existence.

Islamic teaching begins with Adam ﷺ, the ancestor of *Homo sapiens*, who is the first prophet whom Allah guided. Integral to Adam's guidance was confirmation that subsequent generations would also be guided. Islamic belief is that 124,000 prophets were sent to ensure that all nations and tribes would benefit. This is tremendously important if humanity is to be held accountable for its actions. How could people, who had not received clear guidance, possibly be held accountable? Therefore every prophet taught that people should only worship the Divine Perfection of Existence, and should behave decently towards one another.

Allah's final Prophet, Muhammad Mustafa ﷺ, was sent to confirm and re-establish the guidance of previous prophets, and to ensure that Allah's guidance would remain available for all people until the end of human life on earth.

The word 'Islam' has more than one meaning. It may reflect dependence on, and/or, willingness to yield or submit to Divine supremacy. As everything in the heavens and on the earth depends on Allah for its existence and continued life, all things may be described as

being in a state of islam or dependence. An especially respected Christian, who is acknowledged as being truly sincere and devout, may also be described as having submitted, and thus 'In islam within Christianity'. Only when Islam is written with a capital I, does it specifically refer to those who declare that they accept no divinity other than Allah, and that they sincerely intend always to strive and follow the guidance which Allah revealed through His final Prophet Muhammad ﷺ. If practices of other religions differ from these, it is because they have, in some way, become diluted or modified.

The Early Spread of Islam
In AD 622 Muhammad ﷺ and his followers migrated from Makkah to Madinah. This departure (or hijrah) came to mark the beginning of the Muslim era. At Madinah, Muhammad ﷺ organized his followers into a dynamic socio-political group, whose authority was by his death extended over much of the Arabian peninsula.

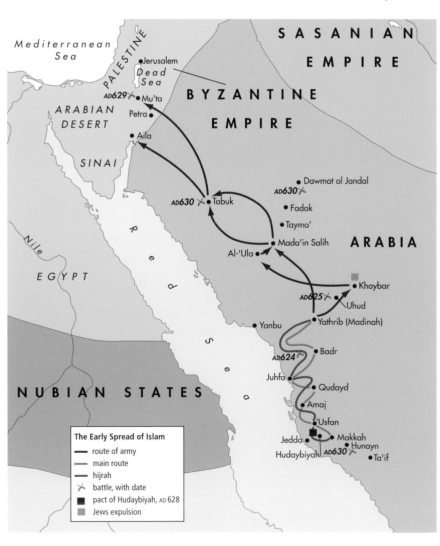

The Early Spread of Islam
— route of army
— main route
— hijrah
⚔ battle, with date
■ pact of Hudaybiyah, AD 628
■ Jews expulsion

POLITICAL, ECONOMIC, SOCIAL AND RELIGIOUS CONDITIONS IN ARABIA

Other than in the Yemen, there was no political organisation in the Arabia of the late sixth and early seventh centuries ad. There were villages, a few towns and a small number of Jewish and Christian settlements, but nomads roamed most of the land. No law or legal structure existed and the only restraint on people was fear of vendetta. Tribal honour meant members were protected whatever their crime, a condition which resulted in incessant warring. Moral authority was only acknowledged when charismatic leadership was respected. While

most worshipped idols, a few still clung to the monotheism brought by Ibrahim ﷺ. Women had no status and female infants were sometimes buried alive. Notwithstanding its illiteracy, Arab society esteemed oratory and particularly valued poetry

Nomads roam the desert landscape with their camels. The camel was a vital part of life in sixth- and seventh-century AD Arabia, prized for its wool, pelt, dung and milk as well as being used for transport.

COLOPHONS

Throughout this section you will see colophons of the Arabic terms of respect used by Muslims:

ﷺ *Sallalahu Alayhi wa aalihi wa Salaam*
May Allah's greetings and blessings be upon him & his progeny
(used immediately after referring to the Prophet Muhammad)

ﷺ *Alayha al-Salaam*
Peace be upon her
(used immediately after referring to Khadijah, Fatimah, Zaynab & Maryam)

ﷺ *Alayhi al-Salaam*
May Allah bless him
(used immediately after referring to a single Imam or Prophet)

ﷺ *Alayhima al-Salaam*
May Allah bless them
(used immediately after referring to two Imams or two Prophets)

ﷺ *Alayhum al-Salaam*
May Allah bless them
(used immediately after referring to three or more Imams or Prophets)

ﷺ *Rahimahu Allah*
May Allah grant him mercy
(used immediately after referring to a single deceased and respected person)

ﷺ *Rahimahum Allah*
May Allah grant them mercy
(used immediately referring to deceased and respected people)

ﷺ *Quddisa Sirroh*
May his soul be blessed
(used immediately after referring to a single deceased and respected scholar)

ﷺ *Quddisa Sirrohuma*
May their souls be blessed
(used immediately after referring to two deceased and respected scholars)

ﷺ *Radi Allahu anhu*
May Allah be pleased with him
(used after referring to a respected companion of the Prophet or the Imams)

The Arabian Peninsula, where Muhammad the Prophet ﷺ was born in AD 570, is dominated by desert at its centre, such as depicted here, with mountains lining the Red Sea in the west and more fertile land to the south.

157

The Early Years of the Prophet Muhammad ﷺ

The Messenger enjoins them to do good and forbids them from evil. He makes all good things lawful and prohibits only those which are shameful. Those who believe, honour and help him, and are guided by the illumination sent with him, will achieve success

Extracted from Qur'an 7:157

Abdullah, Muhammad's 24-year old father, had to travel to Syria on business shortly after his newly wedded wife Aminah had conceived. On his return journey he contracted a fatal illness and died. Muhammad's inheritance from his estate is recorded as being five camels and ten sheep.

THE LIFE OF THE PROPHET MUHAMMAD ﷺ

According to his family, Muhammad ﷺ was born after sunrise on Friday the 17th of Rabi'ul Awwal in the year AD 570; others claim it was on Monday the 12th of that month. Until the official naming, seven days after birth, his mother called him Ahmad. However, at the naming, witnessed by the assembled Hashemite clan, his grandfather, the clan's leader, gave him the name Muhammad, which means 'praiseworthy'.

It was customary for children of Makkan nobility to be entrusted to wet-nurses who lived in the country, away from contagious diseases and pollution. There, they could draw benefit from the fresh desert air, learn traditional customs, culture and the purest form of indigenous Arabic. In accordance with this practice, Muhammad ﷺ was fostered by Halimah, of the Bani Sa'd tribe. Due to a cholera epidemic, he could not be returned to his mother after the suckling period, and it was five years before he finally returned to Makkah.

A short time later, Abdullah's widow took her son to Yathrib, to visit his father's last resting place. On the journey back, Muhammad ﷺ tragically lost his mother. After her death, the household of his paternal grandfather, Abd al-Muttalib, became home to the orphaned six-year-old child.

The inhospitable rocky landscape around Makkah, 72 km (45 miles) from the Red Sea, illustrates why this part of the Arabian Peninsula is called the Hijaz, or 'protected coastline'.

Two years later, when his paternal uncle Abu Talib had inherited the leadership of the Bani Hashim clan, Muhammad ﷺ became ward and a much-loved member of his household. At 12 years old, he accompanied his uncle on a trading trip to Syria, a journey which he remembered as being his most enjoyable ever.

Muhammad ﷺ is recorded as being an unassuming youth with honourable bearing and good character. Reserved and meditative he eschewed the rude sport and profligacy of his contemporaries. This won the approval of his fellow citizens who, by common consent, titled him The Faithful One – Al-Amin. Respected and honoured as being both trustworthy and truthful, he lived a quiet life in the family of Abu Talib.

When Muhammad ﷺ was 20, a visiting trader, cheated of his goods by a resident, remonstrated so poetically and eruditely, that the attention of several young Makkans was captured. They, determined to rectify this wrongdoing, made a covenant between themselves to stand up and protect the rights of the oppressed. In due course they reclaimed the unpaid goods and returned them to their owner. Many years later, the Prophet ﷺ admitted that he still remained faithful to that covenant, called in English, The League of the Virtuous, and said that he would never break it, no matter what inducement was offered. Indeed, the agreement was so firmly established by all of them, that even their descendants continued to regard themselves bound by it.

There has not been a prophet who has not tended his flock. As expressed by John Gay, 'In summer's heat, and winter's cold, he fed his flock, and penn'd the fold.'

Arabic calligraphy of the names Muhammad ﷺ and Ali ؏.

KHADIJAH ؏

When Muhammad ﷺ was 25, his uncle learned that the noble Makkan widow Khadijah ؏, known alternately as Princess of Merchants and The Pure One, was looking for a manager to represent her on the annual Syrian trade expedition. When told that Muhammad ﷺ would probably accept that commission, she sent word that, in view of his reputation for truthfulness, honesty and trustworthiness, she would offer him double the sum normally paid. He accepted, and history records that the enterprise was so successful that she offered him a bonus, in addition to their agreed terms. This however he declined.

It is also recorded that she later let him know that, due to his status and respect within the community, his evident honesty, good manners and truthfulness, she was earnestly inclined to marry him. He said he would need first to consult his uncles. In another report, Khadijah's proposal was delivered by one Nafisah who said, 'O Muhammad, why don't you illuminate the night-chamber of your life with the light of a spouse? Will you respond if I invite you to beauty, wealth, gentleness and respect?'

The widowed Lady Khadijah ؏ is reported to have been 40 when she entered into this, her last marriage.

Revelation in Makkah

The first words revealed to Muhammad z were:

Recite in the name of you Sustainer, who has created humanity
from a germ-cell.

Recite for your Sustainer is The Most Bountiful One,

Who has taught the use of the pen,

and taught what humanity had not known.

Qur'an 96:1–5

The 'Mount of Light' is an almost sterile hill of black stone a few miles north-east of Makkah. From the top of its northern side, one may enter the outer part of a small cave Hira which, for a few feet, is just high enough to stand up in. For several years it had been Muhammad's practice, every now and then, to seclude himself there for a day or so. On such occasions his young cousin would bring him water and food. It was during one of these sojourns that revelation first occurred: the order to recite or formally announce, in the name of the One who Creates and sustains all life, the guidance that was to be revealed to him. In addition, he had to commit it to writing for transmission to later generations and different cultures. He was charged with this duty in his fortieth year, the age when, according to Qur'anic teaching, maturity brings realization of the need to discharge the serious obligations of life.

The Messenger's assignment was to enjoin people to do good and to forbid their evil behaviour. The revelation was to be of spiritual truth and moral standards. For the 13 years he was to remain in Makkah, the Prophet z concentrated on rejecting idolatry and inviting people to accept that a day would come when they would have to account for their actions before Allah Almighty, the One True God. Indeed, that was all that he taught during that period.

THE PROPHET'S EARLY TEACHINGS

For the first three years he restricted his discussions to selected friends and members of his family. For the

Seventh/eighth-century BC manuscript page in characteristic Kufic script, named after Kufah, a town in South Central Iraq. The last line of Surah 10, 'Until Allah gives judgement, and He is the best Judge', to the first line of Surah 11, 'Alif Lam Ra: A book firmly arranged'.

Islamic Expansion AD 632–850
This map shows the expansion of Islam after the prophet Muhammad's death in AD 632 until the end of the early Abbasids in AD 850.

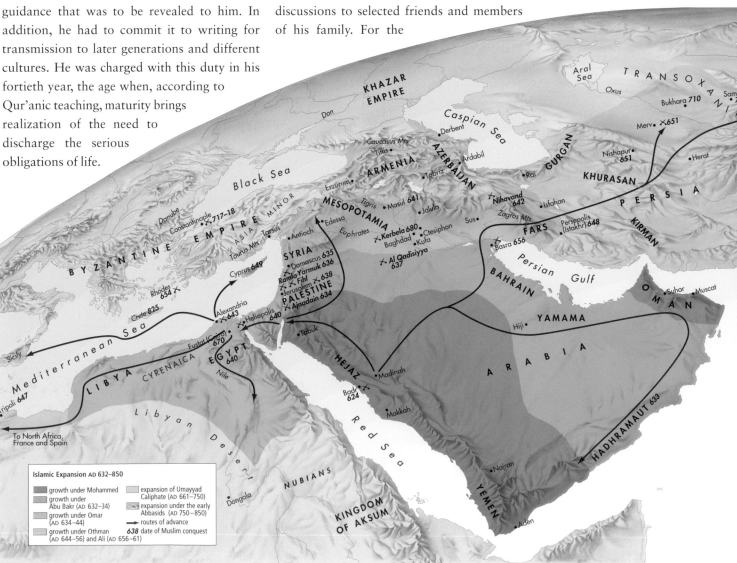

Islamic Expansion AD 632–850

- growth under Mohammed
- growth under Abu Bakr (AD 632–34)
- growth under Omar (AD 634–44)
- growth under Othman (AD 644–56) and Ali (AD 656–61)
- expansion of Umayyad Caliphate (AD 661–750)
- expansion under the early Abbasids (AD 750–850)
- → routes of advance
- **638** date of Muslim conquest

subsequent 10, he appealed to the public at large. While Islam had a limited audience it was not taken seriously by those outside his immediate circle. However, the existing establishment later grew alarmed by its challenge to their authority. No matter how assiduously they harassed or damaged Muslims who had no powerful friends, they could not undermine Muhammad's influence. Qualities of forgiveness, generosity, fairness and unfaltering determination attracted continuing interest and respect. In addition, Muhammad's uncle, Abu Talib, was a man of considerable influence and authority. Before they could deal with Muhammad ﷺ, they had first to contain the power which protected him.

A confederation of tribes drew up a proclamation stating that, unless Muhammad ﷺ was handed to them, his Hashemite clan would be subject to economic and social boycott. The Hashemites refused to comply. However, in recognition of their vulnerability to surprise attack, they left their homes to camp in the safety of a naturally protected gorge on the outskirts of Makkah. After three years, encouraged by

waning interest in Hashemite banishment, several Makkans joined together to annul the boycott and escort the Hashemites home.

Weakened by outdoor life, the Lady Khadijah ﷺ, Muhammad's wife for 24 years, died within 12 months of their return. A month later his uncle and life-long supporter also perished. Muhammad's year of sorrow gave those who hated him opportunity to plot his death. While Ali ﷺ lay in his bed to assure prying eyes he was at home, Muhammad ﷺ migrated to Yathrib.

The Holy Mosque in Makkah encompasses the cube shaped building – Ka'abah – toward which all Muslims face when they pray. It is recorded as being the first house of worship appointed for humanity, and is the most holy mosque of Islam.

The Al-Aqsa Mosque (Dome of the Rock) in Jerusalem. The golden dome screens the rock from which the Prophet ﷺ ascended to the Divine presence. The Al-Aqsa Mosque is the third holiest mosque of Islam.

MUHAMMAD'S FAMILY

Khadijah ﷺ bore Muhammad ﷺ six children. Both sons, Qasim and Abdullah, died in infancy. Their daughters, Zaynab, Ruqayyah and Um Kulthum became respected ladies of Makkah. Fatimah ﷺ, who married Ali ibn Abu Talib ﷺ, the elected fourth Caliph and first of the Twelve Imams, was mother of the second and third Imams, Hasan and Husayn ﷺ.

When Muhammad ﷺ was 30 and fathering his own children, his uncle Abu Talib, in whose home Muhammad ﷺ had lived for the greater part of his life, had a son Ali.

The little boy spent a great deal of time with the other children in Muhammad's house and at the age of five, lived there permanently. He later recounted that the Prophet ﷺ never sought to criticize the things he said or did and would often give him big hugs of affection. He, in return, adored his cousin whom, in his own words, he 'used to accompany, like a young camel following in the footprints of its mother'. Each day, he said, the Prophet ﷺ would draw his attention to one or another virtue which he was then encouraged to emulate.

Revelation in Madinah

Years are remembered by notable events, and as the turning point in Muslim fortunes was the year of Muhammad's migration or *hijrah*, this marks the start of the Islamic Hijri calendar. After he had moved to Yathrib, it became known as, 'the town of the Prophet' – Madinat al-Nabi, or more simply, Madinah.

In his first year in Madinah, Muhammad ﷺ, built the mosque which served as a place of guidance, education and prayer. He next integrated some 300 immigrant Makkans – Muhajirs, and their Yathrib helpers – Ansar, into one united community by formally pairing them as 'brothers in faith', to live together and share resources. Muhammad ﷺ himself pledged brotherhood with Ali ﷺ. To vouchsafe the freedom, order and justice of all inhabitants, he documented the rights and obligations of Muslims and non-Muslims, in the first declaration of human rights of recorded history.

THE RIGHT PATH

During the second year, revelations established: *adhan* – the call to prayer; *wudu* – purification preparatory to commencing a prayerful state; *salat* – the mandatory five daily prayer times; *qiblah* – the Ka'abah in Makkah as the direction to face in offering prayer; *sawm* – fasting for the 29 or 30 days of the month of Ramadan; *zakat al-Fitr* – payment, by the head of households, of 'the cost of a meal' on behalf of everyone in their homes, to ensure that all in the community were able to feast the day after the Ramadan fast ends; Id al-Fitr – the recommendation for Muslims to mark that day, and Id al-Adha – the anniversary of Ibrahim's willingness to sacrifice his son Isma'il ﷺ, with celebration and prayer; and *zakat* – the 2.5% tax on wealth. Also in this year, the Prophet celebrated his daughter Fatimah

Zahra's wedding to Ali ibn Abu Talib ﷺ.

His first grandson Hasan ﷺ was born the following year and his second grandson, Husayn ﷺ in the fourth year. That year their paternal grandmother, Fatimah bint Asad, Abu Talib's widow died. She was the Prophet's aunt and foster mother and the second lady to have accepted Islam. In the fourth year in Madinah, intoxicants became prohibited, and in the fifth, *hajj* – pilgrimage to Makkah – became mandatory for those who can afford it.

SPREADING THE WORD

In 6 AH (AD 628) – Anno Hijri – the sixth year in Madinah, the Prophet ﷺ declared his intention to perform *umrah* – the minor pilgrimage, but the Makkans denied him entry. Notwithstanding that, it was agreed that Muslims would be allowed to spend three days of pilgrimage in Makkah the following year. Accordingly, in 7 AH (AD 629), Muhammad ﷺ performed *umrah* with 2,000 well-disciplined pilgrims.

Instructed to announce that he had been sent as a Messenger and Warner to the whole of humanity, Muhammad ﷺ communicated his commandment to princes, kings, tribal chiefs and other distinguished personalities in 7 AH (AD 629). 185 such communications still exist. He sent ambassadors to the Roman and

Arabic calligraphy of the name Husayn ﷺ.

Arabic calligraphy of the name Fatimah ﷺ.

Madinah's green domed Mosque of the Prophet is the second most holy mosque of Islam. The undoubted heart of this mosque is the tomb of the Prophet Muhammad ﷺ himself.

Byzantine empires, Persia, Ethiopia, Egypt, Yemen, Bahrain and Jordan.

In 8 AH (AD 630) Muhammad ﷺ was granted governance of Makkah and cleared the Ka'abah of idols. 10 AH (AD 632) was marked by delegations to Madinah, to accept Islam and pledge allegiance to the Prophet ﷺ. It is also the year of his 'Farewell *hajj*' in which an estimated 100,000 accompanied him. He died in 11 AH at the age of 63.

ESTABLISHING THE FUNDAMENTALS

Revelation in Madinah provides the basis for Islamic acts of worship, contract, marital regulation and all other aspects of Islamic law.

In his *hajj* address Muhammad ﷺ said, 'Your person and property is honoured and any transgression is strictly prohibited. You will soon return to Allah and have your good and bad deeds judged. Those who hold things in trust should return them. Usury is prohibited in Islam. None should oppress nor be oppressed. Your women have rights over you and you have rights over them. Treat them with kindness and love and provide them with comfortable means of life. They are only lawful for you according to His laws. Hear my words carefully and ponder them! I leave you two memorable

things, one the Book of Allah, the other my example, exemplified by my progeny. If you abide by them you will not go astray. Those present should communicate these words to those who are absent. Today, I have banned all customs and beliefs of the "Age of Ignorance".'

At Ghadeer Khum, just prior to the pilgrims dispersing on their separate ways, the Prophet ﷺ raised Ali's hand and repeatedly announced, 'Ali is master of those over whom I am master.' Thereafter he received the final revelation:

This day I have perfected your religion, bestowed full measure of My blessings and willed your self-surrender to Me to remain your religion. Qur'an 5:3

The fourteenth-century Mamluk, Sultan Hasan Mosque in Cairo. The *mihrab*, or concavity, indicates the direction of prayer toward Makkah. The stepped *mimbar* is the podium from which the Friday address is given.

Arabic calligraphy of the name Hassan ﷺ.

THE FIVE PILLARS

Those who adhere to the elemental beliefs of Islam may be described as Muslim. Those beliefs are sometimes referred to as being the five pillars of Islam.

Sunni sources

According to Bukhari in his 'Sahih', the Prophet ﷺ said that Islam is established upon five pillars:

1 Salah (the daily five proscribed times of communal worship)
2 Payment of Zakat
3 Pilgrimage during the month of Hajj
4 Fasting during the month of Ramadan
5 Declarations of there being no god but Allah, and of Muhammad ﷺ being His Messenger

Sahih Bukhari Chapter of Faith Volume 1 Page 9

Shi'ah sources

According to Koleini in his 'al-Kafi', Imam Muhammad al-Baqir (the fifth Imam) narrated that the Prophet ﷺ (his forefather), said that Islam is established upon five pillars:

1 Salah (the daily five proscribed times of communal worship)
2 Payment of Zakat
3 Pilgrimage during the month of Hajj
4 Fasting during the month of Ramadan
5 Wilayah (guardianship of the faith by leaders, appointed

by Allah to provide error free guidance; with believers' reciprocation by loving them).

Al-Kafi - Volume 2 Page 15
Wassa'il al-Shi'ah - Volume 1 First chapter, Tradition number 1

Shi'ah point out that while Allah guides all of His creation to its own specific perfection; trees automatically bearing blossom and fruit for example, the perfection of humanity can only be arrived at through free will and wise decisions.

(We sent) Messengers to give glad tidings and warnings so that people may have no plea [complaint] against Allah after (the coming of) the messengers

Qur'an 4:165

Thus, Allah ensured that the guidance His prophets delivered would be free of errors, and appointed guides to consolidate those beliefs after the epoch of prophethood had ended. It was clearly necessary that they too would not make errors, if they were to successfully safeguard the sciences and laws of Islam. His error-free appointees, who immediately followed the Prophet ﷺ, are known as m'asumin or error-free Imams.

'People benefit from the guidance of the error-free Imams whenever they find the ability to receive it.'

Islamic Teachings in Brief by Allamah Tabatabai - Page 124 – 125

The Book of Allah

All Muslims agree that the Qur'an is the primary source of Islamic teaching. Although different schools of thought may differ on aspects such as analogy, consensus, public interest, common practice and intellectual reasoning, all agree that, in a very deep sense, Islam is the Qur'an and the Qur'an is Islam.

In Islamic teaching, God is the Creator and the Law giver. As Creator, He is fully aware of how we should behave for our individual and collective success. The Qur'an is His final guidance to humanity. The Qur'an consists of 30 sections, some revealed in Makkah, some in Madinah. One may categorize their content in the following four ways:

1. Belief and creed, e.g.:
- *Allah is the light of heaven and earth. His light analogous to a lamp in a niche (contained) in glass to appear as a shining star....*

  Qur'an 24:35

2. History of previous nations and prophets, e.g.:
- *And when Lot said to his people, 'Surely, your acts of lewdness have never been committed before you.'*

  When Our messengers came to Abraham with the glad tidings ...

To the Midianites We sent their brother Jethro who said, 'O my people, worship Allah, fear the last day and do not create mischief on the earth.

Qur'an 29:28, 31, 36

- *Truly We graced David, (saying) 'O mountains sing Our praise with him, and... (We made subservient to) Solomon, the wind which covers a months journey in a morning ...*

  Qur'an 34:10, 12

3. Moral and social guidance, e.g.:
- *Your Lord has ordered you not to worship any except Him. He commanded you to be good to your parents. Should either reach old age and need care, do not reproach, behave irritably or reject them, but always respond gently. Treat them with humility and tenderness praying, 'Lord be merciful to them; as they were to me when I was little.*

  Your Lord is aware of what is in your heart and how you behave. He is All-forgiving to those who repent.

A class of children in Khartoum, Sudan, being taught the Qur'an. Muslims are exhorted to seek knowledge from the cradle to the grave.

Give close relatives their entitlement, and be generous to travellers in need and the poor; but do not fritter your wealth. Those who squander are, like Satan, ungrateful to the Lord. If you are yourself in need of your Lord's support and have to decline their request, do so with kind words and compassion. Do not be miserly or worthy of reproach, nor so generous that you become destitute.

Qur'an 17:23–29

4 Law. e.g.:

● *O you who believe, when you contract a loan for a fixed term, ensure that it be accurately recorded in writing. No scribe may refuse to do this as Allah commands it be done. Let the borrower dictate terms to safeguard themselves in full awareness of Allah's laws. However, if they are unable to comprehend the terms, suffer some disability, or are unable to dictate, ensure that their guardian does it justly. Then call two reliable witnesses from the community … who should not refuse this duty. Do not hesitate to document contracts be they large or small. This is fairer in the sight of Allah and assures the accuracy of testimony …*

Qur'an 2:282

All Muslim scholars accept that the values and rulings revealed in the Qur'an are without limit and valid for all time. All Muslim scholars agree that because Allah pledged to protect it, not a single word in the Qur'an has been altered.

Men at worship in the Holy Mosque in Makkah. Muslims pray five times daily, quoting the short first chapter of the Qur'an in Arabic over and over again.

The Qur'an is Allah's education, its outcomes are reflected in the lives of people, their environments and relationship with all that is on earth. Learning to read the Qur'an is the first step to their success.

THE IMPORTANCE OF THE QUR'AN

In the words of Imam Ali ☙, 'Then Allah sent him the Book of Light, an inextinguishable illumination of sustained brilliance, a bottomless ocean, an assured route, a never fading beacon and unchanging elucidation of good and evil. Its clarification is unchallengeable, its remedy assured. It is an undiminishing honour and a virtue whose supporters are never abandoned. It is a mine of belief with the very source of knowledge at its core. It is an ocean of justice and the foundation stone of Islam.

It is a valley inexhaustibly irrigated by truth, an assured destination with un-miscible signs for all who seek it. Allah revealed it to quench the thirst of the learned and to bloom in the heart of jurists. It is the highway of the righteous, a salvation and the illumination of darkness.

It is the unbreakable rope of those who hold to it, the honour of those who love it, the peace of those who enter it, and the guidance of those who follow it.'

Sermon 198

The Prophet's Example

Muhammad ﷺ is regarded as the most noble and excellent of Allah's creation, the embodiment of human perfection. As His life evidenced all the virtues and perfection humanity can acquire, He is regarded as the perfect man – Insan al-Kamil. *Hadith* cover the sayings, actions and silent assertions of the Prophet ﷺ which were narrated by his companions or progeny.

Hadith means literally 'a saying, report or account', specifically of what the Prophet Muhammad ﷺ said, or his reaction to what others said and did, recounted by his progeny, household and companions. *Sunnah* means literally 'the model practice and behaviour, custom or observance of the Prophet ﷺ' which Muslims try to follow in their daily lives, religious observance and in their relations with every aspect of Allah's creation. Evidence of his *sunnah* is found within the hadith. A *hadith* may refer to moral conduct, current events, history, future events, the hereafter, legal rulings or any other topic, e.g.:

> The Prophet ﷺ said, 'Humanity is dependant upon Allah; the most loved by Him are those who are of most benefit to His dependants.'
> *Al Kafi* Volume 2 Page 164
> The Prophet ﷺ said, 'Show kindness to the worthy and the unworthy. If you find that they do not deserve it, you at least will have earned it'.
> *Bihar al Anwar* Vol. 74 p. 409
> The Prophet ﷺ said, 'No-one is allowed to carry weapons in Makkah.'
> *Sahih Muslim* Vol. 2 Page 989

ISLAMIC TEXTS

In the Prophet's and his progeny's lifetime, their every word and deed was closely observed by those eager for success in this life and in that yet to come. Many recorded and collected their observations. Some regrettably even fabricated *hadith*. The Prophet ﷺ himself encouraged people to take care that nothing was falsely attributed, and to then disseminate hadith as widely as possible. They were later collected together by numerous scholars to form a major resource for Islamic law.

A crucial and major aspect of this subject is concerned with the degree of reliability and

authenticity of narrations. No Muslim scholar would claim that either the four major collections of Ahl ul-Bayt related *hadith*, or the six major Sunni collections, are necessarily reliable and binding. The main Shi'ah works, known as *The Four Books (al-Kutub al-Arba'a)* are: *Usool al Kafi, Man La Yahdhuruhu al Faqih, Istebsaar* and *Tahtheeb*. The main Sunni works, known as *The Six Books – (al Sihah al-Sittah)* are: *Sahih Bukhari, Sahih Muslim,*

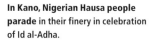
The seeking and imparting of knowledge is an integral part of Islam.

In Kano, Nigerian Hausa people parade in their finery in celebration of Id al-Adha.

After the Id al-Fitr prayer, families in Malaysia visit the graves of departed loved ones to offer prayer for their souls.

Sunan abu Dawud, Jami'al Tirmidhi, Sunan ibn Majah and *Sunan al-Nissa'i*. In addition, there are many other Shi'ah and Sunni collections. While the chapter headings in the above collections are largely the same and many narrations similar, their content is not.

A jurist or *Mujtahid*, therefore, needs to exert substantial time and effort to examine the validity of each *hadith*. The need to verify the authenticity of the chain of narrators led to the development of a new branch of Islamic study, *Ilm al-Rijal* or *Al-Jarh wal taa'dil* i.e., the biographies of men. Some scholarly works on this subject extend to 24 volumes.

When a jurist is not able to find reference in Qur'an or a *hadith* regarding a specific issue, he or she must employ secondary sources such as intellectual reasoning, favoured by the Shi'ah, or analogy, favoured by the majority of Sunnis.

THE EXAMPLE OF THE PROPHET

Muslims, in every age and from every part of the world have strived, and continue to do so, to imitate the perfect example of the Prophet ﷺ in every aspect of their lives. As expressed by the great medieval theologian Al-Ghazali of the tenth century in his *Ihya ulum al-Din*:

'Know that the key to happiness lies in emulating the example of Allah's Messenger ﷺ in everything he did. Doing the things that he did in the way he did them; his activities, rest, approach to eating, sleeping and talking. I do not mention his religious practices, for it goes without saying that these must not be neglected. I draw attention rather to the importance of copying of his customs and practices, for it is only by doing this that unrestricted success becomes possible. For Allah ordered Muhammad ﷺ to, "Tell them, 'If you love Allah, then follow me; Allah will then love you and forgive your sins, for Allah is indeed forgiving and merciful" *Qur'an 3:31*; and "... Accept what the messenger gives you, and refrain from what he has prohibited ... ." *Qur'an 59:7*. That means, sitting when putting your trousers on, standing when winding your turban and beginning with the right foot when putting shoes on ... .'

How Islam is Spread and Lived

People may be physically coerced into doing many things, but they cannot be forced to accept certainty of faith, religion, spiritual doctrine or creed. The spread of Islam, in the form of conversion, is therefore the outcome of mental or spiritual factors, helped occasionally by material circumstances.

The Arab conquests in the early years of Islam, when travel was a lengthy and difficult business, required permanent camps being built in far off lands. Economic and social realities inevitably resulted in these garrisons and towns becoming integrated. By the time such garrisons were no longer required, many troops, already identified with local interests, chose to remain there with their families and friends. A similar pattern of spread resulted from the continued extension and development of trade.

The development of Muslim communities, far away from the centres of Islamic scholarship and learning, inevitably resulted in calls for Islamic teachers and jurists to serve in those areas. Over the years, thousands of Muslim dignitaries travelled far and wide to meet the needs of such societies and establish new centres of learning. At the time of the great slave trade to the Americas, it was not uncommon for spiritual teachers to be taken and later shipped to the new world. There, they too continued their service to the Muslim community and, being literate and learned, often held positions of great trust.

LAW AND ORDER

Perhaps the most interesting aspect of the spread of Islam has been the attraction it held for the oppressed peoples in the areas of its introduction. An appeal due to principles of equality, justice, fairness and clarity of the doctrine 'to encourage good and oppose evil'.

Being interested in trade, Muslim merchants naturally had a great interest in law and order, peace and security, a factor which no doubt encouraged both migration and conversion in those areas. As trading relationships developed between neighbouring centres and nations, the ever expanding Muslim community constituted a vast common market of free trade and development.

In latter years, the spread of Islam has largely been the result of European colonialism. Muslim citizens of various empires doing military service

One of the oldest solid-wood, Malay style mosques at Kampung Laut – Village of the Sea, near Kota Bharu in Malaysia.

Islam Today
Islam is the second largest religion in the world. There are 1,188 million Muslims in 184 countries throughout the world. The map shows the worldwide distribution of Muslims and the spread of Islam during the 20th century.

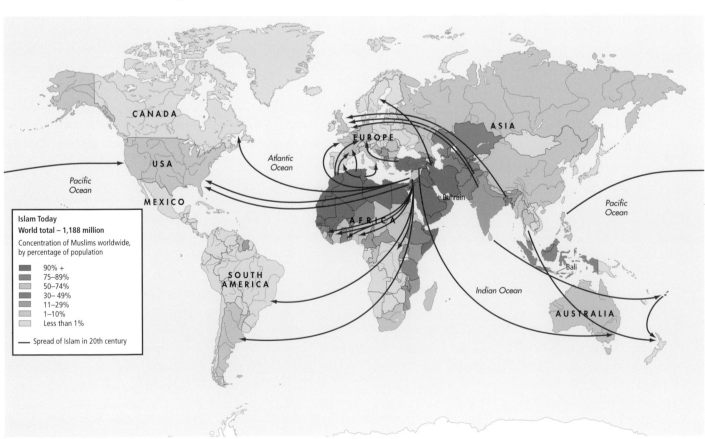

Islam Today
World total – 1,188 million
Concentration of Muslims worldwide, by percentage of population

- 90% +
- 75–89%
- 50–74%
- 30– 49%
- 11–29%
- 1–10%
- Less than 1%

— Spread of Islam in 20th century

in foreign lands, or being translocated to labour in manufacturing or agricultural industries. Those opposed to colonial rule and its restrictions were exiled to far off empire outposts. Muslim merchants, unwilling to accept the yoke of colonialism simply moved to other areas, to establish new commercial centres and re-establish their previous circumstances.

In addition to economic migration, mention needs also be made to the movement of peoples fleeing injustice and persecution, who sought and were granted asylum in a variety of lands. Most notable of these were the expulsions of Muslims from Spain and Sicily, the Balkans and lastly Israel.

As detailed by Dr Ezzati in his *Introduction to the History of The Spread of Islam* there are some 1.5 billion Muslims in the world today. In addition to the populations of over 51 Muslim majority countries, there are large Muslim populations in Asia, including India, China and the Central Asian Republics, Africa, the USA, South America, Australia, the Caribbean and Eastern and Western Europe. These communities, of all colour, race and background, with a variety of tongues and customs, live the Islamic way of life, in every member state of the United Nations.

SHARI'AH

Whether those who accept Islam simply fall in love with it, accept it after careful intellectual examination, or are led to it by Islamic scholars or Sufi Shaykhs, is a matter for further academic study. While it is true to say that zeal and love for Islam in the hearts of Muslims inspires them to discuss it with everyone they come into contact with, it is the injunction to do good and refrain from all that is harmful that makes it a religious duty to invite others to Islam.

In the Arabic language, the word shari'ah means 'the path to be followed'. For Muslims, that path has been established by Allah, hence the word shari'ah is used to denote Islamic law. Peace is to be achieved when human desires do not conflict with that law. Once people are at peace with their Creator, they are at peace with themselves and, it follows, at peace with all of His creation.

The Qur'an does not deny the variety of religions, nor that contradictions might exist between them regarding beliefs and practices. However, it emphasizes the need to recognize the 'oneness' of humanity created by Him, and the need for all to work toward better understanding between followers of different faith.

Enjoying the fun of the fair,
young women ride dodgem cars at the Islamic Relief Games held in Birmingham, UK.

ISLAMIC GROUPINGS

All Muslims
Without exception, Muslims believe:
- in the Oneness of Allah;
- that He sent Prophets as Messengers and Warners to every nation and tribe to teach them to benefit from their time on earth and live in harmony with His creation;
- that He revealed the Qur'an, His final book, to His final Messenger Muhammad ﷺ 'al-Insan al-Kamil – the perfect man'.

Without exception, Muslims are required:
- to face the direction of Makkah and worship Allah five times each day;
- to fast for the month of Ramadan;
- to pay their religious dues;
- if they are able, to go on pilgrimage (*hajj*) once in their lifetime.

Without exception, Muslims accept that:
- existence continues after death;
- a day will come when all have to account for their deeds;
- Allah's creation includes things unseen as well as visible.

Those who declare belief that there is no Divinity other than Allah and conform to the above are, by definition, Muslim.

All Muslims believe they practise Islam correctly, despite their differing interpretations of detail. On matters of practice, Shi'ah Muslims consult contemporary jurists who support the Imamate and Sunni Muslims the opinion of the jurists of the 8th and 9th centuries AD. Examples of such differences can be seen on page 163 in the section on The Five Pillars and on page 166 under the heading Islamic Texts.

SHI'AH
- Shi'ah Muslims derive their name from the Prophet ﷺ who is recorded to have said, 'That one there and his followers – *hatha wa shi'ah tu*', in referring to Ali ﷺ (the first Imam) and his followers. Thus, Shi'ah Muslims follow the 12 '*Masumin*' ﷺ – error-free – Imams' – of Muhammad's progeny, who were Divinely appointed to elucidate the Qur'an and Muhammad's teaching for future generations. They are also known as 'Twelvers', and their jurisprudence as Imamiyyah.
- There are two Shi'ah offshoots, Bohrahs and Zaydi's. They follow different Imams of the same lineage.
- Despite their differences, all these groups believe that they adhere strictly to the example – Sunnah – of the Prophet Muhammad ﷺ.

SUNNI
- The word Sunni comes from 'People of the Sunnah and the masses – *Ahl al-sunnah wal-Jamaah*.' They employed this term to distinguish themselves from those who opposed the manner in which the leadership of the Muslim community was established after the Prophet ﷺ.
- The majority of Sunni Muslims follow the guidance of four schools of Sunni jurisprudence named after Malik ibn Anas, Abu Hanifa, Muhammad al-Shafi and Ahmad ibn Hanbal.
- An offshoot of Hanbali School (Wahabism) prefers to follow the more literal guidance of Muhammad bin Abdel Wahab.
- Despite their differences, all these groups also believe that they adhere strictly to the example – Sunnah – of the Prophet Muhammad ﷺ.
- The offshoot of Hanafi Sunnism, the Qadiani or Ahmadiyya, believe that the term 'Seal of Prophets – *Khataman Nabiyeen*' in Qur'an 33:40, refers to their founder, Mirza Ghulam Ahmad of Qadian. They are therefore not accepted as being Muslim by any Shi'ah or Sunni groups.

SUFISM
- Some Shi'ah, and Sunni Muslims of the four main schools of jurisprudence, interested in the esoteric aspects of Islam, follow Spiritual Masters known as Sufi Shaykhs.

JAINISM

Origins and Practice

The name Jainism comes from Jina, meaning 'victor' over the passions and the self. Jinas, whom Jains call *tirthankaras* attained omniscience by shedding destructive *karma* and taught the spiritual path of happiness and perfection to all humans. Jainism is centred around the Indian subcontinent, and is one of the oldest religions in that region. In recent years thriving Jain populations have developed in the US and Europe.

THE ORIGIN OF Jainism remains untraceable. Jains believe that time rotates in a cycle, descending and ascending. In each half of the cycle 24 *tirthankaras* establish the fourfold order (*sangha*) consisting of monks, nuns, laymen and laywomen; and revive the teachings of the previous *tirthankaras*. The first *tirthankara* in this descending cycle was Risabhdeva, who is traditionally believed to have lived thousands of centuries ago. The twenty-third was Parsvanatha (*c*. 870–770 BC) and the twenty-fourth and last was Vardhamana Mahavira (599–527 BC).

TEACHINGS

Mahavira became a Jina at the age of 42. He attracted a large number of people, both men and women, to his teachings. Those who accepted vows totally (*mahaavrata*) became ascetics. He taught his followers to observe:

- *Ahimsaa*: non-violence and reverence for all life
- *Satya*: truthfulness, communication in a pleasant and non-hurtful manner that is free from falsehood
- *Asteya*: not stealing or taking anything which belongs to others without their permission
- *Brahmacharya*: chastity and control over senses, for the ascetics total celibacy and for the laity faithfulness to one's spouse
- *Aparigraha*: non-attachment to material things

Mahavira was a great reformer and addressed the various problems of the day, such as the caste system, slavery, equality of women, carnal desires, killing or harming life for religious rituals or pleasure of the senses. He taught acceptance of multiple views (*anekaantaavada*) and qualifying dogmatic assertions (*syaadavaada*), a spiritual democracy that made Jains tolerant to others.

SECTS

In the fourth century AD, Jainism developed two major divisions: Digambara (sky-clad ascetics) and Svetambara (white-robed ascetics). With the passage of time, both

An Indian votive painting depicting a Jina seated on an ornate throne. Jains believe that there are 24 Jinas, or *tirthankaras* (meaning victors or conquerors) who showed humans how to attain perfect happiness.

Ornate carvings decorate this ancient Jain temple in the desert near Jaisalmer, Rajastan province, India. The carvings show scenes from the life of Lord Bahubali, one of over one hundred sons born to the first of the *tirthankaras*, Vrishabhanatha. After defeating his older brother in a duel for the kingsom, Bahubali handed the kingdom back and embarked on a quest for enlightenment. After undertaking a severe type of meditation for many years he attained enlightenment, eventually becoming one of the great Jain saints.

Digambara and Svetambara communities have continued to develop, almost independently of each other, into different sects.

PRACTICES

The guiding principle of the Jain practice is their conviction in the phrase *parasparopagrahojivaanam*, meaning interdependence of life on each other. Jains are vegetarians; they care for the environment and are involved in human and animal welfare. They have built beautiful temples all over India and observe many festivals; most are spiritual in nature such as *paryushana* (sacred days of fasting and forgiveness).

They observe six essential duties: equanimity, veneration of the 24 *tirthankaras*, veneration of ascetics, penitential retreat, renunciation, meditation with bodily detatchment, which are meant to enhance their quality of life, physically, mentally and spiritually.

Jainism, though restricted to a minority, continues to be a living tradition. The Jain way of life is not at odds with normal everyday life. It is an ethical doctrine with self-discipline as its core. It does not recognize an Almighty God or a Supreme Being as creator God, but believes in godhood that can be attained by any of us, provided we follow the teachings of the Jina and liberate our souls through self-effort. Jains worship *tirthankaras* as examples and do not ask for any favours.

Jainism is an open religion and irrespective of labels attached to us by birth or otherwise; any person who follows the path of the Jinas is a Jain. The Jain population is about four million worldwide; most Jains and all their ascetics (about 10,000) live in India; 50,000 in North America and 30,000 in the UK.

The body is called a boat,
The soul is called a navigator,
wordly life is called an ocean,
The great sages cross this ocean.

Uttaraadhyayana, 23:73

Devotees pay their respects to a statue of Jain saint Lord Bahubali, during a Jain festival.

SACRED DUTIES

Jains perform penitential retreat (*pratikramana*) daily in the morning and evening to shed the karma that is attracted due to the transgressions of Right Conduct, knowingly or unknowingly. They ask for forgiveness for their transgressions, perform penance, and see that such aberrations are not repeated.

Jains observe *paryushana*, an annual period of atonement and repentance for the acts of the previous year, and of austerities to shed accumulated *karma*. Listening to the Kalpa Sutra (sacred text), taking positive steps to ensure that living beings are not killed, showing amity to fellow Jains, forgiveness to all, austerity and visiting neighbouring temples, these are important activities undertaken during this festival. On the final day (*samvatsari*), Jains seek forgiveness from all for any harm which they have caused and forgive those who have harmed them, saying '*micchami dukkadam*'.

Jain Philosophy

The universe as conceived by Jains has two parts, occupied and unoccupied, and it consists of six substances: the soul, matter, medium of motion, medium of rest, space and time. All except the matter are formless.

The soul is the living being (*jiva*) and the others are non-living substances (ajiva). Both *jiva* and *ajiva* are interdependent and everlasting. It is the attachment of non-living substance (*karma*) to the soul that causes apparent injustices of life, and an unending cycle of birth, death and rebirth in any destiny: heavenly, human, animal and plants or infernal as a mobile being with two to five senses or as an immobile being with one sense. The celestial beings live in the 'upper world' of the occupied universe. Humans, animals and plants, astral bodies and lower kinds of heavenly beings occupy the 'middle world'. The infernal beings live in the lower world.

The Jain way of life aims to shed *karma* attached to the soul and manifest the soul's true characteristics: infinite bliss, infinite knowledge, amity and equanimity. It consists of the coordinated path of the 'Three Jewels': Right Faith, Right Knowledge and Right Conduct. Right Faith is belief in the nine 'real entities' (living being, non-living being, merit, demerit, influx of *karma*, karmic bondage, stoppage of *karma*, shedding of *karma* and liberation); Right Knowledge is a proper grasp of the nine 'real entities'; and Right Conduct is the ethical code, behaviour and actions taught by the Jinas.

KARMA

Jainism describes *karma* as a subtle matter, not perceptible to the senses, found everywhere in the cosmos and having the property of penetrating the soul and clouding its characteristics. The soul's activities cause vibrations in its structure and cause karmic particles to be attracted (influx) to it. If there is karmic matter around the soul, these particles will stick to it, but if it is absent as in liberated souls it will not stick. Benevolent acts cause good *karma* (merit), while sinful acts cause bad *karma* (demerit). Both merit and demerit keep the soul in the worldly cycle, they do not cancel each other out.

Jain temples are scattered all over Girnar Hill in the rural province of Gujarat, India.

The Ranakpur Temple in Rajasthan, India, is not only a centre of Jain worship but also an architectural masterpiece, incorporating natural lighting and ventilation. It has nearly 1,500 carved pillars and 84 separate shrines.

The quantity, size, type and density of karmic particles determine the severity of karmic bondage and the form that the soul will assume in forthcoming births and its inherent passions. Of course, external environments affect these passions, increasing their severity in a complementary way, but Right Conduct can influence the karmic result and reduce suffering. On maturity karmic particles attached to the soul discharge continuously, but as replenishment also takes place, the soul remains in bondage.

LIBERATION

Liberation of the soul from the karmic bondage is a two-stage process: stoppage of karmic flow (blocking of all channels through which *karma* flows by ethical behaviour and control over desires); and shedding the attached *karma* by austerities. When all karmic particles are shed, which may occur after long spiritual development, the soul attains liberation and reverts to its natural state. It ascends to the apex of the universe where it dwells in *siddha silaa*, a liberated soul without material body, enjoying infinite bliss, infinite knowledge, amity and equanimity.

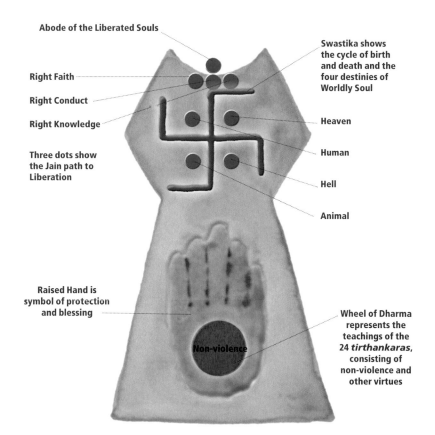

Abode of the Liberated Souls

Right Faith

Right Conduct

Right Knowledge

Three dots show the Jain path to Liberation

Swastika shows the cycle of birth and death and the four destinies of Worldly Soul

Heaven

Human

Hell

Animal

Raised Hand is symbol of protection and blessing

Non-violence

Wheel of Dharma represents the teachings of the 24 *tirthankaras*, consisting of non-violence and other virtues

Mutual Interdependence of all lives

JAIN TEACHINGS

Belief in the self and other realities is Right Faith, their comprehension is Right Knowledge, being without attachment is Right Conduct. These together constitute the way to liberation.

(Tattvartha Sutra 1:4)

Attachment and hatred are the seeds of karma. The wise say that karma is caused by delusion. Karma is the root of birth and death. The wise say that the cycle of birth and death is the cause of unhappiness.

(Uttaraadhyayana 32:7)

By controlling speech the soul achieves mental steadiness and having achieved mental steadiness, the soul with control on speech becomes qualified for self-realization.

(Uttaraadhyayana 29:54)

By controlling the mind the soul achieves the concentration of mind. The soul with the concentration of mind controls the senses.

(Uttaraadhyayana 29:53)

All living beings have to bear the fruit of their karma, either in this life or in future lives. No one can escape the results of their action.

(Uttaraadhyayana 4:3)

All living beings love their life. No one likes to be killed. Those who kill living beings whether they kill or have it killed by someone else or support killing, eventually increase their own enmity and misery.

(Sutrakrutaanga 1:1:3)

The Symbol for Jainism, which represents the suffering that the three worlds (Earth, Heaven and Hell) must endure. The open palm is a symbol of reasurrance, that humans need not be afraid as the path to salvation lies in religion (represented by the Wheel of Dharma), and that after obtaining perfection they may live forever in the Abode of the Liberated Souls.

Interior of the Jain temple in Oxford Street, Leicester, UK, which has become a symbol of Jain unity, a Jain place of pilgrimage and a major tourist attraction for the city of Leicester.

*One knows the nature of substances from Right Knowledge,
Believes in them through Right Faith,
And develops self-control by Right Conduct,
And purifies the soul by austerities.*

Uttaraadhyayana 28:35

JUDAISM

Origins

Judaism was the first religion to profess faith in a single, omnipotent God, with a history dating back over 4,000 years. It shares many of the early traditions and prophets with the later-founded Islam and Christianity. The Hebrew Bible consists of five books widely attributed to have been written by Moses, and which encapsulate the precursory elements of Judaism: the creation myths, Jewish law, and Israelite history. After the Biblical period, Jewish theology and practice were developed by the rabbis.

This sixth-century AD mosaic depicts the menorah, the candlestick used at Chanukah, and the Ark of the Law, which was built by David to contain the stone tablets of the Commandments. The Commandments were received by Moses, the second most important figure in Judaism after Abraham, from God on Mount Sinai, after he led the Exodus from Egypt.

JEWS BELIEVE that Abraham (born c. 2000 BC) was the first to recognize the existence of God; God made a series of covenants with Abraham. Firstly, in return for leaving Ur in Babylon (now Iraq), his native land, Abraham and Sarah, his barren wife, were promised the land of Canaan (today Israel/Palestine) and many descendants. Later, God asked Abraham to circumcise himself, saying that as a perpetual sign of the covenant between God and Abraham's descendants they must circumcise their sons eight days after birth. Soon after he obeyed God's command, Abraham's son Isaac was born.

THE EXODUS FROM EGYPT

Abraham's descendants went down to Egypt *c.*1700 BC to avoid a famine. A few generations later they were regarded as hostile aliens, made into slaves and forced to do hard labour. When the pharaoh ordered their male babies to be killed, God acted upon the covenant he had made with Abraham, Isaac and Jacob and sent plagues upon Egypt when the pharaoh refused to let the people go out and worship their God. Because of the experience of being enslaved and then rescued by God, Judaism later emphasized the importance of freedom and treating the stranger well. In Judaism, redemption when it refers to the past describes being rescued from Egyptian slavery and when it refers to the future means the hope that present-day troubles will be replaced by a time of peace and perfection.

When the Children of Israel (the Biblical phrase for what later became the Jewish people) left Egypt and reached Mount Sinai in the desert, God remade the covenant with the whole nation, giving them the Ten Commandments and many other instructions detailing how they were to serve God. Some influence from Egyptian codes has been perceived in the commandments which Moses, the leader of people through the Exodus and the 40 years in the desert, relayed to the people.

When the Children of Israel returned to the land under Joshua's leadership, they defeated the tribes living there and established themselves. David (who reigned 1006–965 BC), one of the

Let my people go that they may serve me in the wilderness.

Exodus, 7:16

The Journey of Abraham
Abraham was the earliest of the Hebrew patriarchs and was summoned by God to leave his home in Ur and journey to Canaan, where he was to become the father of a nation. Although the Biblical account gives many details of the journey, there is some dispute over his actual route.

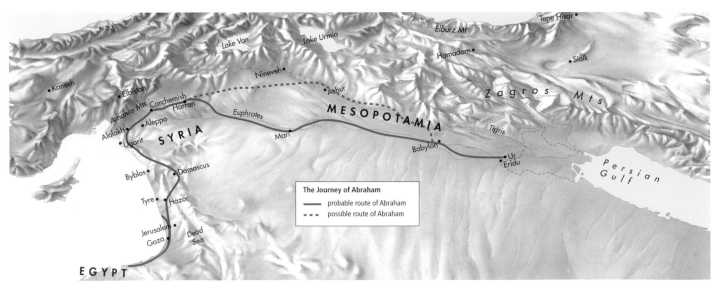

The Journey of Abraham
—— probable route of Abraham
- - - possible route of Abraham

first kings of Israel, erected a tent in Jerusalem to hold the ark containing the two stone tablets of the Ten Commandments. His son Solomon (who reigned 965–928 BC) built an impressive temple; the Bible contains many references to Jerusalem as 'the place I chose to dwell among you'. Jerusalem was captured by the Babylonians in 586 BC and many of the people forced into exile.

c. 2000 BC	Abraham born
c. 1280 BC	Exodus from Egypt and Sinai
c. 1200 BC	Joshua conquers Canaan
c. 1000 BC	David's reign 1006–965 BC
586 BC	Destruction of the First Temple
538 BC	Return and rebuild the Temple
164 BC	Maccabees defeat Syria and rebuild Temple
70 AD	Destruction of the Second Temple
70 AD	Jochanan ben Zakkai founds School at Yavneh
135 AD	Bar Kochba Revolt
200 AD	Redaction of the Mishnah (see p. 176)
c. 600 AD	Redaction of the Babylonian Talmud (see p. 176)

FALL OF JERUSALEM

In 538 BC, the people were allowed to return to the land of Israel by Cyrus of Persia, who had crushed the Babylonian empire, and rebuild the Temple in Jerusalem. The Second Temple was built tall to combine maximum splendour with the dimensions given in the Bible for the portable shrine the Children of Israel carried in the wilderness.

By 44 BC the land was under the control of the Roman Empire. The Romans were normally tolerant of well-behaved local religions but the Zealots, an intemperate minority, refused to accept their rule and revolted. In response, the Romans successfully besieged Jerusalem, destroyed the Temple in AD 70 and martyred many leading rabbis. After a further unsuccessful rebellion against Rome in AD 135 by Simon bar Kochba, many Jews were exiled.

A small number of Jews remained in the land of Israel but the majority of the Jewish people lived scattered across the world. Immediately after AD 70, the major Jewish communities were in Babylon, Egypt and Italy. Today the largest diaspora community is the USA whose Jewish population outnumbers Israel's.

EARLY RABBIS

Yochanan ben Zakkai, a scholar who enabled Jewish teaching to survive and who can be regarded as the originator of Rabbinic Judaism, smuggled himself out of Jerusalem during the siege in a coffin shortly before the destruction of the Temple in AD 70. The Romans permitted him to set up a school at Yavneh on Israel's Mediterranean coast. His students became the first rabbis; they expanded existing commentaries on the Bible and developed a framework of belief which enabled their generation, traumatised by the destruction of the Temple, to continue to live as Jews.

RABBINIC JUDAISM

Judaism as it is practised now rests both on the Bible and on rabbinic development of Biblical ideas. The ancient rabbis in Israel and Babylon said their interpretations of the Bible represented its true meaning, even when these were not literal. For instance they said that 'an eye for an eye' meant paying compensation to the injured party, not injuring them in turn. Another innovation was their belief in the immortality of the soul, possibly because the rabbis in Babylon were influenced by Zoroastrianism, the local religion, in which this was important an important belief.

You shall treat the stranger as the native amongst you, and you shall love him as yourself, for you were strangers in Egypt; I am the Lord your God.

Leviticus, 19:34

The destruction of the Second Temple in Jerusalem in AD 70 by the Romans destroyed the nation of Israel and finalized the Jewish diaspora. The Temple Mount, the Temple's former site is also a sacred site in Islam and remains a focus of religious tensions.

GOD IN JUDAISM

'Eternal One who ruled alone before creation of all forms ... after everything shall end, alone in wonder will God reign.... This is my God who saves my life, the rock I grasp in deep despair, ... My God is close I shall not fear.'(From *Adon Olam*, Ruler of Eternity', final hymn of the Saturday morning service).

Maimonides, a twelfth-century Jewish philosopher and expert in Jewish law, defined 13 Principles of Faith, a brief codification of essential Jewish beliefs; nine deal with the nature of God. God is the creator and guide of the universe, is one, without bodily form, the first and the last, the only focus of prayer, the giver of the Torah (the first five books of the Bible),

omniscient, who rewards those who keep the commandments and punishes those who break them and will resurrect the dead.

Some of God's Biblical names may originally have been associated with Canaanite pagan deities but have taken on a meaning appropriate to Jewish theology. For instance YHVH, the name of God considered too holy to pronounce, is derived from the Hebrew root 'to be' and is linked in later Jewish thought with God's mercy. Shaddai comes from a root meaning 'breast'; there are many breasted pagan goddess figurines which may the source of the name. It is translated 'Almighty' and used in the Bible to describe God as sustainer.

Sacred Texts

Jews are called the 'people of the book' and a great deal of emphasis is placed on the study of the sacred texts in the Jewish faith. Jews believe that the nature of God is revealed through the events of history, and it is only through study that individuals can understand the essence of Judaism for themselves.

THE BIBLE reached its present form soon after the Babylonian exile in the sixth century BC. It is divided into three sections. The first five books – Genesis, Exodus, Leviticus, Numbers and Deuteronomy – are called the Torah or Pentateuch (meaning 'written law'). The Torah records the revelation of God to Moses on Mount Sinai 3,000 years ago. They contain 613 commandments, as well as describing the early history of the Children of Israel. The second section, Prophets, includes the history of settling the Promised Land and the writings of prophets like Isaiah and Hosea. The third section, Writings, contains the psalms, the short books read on festivals including Ruth and Song of Songs, wisdom literature (such as Proverbs and Job) and later historical books like Chronicles and Ezra.

THE MISHNAH

The Mishnah (Repetition) was written down around AD 200. This body of work defined the teachings and legal system intrinsic to the Torah. Tradition says it was compiled by Rabbi Judah the Prince who selected and organized the body of oral law developed during his time. It is divided into six orders or subject areas: Prayer and Agriculture, Festivals, Women, Civil Law, Rituals and Purity. Each of the orders is subdivided: Civil Law includes sections on Damages, Employment Law, Government and Ethics. The Mishnah begins with prayer and its first chapter defines times of prayer; it also begins by referring to the Temple destroyed in AD 70 and ends by referring to the Messiah, whom Jews believe to be the messenger announcing the arrival of a future era of peace and perfection. This looking back to the destruction of what had been the pattern of Jewish life while simultaneously looking forward to future hope and purpose is typical of the Mishnah; one must read between the lines of

the text to understand it fully. It often gives varying opinions, thus validating debate and diversity, and is written in simple, rhythmic Hebrew, easy to learn by heart, showing its origins in an oral tradition.

THE TALMUD

Once the Mishnah was written down, commentators started to analyze why Judah had preferred some existing oral laws to others. The Babylonian Talmud ('learning') was written down around AD 500; it contains the Mishnah and the Gemara (meaning 'completion' of the discussion on each topic). Its redactors also included

The Sephardic Jewish communities in medieval Spain were renowned for their learning and art; this inscription, decorated with mythological animals, comes from a Hebrew manuscript Bible illuminated by Joseph Assarfati at Cervera in 1299.

aggadah, morally improving Bible interpretations and stories about the lives of the rabbis. The Gemara is written in Aramaic, the contemporary vernacular. The Babylonian Talmud deals only with those areas of Jewish law observed in the diaspora, not Temple ritual or agriculture. Its style is discursive; topics beyond the supposed subject are often included in one volume. Its style can be deceptive; an apparent debate may include statements by rabbis who lived generations apart whose views have been interwoven. There is also a Palestinian Talmud which is shorter and considered less authoritative.

THE COMMENTARIES

The process of commentary and debate continued after the Talmud was written down. As it flows from subject to subject and needs expertise to decipher, several commentators on the Talmud also wrote straightforward codes of Jewish law which they believed would be accessible for the uneducated. The most famous

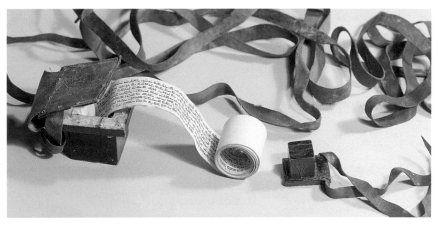

is the *Shulchan Aruch* (*Prepared Table*) by Joseph Caro who lived in Israel in the sixteenth century; it was published with a commentary 'The Tablecloth' noting European Jewish practice wherever it differed. Today, observant Jews, both Orthodox and Reform, still write to the leading contemporary authorities with questions on Jewish law, particularly on issues which did not occur in previous generations and receive replies, collections of which are often published.

Tefillin, **two leather pouches** containing sections of the Torah, are worn during prayer, as is the *tallit*, or prayer shawl. Orthodox Jews may wear the *tallit* constantly; other denominations generally only during prayers and in synagogue.

THE IMPORTANCE OF LEARNING IN JUDAISM

'Learning God's teaching is equal to everything else' (Talmud)

Study has always been very important in Judaism, both to understand what God wants the people to do and as an intellectual joy in itself. It is considered to be as important as prayer as a way of becoming close to God. Scholars were therefore regarded as an elite; matchmakers would rate a good Talmud student highly. Study is not supposed to exist in isolation from deeds of kindness to others, but is supposed to inspire goodness.

This passionate enthusiasm for learning inculcated by studying Jewish texts is thought to explain why Jews have often succeeded as doctors and university scientists.

Jewish literature also includes philosophy, histories, ethical tracts and poetry – liturgical and secular: for example Maimonides' (a twelfth-century Egyptian philosopher and legalist) *The Guide for the Perplexed*, an explanation of Judaism written in Arabic, and Bachya Ibn Pakudah's (an eleventh-century Spanish philosopher) *Duties of the Heart*, a book of religious ethics.

These days education is considered the way to transmit Judaism to future

generations and synagogues and schools try hard to find imaginative ways of teaching. Synagogues offer classes to adults, many Jews travel to Israel to study in their gap year, universities in the diaspora often offer Jewish Studies and more people are studying Talmud now than ever before in Jewish history

Jewish men studying in a synagogue. Study and learning, particularly of the Torah and Talmud, are key elements of Judaism, and scholarship is greatly respected.

Jewish Festivals

The cycle of the Jewish year
includes festivals of joy and times
of mourning, times of contemplation
and times of dancing and happiness.

The prayer book calls Rosh HaShanah 'The birthday of the world', the anniversary of creation. Apples and honey are eaten at home to express the hope that the coming year will be sweet. As well as the new calendar year, Rosh HaShanah begins ten days remembering all wrong-doings from the past year in order to rectify them before the Day of Atonement. The *shofar* or ram's horn is blown repeatedly in synagogue; its harsh sound is believed to open closed hearts to God.

Yom Kippur, the Day of Atonement, is a spiritual cleansing enabling one to start the year afresh. Those physically able – not the young, or ill – abstain from all food and drink for 25 hours; services are held in the evening and from early morning until dark, the synagogue vestments are white; once a year human beings aspire to be like angels who, white-clad, spend all day every day praising God. The liturgy is particularly beautiful and many of the tunes sung are joyful – the congregation pray for forgiveness confident in God's mercy.

'Eternal, Eternal, God of mercy and compassion, slow to anger, generous in love and truth, showing love to thousands, forgiving sin, wrong and failure, who pardons.' (Exodus 34 and Yom Kippur liturgy)

Tu b'Shvat is the New Year of Trees. Traditionally observed by mystics, recently some Jews have enjoyed redeveloping its ecological theme and tree-planting has been an important part of the regeneration of the land of Israel.

DAYS OF PILGRIMAGE

Passover (from the Hebrew *Pesach*), commemorates the exodus from Egypt when God redeemed the people from Egyptian slavery. It is celebrated by a *seder* (a sequence of readings and symbolic actions), described in a special prayer book, the *Haggadah* (recitation), when the events of the Exodus are explained to the children by their parents round their dining table and they eat unleavened bread to commemorate the Children of Israel's hasty departure from Egypt.

Seven weeks after Passover, Shavuot (Pentecost) celebrates the giving of the Ten Commandments at Mount Sinai; the commandments explain to the people how God wishes to be served.

During Succot (Tabernacles) Jews remember living under God's protection during the 40 years in the wilderness. Each family builds a small open-roofed booth and, weather permitting, eats there; the *lulav*, palm fronds, myrtle and willow branches are shaken together with a citron. At the end of the festival, on Simchat Torah (the Rejoicing of the Law), the final chapter from Deuteronomy is read and immediately the cycle of reading the Torah recommences at the beginning of Genesis. The scrolls are processed around the synagogue and there is often much singing, dancing and celebrating.

The festival of Passover commemorates the release of the Hebrews from slavery in Egypt. During the Passover meal, or seder, special foods are eaten in memory of the events of the Exodus, and the youngest child present goes through a ritual question-and-answer process to explain these events.

The *menorah*, an eight-branched candlestick, is lit at Chanukah to commemorate the rededication of the Temple after Greek occupation. The amount of oil present was only enough for one day, but, miraculously, lasted for eight; hence the eight branches of the *menorah*.

DAYS OF THANKSGIVING FOR RESCUE

Purim commemorates the events of the book of Esther which tells how a decree stating that Jews should be killed on a certain date was averted. Jews read the book of Esther, thank God for averting the decree, give to the poor so they can also celebrate, send food gifts to friends and eat and drink. Children dress up, and in Israel there are carnival processions.

On Chanukah Jews light candles, starting with one and adding another daily throughout the eight days of the festival to remember the rededication of the temple in 164 BC after Judah the Maccabbee, his brothers and their small guerrilla forces drove out the Syrians who wanted to control the land that is now Israel due to its key strategic position between Europe and Africa. To complete their conquest of the land the Syrians had desecrated the Temple and forbidden essential Jewish observances like Sabbath and circumcision. The Talmud describes a miracle: once the temple was cleaned and ready to resume services, one day's supply of pure oil for the light kept burning in the Temple lasted eight days until more could be prepared.

DAYS OF MOURNING

On Tisha b'Av, the 9th of Av, Jews remember the destruction of the First and Second Temples by fasting, reading the Book of Lamentations and singing dirges describing other episodes of persecution. Three minor fast days, 17th Tammuz, 10th Tevet and Fast of Gedaliah commemorate stages in the siege and defeat of Jerusalem.

The seven weeks between Passover and Shavuot are a time of mourning when the deaths from plague of students of Rabbi Akiva, a first century rabbi, are remembered; no weddings or parties are held. On Lag b'Omer the plague lifted for a day so mourning restrictions stop.

MODERN FESTIVALS

Three significant events in twentieth-century Jewish history are now commemorated in the calendar: Holocaust Memorial Day (Yom HaShoah), 27th Nissan; the anniversary of the battle of the Warsaw Ghetto, Israel Independence Day (Yom HaAtzmaut) 5th Iyar; and Jerusalem Day, 28th Iyar, the anniversary of the reunification of Jerusalem in 1967.

Purim, celebrated here in Jerusalem, celebrates Esther's saving of the Jews. Toys for children and drink for adults are all part of this happy festival.

THE FESTIVALS

The Jewish calendar is a corrected lunar calendar. There are 365 days in the solar year and 354 in 12 lunar months. An extra month is added in seven years in every 19; this system was worked out during the Babylonian exile – hence the Babylonian names for the months. The festivals vary by four weeks against the civil calendar but the spring festival, Passover, always happens in Nissan (March/April) and no major correction has ever been needed.

THE MONTHS AND FESTIVALS IN ORDER

Months and dates	Festival Names	Months and dates	Festival Names
Tishre (September/October)		*Nissan (March/April)*	
1st & 2nd	Rosh HaShanah	*15th–21st	Passover
3rd	Fast of Gedaliah	27th	Holocaust
10th	Yom Kippur		Memorial Day
*15th–21st	Succot		
*22rd	Simchat Torah	*Iyar (April/May)*	
		5th	Israel
Cheshvan (October/November)			Independence Day
Kislev (November/December)		18th	Lag b'Omer
25th–2nd	Chanukah	28th	Jerusalem Day
Tevet (December/January)		*Sivan (May/June)*	
10th	10th Tevet	*6th	Shavuot
Shevat (January/February)		*Tammuz (June/July)*	
15th	Tu b'Shvat	17th	17th Tammuz
(Extra Adar – leap years only)		*Av (July/August)*	
Adar (February/March)		9th	Tisha b'Av
13th	Fast of Esther		
14th	Purim	*Elul (August/September)*	

*An additional day is observed by Orthodox Jews in the diaspora

Jewish Movements

The Jewish world used to be divided only by geography; each country would have its own foods, tunes for the liturgy and customs. In the last 200 years, Jews have been divided by ideology as well as separated by distance. The division is not only between Orthodox and Reform but between Modern Orthodoxy and Ultra-Orthodoxy.

ULTRA-ORTHODOX Jews are divided into two main groups, Hasidim and Mitnagdim.

HASIDISM

Hasidic Judaism originated in Poland in the eighteenth century. Its founder, known as 'The Besht', an acronym meaning Master of the Good Name, felt the Judaism of his time was too focused on scholarship and scholars. He emphasised personal piety and the presence of God in everything. His disciples developed his ideas and each in turn gathered disciples. Later, different Hasidic sects were named after the places their leader or 'rebbe' lived. The best-known Hasidic sect is Lubavitch who, in particular, emphasize outreach to less observant Jews.

MITNAGDIM

Mitnagdim (opponents) originally criticized the early Hasidim for allowing services to run late with enthusiastic singing and dancing and for over-dependence on rabbis who sometimes exploited their followers. Today the term is used for non-Hasidic, very Orthodox Jews who devote themselves to Jewish learning and live lives of intense piety.

MODERN ORTHODOXY

Modern Orthodox Jews believe that Jewish law was directly dictated by God to Moses and is immutable but that this does not preclude involvement in the non-Jewish world. Rabbi Samson Raphael Hirsch, a leader of nineteenth-century German Orthodoxy, said 'Be a Jew at home and a gentleman out in the street' and encouraged his followers to go to university and reach a high standard of secular as well as Jewish education.

MASORTI (CONSERVATIVE)

In the United States, Conservative Judaism is a major movement; numbers are smaller but

Jewish summer camps and schools, such as this American camp for teenage Hasidic Jews, are a common way for parents to ensure their children receive education in Hebrew and Torah studies as well as conventional schooling. Many synagogues also have weekday classes, scheduled after normal school times.

Judaism Today
Approximately 14 million Jews account for 0.4 per cent of the world's population across 134 countries. The map shows the distribution of Jews throughout the world.

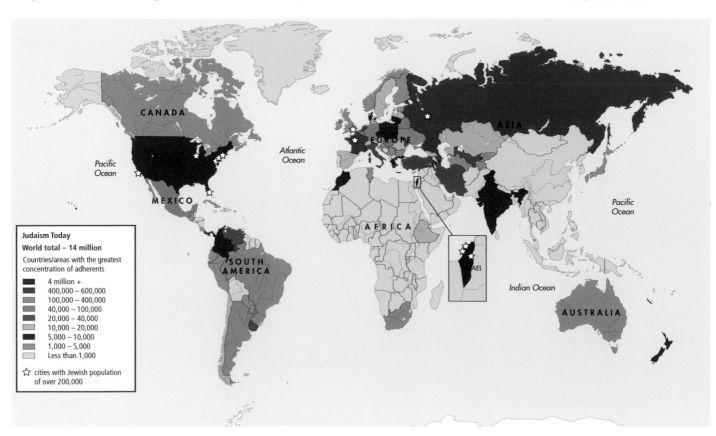

Judaism Today
World total – 14 million
Countries/areas with the greatest concentration of adherents

- 4 million +
- 400,000 – 600,000
- 100,000 – 400,000
- 40,000 – 100,000
- 20,000 – 40,000
- 10,000 – 20,000
- 5,000 – 10,000
- 1,000 – 5,000
- Less than 1,000

☆ cities with Jewish population of over 200,000

increasing rapidly in the UK and Israel. Their services are traditional in style, although women often play a more active role than in Orthodoxy. They recognize that Jewish law has evolved over time but aim to keep within traditional parameters. Sometimes they innovate: they ordain women as rabbis, they annul marriages where the husband refuses to divorce his wife, thus preventing her from re-marrying and they permit driving to synagogue on the Sabbath when it is too far to walk. In Israel, where American ideas are considered alien and in the UK where 'Conservative' has political connotations they call themselves Masorti ('traditional').

REFORM

Early Reform Jews in nineteenth-century Germany and the United States felt the dietary laws and other rituals prevented them from enjoying their new opportunities for integration into the surrounding culture. Some of their innovations were permitted in Jewish law but not customary usage, for instance prayer in the vernacular. They also omitted liturgical references to the return to Zion and reintroduction of Temple sacrifices. Twenty-first-century Reform Jews see more value in observance and have reintroduced some rituals and prayers discarded by their predecessors; the history of last century demonstrated the importance of Zionism (the belief that Jews should have a state of their own). They believe men and women should play an equal role in synagogue life.

LIBERAL

Liberal refers to the more radical of the two progressive Jewish movements in the UK (in pre-war Germany 'Liberal' meant the more traditional wing). Liberal Jews and American Reform Jews – but not British ones – say that the child of a Jewish father, educated as a Jew, should be regarded as Jewish (traditional Judaism says Jewish status is passed on only by the mother). Their services use more English and they have a modern egalitarian formula for divorce.

RECONSTRUCTIONISM

Reconstructionist Jews follow the writings of Mordecai Kaplan (1881–1983), an American thinker who regarded Judaism as a civilization rather than a religion. He encouraged building Jewish community centres so that broader aspects of Jewish culture could flourish and valued the food laws as part of Jewish culture rather than obedience to God's word. He believed that God is transcendent not immanent.

CHAVURAH

Chavurot ('fellowship groups') originated in the 1960s as small, informal groups wanting a more participatory, egalitarian style of service than synagogues then offered. They developed a radical Jewish spirituality, incorporating many New-Age ideas. Participants in their services often sit in a circle rather than in formal rows as in most synagogues; the services often include meditation and breathing exercises. Their religious thinkers have asked whether nuclear electricity can be considered kosher; many of the mediation practices they encourage exist in traditional esoteric Judaism but are not well-known in the mainstream community.

Ultra-Orthodox Jews, such as this congregation in New York, interpret the commandments and Jewish custom as strictly as possible.

Reform Jewish women and children in synagogue. Unlike many Orthodox congregations, Reform groups do not segregate the sexes during worship.

ASHKENAZIM AND SEPHARDIM

Ashkenazi originally meant 'German' although it now includes all European Jews; as the majority in Europe and the United States Ashkenazi customs are usually wrongly assumed to apply to all Jews. Sephardi originally meant 'Spanish'. The Jews expelled from Spain in 1492 proudly maintained their distinctive liturgical and cultural traditions while living among Ashkenazim in the United States and Europe. Sephardi is now also used to describe Jews from North Africa and the Middle East. Both Ashkenazim and Sephardim developed their own tongue which mixed Hebrew and their local language; Ladino mingles Hebrew and Spanish, and Yiddish combines Hebrew and German. In Spain before the expulsion there was a wonderful flowering of Jewish culture known as the Golden Age of Spain which benefited from the poetic and philosophic influences of the surrounding Arabic world; many of the liturgical poems written by Judah HaLevi (c.1075–1141) and Solomon Ibn Gabirol (1020–57) are still in the prayer book and the philosophy written by Moses Maimonides remains influential. The Sephardim never divided into groups with different beliefs as the Ashkenazim did. In Israel the differences between the two communities are being eroded.

Judaism in Practice

Judaism prescribes rituals for all stages of the life cycle and includes commandments to give charity and eat 'proper' or kosher food; all aspects of life connect to God and the commandments God gave to the Jewish people.

Eight days after birth, health permitting, Jewish boys have a *brit milah* ('covenant of circumcision') when they are circumcised and given a Hebrew name for use on religious occasions. Recently, new ceremonies have been written to welcome baby girls into the covenant – without circumcision. A month after birth, first-born baby boys from Orthodox families have a *Pidyon HaBen*, Redemption of the Firstborn; in Biblical times, the firstborn used to be dedicated to God's service, then the tribe of Levi became priests for the whole nation but firstborns are still ceremonially returned to ordinary status.

COMING OF AGE

Boys at 13 and girls at 12 are considered *Bar/Bat Mitzvah*, responsible for their own observance of the commandments and entitled to perform ceremonial roles in synagogue. To celebrate their new adult status, they say the blessings recited over the Torah in the Sabbath morning service and may also read from the Bible, lead the service or prepare a speech on the readings. A celebration follows the service. In Progressive synagogues boys and girls have identical ceremonies; this has led in recent years for a call for greater observance of their religious maturity for Orthodox girls; some now give a speech at the end of the Sabbath service or say Torah blessings in a separate women-only service and some share a ceremony with other girls, perhaps on Sunday in the synagogue hall.

The Bar Mitzvah ceremony, is undertaken by boys at 13, and welcomes them into the community as an adult male. It is celebrated not only by their reading in synagogue, but, conventionally, also by a large and gift-laden private party.

An Orthodox Jewish wedding ceremony. At the end of the ceremony the groom stamps on a glass with his foot as an expression of sorrow for the destruction of Jerusalem in 70 AD.

MARRIAGE

'Therefore a man shall leave his mother and his father and hold fast to his wife, and they shall be one flesh'. (Genesis, 2:24)

Judaism believes that marriage is the happiest and holiest state for human beings. Jewish weddings take place under a canopy, symbolizing the couple's future home. To make the bride and groom happy on their wedding day is regarded as an important responsibility for all their guests. Traditionally the groom gave the bride a ring and a *ketubah* (marriage contract) was written, detailing his responsibilities to her and fixing the alimony to be paid in case of divorce. This is unromantic but practical; at the wedding, the groom loves the bride, believes they will never separate and so may suggest a more generous sum than if the couple wait until the marriage has irretrievably broken down before making financial arrangements. These days marriage is regarded as a more equal responsibility and many non-Orthodox couples exchange rings to symbolize this.

FOOD

The laws for kosher eating are an important part of Jewish life and identity. The commandments listed in the Bible – do not eat blood, do not cook a kid in its mother's milk, do not eat shellfish, do not eat birds of prey, only eat meat from animals with split hooves who chew the cud – were further developed by the rabbis. They instituted *shechitah* (cutting across the arteries of the neck with a sharp knife), a method of slaughter which extracts the maximum amount of blood while minimizing the animal's suffering). They extended the prohibition of cooking a kid in its mother's milk to complete separation of all meat and milk, even prohibiting cooking them in the same vessels or serving them with the same plates and cutlery. Some have suggested that the Biblical laws represent a rudimentary system of hygiene and are now an artificial barrier between Jews and others; others insist that eating is a vital part of life and so part of religious observance; blessing God before eating food prepared according to God's commands helps connect all daily life to the Almighty.

Judaism permits divorce and remarriage in the hope that the second marriage may be more successful but 'the altar in heaven weeps when a man divorces the wife of his youth' (Talmud).

DEATH

Judaism teaches that the soul is immortal. There are many mourning rituals for the bereaved which at first protect them in their loss and then gradually help them return to daily life. At the funeral, the immediate family say the *kaddish*, a prayer praising God. After the funeral the mourners return home and should be brought food, visited and consoled throughout the next seven days. There follow 30 days in which some mourning restrictions still apply. One says *kaddish* for a parent for 11 months and for 30 days for other close relatives; those who attend synagogue to say *kaddish* often find the support of the community and other mourners helpful. On the anniversary of a death, the family light a memorial candle and say *kaddish*.

GIVING TO THE POOR (TSEDAKAH)

Judaism believes giving to the poor is a very important part of religious life. Synagogues often have special funds to support the needy. The medieval Jewish philosopher, Maimonides, defined eight types of charitable giving and said that the highest is enabling the poor to become self-supporting.

Even in civil graveyards, Jews were not normally buried in the same area as Christians, and so many cities have a separate Jewish cemetery, such as this one in Sevastopol, Russia.

Jewish Worship

Worship of God is one of life's central activities for religious Jews.

'The world stands on three things, Torah, worship and good deeds' (Talmud)

'Before you pray, remember any good qualities you have or any good things you have done. This will put life into you and enable you to pray from the heart' (Nachman of Bratzlav, 1772–1811, a Hasidic Rebbe).

AFTER THE DESTRUCTION of the Temple, a prayer ('the service of the heart') replaced animal sacrifices. Known as HaTefillah (the Prayer) or the Shmoneh Esreh (18 Blessings) or the Amidah (Standing Prayer), it starts with three paragraphs in praise of God, continues on weekdays with requests for forgiveness, health, wellbeing and redemption, and always ends with three paragraphs thanking God. On the Sabbath, God's day of rest, petitions are inappropriate; the first three blessings and the last three are said with one middle blessing, thanking God for the gift of Sabbath rest and joy. There are pauses during and at the end of the set liturgy for private meditation. The Amidah is said morning, afternoon and evening.

Morning and evening, Jews say the Sh'ma: 'Hear, O Israel: the Lord our God, the Lord is one, … love the Lord your God with all your heart and with all your soul and with all your might…' *(Deuteronomy, 6:4–5)*. In the prayer book, the Sh'ma is preceded and followed by blessings thanking God for creation, remembering God's love for the Jewish people and hoping for the coming of the Messiah.

The Psalms form a major part of Jewish worship and some are included in all daily and festival services.

Jewish men – and nowadays some women too – cover their head with a *kippah* (skullcap) or hat when they pray as a sign of respect. At the morning service many wear a *tallit*, a large white shawl with a knotted fringe at the corners as a reminder of God's commandments ('make tassels on the corner of your garments … it shall be a tassel for you to look at and remember all the commandments of the Lord…' *Numbers, 15:37–41)*. The numerical value of the knots and

Many Jewish parents choose to send their children to religious schools, such as this one in Stamford Hill, London, where Hebrew, Torah and Talmud study form part of the curriculum.

Major supermarket chains almost all now have a kosher food section to cater to Jewish customers. The kosher laws cover not only what foods can be eaten, but also the preparation of the food and the correct slaughter of animals.

the Hebrew words for the threads equals 613, the number of the commandments in the Bible. The Sh'ma is written out on parchment and contained in small black leather boxes – *tefillin* or phylacteries – worn at weekday morning services by observant Jews on the arm and forehead to fulfil the commandment in Deuteronomy, 5:9: 'Hold fast to these words as a sign upon your hand and let them be as reminders before your eyes.'

THE SABBATH

Shabbat ('rest') is a day on which no creative work is done, following God's example: '... in six days the Lord made heaven and earth, and on the seventh day he rested and was refreshed.' *(Exodus, 31:17)*. This frees time for prayer, singing, walking, eating, studying and enjoying oneself. This day is the crown of the week for a Jew; a day of blessing and happiness. Two candles are lit to usher in the Sabbath; and a cup of wine is blessed to declare the day holy. Best clothes are worn and especially good meals eaten. The main synagogue service of the week takes place on the Sabbath morning. *Shabbat* perhaps derives from the Babylonian *shapattu*, held on the seventh, 14th, 21st and 28th day of the month, when their gods were propitiated.

SYNAGOGUE

There are three Hebrew names for the synagogue, illustrating its three main roles ('synagogue' means the same in Greek): Beit HaKnesset (House of Assembly), Beit HaTefillah (House of Prayer) and Beit Hamidrash (House of Study). Originally, when the second temple was still standing before AD 70, people would meet in the early synagogues to pray at the same times as when the sacrifices were offered. Once the Temple was destroyed in AD 70, the rabbis developed the synagogue as the place of Jewish community socializing, worship and study.

HOME

Much of Jewish observance takes place in the home; a Jew with access to a synagogue but no facilities for home observance would find it harder to live a Jewish life than one with no synagogue available but with a well-equipped Jewish home with a kosher kitchen and all the books and artefacts needed for study and festival observance. Many festivals are observed entirely or mainly at home: the Sabbath meals, the Passover *seder*, the special foods associated with each festival, Chanukah candle-lighting. Ultra-Orthodox Jewish women who have no role in the synagogue beyond catering and perhaps special study sessions say that because they set the religious tone of their home, they have a religious position as influential as their husband's. The home is also the place of private prayer and study and children's early Jewish education.

A female rabbi practises blowing the *shofar* (ceremonial horn), which is sounded on Rosh HaShanah. Whenever the Bible refers to a trumpet, it means a *shofar*, which is made from the horns of any kosher animal, usually a ram or an antelope.

PERFECTING THE WORLD: TIKKUN OLAM

Jews believe that they are God's partners in bringing the world into a state of perfection. Then the world will reach the Messianic Age, the future time of peace and perfection for all described in the prophetical books of the Bible: for instance Isaiah 11:9: 'They shall not hurt or destroy in all my holy mountain: for the earth shall be full of the knowledge of the Eternal as the waters cover the sea.' Therefore actions which increase harmony in the world are encouraged. Some prayer books specify that certain commandments are performed in order to bring the Messiah – in Kabbalistic language, 'to re-unite God and the divine presence (Shechinah)'.

Tikkun Olam was especially important to many Zionists. Pioneers to the land of Israel believed that they had an opportunity to build a qualitatively different country to the diaspora countries they had left; some felt that in Israel Jews could return to the land, 'build and be rebuilt', living a healthier life than the urban existence many had enjoyed – or endured – in the diaspora. A. D. Gordon, farmer, thinker and writer (1856–1922) preached a 'religion of labour and closeness to nature' and provided the ideology for the kibbutz movement whose members share everything – 'from everyone according to their ability, to everybody according to their needs'. Many other social projects in Israel have been developed out of a profound idealism and passion to build a society which fulfils Jewish concepts of justice.

Anti-Judaism

Jesus and his followers were all Jewish, but the two religions quickly became distinct, especially once Jesus' followers started converting non-Jews. By the time the gospels were written down, in order to increase the contrast between Jesus and the Jewish community, his Jewish contemporaries, the Pharisees, were depicted wrongly as hypocrites and legalists although Jews know them to be creative and merciful in their interpretations.

ONCE CHRISTIANITY had become the established religion in Rome, the role of the Romans in the death of Jesus-who used crucifixion as a punishment- was played down and that of the Jews exaggerated. The Romans used crucifixion as a method of capital punishment; post-Biblical Jews rarely used capital punishment for any crime and never crucified. Christians believed that they had inherited God's covenant with the Jews; a common image in medieval iconography is the church as a beautiful upright woman contrasted with the blindfolded synagogue.

In late-medieval times the Jews were attacked as Christ-killers and accused of using the blood of Christian children to make unleavened bread for Passover and bringing plague to the communities in which they lived. Jews were restricted in their

The conditions at Auschwitz, as in other concentration camps, were horrific almost beyond belief. This photograph, taken in 1944, shows the cramped, disease-ridden bunks in which the prisoners slept.

employment; among permitted occupations was money-lending, which made them unpopular with their debtors. Jews were often forced to wear distinctive clothing, expelled from many countries, including England in 1290, attacked during the Crusades in Europe and Palestine and forcibly converted to Christianity.

Persecution of the Jews in Medieval Europe
In late-medieval Europe the Jews were attacked as Christ-killers, restricted in their occupations, forced to wear distinctive clothing, expelled from many countries and massacred.

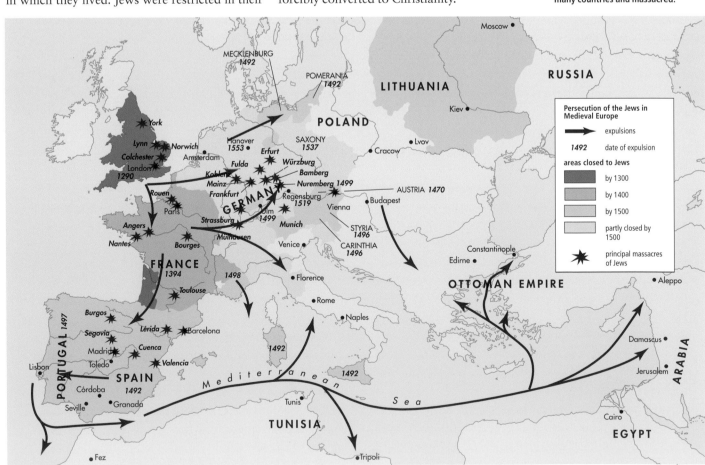

In recent years Christians have recognized the injustice of traditional Christian beliefs about Judaism. In 1965 the Catholic Church published *Nostra Aetate* which said that Jews were not responsible for Jesus' death, nor had God's covenant with them ceased.

Anti-Judaism did not exist only in Christian countries. Muhammad began writing very positively about Judaism, and Jewish influence can be seen in Islam. When the Jews did not convert to Islam he began to criticize them. Jews had protected status in Muslim countries as fellow monotheists and were not subjected to forced conversion but were frequently compelled to wear special clothes and to pay special taxes.

THE HOLOCAUST (SHOAH)

Six million Jews, including 1.5 million children were killed between 1942 and 1945 by Nazi Germany. In Israel this is called the Shoah ('catastrophe'); Holocaust, the term often used in English, means 'burnt-offering'; while many of the victims were cremated, no God would wish to be so served. Adolf Hitler came to power while Germany was suffering economic depression, worsened by the punitive settlements made by the Allies at the end of the First World War. He blamed Germany's misfortunes on the Jews and wanted to make Germany and the countries it held *Judenrein*, 'free of Jews'. It was hard for Jews to get visas to countries not under German control before the Second World War began and impossible thereafter; immigration to Palestine held under the British mandate as the Jewish homeland was restricted in order not to anger the Arabs.

After the Wannsee Conference in 1942 the Nazis tried to develop the most efficient methods of mass killing. Shooting groups, who were first forced to dig a large trench into which they would fall and be buried, was tried but was considered expensive and inefficient. Six death camps were built to which Jews were deported from all over Europe; after harrowing journeys crammed into cattle cars they were herded into 'showers', gassed and their bodies cremated. Other Jews were forced to staff death camps, made to work in labour camps or held in concentration camps; short rations, disease and terrible conditions killed many but some survived to testify after the war about their experiences.

Considering that they were often unarmed and inexperienced fighters, there was considerable Jewish resistance to the Nazis. There were revolts in five death camps and 25 of the ghettoes to which many Jews were deported and forced to labour. Many escaped the ghettoes and joined partisan groups. The Warsaw Ghetto Revolt lasted from 19 April to 15 May 1943. Those unable to resist militarily often focused on spiritual resistance; aware that the Nazis wanted not only to kill Jews but degrade them, they consciously held onto their human dignity.

While many non-Jews helped to carry out the Nazi programme of mass destruction, either by actively participating in the killing or by betraying Jews to the Nazis, others were willing to risk their lives to hide or protect them.

During the Second World War, Jews in Nazi-occupied countries were forced to live in ghettoes. This is the remains of a cemetery in the Jewish ghetto quarter in Prague, Czech Republic, after it was destroyed by the Nazis.

The entrance to the concentration camp at Auschwitz in Poland, where over one million Jews were murdered by the Nazis.

ZIONISM: SOLUTION TO ANTI-SEMITISM OR CAUSE OF IT?

Theodore Herzl, a Viennese Jewish journalist, sent to cover the trial of Alfred Dreyfus, accused of treason on scanty evidence in Paris in 1894, decided that if such blatant injustice could be perpetrated in France, the first European country to grant Jews full citizenship, then the Jews needed a homeland of their own as a refuge from anti-Semitism. He devoted the rest of his life to campaigning to bring a Jewish state into existence. The need for a state where Jews could go as a refuge from persecution was demonstrated as never before by the Holocaust. Herzl's daughter died in Theresienstadt, a Nazi concentration camp.

Since 164 BC, Jews had prayed for the return to the land promised by God to Abraham and his descendants. In the nineteenth century, before Herzl began his political campaign, pioneers had already begun returning to Palestine and were living mostly in the four holy cities Hebron, Jerusalem, Safed and Tiberias. Some Zionists ignored the question of the indigenous Palestinian population; others assumed that it would be possible for Jews and Arabs to live in peace and develop the land together.

After the Six Day War in 1967, Israel took possession of territories which had been relinquished to Arab countries under the terms of a previous United Nations' agreement. These occupied territories have been the source of Jewish-Arab tension ever since, with Israel seeing the areas as vital to their national security, and Arabs struggling to regain political dominance. Despite a 1995 peace treaty between Yitzhak Rabin and Yasser Arafat (leader of the Palestine Liberation Organisation) which planned the withdrawal of Israeli troops and granted zones of self-government to the Palestinians, tensions still run extremely high.

SIKHISM

Origins and Practice

Founded only 500 years ago by Guru Nanak (1469–1539), Sikhism is one of the youngest of the world religio Nanak was succeeded by nine Gurus, a common term in all Indian traditions for a spiritual guide or teach A Sikh (disciple, or seeker of truth) believes in One God and the teachings of the Ten Gurus, enshrined in the holy book, Guru Granth Sahib. Additionally, he or she must go through the Amrit ceremony, the Sikh Baptism, which initiates Sikhs into Khalsa. The purpose of the Khalsa brotherhood is to abolish divisions based on caste, gender, or ethnicity. Fundamental to the faith is fostering compassion for people that are poor or suffering, promoting equality among all people, cultivating a real personal devotion to God and seeking harmony among all human beings.

GURU NANAK founded the Sikh religion after a revelatory experience at the age of about 38. He began to teach that true faith consisted of being ever-mindful of God, meditating on God's Name, and reflecting it in all activities of daily life. Travelling throughout India, Sri Lanka, Tibet and parts of the Arab world he discussed his revelation with people he met, and attracted followers of both Hindu and Muslim faiths. Guru Nanak's teachings of service, humility, meditation and truthful living became the foundation of Sikhism.

The Mughal Empire
Sikhism came into being at a time when the Mughals ruled India and European colonialism was in its infancy. Although at first inconspicuous, Sikhs began to attract attention early in the seventeenth century and this resulted in Mughal hostility, culminating in open warfare by the beginning of the eighteenth century. This map shows the extent of the Mughal ruler's empires as well as the various rebellious factions (the Marathas, the Satnamis, the Rajputs, the Jats and the Sikhs) within the empire at this time.

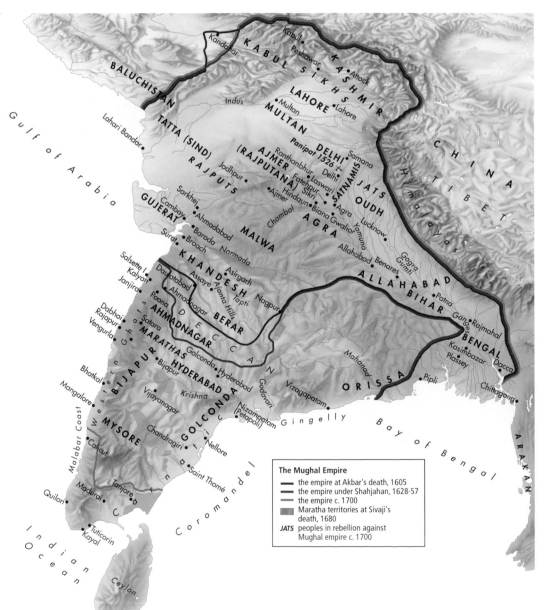

The Mughal Empire
— the empire at Akbar's death, 1605
— the empire under Shahjahan, 1628-57
— the empire c. 1700
▒ Maratha territories at Sivaji's death, 1680
JATS peoples in rebellion against Mughal empire c. 1700

Guru Nanak appointed his successor who was known as Guru Angad and he was followed by eight subsequent Gurus. The last living guru, Guru Gobind Singh, who died in 1708, pronounced the end of the line of succession and ordained the Guru Granth Sahib, the Sikh Holy Scripture, to be the ultimate spiritual authority for Sikhs. The Guru Granth Sahib was compiled and edited by the Fifth Guru, Guru Arjun, in 1604. It occupies the same place in Sikh veneration that was given to the living gurus, and its presence lends sanctity to the Sikh place of worship, the Gurdwara.

THE GURU GRANTH SAHIB

The Guru Granth Sahib contains the writings and hymns of saints and preachers with different religious backgrounds but whose philosophy conformed to the spirit of Sikhism. The entire Sikh holy book is composed in music and poetry. It contains 5,894 hymns, of which Guru Nanak contributed 974, composed in 19 *ragas* (musical modes). The singing of these hymns from Guru Granth Sahib is an integral part of Sikh service.

The Rehat Maryada (Sikh Code of Conduct) published in 1945, regulates individual and corporate Sikh life. Life-cycle events are recognized in Sikhism by naming of the newborn in the gurdwara, the marriage ceremony, and the funeral, following which the body is cremated. Funeral monuments are prohibited. Guru Gobind Singh, the Tenth Guru, instructed his followers to drop their last names, which in India indicate one's caste. All Sikh men, therefore, take the additional name Singh (lion) and women take the name Kaur (princess) to show their acceptance of the equality of all people regardless of caste or gender. Another symbol of the Sikhs' acceptance of universal equality is the *langar*. This is a meal, which is eaten together by the congregation, shared food becoming a social leveller.

A devotional picture of Guru Nanak, the founder of Sikhism. Although born into a Hindu family, his father worked for a Muslim and he had friends from both religions from an early age. After a mystical experience, he began to preach his new vision of faith.

THE GRANTHI

Sikhs do not have a priestly order, monks, or nuns. The Sikh 'clergyman' is the *granthi*, who is encouraged to marry. Sikh congregations are autonomous. There is no ecclesiastical hierarchy. The Akal Takhat heads the five temporal seats of Sikh religious authority in India which debates matters of concern to the Sikh community worldwide and issues edicts which are morally binding on Sikhs. These decisions are coordinated by the SGPC (the Shiromini Gurdwara Parbandhak Committee) which also manages Sikh shrines in India. Format Sikh worship consists mainly of singing of passages of the Guru Granth Sahib to the accompaniment of music. A passage of the holy book is read aloud and expounded upon by the *granthi* at the conclusion of the religious service. The central prayer of Sikhs, Ardas, is recited by the *granthi* and the assembled congregation. This prayer gives a synopsis of Sikh history as well as being a supplication to God. Any Sikh with sufficient religious knowledge is permitted to conduct *gurdwara* worship in the absence of a *granthi*. All are welcome to attend Sikh religious services and to participate in the *langar* served afterwards.

A temple leader in India puts a new flag on the pole for the festival of Baisakhi, celebrating the New Year and the founding of the Khalsa, the sacred brotherhood of Sikhs, by Guru Gobind Singh in 1699. All gurdwaras fly the Sikh flag outside, and the anointing of the pole and raising of a new flag is an annual ritual.

Guru Nanak's Teachings

The three basic tenets of Guru Nanak's teachings are: Naam Japo – constant meditating upon God's Name; Kirt Karo – engage in an honest, non-exploitive labour; and Wand Chakko – share your earnings, out of love and compassion for others.

THE CORNERSTONE of Guru Nanak's teachings was equality. He said that in the eyes of God everyone is equal and God's grace may come to the scholar as well as to the unlettered, high or low, the rich or poor. It does not depend on caste, knowledge or penance. Guru Nanak denounced the idea that spirituality was only for men and not for women. He perceived that there can be no enduring democratic culture unless grounded in recognition of full gender equality. In a society deeply divided by religion, gender and caste, and with widespread intolerance and exploitation, Guru Nanak instituted three practices to promote equality and alleviate suffering. *Sangat* was an invitation to people of all castes and backgrounds to meditate together. Before or after the meditation, he asked people to sit and eat together irrespective of their social background to create a sense equality, called *pangat*. He also started a tradition of free distribution of food to the rich and poor alike at places of worship, named *langar*. These three institutions still exist in Sikh society today.

ULTIMATE SPIRITUAL REALITY

Guru Nanak defined God as a Supreme Spirit, Ultimate Spiritual Reality and he rejected the idea of exclusiveness and uniqueness of any prophets, gods, race or religion. God is loving father, mother, husband, wife, beloved and is seen in every possible relationship. Guru Nanak said, 'God created this universe and revealed himself. To us and in us, God has manifested.' 'As fragrance dwells in a flower, and reflection in a mirror: so does God dwell in every soul.' According to Guru Nanak, the material universe is God's creation. Its origin was in God and its end is in God: it operates within God's Hukam or God's Order or Will. Guru Nanak spoke of innumerable galaxies, of limitless universe, the boundaries of which are beyond human ability to

A Sikh elder reads from the Guru Granth Sahib, the Sikh scriptures, in a gurdwara in Southall, London.

Guru Nanak

Guru Nanak was born in the Punjabi village of Talvandi Rai Bhoi (now Nankana Sahib) in 1469. After a childhood spent in his village he was sent by his father to work in Sultanpur Lodhi. There he had a vision, telling him to renounce everything and venture out and teach the 'Nam' (the word of God). For over 20 years he travelled extensively (see map) and eventually settled down in Kartarpur on the Ravi river where he continued to teach. He died in Kartarpur in 1539. Also shown are the locations of the Five Takhats of Khalsa ('takhat' meaning throne). They are considered to be the seats of Sikh religious authority, and as such are of great significance to the Sikh community.

comprehend. As all creation has the same origin and end, humans must endeavour to live in harmony with God's creation, and nature, by conducting themselves through life with love, compassion, simplicity and justice.

According to Guru Nanak, religion in its true sense is a search for the Ultimate Spiritual Reality and an effort to harmonize with it. The primary purpose of human life is to merge with God under

Guru Nanak
— Guru Nanak's travels
▪ Takhats

the guidance of true Guru, attained through meditating and contemplating on God's presence while still taking an active part in every-day life.

ENLIGHTENMENT

Guru Nanak's ethics of truthful living were directed towards enlightenment rather than redemption. To him enlightenment not salvation was of primary importance, which happens only through God's grace. Enlightenment leads to spirituality, which inspires humans to dedicate his or her life to the service of humanity. Such were the universally applicable ethics of truth and dedication, which Guru Nanak strove to promote as true religion among humankind.

A stall selling Sikh religious merchandise at the Khalsa festival held in Southall, London. The tenth Guru, Gobind Singh, founded the Khalsa in 1699, by baptizing five Sikhs who in turn baptized him. To become a member of the Khalsa means that one has to dedicate ones life to Sikhism.

INITIATION CEREMONY

The tenth and the last Guru, Guru Gobind Singh (1666–1708) initiated the Sikh Baptism ceremony in 1699, giving distinctive identity to the Sikhs. The first five baptized Sikhs were named 'Panj Pyare' ('Five Beloved Ones'), and they in turn baptized the Guru on his request. At the Amrit ceremony, the initiate promises to follow the Sikh code of conduct as an integral part of the path toward God-realization. He or she vows at that time to abstain from the use of tobacco and other intoxicants; to never cut the hair on any part of the body; to not eat the meat of animals killed in a religious or sacrificial manner; to refrain from any sexual contact outside of marriage; and to wear the five symbols of Sikhs.

After this ceremony, the initiate is considered a part of the Khalsa (Belonging to God) brotherhood. Khalsa means a spiritually integrated person alive to his duties both to God and society, and is enjoined to tithe both time and income and to pray and meditate daily. He or she must live a moral life of service to mankind, in humility and honesty. The five symbolic 'K's' worn by the initiated Sikh are: unshorn hair, over which men wear a turban; comb; a steel bracelet; a short sword; and a garment that is usually worn under a Sikh's outer clothes

Sikh adherents participate in the colourful Mayia festival.

Sikh Philosophy

The basic postulation of Sikhism is that life is not sinful in its origin, but having emanated from a Pure Source, the true one abides in it. Nanak wrote: 'O my mind, thou art the spark of the Supreme Light. Know thy essence.' Not only the entire Sikh philosophy, but all of Sikh history flows from this principle. The religion consists of practical living, in rendering service to humanity and engendering tolerance and love towards all. The Sikh Gurus did not advocate retirement from the world in order to attain salvation. It can be achieved by anyone who earns an honest living and leads a normal life.

In Sikhism, time is cyclical, not linear, so Sikhism has no eschatological beliefs. Time is seen as repeated sequences of creation and destruction, and individual existence is believed to be a repeated sequence of birth, death, and rebirth as the soul seeks spiritual enlightenment. Sikhs believe that greed, lust, pride, anger, and attachment to the passing values of earthly existence constitute haumai (self-centeredness). This is the source of all evil. It is a person's inclination to evil that produces the karma that leads to endless rebirth. Haumai separates human beings from God. Sikhism teaches that human life is the opportunity for spiritual union with the Supreme Being; and for release from the cycle of death and rebirth. Enlightenment happens only through God's grace and inspires humans to dedicate their lives to the service of humanity. According to Nanak grace does not depend on caste, knowledge, wisdom or penance. Those who seek it through love, service and humility attain the goal of life.

THE UNIVERSE AND NATURE OF GOD

Guru Nanak defined God as the Ultimate Spiritual Reality and he rejected the idea of exclusiveness of any prophets, gods, race, or religion. To Sikhs, religion in its true sense, is a search for the Ultimate Spiritual Reality and an effort to harmonize with it. Enlightenment, not redemption, is the Sikh concept of salvation.

The material universe is God's creation. Its origin was in God and its end is in God; and it operates within God's hukam (God's Order). Descriptions of the universe and its creation in Sikh scripture are remarkably similar to recent scientific speculation about the universe and its origin. One of the basic hymns in the Sikh Scripture describes the indeterminate void before the existence of this universe. Guru Nanak spoke of innumerable galaxies, of a limitless universe, the boundaries of which are beyond human ability to comprehend.

The nature of God is not to be understood through one's intellect, but through personal spiritual experience. A believer has to meditate upon this belief, in order to experience the existence of God. The emphasis is on mastery over the self and the discovery of the self; not mastery over nature, external forms and beings.

God is Omnipotent, Omniscient and

A Sikh bridegroom and bride at a wedding ceremony in the UK. Arranged marriages are practised within Sikh communities, but less commonly than among Muslims or Hindus.

Omnipresent in Sikhism. He is present in all relationships, directs all events within the universe, and watches over them in the manner of a kind and compassionate parent.

THE SECOND POSTULATE

Humans, practising a highly disciplined life are capable of further spiritual progression. It is important that Sikhs retain the primacy of spirit over material matter, but it is not required that they renounce the world. However, they should reject conspicuous consumption and maintain a simple life, respecting the dignity in all life, whether human or not. Such a respect for life can only be fostered where one can first recognize the Divine spark within oneself, see it in others, and cherish it, and nurture it.

SPIRITUAL DISCIPLINE

Humans have the capability to further their spiritual progression through conscious choice. The method suggested by Guru Nanak is one of spiritual discipline, meditation and prayer, and sharing. Sikhism emphasizes mastering Haumai. This is achieved by developing five positive forces: Compassion, Humility, Contemplation, Contentment and Service (*seva*) without expecting any material or spiritual reward. Sikhism also preaches strong family involvement, in which a person pursuing this spiritual discipline also works to create an atmosphere for other members of the family to progress spiritually.

THE THIRD POSTULATE

The third postulate is that the true end of the human beings is in their emergence as God-conscious beings, who operate in the material world, with the object of transforming and spiritualising it into a higher plane of existence. In this spiritual state individuals are motivated by an intense desire to do good, transforming their surroundings.

Enlightened spirits become benefactors of humanity and the world around them. Such individuals would not exploit another human or sentient being, as each is a manifestation of the eternal and the supreme. In this God-conscious state they see God in all and everything, and a Sikh life is one of harmony with other individuals, beings and forms.

An elder leads the congregation in prayer at a gurdwara in Southall, London. Although congregational leaders tend to be male and middle-aged or elderly, the post is not as formalized as in many religions and others sometimes fulfil their role.

UNITY OF SPIRIT AND MATTER AND THE INTERCONNECTEDNESS OF ALL CREATION

The Sikh view is that spirit and matter are not antagonistic. Guru Nanak declared that the spirit was the only reality and matter is only a form of spirit. Spirit takes on many forms and names under various conditions.

The chasm between the material and the spiritual is in the minds of humans only. It is a limitation of the human condition that spirit and matter appear as duality, and their unity is not self-evident.

"When I saw truly, I knew that all was primeval.
Nanak, the subtle (spirit) and the gross (material) are, in fact, identical."
(Guru Granth Sahib, page 281)

That which is inside a person, the same is outside; nothing else exists;
By divine prompting look upon all existence as one and undifferentiated;
(Guru Granth Sahib, page 599)

As shown at this temple in the UK, the flagpole outside each Sikh gurdwara is anointed with milk by the temple leaders every year at the festival of Baisakhi.

Sikhism Today

There are no denominations in Sikhism, but in the United States in particular there is grouping along language and cultural lines. The majority of Sikhs in the United States are immigrants of Indian origin, speak Punjabi, and have distinct customs and dress that originates in Punjab, India. Sikhs of Indian origin number approximately a half million in North America and approximately 23 million throughout the world.

SIKHS ARE CONCERNED with the creation of a just social order and are committed to social equality and peaceful co-existence.

SIKHISM AND OTHER FAITHS

Interfaith dialogue and cooperation have been a part of Sikhism since Guru Nanak founded the faith. He did not attempt to convert the followers of other religions but, rather, urged them to rediscover the internal significance of their beliefs and rituals, without forsaking their chosen paths. He indicated that because of human limitations, each group grasps only a narrow aspect of God's revelation. The Sikh Gurus were opposed to any exclusive claim on truth, which a particular religion might make. Just as this indicates a pluralistic acceptance of the legitimacy of all faiths, and all that are

valid, it indicates, too, an acceptance of all groups and individuals. Guru Arjun said: 'All are co-equal partners in the Commonwealth with none treated as alien.' (Guru Granth Sahib). Numerous examples suffice to show how this attitude has evidence itself in Sikh history. When compiling the manuscripts that would make up the Guru Granth Sahib, Guru Arjun included hymns written by both Hindu and Muslim religious thinkers. There are, in the Guru Granth Sahib, hymns written by persons considered by Hindus to be untouchables. The holiest of Sikh shrines, the Golden Temple at Amritsar has four doors, each facing a cardinal direction. This was done to indicate that all are welcome. The cornerstone of the Golden Temple was laid by a Muslim holy man. The ninth guru, Guru Tegh Bahadur, died championing the rights of Hindus to practise their own religion.

Sikhism Today
Sikhs are concerned with the creation of a just social order and are committed to social equality and peaceful co-existence. Around 23 million Sikhs of Indian origin constitute 0.4 per cent of the world's population across 21 countries.

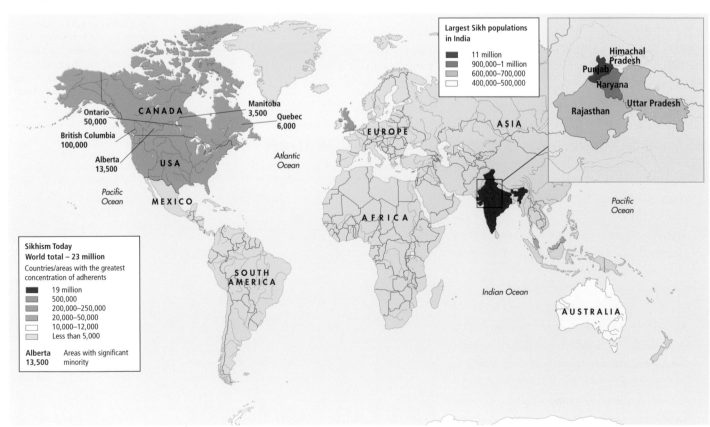

Largest Sikh populations in India
- 11 million
- 900,000–1 million
- 600,000–700,000
- 400,000–500,000

Himachal Pradesh
Punjab
Haryana
Uttar Pradesh
Rajasthan

Ontario 50,000
Manitoba 3,500
Quebec 6,000
British Columbia 100,000
Alberta 13,500
CANADA
USA
MEXICO
Pacific Ocean
Atlantic Ocean
EUROPE
ASIA
AFRICA
Pacific Ocean
Indian Ocean
SOUTH AMERICA
AUSTRALIA

Sikhism Today
World total – 23 million
Countries/areas with the greatest concentration of adherents
- 19 million
- 500,000
- 200,000–250,000
- 20,000–50,000
- 10,000–12,000
- Less than 5,000

Alberta 13,500   Areas with significant minority

campaigns, issues affecting children, AIDS, food and other help for the homeless and displaced. In India particularly, there are many free clinics operated by Sikhs, which accept persons of all religious and castes as patients. In some Western cities, Sikhs have continued that tradition. Since the intrinsic spirit of Sikhism is pluralistic, it has much to contribute towards inter-faith and inter-community accommodation. It is a willing partner in the emergence of a pluralistic world community that preserves the rights of human dignity and freedom for all human beings. In witness of this attitude and spirit, the Ardas, recited at the end of a Sikh religious service ends with the words 'May the whole world be blessed by your grace'.

A cornerstone of the Sikh faith is the concept of seva, the selfless service of the community – not just the Sikh community, but the community of man. Bhai Gurdas, an early Sikh theologian, said: 'Service of one's fellows is a sign of divine worship'. What one does in selfless service is considered to be a real prayer. A Sikh who, with no thought of reward, serves others, performs the truest form of worship, whether he is feeding the homeless or bringing company and compassion to people who suffer.

Sikhism seeks to give humanity a progressive and responsible philosophy as a guide to all of the world's concerns. Believing that there is a part of the divine in all that God created, the interdependence of all generations, species and resources must be recognized. Sikhs advocate preserving what was given to humanity and passing it on in a healthy and robust condition, hence their strong involvement in the environmental movement.

The exquisite Golden Temple at Amritsar, in the Punjab, is the most sacred site in Sikhism. Originally begun by Guru Amar Das, the huge complex has been expanded by other Gurus over the centuries and the original sacred text of the Guru Granth Sahib, was installed here in 1604.

THE COMMUNITY OF HUMANITY

In modern times, the lesson of equality that is taught by the *langar*, the meal eaten together by Sikh congregations, extends beyond caste-obliteration to the acceptance and toleration of people of all races, creeds and nationalities. Sikhs do not disparage other faiths, nor claim sole possession of the truth. Sikhism does not attempt to convert adherents of other faiths. In the West, Sikh congregations belong to local interfaith associations and participate fully in their efforts such as environmental protection

Young Sikhs queue to pay their devotions to the Guru Granth Sahib at a London gurdwara. The Guru Granth Sahib, a collection of scriptures, is considered the symbolic head of Sikhism, and is treated with great respect.

THE HEALTHY, HAPPY, HOLY ORGANISATION

Since the 1960s, however, there has existed a group, generally called the American Sikhs, whose leader is Yogi Harbhajan Singh. American Sikhs are easily distinguished from others by their all white attire and by the fact that turbans are worn by both men and women. This group now numbers about 5,000. The majority of American Sikhs, who refer to their group as 3HO (Healthy, Happy, Holy Organization) know only limited Punjab. Indian Sikhs and American Sikhs are mutually accepting and visit one another's gurdwaras.

TAOISM

Origins

Taoism is the main surviving religion native to China. Its roots lie far back in Chinese shamanism and in philosophy and its name comes from the Chinese word for the way – meaning 'the Way, the very essence, of nature'. It developed into a full-blown religion from the second century AD.

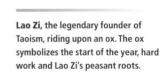

THE EARLIEST KNOWN religion in China is shamanism – the roots of which lie north of China in Siberia. Shamans communicate between the two worlds of the physical world of this earth with its creatures and the spiritual world of the deities. China has the world's oldest recorded shamanic literature including poems of divination from *c*. 1200 BC as well as an entire cycle of Shamanic songs dating from *c*. fourth century BC called the *Chu Ci* (*Songs of the South*). Shamanism was

a major formative force in the early culture of China, creating priestly kings through most of the second millennium BC. These gradually gave way to specifically military and political rulers while the shamans became court magicians and divination experts.

THE ROLE OF SHAMAN

The gradual end of the official courtly role of shamans came as a result of the rise of the Confucian elite. The world of shamans was

Lao Zi, the legendary founder of Taoism, riding upon an ox. The ox symbolizes the start of the year, hard work and Lao Zi's peasant roots.

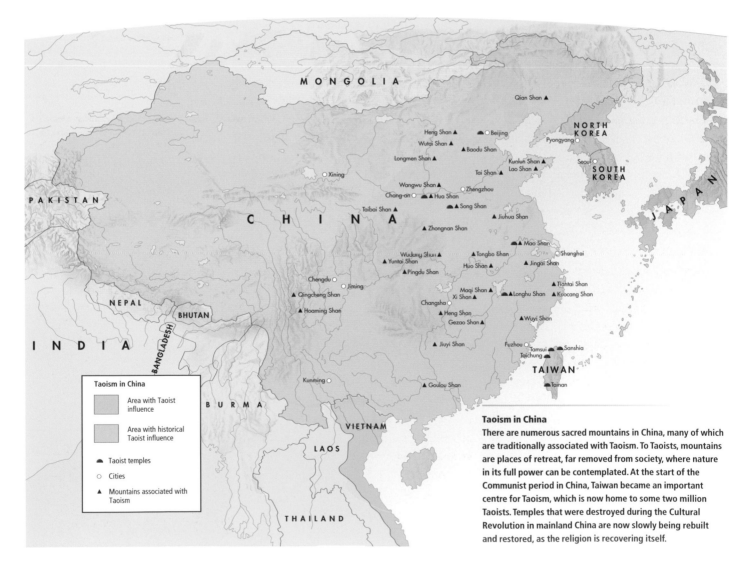

Taoism in China

Taoism in China

Area with Taoist influence

Area with historical Taoist influence

▲ *Taoist temples*

○ *Cities*

▲ *Mountains associated with Taoism*

There are numerous sacred mountains in China, many of which are traditionally associated with Taoism. To Taoists, mountains are places of retreat, far removed from society, where nature in its full power can be contemplated. At the start of the Communist period in China, Taiwan became an important centre for Taoism, which is now home to some two million Taoists. Temples that were destroyed during the Cultural Revolution in mainland China are now slowly being rebuilt and restored, as the religion is recovering itself.

one of spiritual forces, unpredictability and divination. The Confucians, as the main legislative and administrative officials deeply concerned with government law, were the opposite: they sought order, control and logic and saw the shamans as unpleasant leftovers of a primitive worldview – anarchic and disordered. With the rise of the Confucian elite from the fourth century BC onwards, the shamans were gradually but firmly removed from positions of power or authority by the Confucian elite until by the first century BC they had been to all intents and purposes pushed underground.

The essential spirit of shamanism was to resurface in a more 'respectable' form through the rise of a new religion from the second century AD onwards – Taoism.

THE RISE OF TAOISM

While shamanism was declining, the quest for immortality was rising. This was a belief that certain substances or practices could ensure the physical body, and thus the spirit never died. The First Emperor (221–209 BC) was obsessed by this quest. It is another stream of thought and practice, which flowed into the creation of Taoism.

In the second century AD, these streams came together in the rise of a number of shamanic-type charismatic figures who developed a new semi-philosophical framework, within which shamanic practices such as exorcism, combined with the quest for immortality, were expressed anew within a religious philosophy of the Tao.

One of the key moments in the origin of Taoism as a religious movement is usually taken to be an experience of Zhang Dao Ling at some time in the first half of the second century AD when this charismatic healer/preacher – very much within the shamanic tradition – had a vision. In the vision Lao Zi, the reputed author of a major book of philosophy of the Tao, known as the *Dao De Jing*, gave Zhang the power to use his teachings to bind evil forces and heal those who repented of their sins.

Shamans performing a ritual dance at Ichon, South Korea. Taoism originates from Chinese shamanism, and shamans can still be found in some areas of Southeast Asia.

Taoist monk at Hua Shan Mountain. Religious Taoist followers strive for immortality through a combination of philosophy, meditation and liturgy.

THE VIRTUE OF THE WAY

Lao Zi was a philosopher who lived sometime in the sixth century BC and to whom a book of sayings – *Dao De Jing* meaning *The Virtue of the Way* – about the Tao is credited. We actually know virtually nothing about him – the very name just means Old Master. He was one of many hundreds of key philosophers who, from the sixth to fourth centuries BC, explored concepts of the Tao – which simply means 'the Way' as in a path. The Way had originally been used as a moral term – Confucians saw the Tao as the moral path, which the world had to follow to remain balanced. But Lao Zi took this further and explored the Tao as the very origin of nature – the source of the origin

– the very foundation of all reality.

When Zhang Dao Ling claimed that Lao Zi had given him authority over spiritual forces, the key to immortality and the power of the *Dao De Jing* to combat evil, Zhang fused elements of the officially discredited shamanism of the ordinary folk with the quest for longevity and immortality and the philosophical and quintessentially anti-Confucian/elite teachings of philosophers such as Lao Zi. From this strange conglomeration came Taoism – the Way of the Tao, the religion of following Nature's Path, of seeking immortality and of combating the forces of evil spirits.

Taoist Beliefs and Practices

The essence of Taoism is maintaining the balance of nature – of the Tao – through controlling and influencing the forces of yin and yang, exorcising evil spirits and seeking immortality. Taoist priests also act as local priests to many communities, offering advice, prayers and rituals, which maintain local life and offer the individual solace and comfort.

Left: An eighteenth-century boxwood pendant, showing the yin-yang symbol and the sacred trigram, as well as an agate gourd which symbolizes immortality.

TAOISM TEACHES that the world, indeed the entire cosmos is finely tuned and balanced and that the role of humanity is to maintain this balance. Central to Taoism is the creed-like statement found in Chapter 42 of the *Dao De Jing*, the key text of Taoism:

> The Tao is the Origin of the One:
> The one is the Origin of the Two:
> The Two give birth to the Three:
> The Three give birth to every living thing.

In other words, the Tao is the primal source of all unity and existence – the One. From this one comes the twin forces of yin and yang – polar opposites that are locked in a struggle for supremacy, which can never be achieved because they each contain the seed of the other within them. Thus, for example, autumn and winter are yin but inexorably give way to spring and summer, which are yang, which in turn give way to autumn and winter.

THE WAY

In Taoism, the Tao – the Way – moves from being a descriptive term for the relentless cycle of the natural world to being to all intents and purposes the ultimate 'divine' force. The Tao is classically represented in Taoist temples by three statues. These statues – male figures – represent the Tao as the Origin, the Tao as manifest in the human form of the sage Lao Zi and the Tao as Word – as found in the Dao De Jing.

The two forces of yin and yang dominate all existence and from their dynamic, eternal struggle they produce the three of Heaven, earth and humanity. Heaven is yang while earth is yin and their interaction gives rise to the forces which enliven all life. Humanity is the pivot upon which this all hinges. We have the power to throw the

The yin-yang symbol. In Taoism, the Tao is the ultimate whole that defines the universe, and yin and yang are the two opposite halves of that whole. Yin and yang have opposing characteristics; for example, yin is regarded as cold, dark and female, and yang is heat, light and male. However, yin and yang are mutable characteristics, found within one another and created by one another. This leads to different degrees of ying and yang, and means that one does not predominate over the other. yin and yang also have physical manifestations that affect all aspects of life, from ailments of the body to political events.

TAOIST RITUALS

Taoism offers many rituals, charms, prayers and prescriptions for dealing with physical ailments and psychological troubles. It is possible to find a charm to be cited, burnt or ingested for almost any problem. As such it plays the role of priest, psychologist and counsellor for many people.

Taoist rituals are only tangentially related to the major rites of passage such as birth, marriage and death. A traditional Chinese wedding will involve elements of Buddhism, Confucianism and Taoism. Taoism's role is more to do with establishing a relationship between the community and the spirit world – in the way that shamans link the spirit world with the physical. Taoism claims the power to control and shape the behaviour of the spirit world in order to enhance the life of those here on earth. There is still, nevertheless, an element of dealing with unpredictable forces in the Taoist rituals of invoking the spirit world. All of this is seen as part and parcel of maintaining the balance of nature – of the Tao.

cosmos out of kilter by creating too much yin or too much yang, or to balance the cosmos. Taoism embodies this in many of its liturgies and rituals.

Taoism also offers the individual the chance to slough off sins and misdemeanours through rituals of repentance and of exorcism. It also seeks to control the forces of the spirit world, which can break through to harm this world. For example it exorcises or placates ghosts of those whose descendents have not offered the correct rituals to ensure they pass to the spirit world.

IMMORTALITY

One of the most important areas of teaching is the possibility of achieving longevity and even immortality. Taoism teaches that immortality is about ensuring the physical body is transformed into an eternal body through rituals and even diet. The quest for immortality and the supernatural powers which this involves, has been a major facet of the mythology of China and manifests itself today in serious practitioners on sacred mountains and in the extravagant antics, such as flight, of certain figures in popular Chinese movies and stories.

The quest for immortality takes many forms. For some it is the literal quest for certain foods and substances which if eaten will transform the body. For others it is daily meditational practices which encourage the growth of a spiritual body. For yet others it is a life of abstinence and devotion, undertaken as a hermit in the wild, by which the body becomes simply a part of the cosmic Tao and thus can never die.

Local people, Taoist priests and nuns join together to in a colourful procession to celebrate the dedication of a new temple in the Shaanxi province, China.

Lao Zi and Zhuang Zi

The two most formative figures in Taoist philosophy never saw themselves as belonging to a religion called Taoism. Lao Zi lived in the sixth century and Zhuang Zi in the fourth century BC. In their books, the *Dao De Jing* and the eponymous *Zhuang Zi* they explored the understanding of reality through exploring the meaning of the Tao – the Way.

Two characters, one for Zhuang Zi, the fourth-century BC Taoist philosopher, and one for Mo Zi, the fifth-century BC disciple of Confucius inscribed by the contemporary calligrapher Li Jinxue.

L AO ZI LIVED at the same time as Confucius, c. sixth century BC, yet we know virtually nothing about him. That he wrote some of the verses in the *Dao De Jing* seems clear because a certain number are written in the first person. It is likely, however, that the bulk of the *Dao De Jing* are wisdom sayings and commentaries which were originally passed down orally and then came to be associated with the wisdom of Lao Zi. The *Dao De Jing* has been described as a handbook to leadership. Its attitude to such a role is reflected in Chapter 17:

'The highest form of government
is what people hardly even realize
is there..[...]

Next down is the dictatorship
That thrives on oppression and terror –
And the last is that of those who lie
And end up despised and rejected.

The sage says little –
and does not tie the people down:
And the people stay happy
Believing that what happens,
happens, naturally.'

Perhaps the most famous line of all in the *Dao De Jing* sums up the reason why the Confucians, who wanted logic, found the thoughts of the Taoist so hard to handle. It is the quintessential text of doubt and of humility

Below: A Chinese illustration showing a group of scholars copying the sacred text of the *Dao De Jing* and handing it to the emperor.

before the sheer inconceivability of the Origin of all and is the opening lines of Chapter 1:

> 'The Tao that can be talked about is not
>   the true Tao.
> The name that can be named is not the
>   eternal Name.
> Everything in the universe comes out
>   of Nothing.'

ZHUANG ZI

Zhuang Zi takes up this theme of the unknowability of the ultimate and of the inadequacy of language to capture that which is beyond. Zhuang Zi was a rumbustuous character who lived in the fourth century BC and in his book of the same name we find one of the most entertaining, moving and complex characters of ancient philosophy. An inveterate arguer, joker and wit, he takes language to its limits and bursts it through stories and ridicule. Perhaps one of the most famous of his explorations of what is reality is the butterfly dream in chapter 2:

> 'Once upon a time I, Zhuang Zi, dreamt that I was a butterfly, flitting around and enjoying myself. I had no idea I was Zhuang Zi. Then suddenly I woke up and was Zhuang Zi again. But I could not tell, had I been Zhuang Zi dreaming I was a butterfly, or a butterfly dreaming I was now Zhuang Zi?'

Zhuang Zi also introduces a key term in Taoism with the phrase *wu-wei* – translated as 'actionless action'. In Chapter 22 he defines *wu-wei* thus:

> 'One who follows the Tao daily does less
>   and less.
> As he does less and less, he eventually
>   arrives at actionless action.
> Having achieved actionless action, there is
>   nothing which is not done.'

For Zhuang Zi, the Tao is about being natural, about being true to your 'innate nature'. He sees the innate nature as something good and given which becomes distorted when people try to reform others, make them conform to their ideas or do what they think is right. He is anarchic in his approach to authority and dismisses all attempts to control as attacks on the innate and essential goodness of human nature. This strand of optimism about the nature of life runs throughout Taoism and can be seen for example in the Taoist Association of China's statement on ecology:

'Taoism has a unique sense of value in that it judges affluence by the number of different species. If all things in the universe grow well, then a society is a community of affluence. If not, this kingdom is on the decline.'

For both Lao Zi and Zhuang Zi, words and knowledge are secondary to experience and reflection. This is at the heart of the philosophy of Taoism.

The roof of a Taoist temple in China; like most Taoist temples it displays hundreds of different gods for worship.

Taoism Beyond China

Taoism, for centuries only found in China, has in the last 200 years spread wider in Asia and in the last 50 years to the West, at the same time it has undergone the greatest persecution of its history in China.

TAOISM IS THE quintessential Chinese religion and for the majority of its history has been found only within China itself. However, the migration of the Chinese into Southeast Asia over the last 200 years has led to a spread of Taoism and Taoist ideas into many parts of Asia. For example, Malaysia has over 7,500 Taoist temples; Indonesia has now long established-Taoist temples where the Chinese have settled; Singapore has some of the most important centres of Taoism outside China. In many such places, Taoism has merged with local traditions and also offers a home for Buddhist and Confucian ideas and beliefs. It is very much a parochial form of Taoism, lacking the great spiritual centres of Taoism in China such as the sacred mountains or the historic centres like Mao Shan. However it is not uncommon to find Taoism shrines in Southeast Asia which have a stone taken from one of the sacred mountains, especially the greatest Tai Shan, and venerated as a physical link back to China.

Beyond Southeast Asia, the Chinese diaspora has created substantial communities in places such as California, the United Kingdom, Canada and the Netherlands. In such communities, Taoism plays a role though usually as part of the backcloth of traditional beliefs against which life in these Chinese communities is played out. In a few places, specific Taoist centres have come into being but this has usually been linked to the growing interest in Taoism amongst non-Chinese.

THE WEST AND TAOISM

The teachings of Taoism were first sympathetically introduced to the West by returning Christian missionaries and scholarly academics in the late nineteenth century. Since then certain key books, such as the *Dao De Jing* and to a lesser extent the *Zhuang Zi*, have become international best-selling religious classics. The iconography of Taoism, especially the yin/yang symbol has become popular with Westerners who often remain ignorant of the philosophy behind such a symbol but like its 'feel'.

A crowd watches as the Dragon dance is performed to celebrate the New Year in the Chinatown area of Manchester. Rehearsals for the Dragon dance begin months beforehand.

Taoism beyond China
Although for most of its history Taoism has been confined to China, the migration of the Chinese into Southeast Asia over the last 200 years has led to the spread of Taoism and Taoist ideas into many parts of Asia. The Chinese diaspora has also created substantial communities in places such as California, the UK, Canada, the Netherlands, Australia and New Zealand.

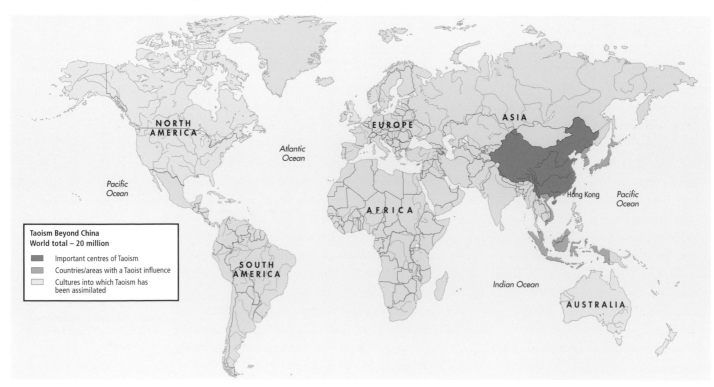

Taoism Beyond China
World total – 20 million
- Important centres of Taoism
- Countries/areas with a Taoist influence
- Cultures into which Taoism has been assimilated

Unlike Buddhism, there has been no serious attempt to missionize the West by Taoist masters. There is no equivalent to the impact of the Dalai Lama on the West nor that of organizations such as the Hare Krishnas. Instead, Taoism has few centres but great appeal as something which individuals engage with at their own pace and with their own integrity. In North America and to a much lesser degree in the United Kingdom and Europe, there are a few Taoist centres and movements but they are very small and modest in their goals. There has instead been a spread of Taoist ideas into the wider culture of the West. The use of the yin/yang symbol has been noted, but the ideas of Feng Shui and Traditional Chinese medicine, both rooted to a certain degree in Taoism, have become very popular and are often used by people who would see themselves as belonging to Christianity or Judaism for example, but who find these 'Taoist' ideas helpful.

THE STUDY OF TAOISM

Scholarly study of Taoism is also quite a small field but is having an impact beyond its modest scale. For while the West has been collecting information and analyzing Taoism, the faith was almost wiped out during the Cultural Revolution in China from 1966–76. During this period, virtually all Taoist temples were closed; thousands destroyed; up to 95 per cent of all statues destroyed and Taoism as an organized faith very nearly died out. Mao launched the Cultural Revolution to destroy the vestiges of China's past. He very nearly succeeded.

As a result, it has been only since *c.* 1980 that Taoism has been able to reorganize itself and slowly try to get its temple sites restored to it. In the process, it has lost much of its traditional scale and even its understanding of the deities and of Taoist practice. To some degree it has had to look to the West for accounts and resources to rebuild its presence in China. It is also true to say that as a result of the Cultural Revolution, many of the practices and deities associated with the Imperial world of ancient China have died out and no-one is particularly interested in reviving them. Instead, the most popular deities being worshipped and supported at Taoist temples in China are those to do with wealth, health, success and fertility. It is therefore outside mainland China that one finds the imperial deities such as the City God or the Jade Emperor of Heaven worshipped.

To a certain degree Taoism is going through one of the most challenging and radical stages of its long history. Structures and beliefs, which have remained unchanged and unchallenged for centuries, have been thrown into sharp relief by both the persecution of Taoism in China and by the encounter with interested but questioning Western thought and practice.

An elderly Taoist priest at the Shangqing Gong temple at the top of the sacred Qingcheng (Green City) mountain in Sichuan province, China. There are five major Taoist sacred mountains and hundreds of more locally famous ones, such as Qingcheng.

Zoroastrianism

Like Judaism, Christianity and Islam, Zoroastrianism is a monotheistic religion that still survives today, albeit with a relatively small number of followers. There are only a few hundred thousand practising Zorastrians left in Iran, where the religion first emerged, with the largest group being the Parsees in India who number around 125,000. It is thought by some to have been founded around 1200 BC; by others around 588 BC by Zarathustra, later known as Zoroaster. Its first adherents were the pastoral nomads of the ancient Afghanistan-Persian border areas. Subsequently, Zoroastrianism became the chief faith of Persia before the arrival of Islam.

THE RELIGIONS OF India and Persia in Zarathustra's time were polytheistic. Zarathustra, who was probably a priest in what is now Iran, formulated a new religion that attempted to concentrate the many gods of these faiths into one, Ahura Mazda, meaning Wise One. Ahura Mazda, it seems, appeared to Zarathustra in a vision and appointed him to preach *asha*, the truth. Creator of the universe and the cosmic order, Ahura Mazda brought two spirits into being. One was the spirit of truth, light, life and good, Spenta Mainyu. The other was Angra Mainyu, the spirit of darkness, deceit, destruction and death. World history comprises the ongoing cosmic struggle between the two Mainyus. Ahura Mazda is therefore not omnipotent, but he and Angra Mainyu represent the contest between good and evil, or *asha* (truth) and *druj* (lies), which is weighted in favour of the former. Humans must join the cosmic struggle, bringing both body and soul to the great contest, but they must not debilitate themselves by fasting or celibacy, both of which are forbidden in Zoroastrianism. Zarathustra's monotheistic concept did not make Ahura Mazda the only focus of faith. There were also the souls known as Fravashis, which are venerated by Zoroastrians. The Fravashis also participate in the cosmic struggle as and when their aid is enlisted. In this, the Fravashis resemble the saints of Roman Catholicism.

Zoroaster, the founder of Zoroastrianism, dying ritually in flames, as imagined by a nineteenth-century French illustrator.

sacred fire that must never be allowed to go out. The architecture of the temples is designed to reflect this. The fire must also never be contaminated, and the Zoroastrian laity are forbidden to touch the fire. Priests are responsible for fuelling the fire, and must constantly purify themselves to avoid contamination. This includes wearing a mask or Padan, which covers the nose and mouth.

THE GATHAS AND THE ATTRIBUTES

The Gathas is a set of 17 hymns written by Zarathustra himself. Other texts were later added, but many were destroyed in the persecutions that followed invasions of Persia by the ancient Greeks, the Muslims and the Mongols. The language of the Gathas is a very ancient tongue, Avestan, which resembled

FIRE AND DIVINITY

Ahura Mazda is represented by fire, which is believed to be a manifestation of the power of creation and God's divinity. Fire is a sacred element of Zoroastrianism, and is used in all religious ceremonies. The focal points of worship are the fire temples, which house a

A bas-relief from the Achaemenid necropolis of Naqsh-i-Rustam, Iran, showing the Persian king Ardashir I (AD 224–243), receiving a ribboned crown from the good deity Ormuzd as a symbol of his rule.

Sanskrit, the language of the Aryans of India. It was in the Gathas that Zarathustra presented Ahura Mazda as the sole transcendent god who created the world through his divine Attributes. Zarathustra did not name a particular number of Attributes, but they have been specified as seven, known as Amesha Spentas, or Bounteous Immortals, all of which include an attribute of Ahura Mazda and human virtue as well. The seven Attributes start with Vohu Manah, or good thought. Asha Vahishta represents justice and truth, Kshathra stands for dominion, Spenta Armaiti for devotion and serenity. Wholeness, or Haurvatat, is the fifth Attribute, followed by Ameretat, immortality, and the good spirit, Spenta Mainya, creative energy. In the Gathas, the Attributes are sometimes personified, or sometimes exist simply as ideas. The basic concept in Zoroastrianism is dedication to moral excellence and ethics, as expressed in the motto 'good thoughts, good words, good deeds'.

ZOROASTRIAN WORSHIP AND BELIEFS

Zoroastrian ceremonies centre round a sacred fire, but only as a symbol on which the acts of worship are concentrated. There is no belief in reincarnation or in karma, divine judgement of acts performed during life. Rather, humans are judged on the basis of whether good or evil predominated in their lives. After that, souls are consigned to Heaven, the best existence, or Hell, the worst existence. Zoroastrianism, a fundamentally optimistic faith, teaches that collectively, the good done by humanity will transform the world into a heavenly utopia, and when time ends, all souls,

I, who have set my heart on watching over the soul, in union with Good Thought, and as knowing the rewards of Mazda Ahura for our works, will, while I have power and strength, teach men to seek after Right.

From the Ahunaviati Gatha

The Kabah-e-Zardoucht, or Zoraster's cube, a black and white stone tower at the Achaemenid necropolis. It was erected by the Persian king Darius I (521–486 BC) to house the sacred flame of Zoroastrianism.

THE TOWERS OF SILENCE

Death and dead matter are polluting elements in Zoroastrianism and disposal of dead bodies have been traditionally carried out at private ceremonies within the Dakhma-nashini, better known as the Towers of Silence. This reflects the revulsion for dead bodies that was a feature of the ancient Aryan culture of northern India, and Aryan ideas, in fact, permeate the Zoroastrian ceremonies. The only people who can touch a body which, it is believed, is filled with the evil spirit of putrefaction up to three hours after death, are specially designated corpse-bearers. The body is first bathed in the urine of a white bull, the clothes are destroyed and are replaced by special religious dress, the Sudreh-Kusti. After the Geh-Sarna ceremony, which is designed to fortify the dead soul, family members make their farewells and the body is placed on a stone slab. A dog, which can chase away evil spirits, is brought in to look on the face of the dead person. The body is then taken to a circular stone structure, the Dakhma. The corpse is then left for disposal by a combination of the sun, the rain and the vultures, a process that can take up to a year. This practice is increasingly rare among modern Zoroastrians, and disposing of the dead in Dakhmas has been replaced by burial or cremation.

New Religions
East Meets West

The deepest encounter between East and West has taken place between western Christianity and Indian religions, particularly Hinduism. Hinduism has many deities, many sacred books, no Church, and acknowledges that any religion can be a road to the ultimate God. Christianity has the Bible, the Church, and implies there is only one way to God. Nevertheless the dialogue between these two apparent opposites has not been a dialogue of the deaf.

WHEN THE FIRST Western imperialists, the Portuguese, landed on the coast of what is now the Indian state of Kerala in the sixteenth century, they were surprised to find Christians who claimed their forefathers had been converted by St Thomas the doubter, one of the 12 disciples. The tradition that the apostle preached and was martyred in India is so deeply embedded in South Indian Christianity that it cannot be lightly dismissed. The Thomas Christians formed a self-contained community making little or no effort to disturb Hindus in their beliefs. But the Portuguese missionaries brought the intolerance of Western Christianity with them, teaching that there was only one Church and no salvation outside it. This first meeting between Western Christianity and India divided the Christians of Kerala, taught them to decry Hinduism, and rejected any dialogue with other religions. The missionaries who spread throughout India under British rule also preached Christianity as the only true religion and brought their own doctrinal differences with

An itinerant Christian preacher in India during the nineteenth century. At first the British in India largely respected the native religions, but during the nineteenth century evangelical movements grew in power and many European missionaries were sent to attempt to convert the 'heathen' Indians.

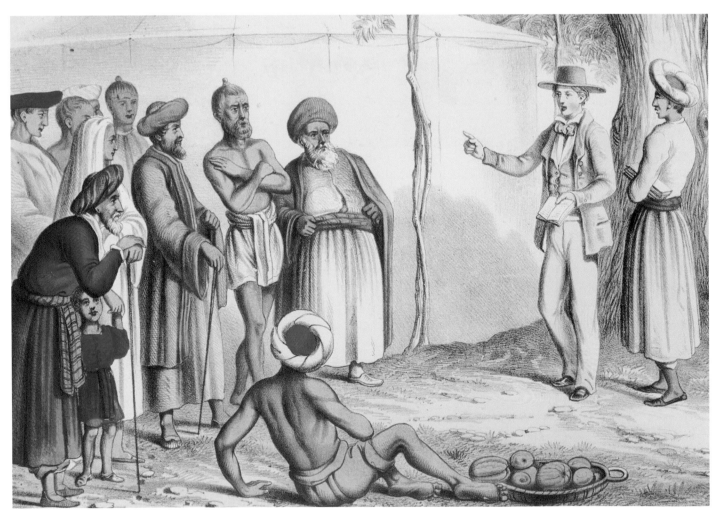

them. But the Western missionaries' attempt to convince Hindus that they were in error had little success and by the end of the nineteenth century missionaries were beginning to realize that there had to be a meeting with Indian religions. The World Missionary Conference in Edinburgh in 1910, the first 'ecumenical' gathering of Christians from many traditions, acknowledged the harm done by 'missionaries who have lacked the wisdom to appreciate the nobler side of the religion which they have laboured so indefatigably to replace'.

DIALOGUE BETWEEN EAST AND WEST

From the early days of the British Raj there were laymen who rejected the missionaries' scornful attitude to Hinduism. Warren Hastings, the eighteenth-century Governor of Bengal, supported the foundation of the Bengal Asiatic Society, which produced a number of outstanding scholars of Indian languages, religion, and culture. One, William Wilkins, translated the Bhagvad Gita, the Hindu scripture which deeply influenced Mahatma Gandhi two centuries later. In the nineteenth century, Max Muller, a German scholar, settled in Britain and achieved world renown for his translations of the Hindu texts. Although a Christian, he was a powerful advocate of the wisdom of the Vedas. At the same time some Hindus pleaded for a dialogue with Christianity and Western culture. The most renowned was Vivekananda, a Swami Hindu holyman, who made a deep impression on the historic World Parliament of Religions in

Chicago in 1893. He once wrote, 'India must bring out her treasures and through them broadcast among the nations of the earth and in return be ready to receive what others have to give her.'

THE TWENTIETH CENTURY

During the twentieth century there have been numerous Christian teachers who have been deeply influenced by Hinduism. One of the most widely read is Bede Gritffiths, a British Benedictine monk who came to India and founded an Ashram where he lived until his death. His book, *The Marriage of East and West*, summarizes the influence of the East on his Christianity. There are many Hindus who have acknowledged a debt to Christianity, the most famous being Mahatma Gandhi. In the last half of the twentieth century, both Hinduism and Buddhism found many followers in the West who saw in those religions a more spiritual religion than Western Christianity, a religion which valued experience rather than doctrine.

The Indian pacifist leader Mahatma Gandhi (1869–1948) eating a final meal before preparing to fast in protest of the British occupation of India, 1939.

A Shinto priest at the Maple Tree festival at the Arashaiyaina River, Japan. The Shinto religion reveres nature, with all creation regarded as the expression of spiritual power.

THE EAST AND THE ENVIRONMENT

In the last decades of the twentieth century there was a meeting between Western environmentalists and Eastern religious thought. The environmentalists acknowledged that Western attitudes towards the environment were based on theology and philosophy, which elevated humans above the rest of creation, and regarded nature as a resource for us to exploit. In Eastern religions they found a theology which regarded humans as part of nature and taught that it was our duty to live in harmony with all creation. The difference was acknowledged by many Christian theologians too. Diana Eck, an American theologian for instance, wrote, 'most of us in the Christian tradition have not let the icons of nature become a powerful part of our theology. There is no part of nature that carries for Christians the cultural and mythic energy of the Ganges.' It is this respect for nature, this search for harmony between humans and the rest of creation, which may well be the most profound outcome of the meeting between East and West in the twenty-first century.

207

New Religious Movements

New religions are a challenge to both secularism and organized religion. They manifested in the West as marginal, counter-cultural movements, but the ideas and practices of Eastern-based and New Age movements have increasingly influenced mainstream society. New religions are also found worldwide, particularly in Africa, Japan, Indonesia and South America. Other 'new' religions may not be new in the strictest sense, with their basis in the older religions (such as Buddhism and Christianity). These religions have found new interpretations within a new audience, who live in a vastly different social context to the ones in which such religions first emerged.

THE LATE TWENTIETH century witnessed an upsurge of new religions – at a time when the triumph of science-based secularism seemed almost complete. However, new religions flourish at times of rapid social change, while organized religion adapts more slowly and so may fail to provide leadership and inspiration. Faced with the challenges of the post-war technocracy, the churches and synagogues were widely perceived, especially by young people, as irrelevant and out of touch.

Rejection of traditional Western religion by young people led to a quest for alternative spiritual traditions, and psychology created a new vocabulary and awareness of the inner self. Thousands of seekers were visiting Asia, and discovering that Hindu and Buddhist meditation provided a more systematic methodology for deeper spiritual experience, particularly as taught by gurus.

The first guru to popularize meditation was Maharishi Mahesh Yogi, who brought Transcendental Meditation to the West in 1958. The other most popular movements of the time were ISKCON (International Society for Krishna Consciousness), the Divine Light Mission (later Elan Vital) and the Osho movement. Osho created an innovative synthesis between psychology and meditation, which directly influenced contemporary interest in personal development.

Maharishi Mahesh Yogi, who brought Transcendental Meditation to the West in 1953 and became a popular guru during the 1960s.

WHY PEOPLE JOIN NEW RELIGIONS

Whereas earlier sectarian movements, and many in the developing world today, particularly Africa, appeal to the poor and oppressed, the typical membership of new religions in the West comprises well-educated, middle-class, youngish men and women, dissatisfied with received values and actively seeking spiritual growth. Self-development has sometimes been condemned as narcissistic, but adherents find it a valid, effective path to God. While many movements are sects of world religions, many others are syncretic; for example, Japanese religions often combine elements of Buddhism and Shinto, sometimes along with Christianity or positive thinking.

New religions have often been portrayed negatively as dangerous 'cults', led by gurus practising mind control, an image fuelled by a series of pre-millennial tragedies such as the siege at Waco in Texas, where David Koresh, leader of the Branch Davidians, died in a fire along with many of his followers, including children. There have been some abuses of power such as coercion, deception, financial and sexual misdemeanours in the more authoritarian movements, particularly Christian-based movements including the Unification Church (Moonies) and the Jesus Army – but such problems are also found within organized religions. New religions have been accused of breaking up families, but they also offer a new tribal identity to survivors of dysfunctional nuclear families. One of the greatest benefits described by members is living in a community of kindred spirits. Of the tens of thousands of new religions worldwide, the majority coexist peacefully within society.

Members of the Jesus Army, a radical offshoot of the Christian Pentecostal movement founded in 1970, baptizing new converts in Trafalgar Square, London.

THE NEW AGE AND THE HOLISTIC REVOLUTION

New religions arose as marginal groups in society, but also at the leading edge; their impact extends beyond the numbers of people involved. They function as crucibles for socio-spiritual experiments of which the more successful have been taken up by mainstream society, particularly through the New Age.

New Age is an umbrella term covering a range of spiritual groups and communities, such as Findhorn in Scotland, but it also represents a shift in values. William Bloom, one of the founder-shapers of the New Age in Britain, has summarized the philosophy of this holistic revolution: 'The purpose for each of us is to achieve integration and fulfilment within a holistic and intimately interdependent world in which consciousness and matter are one.' Some key values (shared with pagan movements) are reverence for nature (including environmental activism, animal rights and organic farming), the goddess and divine feminine, emotional intelligence, higher consciousness, and a shift from 'religion' to 'spirituality'. The beliefs and practices of new religions and the New Age have increasingly pervaded homes, workplaces, medicines, and the arts, helping transform secular society.

GURUS

One of the most contentious aspects of new religions is the master–disciple relationship, which is prone to exploitation by some of the more unscrupulous leaders. Gurus can be immensely charismatic leaders, who claim to derive their authority by divine appointment or the possession of esoteric knowledge. They offer enlightenment to their followers, but often the price is total obedience. In Asia, the guru is a revered figure, supported by tradition, whose role varies from spiritual teacher to manifestation of God. The relationship with followers is parent–child, requiring responsibility and direction from guru, trust and submission from devotee. However, the meeting between Asian gurus from more longevous religions and their new Western disciples can lead to problems such as culture clash. Some commentators have objected to the high status accorded the guru, which seems blasphemous in Christian terms and anti-democratic. Although not unique to new religions, there have been various examples of abuses of power – among Asian and Western gurus, but also among Christian priests – particularly sexual exploitation by male leaders of their female followers. Submission combined with intense devotion carries a high risk, yet paradoxically may also lead to a higher freedom. When the guru–disciple relationship works well, as it often does, the reward is ecstatic mystical experience: a transmission beyond words. The master then becomes a midwife facilitating a spiritual rebirth.

Baha'i

The Baha'i Faith is an independent monotheistic religion with a worldwide population of some seven million people. They come from more than 2,000 different tribal, racial and ethnic groups and live in 235 countries and dependent territories. It originated in Iran in 1844 and has its own sacred scriptures, laws, calendar and holy days.

THE BAHA'I FAITH teaches that the Founders of the world's major religions, including Krishna, Buddha, Zoroaster, Abraham, Moses, Jesus Christ and Muhammad, are divine Teachers sent by one God to educate humanity through teachings and laws suited to its stage of development. The Baha'i Faith recognizes two additional Teachers for this age: the Bab and Baha'u'llah. Baha'is believe that religious revelation will continue in the future to provide guidance to 'an ever-advancing civilization'.

In 1844 the Bab ('the Gate') founded the Bábí Faith. His main purpose was to prepare humanity for the imminent appearance of another divine Teacher who would lead humanity into an age of universal peace. In 1863, Baha'u'llah ('the Glory of God') announced that He was the figure foretold by the Bab, and the Baha'i Faith was born. The Faith's unity has been preserved through the provisions of a written Covenant, which established the Faith's principles of succession and institutional authority. There are no clergy in the Baha'i Faith. The Baha'i community governs itself by elected councils at the local, national and international levels, and only Baha'is are permitted to contribute to the funds of their Faith. Baha'is in Iran have suffered persecution for their beliefs since the Faith's earliest days.

UNITY

The main theme of Baha'u'llah's revelation is unity. He taught that 'the earth is but one country, and mankind its citizens'. His writings contain principles, laws and institutions for a world civilization, including: abandonment of all forms of prejudice; equality between the sexes; recognition of the common source and essential oneness of the world's great religions; elimination of the extremes of poverty and wealth; universal compulsory education; responsibility of each individual to search independently for truth; establishment of a world federal system based on principles of collective security; and recognition that religion

The shrine of the Bab in Haifa, Israel. Erected in 1953, it contains the remains of the Bab, the forerunner of Baha'u'llah.

Baha'i
The Baha'i faith originated in Iran, and is an independent monotheistic religion with a worldwide population of seven million people.

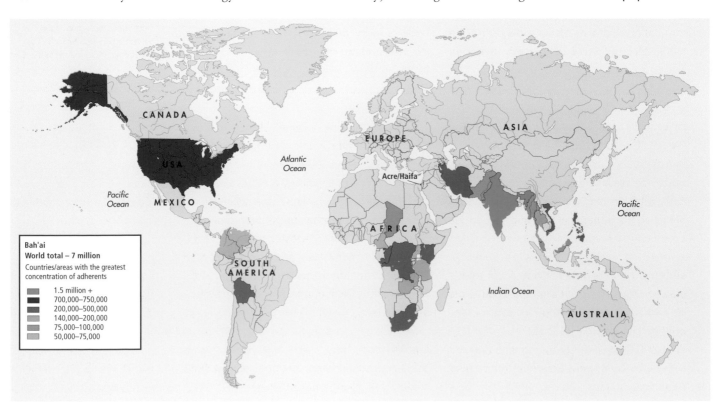

CANADA

USA

MEXICO

Pacific Ocean

Atlantic Ocean

EUROPE

Acre/Haifa

ASIA

AFRICA

SOUTH AMERICA

Indian Ocean

Pacific Ocean

AUSTRALIA

Bah'ai
World total – 7 million
Countries/areas with the greatest concentration of adherents

- 1.5 million +
- 700,000–750,000
- 200,000–500,000
- 140,000–200,000
- 75,000–100,000
- 50,000–75,000

is in harmony with reason and scientific knowledge. Because of its commitment to these ideals, the Baha'i community has been an active supporter of international organizations such as the United Nations. Service to humanity is another central teaching of the Baha'i faith, which has led Baha'is to initiate thousands of social and economic development projects – most of them modest, grassroots efforts such as schools, village healthcare campaigns and environmental projects – around the world.

The Baha'i World Centre in the Acre/Haifa area of Israel has been both the spiritual and administrative centre of the Baha'i Faith since Baha'u'llah was exiled there in 1868. The Shrines (burial places) of the Bab on Mount Carmel in Haifa and of Baha'u'llah near Acre are the two holiest places on earth for Baha'is.

BAHA'U'LLAH

Baha'u'llah, which is Arabic for 'the Glory of God', is the title adopted by the Founder of the Baha'i Faith, Mirza Husayn-'Ali' (1817–92). Born into a noble family in nineteenth-century Iran, Baha'u'llah refused the political position offered to him when He was a young man and chose instead to spend His wealth caring for the poor and the sick. He became an early follower of the Bab, a young merchant from Shiraz who claimed to be the bearer of a new religion destined to renew Persian society.

In 1852, while imprisoned in Tehran for his belief as a follower of the Bab, Baha'u'llah received the first intimations of the mission foretold by the Bab. Upon his release from prison, Baha'u'llah was exiled to Baghdad and, in 1863, declared there that he was the long-awaited Messenger of God. The vast majority of the Bab's followers accepted this declaration and so the Baha'i community was born.

The key points of Baha'u'llah's message can be summed up as global unity and justice. He taught that there is only one God who has revealed his will through a series of divine Teachers. While the social teachings of the great religions they founded differ according to the time and place

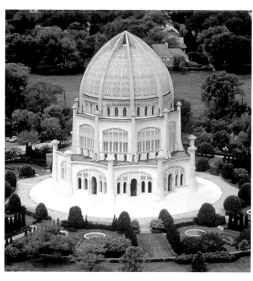

A Baha'i temple in Chicago, Illinois. Almost all major cities in the USA and Europe have at least one Baha'i place of worship.

they were delivered, the spiritual essence of all faiths is the same: that the purpose of all human beings is to know and worship their Creator. In this age, humanity is capable of recognizing the oneness of God, religion and the human family. Baha'u'llah called upon the world's secular and religious leaders to devote all their energies to the establishment of universal peace. He wrote: 'my object is none other than the betterment of the world and the tranquility of its peoples'.

Before His death in 1892, Baha'u'llah provided for the succession of leadership of the Baha'i community, ensuring its unity and protecting it from schism. His eldest son, Abbas Effendi (who adopted the title Abdu'l-Baha, which means 'servant of the Glory'), was appointed the head of the Baha'i Faith and the sole authorized interpreter of Baha'u'llah's writings. This act enabled the Baha'i community to pass through the first century of its existence with its unity firmly intact, in the face of both external and internal challenges.

Abdu'l-Baha (1844–1921), the oldest son of Baha'u'llah, the founder of the Baha'i faith. He took over the movement after his father's death and brought its teachings to the West.

ABDU'L-BAHA

Abbas Effendi, known as 'Abdu'l-Baha' (Arabic for 'servant of the Glory'), was born on 23 May 1844 – the same night that the Bab first declared his mission. He was the eldest son of Baha'u'llah and was only eight years old when his father was first imprisoned. He accompanied Baha'u'llah through 40 years of exile and imprisonment, and as he grew into adulthood he became not only his Father's closest companion but also his deputy, his shield and his principal representative to the political and religious leaders of the day. Abdu'l-Baha's leadership, knowledge and service brought great prestige to the exiled Baha'i community.

After the passing of Baha'u'llah on 29 May 1892, Abdu'l-Baha became the leader of the Baha'i community, the position to which he had been formally appointed by Baha'u'llah. In this way, the question of religious succession that has plagued other faiths was avoided. Through his will and testament, Baha'u'llah prevented schism and established a firm foundation for the further development and progress of his faith by preserving the integrity of his teachings. It was Abdu'l-Baha who first took the Baha'i message to the West, visiting Europe and North America, where the Teachings found many supporters and the worldwide spread of the faith began.

Rastafarianism

Rastafarianism is a loosely organized religio-political movement inspired by the 'black power' teachings of the Jamaican Marcus Garvey (1870–1940). Garvey taught that black Caribbeans were the lost tribes of Israel and that all black people in the Western world should shake off the oppression of the white man and return to Africa, the promised land.

Marcus Garvey (1870–1940), the Jamaican demagogue and preacher whose teachings on black power formed the basis of Rastafarianism.

ACCORDING TO GARVEY, the Bible showed that an African king would be crowned as the Messiah; Ethiopia was of special significance. A belief in Ethiopia as the cradle of civilization and site of a future utopia was popularized among black Jamaicans in the nineteenth century, taking inspiration from the biblical prophecy that 'Ethiopia shall soon stretch forth her hands unto God'. With Garvey, Ethiopianism achieved its fullest development. Many blacks saw the 1930 coronation of Prince Ras Tafari Makonnen as Emperor of Ethiopia as the fulfilment of Garvey's prophecy. The Emperor, who took the name Haile Selassie (Power of the Trinity), was hailed as God or Jah, the divine saviour of the black people, and the Rastafarian movement began.

In the 1950s Rastafarianism began to spread throughout the Caribbean, playing a major role in left-wing politics, and then to the United Kingdom and the USA. In the 1970s the music of reggae artist Bob Marley (1945–81) helped to spread the Rastafarian movement worldwide. Over the following years, thousands of reggae recordings with titles such as 'Africa is Paradise', and 'Rasta Never Fails' acted as vehicles for the message and spirit of Rastafari. Today there are thought to be up to a million Rastas worldwide including in many European and African countries as well as in Australasia and elsewhere. Since the 1950s some Jamaican Rastafarians have lived in Ethiopia on land donated by Haile Selassie in thanks for the support of the African diaspora when the Italians invaded Ethiopia in 1935. Although the vast majority of Rastas are black, a few are Afro-Chinese and Afro-East Indian and some are white.

Haile Selassie's death in 1975 caused a crisis of faith. Some Rastafarians thought his death was a fabrication, others that it was part of a Babylonian (white man's) conspiracy. For Rastafarians, Babylon is the antithesis of Ethiopia and refers to the biblical kingdom that enslaved the nation of Israel. Some Rastas believe their saviour remains present in spirit, others that he will be resurrected.

Rastafarianism
Rastafarianism originated in Jamaica, but it soon spread to the rest of the Caribbean, to the eastern USA, the UK, Australia, New Zealand and beyond.

Rastafarianism Today
World total – 1 million
Countries/areas with the greatest concentration of adherents

- Over 100,000
- Over 14,000
- Over 5,000
- 500–1,000
- Minimal number

BELIEFS AND PRACTICES

The Rasta belief system is very loosely defined. Emphasis is placed on a natural, straightforward lifestyle, on coming to know Jah (God) in every aspect of life, and on the individual's subjective interpretation of core themes: the belief that repatriation to Africa is the key to overcoming white oppression, non violence, a belief in the divinity of Haile Selassie and a condemnation of Babylon (the white power structure). Ethiopia is sometimes understood literally as an earthly paradise, sometimes as a symbol of a time when black oppression will cease. The concept of 'I and I' is central to the movement and expresses the concept of oneness – God within all of us, and all of us as one people. The movement rejects Christianity although a majority of first generation Rastas were Christians or came from Christian homes.

There are two highly organized sects within Rastafarianism, the Bobos and the Twelve Tribes of Israel (to which Bob Marley belonged). However, most Rastas prefer to live their own individual Rasta philosophy without belonging to an organization.

SYMBOLS

The wearing of dreadlocks (hair grown long, matted and twisted into coils) sets Rastas apart from Babylon and is supported in the Bible: 'They shall not make baldness upon their head, neither shall they shave off the corner of their beard, nor make any cuttings in the flesh' (Leviticus 21:5). Rastafarians can also be recognized by wearing the colours of their

religion: red, gold and green. Red symbolizes the blood of martyrs, gold the wealth of the homeland, and green the beauty and vegetation of Ethiopia. Sometimes black is used to represent the colour of Africans. The lion is also a prominent symbol. It represents Haile Selassie, the conquering Lion of Judah.

Prince Emmanuel, a Rastafarian community leader. Some Rastafarians take honorific titles in memory of Haile Selassie's status as Emperor of Ethiopia.

An Ethiopian banknote bearing the face of Ras Tafari Makonnen (1892–1974), who took the name Haile Selassie upon becoming Emperor of Ethiopia. Selassie remained an Orthodox Christian all of his life and was somewhat baffled at being worshipped by the Rastafarians.

RASTAFARIAN RITUALS

There are two main Rastafarian rituals: reasonings and the *binghi*. The reasoning is an informal gathering at which a small group of brethren generally smoke the holy weed, ganga (marijuana), and engage in discussion. Whoever lights the pipe says a short prayer and then the pipe is passed around the circle until everyone has smoked. The reasoning ends when the participants have all, one by one, departed. The ganga or 'wisdom weed' is smoked for religious reasons or to aid meditation; some do not use it at all. A number of Biblical texts are cited to support use of the herb including '...thou shalt eat the herb of the field' (Genesis 3:18).

The *nyabinghi* or *binghi* ritual includes drumming (believed to be the voice of Jah), chanting, dancing and praise to Jah Rastafari. *Binghi* rhythms inspired reggae and Bob Marley incorporated its drumming and chants into his music. Considered the most inspirational meeting of Rastafarians, the *binghi* is held on special occasions including the coronation of Haile Selassie (2 November), his ceremonial birthday (6 January), his 1966 visit to Jamaica (25 April), his personal birthday (23 July), emancipation from slavery (1 August), and Marcus Garvey's birthday (17 August). *Binghis* can last for several days and in Jamaica bring together hundreds of Rastafarians from all over the country.

Contemporary Paganism

Paganism is an umbrella term for a variety of spiritualities that venerate nature. Most Pagans practice what they see as pre-Christian or non-Christian traditions, incorporating all aspects of the natural world within a divine and ever-changing unity. Pagans are usually polytheists seeing their deities as separate entities but also part of an all-embracing totality of existence.

INFLUENCED BY nineteenth-century Romanticism and its valuing of individual experience and spiritual interpretations of the world, contemporary Paganism can be seen as a reaction against the Enlightenment celebration of reason. The term 'pagan' derives from the Latin *paganus*; *pagus* was a country district, and *paganus* came to refer to a 'country dweller'. 'Pagan' was originally a neutral term but took on a pejorative meaning among Christians in the fifth century when it became used to designate non-Christians. Modern Pagans have claimed the word as part of a critique of Christianity, which many say is patriarchal, seeking to control both women and nature. By contrast, Pagans give positive values to both, claiming that mastery of women and the domination of nature is interconnected. The psychology of Carl Jung (1875–1961) has been formative in a revaluation of 'the feminine' as a repressed psychological principle. A feminine focus has been strengthened further by the 1960s women's movement. Many feminists sought to reinterpret canonical religious texts of the Judeo-Christian tradition by editing out what they saw as patriarchal elements, others turned to the goddess – as representative of 'feminine aspects of the sacred' – arguing that formal religion had repressed this part of holiness. Many Pagans view the root of the current environmental crisis as being located in a patriarchal scientific worldview that conceives of nature as a machine rather than as a living organism.

MANY PAGAN PATHS

Being eclectic and including many different spiritual paths, Paganism comprises witchcraft, druidry, heathenism and Western shamanism amongst others. Modern witchcraft or 'wicca' was created in the 1940s and 1950s by a retired civil servant named Gerald Gardner (1884–1964) who mixed ceremonial magic with folk beliefs. Various versions of

The spirit world ... is not separate from the earth we walk upon, not some convenient semi-detached housing estate down the road you can drive away from when the tone of the neighbourhood starts to crumble. The spirit world is here beside us, always; and unseen, often unguessed, it touches and changes the world of physical forms that we live in. Our actions, in turn, change the spirit world and we can work to lighten our awareness of it....

Gordon MacLellan, 'Dancing on the Edge: Shamanism in Modern Britain', in *Paganism Today*

A white witch performing a Wicca ceremony. The Wicca movement is based on ancient Pagan rituals of magic and folklore.

witchcraft have developed from Gardner's writings, and contemporary witches are subdivided into: Gardnerians, those who derive their ways of working from Gerald Gardner; Alexandrians, practitioners of Alex Sanders' (1926–88) specific mixture of witchcraft and Kabbalistic magic; and feminist witches, those who see in witchcraft a means of overcoming patriarchal oppression.

Not much is known about the ancient druids, the Celtic spiritual leaders. Celtic beliefs were localized and few generalizations may be made, but the druids have been imagined in different periods from the Renaissance on. Modern druids believe Druidry to be one of the nature religions of the United Kingdom and worship the natural forces of the earth through the creative arts. The love and inspiration of nature is called 'Awen', and it is the role of bards to encourage the flow, and ovates to divine its process through tree lore and runes. Likewise, Heathens – practitioners of Anglo-Saxon, German and Scandinavian traditions – attempt to recapture an ancient way of life through mythology and the twelfth- and thirteenth-century sagas of Icelander Snorri Sturluson (1179–1241). The main northern tradition is known as 'Odinism' after the principle god Odin, or Asatru, meaning 'loyalty or troth to the gods'. By contrast, Western shamans often turn to non-Western indigenous religious beliefs for inspiration. Native American traditions being especially popular.

Druids celebrating the Summer Solstice at Stonehenge, UK. Druidry was revived in the eighteenth and nineteenth centuries when antiquarians such as William Stukeley and John Aubrey theorized that Stonehenge and Avebury were Druidic monuments. For modern Druids the Summer Solstice is still the highlight of the religious calendar, and holds deep spiritual significance. The sun is at its highest point, and sunlight is at its maximum, imbuing fertility upon the whole of nature.

Below: A protestor against the Newbury Bypass demonstrates in Penn Wood, England. Neo-paganism is strongly linked with the modern environmentalist movement.

CELEBRATING NATURE

A Pagan view of the world sees a relationship with the whole of nature; it places the individual within a wider connecting pattern, often visualized as a web in which all aspects of creation are seen to be in constant flux and motion. This is a dynamic and pervasive worldview where spirits coexist with everyday material reality. Many Pagans celebrate a seasonal myth cycle whereby the process of nature – birth, maturation and death – are portrayed in dynamic interaction with goddesses and gods, as personification of the powers of the cosmos. At eight points in the year – usually **Samhain** (31 October), Winter Solstice (22 December), **Imbolg** (2 February), Spring Equinox (21 March), **Bealtaine** (30 April), Summer Solstice (22 June), **Lughnasadh** (31 July), Autumn Equinox (21 September) – the changing aspects of practitioner and the gods are celebrated. This involves an interaction with the web of life as spiritual experience, linking the individual with the whole cosmos. Feeling connected to the whole of nature leads some Pagans to an involvement in environmental campaigns and, in some cases, to radical

protest against any planned destruction of the countryside. Increasingly, environmental concerns are seen to be an important spiritual component of modern Paganism.

The Culture of the West

In the West a culture has emerged which shares many of the characteristics of religions elsewhere in the world. It is called secularism, and though it specifically repudiates any attempt to apply any sense of the supernatural to its interpretation of the world, it uses similar techniques to impose intellectual and moral order on the chaos of existence.

WESTERN SECULARISM has its own revealed truths and unexamined assumptions. Among its key values are democracy, capitalism, scientific scepticism, individualism, tolerance, human rights, freedom of choice and the separation of Church and State. All this has its roots in a Judeo-Christian inheritance but, since the Enlightenment, it has been shaped by a mix of other influences – science, rationalism and the reductive determinism of Darwin and Freud.

For two centuries, secularism asserted the possibility of human perfectibility. Utilizing a philosophy which denied the existence of any values outside the natural order, it held the natural sciences to be the highest form of human knowledge. The practical changes it wrought freed energies which produced the industrial revolution, the modern democratic state, unprecedented levels of economic growth and a high culture of science, art and learning. And it brought social progress which undermined inherited privilege and improved the material life of ordinary working people. Such evolution would continue, suggested thinkers like the German sociologist Max Weber (1864–1920), who spoke of an irreversible 'shift to rationalization'. And as human beings became more rational they would have no need for religion. 'From myths to maths' was the cry.

MODERNITY

But the liberal assumption that humanity was steadily progressing to a more enlightened and tolerant state had been called into question halfway through the twentieth century. The science, capitalism and modernity which brought antibiotics, foreign holidays and consumer gadgets also brought nuclear weapons, the gas chamber, pollution and toxic waste. Contradictions and paradoxes began to emerge. With individualism came imperialism – military, economic and cultural. Out of capitalism came communism. With democracy

Max Weber (1864–1920) was born in Erfurt in Germany. He was an extremely influential sociologist who believed that as people became more sophisticated in their thinking, their need for religion would diminish.

came a free market whose dominance became an unquestionable ideology. Throughout the previous three centuries the freedom of individuals and markets had seemed indivisible but now tensions surfaced between the two. The emphasis upon individual self-interest created wealth but tended to atomize society with increases in family breakdown and in rates of crime and violence. As capitalism developed, advertising and designer branding constantly generated insatiable new levels of demand. Those who had once regarded themselves primarily as citizens began to see themselves chiefly as consumers. Morality, which once had been, like language, a shared enterprise, became the province of private conscience.

All this impacted upon the rest of the world. In developing nations – particularly in India, sub-

Saharan Africa and parts of Latin America – the forces that produced innovation and independence in the West brought chiefly imitation and dependence for the Third World. What were seen as liberating influences at home was perceived as an aggressive assault abroad. As the twentieth century continued, the forces of economic globalization only exacerbated this divide and the sense of alienation which went with it. Under the slogan of multi-culturalism, what often arrived was an impoverished mono-culturism.

SCIENTIFIC RATIONALISM

As the twentieth century progressed, many felt that the revolution of scientific rationalism had left a void at the heart of modern culture. Some, like Sartre and Camus celebrated it, but most lamented it, or at least felt uneasy at the 'God-shaped hole' which had been left behind. But as the Age of the Enlightenment finally gave way to that of post-modernism it became clear that the offspring of modernism – science, capitalism, individualism and democracy – were merely enabling mechanisms. Liberalism was what British philosopher Alistair McIntyre (b. 1929) called a 'second order morality': it sets up a framework within which other virtues can flourish, but it does not create them. A society whose moral capital had been formed by centuries of Judeo-Christian tradition became a multi-faith pluralistic society with no common store of values on which to draw. As a result, society became increasingly a conflictual forum in which ethnic communities, religious associations, single issue pressure groups and a host of others pressed their disparate claims on the state – which increasingly seemed to lack the core of shared values it needed to adjudicate on disputes between such members.

Religion was no longer replenishing this moral capital. For two centuries the institutional churches had been in decline. Membership of Protestant churches in Britain fell from 22 per cent of British adults in 1900 to six per cent 100 years later. Yet statistics also show that if organized religion was in decline, belief was not. The 1990 European Values Survey revealed that, though most people did not expect answers from the church, the number who regularly feel the need for prayer, meditation or contemplation was 53 per cent – three per cent up on a decade earlier. And the percentage of the population which emerged as avowedly atheist remained only steady at around four per cent. Everywhere religion was taking new fissiparous forms. Fundamentalism was on the rise. Environmentalism took on a religious dimension. Sects, cults and new religious movements blossomed. The children and grandchildren of the West's immigrant communities began to shape new Europeanized forms of the old religions, most particularly of Islam, stripped of the customs and traditions the older generation brought from the Third World. New Age spiritualities were experimented with by as much as a quarter of the Western population. There was a flowering of what was described as 'vague faith' in new folk practices, such as the building of roadside shrines for those killed in traffic accidents or in the response to the death of public figures like the Princess of Wales. It became known, dismissively, as 'pick and mix' religion but it was no less potent for that. Beliefs, said sociologists of religion were of an increasingly individualised and unorthodox nature.

Even science was forced to take note. Biogenetic structuralists began to suggest that there was something in the gene-proteins of human DNA which was pre-programmed to seek after the sacred. Even in the secular West, religion would not go away.

Congregation at a joint Methodist and Baptist church in Taffs Well, Wales. Many denominations, especially those derived from the mainstream Protestant tradition, now hold joint services and sometimes share church space, due to falling attendance levels.

Flowers placed outside Kensington Palace after the death of Diana, Princess of Wales, in September 1997. Diana's death seems to have revived a folk tradition of placing flowers in public spaces as a memorial.

Religion in the Modern World
Conflict of Ideologies

For all its strength – or perhaps because of it – the culture of the West provoked a number of religious and ideological reactions. The most dramatic of these was fundamentalism. More moderate religious forces also increasingly challenged many modernist Western assumptions. But, in this clash of ideologies, the secular West was always the benchmark for religion's responses.

A Muslim Palestinian passes the fourth station of the Cross on the Via Dolorosa, the road that Jesus is supposed to have taken to the Crucifixion, in Jerusalem. Jewish graffiti has been scribbled on the door.

FUNDAMENTALISM FIRST arose early in the twentieth century among some Protestants in the United States who used the term as one of approval to distinguish themselves from more liberal Christians who were, in their opinion, distorting the faith. Its five fundamentals were: the literal inerrancy of the Bible, the divinity of Jesus Christ, the Virgin Birth, the physical resurrection and bodily return of Christ, and the idea that the Atonement would happen on an individual level rather than be a universal phenomenon.

From the outset it defined itself as a reaction against modernism, and yet it was itself very modernist in the rationalism it applied to religion and its insistence that the Book of Genesis is scientifically sound it its every detail. The literalism it applied to the Scriptures went back to the fundamentals in a peculiarly modern way.

CO-EXISTENCE

In previous ages Christians had been happy to allow two ways of looking at the world to co-exist. Religion primarily located itself in a style of thinking which reached into the deeper layers of the human mind concerned with meaning; its tools were aesthetic – myth, rituals, poetry, music, art – and it took as its norm an allegorical mystical understanding of Scripture. More day to day concerns were governed by an approach which was empirical and rational, and concerned itself with the mechanics of how things got done, and could be made to happen

The Revival of Religious Conflict
By the 1960s religion seemed to be in decline across the world. In the last 30 years, however, it has revived remarkably, and conflict and violence have returned with it. Although religion is not always the major factor in conflicts, its role is increasing. Other contributing factors may include territorial, politcal or ethnic issues.

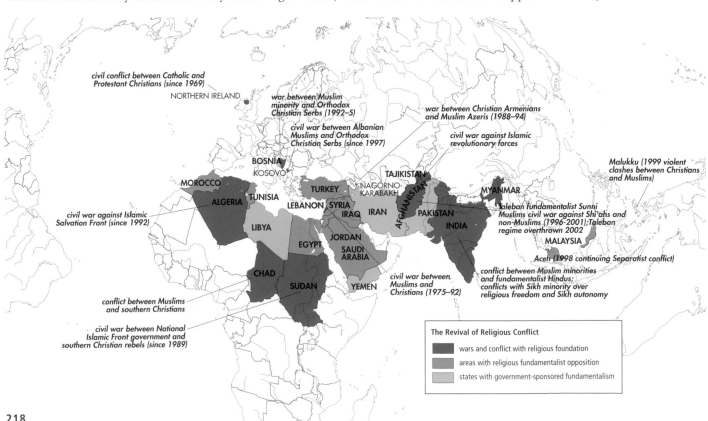

civil conflict between Catholic and Protestant Christians (since 1969)
NORTHERN IRELAND

war between Muslim minority and Orthodox Christian Serbs (1992–5)

civil war between Albanian Muslims and Orthodox Christian Serbs (since 1997)

war between Christian Armenians and Muslim Azeris (1988–94)

civil war against Islamic revolutionary forces

BOSNIA
KOSOVO

MOROCCO

TURKEY

TAJIKISTAN

NAGORNO-KARABAKH

Malukku (1999 violent clashes between Christians and Muslims)

MYANMAR

ALGERIA   TUNISIA   LEBANON   SYRIA   IRAN   PAKISTAN

civil war against Islamic Salvation Front (since 1992)

LIBYA   IRAQ   AFGHANISTAN   INDIA

Taleban fundamentalist Sunni Muslims civil war against Shi'ahs and non-Muslims (1996-2001);Taleban regime overthrown 2002

JORDAN   EGYPT   SAUDI ARABIA

MALAYSIA

Aceh (1998 continuing Separatist conflict)

CHAD   SUDAN   YEMEN

civil war between Muslims and Christians (1975–92)

conflict between Muslim minorities and fundamentalist Hindus; conflicts with Sikh minority over religious freedom and Sikh autonomy

conflict between Muslims and southern Christians

civil war between National Islamic Front government and southern Christian rebels (since 1989)

The Revival of Religious Conflict
- wars and conflict with religious foundation
- areas with religious fundamentalist opposition
- states with government-sponsored fundamentalism

more efficiently. It could not assuage human pain or sorrow or explain the meaning of life, and did not try to. The difficulty came when the Enlightenment, with its science and sceptical rationalism, came to regard reason as 'true' and myth as 'false' and superstitious. Alarmed by this, fundamentalists tried to insist that religious truths were in fact true literally and scientifically. Their mythology became an ideology. And science and religion went head-to-head in the trial of John Scopes, in Tennessee in 1925, who had been teaching schoolchildren Darwin's theory of evolution. Scopes was convicted, but fundamentalism was the real loser in the case. Creationists have since been forced to create ever more elaborate justifications for their position.

But the pull of such a radical response to secular modernism has continued to be powerfully felt, and not just in the Bible Belt of the United States. Though many scholars argue the term fundamentalist is not theologically accurate when applied to other religions, similar visceral reactions to secularism have been felt in other faiths where traditional ideals and beliefs come into conflict with Western values. In Judaism, Islam, Hinduism, Buddhism and even Confucianism, something similar has been found – and with sometimes violent consequences. Fundamentalists have in Iran toppled a government: in Israel and Egypt they shot their own presidents; in India they caused the death of thousands in riots; in Afghanistan they shrouded the entire female population in veils and chadours on pain of death; in Indonesia they fed bloody tribal conflicts; in the United States they killed doctors who work in abortion clinics and in the United Kingdom they forced a leading writer, Salman Rushdie, into hiding for years with death threats.

To characterize each of these as fundamentalist disguises some key differences. Christian fundamentalists tend to focus on issues of doctrine – which is why there are such intense clashes between evangelical missionaries and the Roman Catholic Church in Latin America. By contrast their Jewish and Muslim counterparts are more concerned with practice – and with observing their revealed law more rigorously than ever before. Then again, Hindu zealots, who in 1992 destroyed the 400-year-old Muslim mosque in Ayodhya and have persecuted both the Muslims and Christian minorities, have developed a fundamentalism much more akin to a religious nationalism.

EXCLUSIVISM

What these all have in common is a new exclusivism which was previously alien to all the major faiths. Ancient Hinduism was tolerant in its own way, as was medieval Muslim civilization, and there was an open-mindedness to the traditional practice of Judaism and Christianity which is lacking in modern fundamentalists driven by resentment, rage and revenge. In all this the focus of the discontent is largely the culture of the West, though in India fundamentalists also kick against a Muslim incursion eight centuries ago, and in Afghanistan the fanatics, disdain for anything non-Islamic extended even to ancient religious artefacts, including the world's biggest statues of the Buddha which were blown up in 2001. All these fundamentalisms share a sense of domination and humiliation by Western cultue, in particular the economic and military power of the United States which is widely regarded in the Arab world as 'the Great Satan'. This antipathy reached a terrifying climax on 11 September 2001 when terrorists, claiming to act in the name of Islam, crashed two planes into the World Trade Center in New York and one into the US military headquarters in the Pentagon, Washington DC. More than 4,000 people died. In response, the United States launched a 'war on terrorism'.

Yet this clash of ideologies is not restricted to those who see the West as the enemy in a cosmic war between good and evil. Western culture is far from homogenous and there have been many internal critiques of its dominant ideology. Whether or not religion dies away further in the West there is no doubt that internal Western ideological and moral differences will continue to be coloured for some time yet by a dialogue between religious and secular values.

Taleban rebels outside Kabul, Afghanistan, during the Taliban's sweeping conquest of the country in 1996. The Taliban went on to impose one of the most hardline fundamentalist Islamic regimes ever known, banning women from appearing in public, medicine and any form of education, as well as virtually all music and art.

Multi-faith Societies

A multi-faith society, meaning a society in which there is more than one religion, is not a recent phenomenon. India for instance has provided a home for all the major world religions for many centuries. The court of the sixteenth-century Muslim Emperor Akbar was multi-faith, and the emperor himself took a great interest in all religions even trying to evolve a synthesis of them to bring faiths together in harmony. Historically, China has been a multi-faith society too and even today has five major religions, although as a Communist country it is officially atheist.

IN THE SECOND half of the twentieth century migration, from Asia, Africa and the Caribbean has introduced different religions into many European countries which were formerly regarded as mono-faith Christian societies. Those European countries had minorities such as Jews for many centuries, but it was only with the twentieth-century migrations that they came to regard themselves as multi-faith societies. With their non-Christian faiths, the migrants also brought different cultures and were of a different colour to the majority white population. These three factors have created difficulties in absorbing the migrants from Asia, Africa and the Caribbean.

A poster calling for religious harmony in Madras, India. It shows symbols of the three major religions of India: Hinduism, Islam and Christianity.

WAYS OF LIVING TOGETHER

There are at least three different ways in which countries today live with more than one faith. Some demand that everyone should accept the dominance of one faith and only allow minorities to carve out limited spaces for themselves. No minority is allowed any rights which dilute the mono-faith character of society. Countries which define themselves by their religion, such as Pakistan which has declared itself to be an Islamic nation, fall into that category. In Pakistan, non-Muslims do not share the same voting rights as Muslims, and while they do have freedom of worship they live under the fear of offending against the stringent laws forbidding blasphemy against Islam. In Western European countries there are politicians who take a similar, but less draconian line. While not opposing freedom of worship they do demand that minorities conform to 'the national culture' and would usually describe that culture as Christian.

Mahatma Gandhi openly proclaimed his faith in Hinduism, India's majority religion and his pride in its contribution to the culture of his country. But at the same time the Mahatma rejoiced in India's multi-faith tradition and gave his life for promoting harmony between Hindus and Muslims. It is the Mahatma's model that most European countries follow. In the United Kingdom, for instance there is still an established Church, but wherever there are communities which are not Christian there are mosques, temples or gurudwaras. All major political parties accept the rights of minority religions and from time to time acknowledge their contributions to society.

Some multi-faith countries have declared themselves to be secular in order to distance their governments from any association with the majority religion. Secular India allows complete freedom of worship and of religious practice but although 80 per cent of Indians are classified as Hindus, neither they nor any other religion is permitted to play any role in public life and Hinduism is not treated as the national religion. The constitution commits the government to treating all religions equally in every respect. But the word secular can lead to the impression that the official policy is opposed to all religious belief. At the same time the declaration of a country as secular can create a sense of grievance among believers in the majority faith who feel that some recognition of the past and present contribution their beliefs, traditions and culture have made should be acknowledged. Both these problems have arisen in India.

Mahatma Gandhi and other members of the resistance movement against the British march to Jalalpur in 1930, protesting against the Salt Tax. Gandhi's life was dedicated to the promotion of the multi-faith society, showing that people of different faiths could live side by side in the same country.

CO-OPERATION AND RECONCILIATION

In part at least because of the increase in multi-faith societies, leaders of world religions are now far more ready not just to talk but to see good in each other. Christian Churches traditionally interpreted the words of Jesus in St John's gospel, 'I am the way the truth and the life, no man cometh to the father but by me' as meaning that Christianity was the only way to God, that it had a monopoly of the truth. Now the Western churches acknowledge that there are universal truths to be found in all the historic religions. They face a difficult theological balancing act in allowing truth to other religions while at the same time teaching the unique nature of Jesus, but it is a balance they are trying to keep. During his papacy Pope John Paul II has gone out of his way to promote understanding and to heal historic wounds between the Roman Catholic Church, other Christian Churches and other faiths too. But religious tensions, which can all too easily lead to violence, survive in almost all multi-faith societies. The best hope for harmony lies in the reconciliation and mutual respect that the Pope and other religious leaders are promoting.

The Cao Dai Temple, Saigon, Vietnam, which has represented a synthesis of three religions, Confucianism, Taoism and Buddhism, since it was built in 1926.

Science and Religion

The Scientific Revolution signalled, for some, the death of God and the replacement of worn-out superstitions with theories, measurements and calculations. But, while science and religion might offer competing answers to ultimate questions, they have not always engaged in war. Rather, their paths to absolute truth have often intertwined, innovations in one leading to developments in the other.

ASTRONOMY, THE MOST ancient science, was inspired by the desire to decipher the divine mysteries of the heavenly bodies while the progress of modern science was smoothed by the Biblical teaching that the natural world is a creation, that creation can be known and that history is linear. Many of the founders of modern western science were Christians seeking to demonstrate that humans lived in an orderly universe. But, while Nicolaus Copernicus (1473–1543) and Isaac Newton (1642–1727) were both Christians, they were also inspired by alchemy, an ancient mystical-scientific tradition that sought to uncover nature's secrets and which, for some, promised to reveal the mystery of eternal life. In modern times, alchemy continues to be a focus for various alternative mystical paths.

As the scientific worldview increasingly came to dominate, especially in intellectual circles, so too did an image of God as the rational architect of an ordered world, a type of divine 'watchmaker'. The publication of Charles Darwin's *On the Origin of Species* in 1859 offered what many considered to be a fatal blow to the design argument, stressing as it did natural selection and chance mutation (see box). At the same time, it spurred some Christians to renew their efforts to read the Bible as if it were a scientific manual. Other religions similarly find scientific truths in their sacred texts; Islam, for example claims that the Qur'an contains the basics of embryology, citing verses such as 23:12-16 which describe the development of a child from a tiny drop in the womb.

A RESPONSE FROM THE NEW RELIGIONS

In opposition both to the dominant scientific paradigm (notably orthodox medicine) and to mainstream Christianity, a number of new religions emerged, drawing on pseudo or alternative science. The 'New Thought'

movement, which arose in the United States in the mid-nineteenth century, taught that 'Every phenomenon in the natural world has its origin in the spiritual world'. New Thought drew on a variety of sources, including the teachings of Anton Mesmer, an eighteenth-century physician who made scientific claims for the existence of a universal life force and whose practice of Mesmerism, based on this belief, was a forerunner of hypnotism. New Thought

A 1570 painting of an alchemist's laboratory. Alchemy, which combined practical science with mystical thinking and quests for elusive magical substances, was thought to provide a way of understanding nature's secrets and, many believed, held the key to eternal life.

influenced movements from Christian Science to Spiritualism and the New Age. Both Christian Science and Spiritualism are Christian-based movements which arose in the nineteenth century; the former focuses on spiritual healing and the latter on communication with spirits of the dead. The New Age is an umbrella term for a myriad of movements, groups and teachings which have in common the belief that the inner self is the source of the divine. In the twentieth century, the scientific community's Gaia Hypothesis, which stresses the interconnectedness of creation rather than the dominance of man over nature, was hugely influential in Neopaganism. Other new religions seek to have their claims validated by mainstream science. Transcendental Meditation, for example, claims to have been the subject of reports in more than 100 scientific journals. Still others take inspiration from science fiction; the founder of the Raelian UFO religion teaches that 'science should be your religion' and tells how he witnessed a flying saucer land and met its small, greenish occupant.

Today, many scientific studies which seemed to give reason for scepticism and even atheism have been shown to be either misleading or mistaken. One recent development, the 'Anthropic Principle', gives compelling evidence for a Creator, arguing that the universe seems to have been designed to support life. Perhaps Newton was right when he said that a little knowledge leads away from God, but much knowledge leads towards Him.

Charles Darwin, who proposed the theory of evolution in *The Origin of Species*. Darwin largely shunned the religious controversy caused by his work, leaving public argument to disciples such as the biologist Thomas Huxley (1825–1895).

THE SCOPES TRIAL

From the publication of Darwin's *On the Origin of Species* in 1859, conservative Christians in the United States led the fight against evolutionary teaching. In 1925 Tennessee passed the Butler Act, making it illegal 'to teach any theory that denies the Story of Divine Creation of man as taught in the Bible, and to teach instead that man has descended from a lower order of animal'.

John Scopes, a Tennessee High School science teacher taught the forbidden doctrine and was arrested. The ensuing so-called Scopes or Monkey Trial was heralded as the original 'trial of the century' and represents one of the deepest and most persistent conflicts of modern American culture. Swamped with hundreds of reporters, it became the topic of conversation as far away as Italy, Russia, India and China.

The jury found Scopes guilty. The Tennessee Supreme Court later reversed the judgement on a technicality but upheld the constitutionality of the Butler Act. Editors excised any serious treatment of evolution from science textbooks and the teaching of evolution effectively disappeared from the nation's public schools until the 1960s.

Today, polls indicate that around half of adult Americans and a quarter of college graduates continue to doubt Darwinian explanations of human origins.

John Scopes was the high school teacher who, in 1925, agreed to challenge the Tennessee state legislatures law forbidding the teaching of evolution, leading to the famous Scopes Trial, which eventually resulted in the law being overturned.

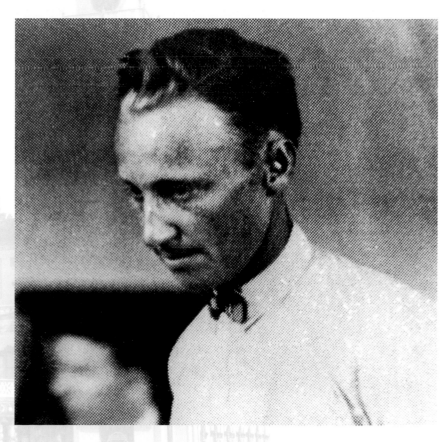

Women and Religion

Women have usually played a subordinate role in patriarchal world religions, but have been revered as mystics and even leaders in many new religions and sects. Feminists are campaigning successfully for the right to ordination. However, many women are leaving organized religion to join goddess spirituality movements, which offer a more holistic spirituality, with intrinsic respect for traditionally feminine qualities such as fertility and creation, which in turn encompass a respect for life, nature and the female gender.

WOMEN HAVE ALWAYS been interested in religion and spirituality, but have usually been disparaged, excluded and oppressed by organized religion. Sometimes it seems that the only salvation offered is to become submissive wives and gain redemption through the suffering and sacrifice of childbirth, or occasionally as virgin martyrs. The founders of world religions exemplified progressive, compassionate attitudes to women, but their reforms were subverted by priesthoods and theologians into orthodoxies supporting the misogyny of patriarchal societies. As the prominent feminist theologian Mary Daly says: 'Even if in Christ there is neither male nor female, everywhere else there certainly is.' Liberal traditions have promoted greater equality, but even in interfaith dialogue the main speakers, events and publications are by men and the theology displays an androcentric bias.

There are very few examples of women in positions of formal authority and leadership, although the medieval abbess Hildegard of Bingen (1098–1179) was a preacher, poet, scientist, composer, healer, administrator and counsellor to kings and popes. Women have always been more active on the margins as saints and mystics. Muhammad's daughter Fatima (AD 616–662) is often recognized as the first Muslim mystic, and Rabia (AD 717–801) one of the most prominent Sufi mystics. A few women have risen as founders and leaders of religious groups, such as the Quaker Mother Ann Lee (1736–1784). In esoteric tradition, 'feminine' qualities such as intuition and sensitivity are valued; women are believed to possess greater magical power, and have excelled as psychics and healers, shamans and seers.

FEMINIST THEOLOGY

Within the 1970s women's movement, religion was initially rejected as irrelevant and irredeemably patriarchal. However, many

A Jewish wedding with a female rabbi. Both the Reform and Conservative denominations of Judaism now ordain women.

women wanted to participate as equal members and priests; they therefore began to challenge religious sexism. Feminist theology developed mainly within Christianity and to some extent Judaism, but its aims and methods are being increasingly adopted within other world religions, particularly Hinduism and Western Buddhism. It operates by questioning practices that keep women subordinated and excluded from the priesthood and policy-making; also by criticizing values, in particular masculine language and symbolism for God. Practical measures include reinterpreting and rewriting sacred texts, reclaiming forgotten or undervalued women as heroines and role models, creating gender-inclusive liturgy.

Some women take a reformist position, working to achieve equality within their tradition. The feminist theologian Rosemary Radford Ruether includes pre-Christian goddess religion, heretical traditions and ecofeminism in her prophetic-liberationist vision. More radical feminists such as Mary Daly have moved beyond the fold as post-Christians. Other women who reject organized religion join new religions that give more power to women, such as the Osho movement and the Brahma Kumaris, or join pagan goddess-worshipping movements, particularly Wicca and feminist witchcraft.

PRIEST/ESSES

The key issue in feminist theology is ordination for women. In many ancient religions, the goddess was served by priestesses, and her messages were channelled through female oracles. Women performed priestly functions in early Buddhism and Christianity, but were disenfranchized after patriarchal routinization. Women are campaigning vigorously for the right of ordination in both Christianity and in Buddhism, especially Mahayana Buddhism. Arguments based on theology and tradition have been successfully refuted, to the point where women can become rabbis in Reform and Conservative Judaism, and priests (though not always bishops) in many Christian denominations.

Many of those who are frustrated by traditional religions are joining goddess-worshipping pagan groups. Wiccan covens are led by a priest and priestess, but the priestess usually takes precedence and controls the ritual, while feminist witchcraft includes groups where women are the sole priests and the goddess alone is worshipped.

Women are often priestesses in African-derived magical religions such as voudoun and obeah. One 'Mambo' or voodoo priest, is shown here in a painting by Hector Hyppolite (1894–1948).

GODDESS SPIRITUALITY

The most obvious manifestation of sexism in the monotheistic religions is the lack of any female person or element in the concept of divinity. Some Jewish and Christian feminists are reclaiming Lilith (Adam's legendary first wife revisioned as the Creatrix) and Hochmah/Sophia, the Biblical figure of Wisdom and exemplar of the divine feminine. The Virgin Mary is also widely elevated in popular devotion and sometimes revisioned as a mother goddess, though she is also felt to be an unsuitable role model for modern women. Women's spirituality movements have rediscovered many Greek, Egyptian, Celtic and African goddesses as symbols of creativity, healing and empowerment. Hinduism offers a rich multiplicity of images from the gentle beauty of Uma to the fearsome power of Kali.

The goddess is the central theme of thealogy (goddess theology), though there is disagreement regarding her meaning and status – whether she is a literal deity, personification of Mother Earth (Gaia), or psychological symbol (the 'goddess within'). Uniting the women's spirituality movement is the vision of a holistic spirituality, which will heal and reintegrate the duality between body-spirit, male-female, humanity-nature. All goddess worshippers agree that 'We don't want God with a skirt' – a feminized version of the Judeo-Christian transcendent, despotic deity. In the words of Starhawk, American feminist witch: 'The Goddess does not rule the world; she is the world.'

The Virgin Mary, as pictured here, is one of the world's most important female religious icons, especially for Catholics.

Chronology

	100,000 BC	50,000 BC	25,000 BC	10,000 BC	8000 BC	6000 BC
AFRICA **BC**	100,000: Earliest evidence of modern man in eastern and southern Africa.		25,000: Evidence of rock art in Tanzania.	8500: Evidence of rock art in Saharan region.		c. 6000: Earliest cultivation of cereal, northern Africa.
AMERICAS **BC**		30,000: Earliest human settlement in the Americas, Brazil.		10,000: Human settlement reaches southern tip of South America. 8500: Evidence of crop cultivation, Peru.	7000: Crop cultivation begins in Tehuacán Valley, Mexico. 7000: Beginning of manioc cultivation, Amazon. 7000: Semi-permanent settlements in North America; some crop cultivation.	
ASIA **(EXCLUDING NEAR EAST)** **BC**		50,000: First settlement of Australia by migrants originating from Southeast Asia.	25,000: Expansion of settlement in New Guinea Highlands and Australia.	9000: Early Chinese pottery.	7000: Agriculture begins, New Guinea. c. 7000: Evidence of rice cultivation, China.	
EUROPE **BC**		35,000: Beginning of Upper Palaeolithic. Appearance of modern man in Europe. 30,000: Earliest cave art in southern France; stone carvings, for example Venus figures, in Spain.			7000: First farming in Aegean and Greece; Iberia and Low Countries 5000; Britain and Scandinavia 4000.	
NEAR EAST **BC**				9000: Sheep first domesticated in northern Mesopotamia. 8350: First walled town (Jericho) founded.	8000: Evidence of domesticated crops (pulses and cereals) in the Fertile Crescent. 7000: First pottery. 7000: Early settlers in Canaan region.	

5000 BC	4000 BC	3000 BC	2000 BC	1800 BC	1600 BC
	4000: North African populations migrate south and east. 3100: Emergence of Egyptian state; new capital at Memphis.	3000: Evidence of Egyptian hieroglyphics. c. 2686: 'Old Kingdom' in Egypt begins (age of the pyramids). 2590: Great pyramid at Giza built. 2150: Collapse of Egyptian Old Kingdom. 2040: Middle Kingdom established, Egypt.	c. 1990: Egyptian conquests of Nubia. 1990: Middle Kingdom rulers buried in pyramids.	1783: Fall of Middle Kingdom, Egypt.	1539: New Kingdom begins, Egypt.
5000: Maize first cultivated in Tehuacán Valley, Mexico.		3000: Maize cultivation reaches South America. 2500: Large, permanent settlements established in South America.	2000: First metal-working in Peru.		1500: Beginning of the Olmec civilization, Mexico (to c. AD 200).
5000: Rising of sea levels results in New Guinea and Tasmania being separated from Australia.		3000: First agricultural settlements, Southeast Asia. c. 2500: Beginnings of Indus Valley culture; development of urban civilization.		c. 1750: Collapse of Indus Valley civilization. c. 1650: Indo-Ayrans begin to arrive in India.	c. 1520: Beginning of Shang dynasty, China. 1500: Settlers migrate from Indonesia to Melaneisa and Polynesia. c. 1450: Development of Brahma worship; composition of the Vedas begins.
	3200: First wheeled vehicles. 3200: Megalithic standing stone circles, mainly in Britain and north-west France.	3000: Walled citadels built in Mediterranean area. 2950: Main phase of construction of Stonehenge. 2300: Beginning of Bronze Age.	2000: Beginning of Minoan civilization, Crete.		1600: Beginning of Mycenaean civilization, Greece.
c. 5000: Colonization of Mesopotamian alluvial plain; irrigation is practised.	c. 4000: Bronze casting begins; plough first used. 3300: Settlers from Anatolia arrive in Sumeria; first city-states built. 3100: Temples at Uruk constructed; ceremonial complexes built as centres of early Mesopotamian cities. 3100: Invention of cuneiform script, Mesopotamia.	2200: Ziggurats first built in Mesopotamia. c. 2200: Old Empire begins, Babylonia (to c. 1750).	2000: Myths of Gilgamesh written in Sumerian language on clay tablets. 2000: Birth of Abraham. c. 2000: Hittites invade Anatolia and found empire.	1650: Hittite kingdom founded, Anatolia.	

	1400 BC	1200 BC	1000 BC	800 BC	600 BC	500 BC
AFRICA	1352: Reign of Akhenaten, Egyptian pharaoh, begins (to 1336). 1322: Death of Tutankhamun; buried in Valley of the Kings, Egypt. c. 1280: Exodus from Egypt and Sinai.	1156: Death of Rameses III, Egyptian pharaoh. 1069: End of New Kingdom, Egypt.		664: Late Period begins, Egypt.		500: Nok Culture in Nigeria.
AMERICAS				700: Chavin de Huantar civilization emerged, Andes (to c. 200).		c. 500: Beginning of Zapotec civilization, Mexico (to c. AD 700); foundation of Monte Albán, Zapotec capital city. 500: First hieroglyphics, Zapotec culture, Mexico. 200: Rise of the Mochica civilization (to c. AD 650).
ASIA (EXCLUDING NEAR EAST)		1030: Zhou dynasty overthrows Shang dynasty.	1000: Villages of round stone houses established, southern Australia.	800: Composition of Upanishads begins. 771: Collapse of Zhou dynasty, China; Eastern Zhou begins. c. 660: Jimmu, Japan's legendary first emperor. 605: Birth of Lao Zi (traditional founder of Taoism).	566: Birth of Gautama Siddhartha (the Buddha). 551: Birth of Confucius. 520: Death of Lao Zi. 527: Death of Mahavira, founder of Jainism.	500: Wet-rice agriculture, Japan. 500: Beginnings of Shinto, Japan. 486: Death of the Buddha. 479: Death of Confucius.
EUROPE		1150: Collapse of Mycenaean Greece.	1000: Beginning of Iron Age (Central Europe). 1000: Etruscans arrive in Italy.	800: Beginning of Celtic Iron Age (Hallstatt). 800: Rise of Etruscan city-states, Italy. 700: End of Greek 'Dark Age'; beginnings of rise of Greek city-states. 753: Foundation of city of Rome.	580: Birth of Pythagoras. 509: Tarquinus Superbus, last of Rome's Etruscan kings, is expelled; Roman Republic established.	480: Second stage of Celtic Iron Age (La Tène). 480: Beginning of Classical Period, Greece. 450: Apogee of Athens as most powerful city-state, Greece. 432: Completion of the Parthenon, Athens.
NEAR EAST		1200: Collapse of Hittite empire. 1200: Israelites reach Canaan; beginning of Israelite religion (worship of Yahweh).	1000: Kingdom of Israel emerges with Jerusalem as capital. 990: Israelites defeat Canaanites. 950: Destruction of Canaanite altars and idols by King Solomon of Israel; First Temple built, Jerusalem.	746: Establishment of Assyrian empire (to 612). 705: Nineveh becomes capital of Assyria. 668: Beginning of reign of King Ashurbanipal, Assyria (to 627). 625: Neo Empire founded, Babylon (to 539).	551: Death of Zarathustra. 550: Foundation of Persian empire. c. 588: Zoroastrianism becomes official religion in Persia. 586: Babylonian capture of the Jews; destruction of the First Temple, Jerusalem.	

400 BC	300 BC	200 BC	100 BC	50 BC	AD 1
323: Ptolemaic Period, Egypt (to 30).				30: Egypt becomes Roman province.	**AD**
					AD 1: Rise of settlement in southwest North America. 1: Complex cultures emerge in Pacific Northwest.
383: Second Buddhist Council. 371: Birth of Mencius (follower of Confucius).	298: Birth of Xun Zi (follower of Confucius). 250: First urban settlements, Southeast Asia. 221: Qin dynasty unites China; Great Wall built. 206: Han dynasty reunites China (to ad 9).		100: Indian religions spread to Southeast Asia.	50: Jainism spreads into southern India.	**AD** 25: Later Han dynasty (to AD 220), China.
399: Death of Socrates. 390: Celts sack Rome.	264: Punic Wars, Mediterranean. 250: Rome controls all peninsular Italy. 206: Rome controls Spain.	200: Arrival of mystery religions in Rome 146: Greece under Roman domination.		48: Julius Caesar conquers Gaul. 46: Introduction of Julian Calendar. 27: Collapse of Roman Republic; beginning of Roman Empire.	**AD** 43: Roman invasion of Britain.
				6–4 BC Birth of Jesus Christ.	**AD** 31: Crucifixion of Jesus Christ. 46: Beginning of St Paul's missions (to 57).

	AD 50	AD 100	AD 200	AD 300	AD 350	AD 400
AFRICA	50: Expansion of Kingdom of Axum (Ethiopia) begins.	150: Domination of the Sudan by Berber and Mandingo tribes begins.				400: First towns in sub-Saharan Africa. 429: Vandals establish kingdom in north Africa.
AMERICAS		100: Nasca culture, Peru (to c. 650). 100: Rise of urban metropolis of Teotihuacán, Mexico. 150: Pyramid of the Sun constructed, Teotihuacán, Mexico.		300: Rise of Maya civilization, Mesoamerica (to c. 900).		
ASIA **(EXCLUDING NEAR EAST)**		125: Third Buddhist Council; acceptance of Buddha image. 150: Buddhism spreads to China.	220: Collapse of Han dynasty, China. 280: Western Qin dynasty unites China. 285: Confucianism introduced in Japan.	300: Foundation of Yamato state, Japan.		400: Settlement of Hawaiian islands.
EUROPE	64: Roman massacre of Druids, Anglesey, North Wales; beginning of persecution of Christians.	117: Roman Empire at its apogee. 125: Building of Hadrian's Wall, Britain.	200: Beginning of Mithraism.	313: Edict of Milan: toleration granted to all religions in Roman Empire. 325: Council of Nicea called by Emperor Constantine; date of Easter is fixed. 330: Constantinople established as capital of eastern Roman Empire.	381: Christianity made official religion of the Roman Empire. 392: Pagan ceremonies banned in Roman Empire. 395: Division of Roman Empire into western branch (led to Roman Catholic and later, Protestant churches) and eastern branch (led to Orthodox churches of Greece, Russia and Eastern Europe).	410: Sack of Rome by Visgoths. 449: Invasion of Britain by Angles, Saxons and Jutes begins. 476: Deposition of las Roman emperor in west.
NEAR EAST	70: Destruction of the Second Temple, Jerusalem; Jewish diaspora begins.					404: Latin version of the Bible completed.

AD 500	AD 600	AD 650	AD 700	AD 750	AD 800
0: Arrival of Bantus southern Africa; troduction of omesticated cattle d iron.	600: First known state in Ghana, western Africa. 641: Arab conquest of north Africa.				

0: Buddhism troduced from Korea Japan. 9: China reunified der Sui dynasty.	607: Chinese cultural influence of Japan begins. 618: Tang dynasty unifies China. 645: Introduction of Buddhism to Tibet.	650: All major Polynesian islands settled.		780: Construction of Javanese Buddhist temple at Borobudur begins.	802: Kingdoms, including Angkor, Cambodia, founded in Southeast Asia.

0: Germanic oples migrate stwards to England d France; spread of ermanic religions. 0: Gregory the Great tends papal power.				787: First Viking raid recorded	800: Charlemagne crowned emperor in Rome; beginning of Holy Roman empire.

1: Birth of uhammad.	610: Quranic verses revealed to Muhammad. 622: First *hijrah* by Muhammad to Makkah ; beginning of Muslim calendar. 632: Death of Muhammad. 632: Beginning of period of Orthodox Caliphs (to 661); collation of the Qur'an.	661: Umayyad Arabia. dynasty begins (to 750); spread of Islamic empire.		750: Abbasid dynasty begins (to 1258).	

	AD 850	AD 900	AD 1000	AD 1100	AD 1200	AD 1250
AFRICA		900: Settlement of Arabs on eastern coast. 969: Foundation of Cairo by Fatimids.			1200: Construction of rock-hewn churches, Ethiopia. 1200: Rise of Mali, west Africa.	1250: West African empire of Benin emerges.
AMERICAS		900: Rise of Toltec civilization, Mesoamerica (to c. 1200).	1000: Rise of Chimú civilization, Andes (to c. 1470).	1100: Toltec capital Tula founded. 1100: Height of Pueblo culture, North America.		
ASIA (EXCLUDING NEAR EAST)	850: Colonization of New Zealand by Polynesian settlers.	900: Large-scale construction of Hindu temples, India.	1000: Construction of Easter Island statues begins.	1130: Zhu Xi born (influential figure in Neo-Confucianism). 1150: Construction of Buddhist temple of Angkor Wat, Cambodia. 1175: Muhammed Ghuri invades India and begins the establishment of a Muslim empire.	c. 1200: Zen Buddhism founded in Japan. 1200: Rise of Polynesian chiefdoms.	
EUROPE		989: Foundation of Russian Orthodox church.	1054: Great Schism begins. 1066: Norman conquest of England. 1073: Gregory VII elected pope; beginning of conflict between Empire and Papacy. 1095: Pope Urban II makes the call to Holy Wars. 1096: Beginning of the First Crusade.	1198: Innocent III becomes pope.	1232: Establishment of the Inquisition.	
NEAR EAST		935: Qur'an finalized.	1099: Crusader knights capture Jerusalem.			1258: Mongols sack Baghdad; Abbasid caliphs remain as spiritual leaders (until 1517); further spread of Islam.

AD 1300	AD 1350	AD 1400	AD 1450	AD 1500	AD 1530
		1400: Manufacture of bronze artefacts begins, Benin. 1415: Beginning of Portuguese empire in Africa.	1492: Conquest of north African coast by Spanish.	1505: Portuguese trading posts established, east Africa. 1520: Beginning of slave trade to New World from West Africa.	
	1350: Rise of Aztec civilization, Mesoamerica (to c. 1521); Aztec capital Tenochtitlán founded. 1350: Collapse of Pueblo culture, North America.		1438: Establishment of Inca empire. 1470: Chimú kingdom conquered by Incas. 1492: Christopher Columbus discovers New World. 1498: Columbus discovers South America.	1519: Spanish under Hernán Cortés arrive in Mexico. 1521: Aztec empire destroyed by Spanish.	1532: Spaniards destroy Inca empire under Francisco Pizarro.
			1469: Birth of Nanak first Sikh Guru.		1539: Death of Guru Nanak.
	1378: Great Schism in the Papacy. 1378: Urban VI becomes pope.		1492: Jews expelled from Spain.	1517: '95 Theses' posted by Martin Luther on church door at Wittenberg. 1519: Charles V of Spain and Netherlands, elected Holy Roman Emperor. 1521: Martin Luther excommunicated; beginning of Protestant Reformation. 1523: Clement VII becomes pope. 1517: Ottoman Turks take over Caliphate (until First World War).	1534: Paul III becomes pope; Henry VIII establishes Church of England and breaks with Rome. 1536: Jean Calvin publishes Institutes of the Christian Religion. 1540: Ignatius Loyola founds the Society of Jesus (Jesuits). 1545: Council of Trent.

	AD 1550	AD 1600	AD 1700	AD 1750	AD 1800	AD 1850
AFRICA		1652: Dutch colony founded, Cape Colony.	1700: Rise of Ashanti power (Gold Coast).		1807: Slave trade abolished (within British empire). 1822: Colony for freed slaves established in Liberia.	1852: South African Republic established. 1869: Suez canal opens.
AMERICAS		1607: First permanent English settlement in North America (Virginia, Jamestown). 1620: Puritans reach New England in the Mayflower. 1625: New Amsterdam (New York) founded by Dutch settlers.	1724: Vitus Bering explores route between Siberia and North America.	1775: American Revolution. 1776: American Declaration of Independence. 1783: American Independence recognized by Britain.	1830: Joseph Smith founds the Church of Jesus Christ of Latter-day Saints (Mormons), USA. 1830: President Jackson orders mass relocation of native peoples, USA.	1861: American Civil War begins (to 1865). 1863: Seventh Day Adventists founded. 1863: Slavery abolished, USA. 1867: Dominion of Canada established. 1870: Birth of Marcus Garvey. 1872: Jehovah's Witnesses founded.
ASIA (EXCLUDING NEAR EAST)		1629: First Europeans on Australian soil. 1645: Discovery of New Zealand. 1669: Tenth and final Guru, Gobind Singh forms Khalsa ('Pure Ones') of Sikhism.	1707: Guru Gobind Singh dies.	1788: British colony of Australia founded.	1801: 'Kingdom of Lahore' proclaimed by Ranjit Singh. 1840: New Zealand annexed by Britain.	1850: Britain grants Australian colonies responsible government. 1856: Britain grants New Zealand responsible government.
EUROPE 1582: Gregorian Calendar introduced. 1598: End of religious wars in France after Nantes Edict.		1652: George Fox establishes Religious Society of Friends (Quakers).	1738: John and Charles Wesley found the Methodist movement.		1806: Abdication of Emperor Francis I; end of Holy Roman Empire.	1859: Charles Darwin publishes *On the Origin of Species*.
NEAR EAST					1844: Bah'ai faith established, Persia.	

AD 1875	AD 1900	AD 1925	AD 1950	AD 1975	AD 1990
1885: Belgium acquires the Congo. 1899: Boer War (to 1902).		1930: Ras Tafari (Haile Selassie) crowned as emperor, Abyssinia. 1935: Italy conquers Abyssinia (Ethiopia). 1941: Haile Selassie restored to the throne, Abyssinia. 1942: Apartheid programme begins, South Africa.	1974: Haile Selassie dethroned.	1975: Death of Haile Selassie.	1990: Nelson Mandela freed. 1994: Nelson Mandela first black president of South Africa.
1876: Battle of the Little Bighorn, USA. 1890: Battle of Wounded Knee, USA.	1921: African Orthodox Church founded.	1940: Death of Marcus Garvey.	1950s: Spread of Rastafarianism, Caribbean, USA. 1958: Maharishi Yoga introduces Transcendental Meditation, USA. 1965: ISKON (Hare Krishna movement) founded, USA.	1975: Indian Self-Determination Act is passed, USA.	
	1911: Collapse of imperial China.	1947: Indian independence declared. 1948: Assassination of Mahatma Ghandi. 1949: China becomes Communist.	1959: Dalai Lama escapes from Tibet to India. 1966: Mao Zedong's Cultural Revolution begins, China.		
		1941: 'Final solution' initiated by Nazis.	1958: Maharishi Yoga introduces Transcendental Meditation, Western Europe. 1970: Jesus Movement established.	1978: John Paul II becomes pope.	1995: Swaminarayan Hindu Mandir, temple of the Swaminarayan Movement, opened, England.
1897: Jewish Zionist movement founded by Theodore Herzl.		1948: Establishment of state of Israel.			

Glossary

ABORIGINAL RELIGION Usually refers to the religion of the indigenous peoples of Australia.

AGES OF MAN In Greek mythology, the five races of humans created by Zeus. The first race, the Race of Gold, was succeeded by those of Silver, Bronze, Heroes and Iron (the current race).

ALLAH The one true god in the religion of Islam. As the Arabic word for God, 'Allah' is also used by Arab Christians.

AMISH Christian Protestant movement founded in Europe in the late seventeenth century. Followers, renowned for their austere, separatist lifestyle, later settled in the United States and Canada.

ANABAPTISTS A persecuted radical Protestant group which arose during the Reformation in sixteenth-century Europe. Followers believed that only adults should be baptized and that they should live apart from the wider society.

ANCESTOR WORSHIP The veneration of the dead by their relatives. It plays an important part in many religions including those of China and Africa.

ASCETICISM The practice of self-denial in order to reach a higher spiritual level. Found in many religions, it includes fasting, self-mortification and celibacy.

ASHRAMA Within Hinduism, one of the four stages of life: student, householder, hermit and renunciate.

AVATAR Within Hinduism, the incarnation of a deity as a human or animal in order to help humanity. The best-known avatars are those of Vishnu.

ARYAN A people who settled in Iran and northern India in pre-history. In the nineteenth century the idea of a superior 'Aryan race' arose; the term was used by Adolf Hitler to designate a super-race and to legitimate his persecution of non-Aryans.

AZTECS Rulers of a vast empire in Mexico from the fifteenth century until the Spanish capture of their capital in 1521.

BABYLONIA An ancient region of southeastern Mesopotamia; at its height, a great and culturally influential empire. Its last great ruler was Nebuchadnezzar II (reigned 605–562 BC), best remembered for the Babylonian captivity of the Jews.

BAHA'I A religion founded in the nineteenth century by Baha'u'llah (Glory of God) in Iran. Its roots lie in Shi'ite Islam but it differs in a number of significant ways – for example in teaching that more prophets follow Muhammad.

BAPTISM Christian initiation ritual usually involving water to signify the initiate's spiritual purification.

BHAKTI In Hinduism, devotion to a deity. Krishna is a popular object of bhakti.

BIBLE Sacred text of Judaism and Christianity. The Christian Bible consists of both the Old and New Testaments whereas the Jewish Bible comprises only the former.

BODHISATTVAS In Buddhism, enlightened beings who have postponed their buddhahood in order that they might lessen the suffering of others.

BON The indigenous religion of Tibet which today exists as a synthesis of the original doctrines and Buddhism, introduced from the seventh and eighth centuries AD.

BUDDHA The Awakened or Enlightened One. The historical Buddha (Siddhartha Gautama), founder of Buddhism, was born in India in the sixth century BC.

BUDDHISM A movement arising from the teaching of Siddhartha Gautama in the sixth century BC. The Mahayana school or 'Great Vehicle' developed from the first century AD, emphasizing the alleviation of suffering for all. The Theravada school is conservative by comparison. The Chan tradition was founded in China in the early sixth century AD and appeared in Japan in the ninth century where it is known as Zen.

CANAANITES People who inhabited the region often referred to in the Bible as Canaan comprising what used to be Palestine as well as what is now Syria and Lebanon.

CANNIBALISM The ritual eating of human flesh, widespread until modern times in some cultures. It was seen as a means of obtaining special supernatural powers and often formed part of religious rituals.

CATHEDRAL The official church of a bishop or archbishop.

CELTS A people whose culture can be traced back to 1200 BC. Around 500 BC they moved from central Europe eastwards into Asia Minor and westwards into Gaul, Spain and Britain. Priests known as Druids oversaw their religious traditions.

CHRISTIANITY Broadly, the religion which arose from the teachings of Jesus Christ and which has as its core the belief that he was sent to earth by God to bring salvation to humanity.

CHRISTMAS In Christianity, the feast of the birth of Christ, held on 25 December.

CHURCH Refers to all Christians, to their major divisions, denominations and gatherings (e.g. Methodist Church) and to the buildings where congregations meet.

COMMUNION In Christianity, the sacrament of thanksgiving (sometimes called the Eucharist or Mass) which commemorates Jesus' last meal with his disciples. It can also refer to the fellowship of all Christians and to a particular Christian church or group of churches (e.g. Anglican Communion).

CONFIRMATION In Christianity, a public commitment to the faith by mature believers.

CONFUCIANISM Considered a religion by some, a philosophy by others, it is a system of ethics stressing respect and restraint which was founded in China about 500 BC by Confucius.

COSMOLOGY Beliefs about the structure of the universe.

CREED A statement of religious belief. In Christianity, the Apostles' Creed and the Nicene Creed are the most popular.

CRUCIFIXION A death penalty widely used by the Romans which involved fastening the victim's arms and legs to a cross or stake and leaving him to die. In Christianity, Jesus was crucified by the Romans under Pontius Pilate.

CULT Traditionally, a style of worship and its associated rituals. More commonly used to describe a religious group characterized by relatively small size and existing in a state of tension with the host society. In popular usage, a dangerous or destructive religious movement.

DAO DE JING The Virtue of the Way, which forms the basis of Taoism. Traditionally written by Lao Zi during the sixth century BC, scholars date it two to three centuries later.

DEITY A god or goddess; a supernatural being.

DHARMA In Buddhism, the teachings of the Buddha or established or natural law. In Hinduism it means universal law or, for the individual, the moral norm.

DIASPORA The dispersion of Jews after the Babylonian exile from Israel of 586 BC, or those living outside Palestine or present-day Israel.

DIVINATION Any method of predicting future events whether through 'reading' the stars, runes or the entrails of animals.

DIWALI The Hindu Festival of Lights celebrating the return of the deities Rama and Sita to Ayodhya. It is accompanied by fireworks and the exchange of gifts.

DOGMA A truth defined by a religious group and believed to be essential to its teachings.

DUALISM The belief that everything is divided into good and evil – whether beings, deities or concepts.

EASTER Easter Sunday, the most important day of the Christian calendar, commemorates Jesus' resurrection.

ECUMENISM The promotion of understanding between traditions within a single religion. The term is used most commonly within Christianity.

ENLIGHTENMENT Movement emphasizing human reason and rational scientific enquiry which arose in the eighteenth century across much of western Europe and North America. In France, many of the enlightenment philosophers attacked established religion.

EPISCOPALIAN Member of the Episcopal Church in the United States which descended from and remains associated with the Church of England.

ETHICS The study of human values and moral conduct.

EVANGELISM Usually an organized attempt to propagate the 'good news' of Jesus Christ, whether through preaching or private conversation.

FAITH An attitude of trust and certainty relating the worshipper to his or her God or religion. While central to, for example, Islam and Christianity, in Hinduism correct behaviour is more important.

FASTING Forgoing food and/or water for a period of time in order to advance spiritually. Muslims are expected to fast completely between sunrise and sunset during Ramadan.

FESTIVALS Originally religious celebrations which included sacred communal feasts, hence their name. Many festivals are connected with rites of passage or seasonal celebrations.

FETISH An object believed to have supernatural powers and hence worshipped.

FUNDAMENTALISM Originally, a Christian movement which arose in the United States in the early twentieth century. Followers abided by The Fundamentals, tracts which laid down the 'fundamentals' of Christianity and insisted on strict rather than metaphorical interpretations of the Bible. More generally, the term refers to the conservative wing of religions. Amongst non-fundamentalists the term can be used to imply intolerance and anti-intellectualism.

FUNERAL RITES Rituals which mark an individual's death and others' grief and aim to help the transition back to everyday life.

GAULS Ancient Celtic people who inhabited modern-day France and parts of Belgium, western Germany and northern Italy.

GENEALOGY The study of family origins and history. Followers of the Church of Jesus Christ of Latter Day Saints (Mormons) are particularly interested in genealogy due to their belief that their dead ancestors might be saved by being traced and ritually baptized.

GOD The supreme being, creator of the universe, or simply a deity.

GURU A Sanskrit word commonly used in Eastern religions meaning teacher, honoured person or saint.

HARE KRISHNA The name commonly given to the International Society for Krishna Consciousness (ISKCON), a movement founded by A.C. Bhaktivedanta Swami Prabhupada in the United States in 1965. The movement has its roots in Vaishnava Hinduism and has devotion to Krishna at its core.

HASIDISM A Jewish religious movement founded by Baal-Shem-Tov in the eighteenth century. The Hasidim believe that religious devotion is more important than scholarly learning.

HEAVEN Often regarded as a blissful upper realm. In Islam, Judaism and Christianity it is where, after death, the worthy will see God face to face.

HELL In many religions a realm of the dead, sometimes a place of eternal torment. Within Christianity, various groups believe individuals' beliefs or actions cause them to be sent there after death. Today, more groups describe hell as isolation from God.

HINDUISM Term originally invented by Europeans to describe the religions of India.

HITTITES An ancient Indo-European people who appeared in Anatolia at the beginning of the second millennium BC and who for around 200 years were one of the dominant powers of the Middle East.

HOLOCAUST The term means massive destruction; it usually refers to the German Nazi regime's extermination of some six million Jews during Second World War.

HUMANISM Generally used to indicate concern with humans rather than with nature or the supernatural. The movement developed in northern Italy during the fourteenth century. In the nineteenth century humanism sometimes amounted to a secular religion.

ICONOGRAPHY Study of visual art, including religious symbolism.

IMMORTALITY The continued spiritual existence of individuals after death.

INCARNATION The concept that God became a man and dwelt among other humans.

INCAS South American Indians who in the fifteenth century expanded from their capital at Cuzco to rule over a vast empire which was lost to the Spanish by 1532.

INDIGENOUS RELIGION A 'home-grown' religion, one originating in and associated with a particular region, such as the Shinto religion of Japan.

ISLAM The word means 'submission' – to Allah, the one true God. The religion was founded in the seventh century AD by the Prophet Muhammad to whom the Qur'an (Islam's sacred text) is said to have been revealed. Today, Islam is the second largest religion in the world.

JAINISM Religion founded in the sixth century BC by Mahavira. It places great emphasis on ahimsa (the principle of non-violence) and austerity in order to dispel karma (actions). Most of its followers are based in India.

JEHOVAH'S WITNESSES A millenarian movement (belief in the imminent return of Christ) founded in the United States in 1872 by Charles Taze Russell. Members are expected to devote significant amounts of time to door-to-door witnessing.

JUDAISM Generally, the religion of the Jewish people. The term is sometimes used to refer to the form the religion took following 70 AD when the traditional teachings were laid down by the rabbis.

KARMA In Indian tradition the actions or effects of actions that an individual accumulates. Karma is believed to enmesh individuals in the cycle of death and rebirth and to determine their state when they are reincarnated.

LENT Within Christianity, a period of fasting and spiritual preparation beginning on Ash Wednesday and finishing 40 days later at Easter. It commemorates Christ's 40 days in the wilderness.

LUTHERANISM The Protestant beliefs and practices derived from Martin Luther (1483–1546). Luther's belief that salvation could be achieved by faith alone rather than by works provoked a break with the church in Rome. Lutheranism is the main faith in Scandinavian countries, the main Protestant Church in Germany and is strong in North America.

MAORIS Polynesian people of New Zealand who traditionally arrived in waves from about 850 AD and finally in the fourteenth century in a 'great fleet' from Hawaiki, a mythical land (Tahiti).

MEDITATION The practice of bringing an individual to a trance-like state in which he or she can achieve enlightenment or liberation. Numerous different methods are used.

MELANESIA One of the three main divisions of Oceania in the southwest Pacific Ocean. It includes the Solomon Islands, the Admiralty Islands and Fiji.

MESOPOTAMIA The so-called 'cradle of civilization', home to some of the earliest cities and the invention of writing. It occupied the region between the Tigris and Euphrates rivers.

MESOAMERICA The area between the present-day United States and South America which, up until the sixteenth century, was home to highly developed civilizations including the Olmecs, Toltecs, Mayans and Aztecs.

MESSIAH Derived from the Hebrew for 'anointed one'. In Judaism, the messiah will come before the resurrection of the dead and the judgement of mankind. In Christianity, the title refers to Jesus.

METHODISM Christian movement originating in England as part of the eighteenth century Evangelical Revival. It aimed to reform the Church of England and was led by John Wesley and George Whitefield. In time, it became a separate church.

MISSIONARY A general term for someone who aims to spread their religion. More specifically, those who strive to win converts to Christianity.

MONASTERY The residence of a religious order, particularly one of monks.

MONK A man who separates himself from the wider society in order to follow the religious life full-time.

MONOTHEISM Belief in the existence of only one deity. The three great monotheistic religions are Judaism, Christianity and Islam.

MORMONS Founded by Joseph Smith in New York state in 1830, the Church of Jesus Christ of Latter-day Saints (commonly called Mormons after their sacred Book of Mormon) teaches that Jesus spent time in Central and South America after his crucifixion. Their key belief is that they represent a restoration of the original Christian church.

MOSQUE The Muslim place of worship; it translates as 'place of prostration'.

MYSTERY RELIGIONS Term for a group of religions from the ancient Mediterranean world all of which emphasized a central 'mystery' (often concerning fertility and immortality), for example the Dionysian mysteries.

MYTH A story that is not literally true, but which usually illustrates fundamental religious truths.

NIRVANA Buddhist term for a state where all suffering and its causes cease.

NONCONFORMIST Term usually designating Protestant dissenters from the Church of England including Quakers, Baptists, Methodists and Presbyterians.

NUN Woman who belongs to a monastic religious order or group.

OCEANIA Collective name for the 25,000 or so islands of the Pacific. It is usually divided into Micronesia, Polynesia and Melanesia.

ORAL TRADITION The verbal dissemination, from one generation to the next, of a people's ancestry and cultural history, including religious beliefs.

ORDINATION A formal church ritual that recognizes and affirms that God has called a person into professional ministry.

ORTHODOX CHURCH Term used for the eastern Christian churches after they split from the Roman Catholic Church in 1054 AD. Most Orthodox Churches are related to a particular country, such as the Russian Orthodox and Greek Orthodox.

PAGANISM Generally, any nature-oriented religion although sometimes used to refer to ancient religions such as those of Greece or Egypt or to any religion considered 'unofficial'.

PALI CANON The earliest and, for Theravada Buddhists, the most authoritative sacred texts of Buddhism, transmitted orally from the time of Gautama Buddha (sixth/fifth century BC) until written down in the first century BC.

PANTHEON Term which has come to mean a particular people's group of deities. For example, the ancient Egyptian pantheon included Isis and Osiris.

PARABLE Originally, an enigmatic or metaphorical saying; the term came to refer to a story illustrating a particular religious or ethical point.

PARADISE Usually, a beautiful enchanted garden brimming with life and symbolizing a time of bliss and plenty. Paradise is found in many traditions including the Sumerian Dilmun, the Bible's Garden of Eden (also mentioned in the Qur'an), and China's Isles of the Blessed.

PASSOVER The most important feast of the Jewish calendar celebrating the Hebrews' escape from slavery in Egypt, usually dated to the mid-thirteenth century BC.

PENTECOSTALISTS In Christianity, a movement which began in the United States in the early twentieth century and teaches that, following conversion, Christians can be baptized in the Holy Spirit, a phenomenon characterized by glossolalia or speaking in tongues.

PERSIA Country in the Middle East known, since 1935, as Iran.

PILGRIM A religiously motivated journey to a sacred site, widespread since ancient times. The *hajj* of Muslims to Makkah is perhaps the most renowned pilgrimage.

PLURALISM A situation in which no single group holds a monopoly in the definition of beliefs, values and practices.

POLYTHEISM Belief in the existence of more than one deity.

PRAYER The attempt to communicate with the divine or supernatural, undertaken either privately or communally.

PRIEST Someone who holds an 'official' religious role and who celebrates the religion's rituals, practices and beliefs.

PROPHECY Broadly, a prediction of the future. In ancient times the oracle at Delphi was particularly famous for its prophecies. Moses is regarded by the Jews as the greatest prophet whereas in Islam both Jesus and Muhammad are seen as prophets. Today, prophecy plays an important part in Pentecostal and Charismatic Christianity.

QI In Taoism, the vital energy or life force which pervades the universe and in the body is centred near the navel.

QUR'AN The sacred book of Islam, the word of God revealed to the prophet Muhammad in the seventh century AD.

RABBI In Judaism, primarily a teacher and interpreter of the Torah and a spiritual guide of the congregation and community.

RAMADAN The ninth month of the Islamic calendar during which all Muslims should fast during daylight hours.

RASTAFARIANISM A religious movement founded in Jamaica in the early twentieth century. It takes inspiration from the Back to Africa movement, preaches the divinity of the Ethiopian Emperor Haile Selassie (1892–1975) and draws on the Bible's Old Testament.

REINCARNATION The belief that when a person dies, their soul is reborn into another living being. Buddhists and Hindus are among those who believe in reincarnation.

RESURRECTION In Christianity, the doctrine that Jesus overcame death on Easter Sunday. Islam also teaches the resurrection of the body.

RITUALS Symbolic words and/or actions which represent religious meanings, and are often performed during religious services.

ROMAN CATHOLICISM The Christian Church headed (temporally) by the Pope whose authority is said to descend from Jesus through the apostle Peter. It is the largest Christian faith group.

SACRAMENT In Christianity, a sacred ritual believed to be performed with the authority of Jesus. Most Protestants accept two sacraments (baptism and the eucharist) whereas the Roman Catholic and Orthodox Churches accept seven (baptism, confirmation, penance, the eucharist, matrimony, ordination and extreme unction).

SACRIFICE A religious ritual in which an object is offered to a divinity in order to establish, maintain or restore a right relationship of a human being to the sacred order.

SAINT A holy person appealed to, after his or her death, in prayers. In Roman Catholicism, there is a complex structure for saint-making; in Protestantism a saint is generally regarded as one of the early leaders of the church.

SAKTISM Within Hinduism, the worship of Sakti, the supreme female creative energy, often as personified in the goddess Devi.

SEVENTH DAY ADVENTISTS A Protestant sectarian movement founded in 1863 and central to which is a belief in Christ's imminent return. Seventh Day Adventists also believe that the sabbath should be celebrated on a Saturday.

SHAMAN Originally from central Asia and Siberia, shamans act as intermediaries between people and the spirit world.

SHAMANISM The practice of connecting in an ecstatic trance state with the spirit world, usually with the aim of healing others.

SHI'ITES One of the two great branches of Islam (the other being the Sunnis). Shi'ites conflict with Sunnis over who should have succeeded the Prophet. Shi'ites insist on the importance of descent from Muhammad's family. Less than 15 per cent of Muslims are Shi'ites although it is the dominant body in Iran.

SHINTO The indigenous religion of Japan which originated at least as early as 500 BC and is composed of huge variety of myths and rituals.

SHRINE A building or place considered holy by a religious group, sometimes because it houses a religious object.

SIKHISM A religion generally viewed as a blend of Hinduism and Islam. Sikhs believe in a single deity and follow the teachings of the Ten Sikh Gurus, starting with Guru Nanak in 1469.

SUFISM A mystical branch of Islam which can be traced back to the eighth century.

SUNNI The dominant branch of Islam, comprising more than 80 per cent of Muslims worldwide.

SYNAGOGUE Judaism's main place of public assembly used for worship, study and community affairs.

SYNCRETISM A religion or belief system created from concepts from two or more religions.

TABOO A restriction or ban on things seen as sacred or powerful.

TANTRISM Buddhist practice which aims at direct experience of the enlightened self through symbols, visual images, repetition of sounds, prescribed movements and empahsized sexo-yogic practices.

TAOISM Religion traditionally founded in China by Lao Zi in the sixth century BC. The goal of Taoism is harmony with the universe.

TEMPLE The term used by Buddhists, Hindus and others to refer to their house of worship.

THEOLOGY The systematic study of God and, more generally, religion.

TORAH The first five books of the Hebrew Bible (Old Testament): Genesis, Exodus, Leviticus, Numbers and Deuteronomy.

TRINITY The Christian belief that God is both one and three: Father, Son and Holy Spirit.

VEDAS India's oldest sacred texts to which superhuman origins and divine authority are ascribed. The word means knowledge or sacred teaching.

VOODOO Religion emanating from West Africa which combines magical and animistic practices with some elements of Roman Catholicism.

WORSHIP Very broadly, the response to whatever is considered holy, for example prayers, songs and sermons.

YIN AND YANG Ancient Chinese symbol depicting the balance of the two great forces in the universe: negative and positive, feminine and masculine. Each has within it the embryo of the other.

YOGA General term for spiritual disciplines practised in Indian religions with the aim of release or liberation.

ZIONISM Movement formally established in 1897 for founding a Jewish national home in Palestine. Since the foundation of Israel in 1948 it has continued to seek support for the state.

ZOROASTRIANISM Religion founded by the prophet Zarathustra (later Zoroaster) in Persia. Dates of its foundation are not clear; some believe it to be *c.* 1200 BC, others date it 588 BC. According to Zoroaster, the supreme god Ahura Mazda is in constant battle with Ahriman, the force of evil.

Bibliography

ROOTS OF RELIGION

Burl, Aubrey, *A Guide to the Stone Circles of Britain, Ireland and Brittany*, Yale University Press, New Haven, 1995

Chauvet, Jean-Marie, Deschamps, Eliette Brunel and Hillaire, Christian, *Chauvet Cave*, Thames and Hudson, London, 1996

Hutton, Ronald, *Pagan Religions of the Ancient British Isles*, Blackwell, Oxford, 1991

Levy, G.R., *The Gate of Horn*, Faber, London, 1963

O'Brien, Joanne and Palmer, Martin, *State of Religion Atlas*, Simon & Schuster, London, 1993

O'Shea, Stephen, *Perfect Heresy*, Profile Books, London, 2000

ANCIENT EGYPT

Hart, George, *A Dictionary of Egyptian Gods and Goddesses*, Routledge and Kegan Paul, London, 1986

Hart, George, *Egyptian Myths*, British Museum Publications, London, 1990

Hornung, Erik, trans. by John Baines, *Conceptions of God in Ancient Egypt: the One and the Many*, Routledge and Kegan Paul, London, 1983

Meeks, Dimitri and Favard-Meeks, Christine, translated by G. M. Goshgarian, *Daily Life of the Egyptian Gods*, John Murray, London, 1997

Quirke, Stephen, *Ancient Egyptian Religion*, British Museum Press, London, 1992

ANCIENT NEAR EAST

Crawford, Harriet, *Sumer and the Sumerians*, Cambridge University Press, Cambridge, 1991

Gibson, John C. L. and Driver, Geoffrey Rolles, *Canaanite Myths and Legends*, Continuum International, 1978

Hardy, Friedhelm (ed.), *The World's Religions: the Religions of Asia*, Routledge, London, 1990

Holloway, Steven W., *Assur is King! Assur is King!*, Brill Academic Club, 2001

King, L. W. (ed.), *The Tablets of Creation*, BookTree, 1998

Kramer, Samuel Noel, *Sumerian Mythology*, University of Pennsylvania Press, 1998

Oppenheim, A. Leo, *Ancient Mesopotamia*, University of Chicago Press, Chicago, 1977

Smart, Ninian (ed.), *Atlas of World Religions*, Oxford University Press, Oxford, 1999

GREECE

Austin, M. M. and Vidal-Naquet, P. (eds.), *The Economic and Social History of Ancient Greece: An Introduction*, Batsford, London, 1977

Boardman, John, *The Greeks Overseas: Their Early Colonies and Trade*, Thames and Hudson, London, 2nd edn., 1980

Boardman, John, *The Oxford History of Classical Art*, Oxford University Press, Oxford, 1993

Carpenter, T. H., Art and Myth in Ancient Greece, Thames and Hudson, London, 1996

Castleden, Rodney, *Minoans: Life in Bronze-Age Crete*, Routledge, London, 1990

Graves, Robert, *New Larousse Encyclopedia of Mythology*, Hamlyn, 1968

Green, Peter, *Alexander to Actium: The Hellenistic Age*, Thames and Hudson, London, 1990

Murray, Oswyn, *Early Greece*, Fontana, London, 1980

Renfrew, Colin, *The Emergence of Civilization: The Cyclades and the Aegean in the Third Millennium BC*, Methuen, London, 1972

Scarre, Christopher and Fagan, Brian M., *Ancient Civilizations*, Longman, Harlow, 1997

ROME

Boardman, John, *The Oxford History of Classical Art*, Oxford University Press, Oxford, 1993

Carcopino, Jacerome (tr. Lorimer, E. O.), *Daily Life in Ancient Rome: The People and the City at the Height of the Empire*, Penguin, London, 1991

Graves, Robert, *New Larousse Encyclopedia of Mythology*, Hamlyn, 1968

Liberati, Anna Maria and Bourbon, Fabio, *Splendours of the Roman World*, Thames and Hudson, London, 1996

Scarre, Christopher and Fagan, Brian M., *Ancient Civilizations*, Longman, Harlow, 1997

NORTHERN EUROPE

Davidson, Hilda Ellis, *The Lost Beliefs of Northern Europe*, Routledge, London, 1993

Jones, Prudence and Pennick, Nigel, *A History of Pagan Europe*, Routledge, London, 1995

Pennick, Nigel, *Celtic Sacred Landscapes*, Thames and Hudson, London, 2000

Trinkunas, Jonas (ed.), *Of Gods and Holidays. The Baltic Heritage*, Hverme, Vilnius, 1999

Vana, Zdenek, *Mythologie und Götterwelt der slawischen Völker. Die geistigen Impulse Ost-Europas*, Urachhaus Johannes M. Mayer, Stuttgart, 1992

CENTRAL AND SOUTH AMERICA (ANCIENT RELIGIONS)

Clendinnen, I., *The Aztecs*, Cambridge University Press, Cambridge, 1991

Cobo, Father B., (ed. & trans. Hamilton) *Inca Religion and Customs*, University of Texas Press, Austin, 1990

Howland, J. (ed.), 'Inca Culture at the Time of the Spanish Conquest', *Handbook of South American Indians*, Vol. 2, 1946

Miller, M. and Taube K., *The Gods and Symbols of Ancient Mexico and the Maya*, Thames and Hudson, London, 1993

Pasztory, E, *Pre-Columbian Art*, Weidenfeld & Nicolson, London, 1998

Sahagun, Fray B de, (trans. by Anderson, J.O. & Dibble, C.), *Florentine Codex: General History of the Things of New Spain*, (13 vols.), School of American Research, Santa Fe, New Mexico, 1950–82.

Schele, L and Miller, M.E., *The Blood of Kings*, Thames and Hudson, London, 1992

Tedlock, D. (trans), *Popol Vue: the Mayan Book of the Dawn of Life*, Simon and Schuster, New York, 1985

OCEANIA

Bonnemaison, J., *The Tree and the Canoe*, University of Hawaii Press, Honolulu, 1994.

Damon, F. and Wagner, R.. (eds.), *Death Rituals and Life in the Societies of the Kula Ring*, Northern Illinois University Press, 1989.

Goldman, I., *Ancient Polynesian Society*, University of Chicago Press, Chicago, 1970

Hocart, A. M., *Kings and Councillors*, University of Chicago Press, Chicago, 1970

Lawrence P., *Road Belong Cargo*, Manchester University Press, Manchester, 1956

Lawrence, P. and Meggitt, M. (eds.), *Gods, Ghosts and Men in Melanesia*, Oxford University Press, Melbourne, 1965

Sahlins, M., *Historical Metaphors and Mythical Realities*, University of Michigan Press, 1976

Thomas, N., *Planets around the Sun*. Oceania Monographs no. 31, Oceania Publications, Sydney, 1986

Wagner, R., *Asiwinorong*, Princeton University Press, 1986

Wagner R., *Habu*, University of Chicago Press, Chicago, 1972

AUSTRALIA

Berndt, R., *Kunapipi*, Cheshire, Melbourne, 1951

Berndt, R., and Berndt, C., *The World of the First Australians*, Rigby, Adelaide, 1985

Durkheim, E. *The Elementary Forms of the Religious Life*, Allen and Unwin, 1915

Eliade, M., *Australian Religions An Introduction*, Cornell University Press, Ithaca, 1973

Howitt, A. W., *Native Tribes of South East Australia*, Macmillan, London, 1904

Maddock, K., *The Australian Aborigines: A Portrait of their Society*, Penguin, 1972

Munn, N., *Walbiri Icongraphy*, Cornell University Press, Ithaca, 1973

Stanner, W. E. H., 'The Dreaming', *Reader in Comparative Religion*, Vogt, E. and Lessa, W. (eds.), Peterson, Evanston, 1958

Strehlow, T., *Aranda Traditions*, Melbourne University Press, Melbourne, 1947

Warner, L., *A Black Civilization*, Harper, New York, 1958

MAORI

Barlow, C., *Tikanga Whakaaro: Key Concepts in Maori Culture*, Oxford University Press, Auckland, 1991

Grace, Patricia, *Potiki*, Women's Press, London, 1987

Harvey, Graham (ed.), 'Art Works in Aotearoa' and 'Mana and Tapu: Sacred Knowledge, Sacred Boundaries', *Indigenous Religions: a Companion*, Cassell, London/New York, 2000

Harvey, Graham (ed.), 'Maori Religion' (by Tawhai, T.P.), *Readings in Indigenous Religions*, Continuum, London/New York, 2002

Reedy, Anaru (ed.), *Nga Korero a Mohi Ruatapu (The Writings of Mohi Ruatapu)*, Canterbury University Press, Christchurch, 1993

Sutherland, Stewart and Clarke, Peter (eds.), 'Maori Religion', *The Study of Religion, Traditional and New Religion*, Routledge, London, 1988

NATIVE NORTH AMERICANS

Bordewich, Fergus M., *Killing the White Man's Indian: Reinventing Native Americans at the End of the Twentieth Century*, Anchor Books/Doubleday, New York/London, 1997

Rajotte, Freda, *First Nations Faith and Ecology*, Cassell, Anglican Book Centre, United Church Publishing House, 1998

Versluis, Arthur, *Native American Traditions*, Element, 1994

Wright, Ronald, *Stolen Continents: The New World Through Indian Eyes*, Penguin Books, London, 1993

CENTRAL AND SOUTH AMERICA (INDIGENOUS RELIGIONS)

Hugh-Jones, C., *From the Milk River: Spatial and Temporal Processes in Northwest Amazonia*, Cambridge University Press, Cambridge, 1979

Hugh-Jones, S., *The Palm and Pleiades: Initiation and Cosmology in Northwest Amazonia*, Cambridge University Press, Cambridge, 1979

Myerhoff, B., *Peyote Hunt: the Sacred Journey of the Huichol Indians*, Cornell University Press, London, 1974

Reichel-Dolmatoff, G, *Amazonian Cosmos: the Sexual and Religious Symbolism of the Tukano Indians*, Chicago University Press, Chicago, 1971

Rostas, S, 'A Grass Roots View of Religious Change Amongst Women in an Indigenous Community in Chiapas, Mexico', *Bulletin of Latin American Studies*, Vol. 18, No 3, pp. 327–341, 1999

Tedlock, B, *Time and the Highland Maya*, University of New Mexico Press, Albuquerque, 1982

Watanabe, J., *Maya Saints and Souls in a Changing World*, University of Texas, Austin, 1992

AFRICAN TRADITIONAL RELIGIONS

Achebe, Chinua, *Things Fall Apart*, Heinemann, London, 1958

Iliffe, John, *Africans: The History of a Continent*, Cambridge University Press, Cambridge, 1995

Mbiti, John, *Introduction to African Religion*, Heinemann, London, 1991

Ray, Benjamin, *African Religions: Symbol, Ritual and Community*, Prentice-Hall, New Jersey, 1999 (second edition)

Samkange, Stanlake, *The Mourned One*, Heinemann, London, 1975

Thiong'o, Ngugi wa, *The River Between*, Heinemann, London, 1965

Visona, Monica B. et al, *A History of Art in Africa*, Thames and Hudson, London, 2000

Zuesse, Evan M., *Ritual Cosmos: The Sanctification of Life in African Religions*, Ohio University Press, Ohio, 1979

SHINTO

Bocking, B., *A Popular Dictionary of Shinto*, Curzon Press, London, 1997

Breen, J. (ed.), *Shinto in History: Ways of the Kami*, Curzon Press, London, 2000

Harris, V. (ed.), *Shinto: The Sacred Art of Ancient Japan*, British Museum, London, 2001

Nelson, J.K., *A Year in the Life of a Shinto Shrine*, University of Washington Press, Washington, 1996

Ono, S., *Shinto, the Kami Way*, Charles Tuttle, Boston, 1962

Reader, Andreasen & Stefansson (eds.), *Japanese Religions Past and Present*, Japan Library, Japan, 1993

Reader, I., *Religion in Contemporary Japan*, Macmillan, London, 1990/University of Hawaii Press, Hawaii, 1991

BUDDHISM

Austin, Jack, (trans), *The Dhammapada*, The Buddhist Society, London, 1988

Besserman, Perle and Steger, Manfred, *Crazy Clouds; Zen Radicals, Rebels and Reformers*, Shambhala, Boston, 1991

Blofeld, John, *The Way of Power, A Practical Guide to the Tantric Mysticism of Tibet*, George Allen and Unwin, London, 1970

Fowler, Merv, *Buddhism, Beliefs and Practices*, Sussex Academic Press, Brighton and Portland, Oregon, 1999

Gethin, Rupert, *The Foundations of Buddhism*, Oxford University Press, 1998

McConnell, John A., *Mindful Mediation, A Handbook for Buddhist Peacemakers*, Buddhist Research Institute, Mahachula Buddhist University et al., Bangkok, 1995

Pym, Jim, *You Don't have to Sit on the Floor; Bringing the Insights and Tools of Buddhism into Everyday Life*, Riders, London, 2001

Reps, Paul, *Zen Flesh, Zen Bones*, Pelican Books, Harmondsworth, 1971

Suzuki, Shunryu, *Zen Mind, Beginner's Mind, Informal Talks on Zen Meditation and Practice*, Weatherhill, New York and Tokyo, 1996

Unno, Taitetsu, *River of Fire, River of Water; An Introduction to the Pure Land Tradition of Shin Buddhism*, Doubleday, New York, 1998

CHRISTIANITY

Bowker, John (ed.), *The Oxford Dictionary of World Religions*, Oxford University Press, Oxford, 1997

Burridge, Richard, *Four Gospels, One Jesus?*, SPCK, London, 1994

Cohn-Sherlock, Lavinia, *Who's Who in Christianity*, Routledge, London, 1998

Hinnells, John, *Who's Who in World Religions*, Penguin, London, 1996

Lenman, Bruce P., *Chambers Dictionary of World History*, Chambers, London, 2000

McManners, John (ed.), *The Oxford Illustrated History of Christianity*, Oxford University Press, Oxford, 1990

Porter, J.R., *Jesus Christ. The Jesus of History, The Christ of Faith*, Duncan Baird Publishers, London, 1999

Pritchard, James, *The Times Atlas of the Bible*, Times Books, London, 1987

CONFUCIANISM

Chu His, *Learning to be a Sage*, University of California Press, Berkeley, 1990

Confucius, *The Analects*, (trans. D.C. Lau), Penguin Books, Harmondsworth, 1979

De Bary, William Theodore (ed.), *Sources of the Chinese Tradition*, Columbia University Press, New York, 1950

Fung Yulan, *A Short History of Chinese Philosophy*, The Macmillan Company, New York, 1948

Hsun-tzu (Xun Zi), *Basic Writings*, Watson, Burton (trans.), Columbia University Press, New York, 1961

Mencius, *The Book of Mencius*. (trans. D.C. Lau), Penguin Books, Harmondsworth, 1970

The Book of Songs, Houghton Miflin, Boston/New York, 1937

Three Ways of Thought in Ancient China, George Allen and Unwin, London, 1939

Waley, Arthur, *The Analects of Confucius*, George Allen and Unwin, London, 1938

Yang, C. K., *Religion in Chinese Society*, University of California Press, Berkeley and Los Angeles, 1961

HINDUISM

Jagannathan, Shakunthala, *Hinduism – An Introduction*

Nikhilananda, Swami, The Upanishads,

Prinja, Naval K., *Explaining Hindu Dharma*, Vishwa Hindu Parishad, UK

Shreemad Bhagvat Gyan Yagna Souvenir, Gujarat Hindu Society, Preston, UK

Yogananda, Paramhansa, *Autobiography of a Yogi*,

ISLAM

Al-Khui, Al-Sayyid Abu Al-Qassim Al-Musawi, *The Prolegomena to the Qur'an*, Oxford University Press

Diouf, Sylviane A., *Servants of Allah – African Muslims Enslaved in the Americas*, New York University Press

Ezzati, Dr Abul-Fazl, *An Introduction to the History of The Spread of Islam*, The Ahl ul Bayt World Assembly, Islamic Republic of Iran

Humphreys, R. Stephen, *Islamic History: A Framework for Inquiry* (revised edition), I. B. Tauris & Co. Ltd./Princeton University Press

Kathir, Ibn, *The Life of the Prophet Muhammad*, Garnet Publishing Ltd

Levtzion, Nehehia & Pouwels, Randall L. (eds.), *The History of Islam in Africa*, James Currey Ltd

Lings, Martin, *Muhammad*, George Allen & Unwin/Islamic Texts Society

Madelung, Wilferd, *The Succession to Muhammad*, Cambridge University Press

Nahj al-Balaghah, *Sermons, Letters and Sayings of Amir al-Mu'minin, Ali ibn Abi Talib u*, Ansariyan Publications, Islamic Republic of Iran

Schimmel, Annemarie, *And Muhammad is His Messenger*, The University of North Carolina Press

Siddiqi, Muhammad Zubayr, *Hadith Literature*, Islamic Texts Society

Subhani, Ja'far, *The Message*, Islamic Seminary Publications Pakistan

JAINISM

Dundas, P., *The Jains*, Routledge, London, 1992

Jain, K., *Lord Mahavira and His Times*, Motilal Banarsidass, Delhi, 1974

Jaini, P., *The Jaina Path of Purification*, University of California, Berkeley, 1979

Sangave, V., *Jaina Community, a Social Survey*, Popular Prakashan, Bombay, 1980

Schubring, Walther, *The Doctrine of the Jainas*, Motilal Banarsidass, Delhi, 1962

Shah, Natubhai, *Jainism: The World of Conquerors* (2 vols.), Sussex Academic Press, Brighton, 1998

JUDAISM

Babylonian Talmud, (Hebrew and English edition), Soncino Press

Gilbert, Martin, *The Dent Atlas of Jewish History*, Dent, 1993

Greenberg, Irving, *The Jewish Way: Living the Holidays*, Simon and Schuster, London, 1993

Jacobs, Louis, *The Jewish Religion: A Companion*, Oxford University Press, Oxford, 1995

Landau, Ronnie S. and Tauris, I.B., *The Nazi Holocaust*, London, 1992

Mendes-Flohr, Paul and Reinharz, Jehuda, *The Jew in the Modern World: A Documentary History*, Oxford University Press, Oxford, 1980

Plaut, Gunther, *Torah, A Modern Commentary*, UAHC Press, 1981

Polaikov, Leon, *The History of Anti-Semitism* (3 vols), Littman Library, 1955

Roden, Claudia, *The Book of Jewish Food: An Odyssey from Samarkand and Vilna to the Present Day*, Penguin, London, 1996

Roth, Cecil (ed.), *Encyclopedia Judaica*, Keter Publishing, Jerusalem, 1972

SIKHISM

Joshi, L.M. (ed.) *Sikhism*, Punjabi University, 1990

Kaur, Sahib, *Sikh Thought*, Sundar Printers, 1986

Sambhi, Piara Singh and Cole, W.O., *The Sikhs*, Vikas Publishing House, 1978

Singh, Dr S., *Philosophical Foundations of the Sikh Value System*, Gurmat Publishers, 1982

Singh, Kapur, *Guru Nanak's Life And Thought*, Guru Nanak Dev University, 1991

TAOISM

Kohn, Livia (ed.), *The Taoist Experience*, State University of New York Press, New York, 1993

Schipper, Kristofer, *The Taoist Body*, University of California Press, Berkeley, 1993

Palmer, Martin (trans.), *Chuang Tzu*, Penguin/Arkana, London, 1995

Palmer, Martin, Ramsay, Jay and Man Ho, Kwok, *Tao Te Ching*, Chrysalis, London, 2002

Wong, Eva, *Taoism*, Shambala, Boston, 1997

ZOROASTRIANISM

Clark, Peter, *Zoroastrianism*, Sussex Academic Press, 1998

Hardy, Friedhelm (ed.), *The World's Religions: the Religions of Asia*, Routledge, London, 1990

Kapadia, S. A., *Teachings of Zoroaster and the Philosophy of the Parsi Religion*, R. A. Kessinger Publishing Company, 1998

Oppenheim, A. Leo, *Ancient Mesopotamia*, University of Chicago Press, Chicago, 1977

Smart, Ninian (ed.), *Atlas of World Religions*, Oxford University Press, Oxford, 1999

EAST MEETS WEST

Basham, AL., *The Wonder That Was India*, Sidgewick & Jackson, London, 1967

Eck, D., *Encountering God*, Penguin, London, 1985

Gombrich, R., *Mahayana Buddhism*, Routledge, London

Gombrich, R., *Theravada Buddhism*, Routledge, London

Grifiths, B., *A New Vision of Reality: Western Science, Eastern Mysticism and Christian Faith*, Collins, London, 1989

Grifiths, B., *The Marriage of East and West*, Collins, London, 1983

Krishnan, R., *The Hindu View of Life*, Allen & Unwin, 1927 (HarperCollins, India, 1993)

Lipner, J., *Hindus*, Routledge, London, 1994

Panikkar R., *The Unknown Christ of Hinduism*, Darton Longman & Todd, 1964

Zaehrer, R.C, *Hinduism*, Oxford University Press, Oxford, 1966

NEW RELIGIOUS MOVEMENTS; WOMEN AND RELIGION

Barrett, David, *The New Believers,* Cassell, London, 2001

Bloom, William, *The Penguin Book of New Age and Holistic Writing,* Penguin, London, 2001

Christ, Carol and Plaskow, Judith, *Womanspirit Rising: A Feminist Reader in Religion,* HarperCollins, New York, 1992

Daly, Mary, *Beyond God the Father: Toward a Philosophy of Women's Liberation,* Beacon Press, Boston, 1985

Gallagher, Ann-Marie, *The Way of the Goddess,* HarperCollins, London, 2002

King, Ursula, *Women and Spirituality,* Macmillan, London, 1995

Orr, Emma Restall, *Druid Priestess,* HarperCollins, London, 2000

Osho, *Autobiography of a Spiritually Incorrect Mystic,* St Martin's Press, New York, 2001

Puttick, Elizabeth, *Women in New Religions,* Macmillan, London, 1997

Starhawk, *The Spiral Dance,* HarperCollins, San Francisco, 1989

BAHA'I

Bahá'í International Community, *Bahá'u'lláh*, Office of Public Information, 1991

Esslemont, John, *Bahá'u'lláh and the New Era*, Bahá'í Publishing Trust, Wilmette, 1990 (5th rev. ed.)

Ferraby, John, *All Things Made New*, Bahá'í Publishing Trust, London, 1987 (2nd rev. ed.)

Hatcher, William S. and Martin, J. Douglas, *The Bahá'í Faith: The Emerging Global Religion*, Bahá'í Publishing Trust, Wilmette, 1998 (rev. ed.)

RASTAFARI

Barrett, L., *Rastafarians: Sounds of Cultural Dissonance*, Beacon Press, Boston, 1988

Campbell, H., *Rasta and Resistance: From Marcus Garvey to Walter Rodney*, Africa World Press, Trenton NJ, 1987

Cashmore, E., *The Rastafarians*, Minority Rights Group London, 1984

Cashmore, E., *Rastaman: The Rastafarian Movement in England*, G. Allen and Unwin, London, 1979

Chevannes, B., *Rastafari: Roots and Ideology*, Syracuse University Press, Syracuse, 1994

Clark, P., *Black Paradise: The Rastafarian Movement*, Borgo Press, San Bernadino, 1994

CONTEMPORARY PAGANISM

Adler, M, *Drawing Down the Moon*, Boston, Beacon Press, 1986 (1979)

Harvey, G., *Listening People, Speaking Earth*, Hurst & Co., London, 1997

THE CULTURE OF THE WEST

Bowker, John (ed.), *The Oxford Dictionary of World Religions*, Oxford University Press, Oxford, 1997

Bruce, S., 'Religion in Britain at the close of the 20th century', *Journal of Contemporary Religion*, vol. 11, no 3, p. 264, 1996

Kerkhofs, Jan (ed.), *European Values Survey*, Louvain, 1990

MacIntyre, Alasdair, *After Virtue*, second edition, Duckworth, London, 1985

Vallely, Paul (ed.), *The New Politics: Catholic Social Teaching for the 21st century*, SCM Press, London

CONFLICT OF IDEOLOGIES

Armstrong, Karen, *The Battle for God: Fundamentalism in Judaism, Christianity and Islam*, HarperCollins, London, 2000

Bowker, John (ed.), *The Oxford Dictionary of World Religions*, Oxford University Press, Oxford, 1997

MULTI-FAITH SOCIETIES

Bellah, R., *Beyond Belief: Essays on Religion in a Past Traditional World*

Hart, D., *One Faith: Non-Realism & The World Faiths*, Mowbrary, 1995

Hinnells, J.R., *A Handbook of Living Religions*, Viking, 1984 (Penguin, 1985)

Kung, H. et al, *Christianity and the World Religions*, Collins, London, 1987

Smart, N., *The World's Religions*, Cambridge University Press, Cambridge, 1989

SCIENTIFIC RELIGIONS

Barbour, I. G., *When Science Meets Religion*, HarperSanFrancisco, San Francisco, 2000

Brooke, J. H. and G. N., *Cantor Reconstructing Nature: The Engagement of Science and Religion*, T &T Clark, Edinburgh, 1998.

Fraser, Caroline, *God's Perfect Child: Living and Dying in the Christian Science Church*, Metropolitan Books/Henry Holt & Company, New York, 1999

Gilbert, J. B., *Redeeming Culture: American Religion in an Age of Science*, University of Chicago Press, Chicago, 1997

Gould, S. J., *Rocks of Ages: Science and Religion in the Fullness of Life*, Ballantine, New York, 1999

Haught, J. F., *Science and Religion: From Conflict to Conversation*, Paulist Press, New York, 1995

Lindberg, D. C. and Numbers, R. L. (eds.), *God and Nature: Historical Essays on the Encounter between Christianity and Science*, University of California Press, Berkeley, 1986

Ward, K. *God, Chance and Necessity*, Oneworld Publications, Oxford, 1996

GLOSSARY

Barrett, David B. (ed.), *World Christian Encyclopedia: A Comparative Survey of Churches and Religions in the Modern World* (2 vols), 2001

Hinnells, J. (ed.), *The New Penguin Handbook of Living Religions*, Penguin, Harmondsworth, 2000

Melton, G. J., *The Encyclopedia of American Religions* (4th ed.), Gale, Detroit, 1993

Schuhmacher, S. and Woerner, G. (eds.), *The Rider Encyclopedia of Eastern Philosophy and Religion*, Rider, London, 1989

Smart, Ninian, *The World's Religions*, Cambridge University Press, Cambridge, 1992

Index

SUBJECT

Acknowledgements

Thanks to James Palmer

Thanks to Matthew Weinberg for all his help and advice (*Baha'i*)

Shree Sanatan Mandir, Leicester: with thanks to the management for their kind support (*Hinduism*)

Preet Majithia for typing and infectious enthusiasm (*Hinduism*)

Mrs Kirti Majithia MA (Sanskrit) for her support with her Sanskrit language background and study of Bhagavad Gita (*Hinduism*)

Thanks to Susanna Rostas for all her assistance (*Central and South America*)

Thanks to Monica

Thanks to Christine Kidney

All Biblical references are taken from the English Standard Version (Crossway Bibles, Wheaton, Illinois, 2001)

Picture Credits

AKG: 11 b, 196, 198 r, 200 b

Amar Hegedus 160,

Art Archive: 8t, 8 b, 9 t,10 t, 10 b, 11 t, 12 b, 12 t, 13, 15 t, 15 b, 17 t, 18 t, 19 t, 20 t, 23 t, 24 t, 27 b, 28, 29 t, 29 b, 30, 33 t, 33 b, 34 t, 34 b, 35, 37 t, 37 b, 38, 39 tm, 39 tr, 39 b, 40 t, 40 b, 41, 43 t, 52, 53, 54, 55 t, 57, 63 b, 65, 71, 74, 77, 77, 78 t, 86, 88 t, 90 t, 93, 95 t, 106, 108, 113 t, 114, 115 t, 115 b, 116, 117, 123 t, 130, 131 t, 133 b, 132, 133 t, 133 b, 139 b, 140 t, 141, 144, 145, 175, 176, 178, 187 b, 204, 205 t, 205 b, 206, 213 b, 221 t, 222, 225 t, 225 b

Baha'i World Centre: 211 t

Christies Images: 19 b, 68 t,76, 89, 119 l

Chloë Sayer: 52, 82, 83 t

Circa Picture Library: 140 b, 197 b, 199, 203

Dipak Joshi: 146, 147 t, 149, 153 t, 153 br

Dr N.K. Shah: 173

Foundry Arts: 53 t, 81 t, 173 t, 210, 211 b

Graham Stride: 26, 70 b, 100, 103 t, 105 t, 105 b, 107 b, 110, 111 b, 152, 172 b

Hutchison Library: 81

Image Select: 61 (all); FPG International 70; Giraudon 50;

Impact: 14, 16 t, 68 b, 69, 72 t, 72 b, 75, 80, 87 t, 87 b, 88 b, 90 b, 91, 93, 94, 95 b, 96, 97 t, 97 b, 98, 99, 101, 102, 103 b, 109 b, 112, 113 b, 118, 119 r, 120, 121 t, 121 b, 122, 124, 125 t, 127 t, 134, 135, 136 t, 136 b, 137, 142, 143, 148 b, 150, 151 t, 151 b, 154 t, 155 t, 155 b, 170 b, 172 t, 180, 181 t, 182 b, 184 t, 184 b, 187 t, 189 t, 189 b, 190, 191 t, 191 b, 192, 193, 194, 195 t, 195 b, 197 t, 201, 207 b, 209, 215 t, 215 b, 217 t, 217 b, 218, 219, 220

Jak Kilby 156, 157 t, 157 b, 158, 159 t, 161 t, 161 b, 162 (all), 163, 164, 165 (all), 166 (all), 167, 168, 169 (all)

Mary Evans 43 b, 47 b, 125 b, 126, 138, 139 t, 186

South American Pictures/Tony Morrison: 57

Still Pictures: Walter H. Lodge 99 t

Susanna Rostas: 56 m, 83 b, 84, 85 t, 85 b

Tara Lewis: 59

Topham: 9 b, 17 b, 19 m, 21, 22 t, 23 b, 25 l, 25 r, 27 t, 31, 32, 36, 44, 45, 51, 58, 73, 75, 104, 107 t, 109 t, 111 t, 123 b, 127 b, 128, 129 b, 129 t, 148 t, 153 bl, 154 b, 171, 177 t, 177, 179 t, 179 b, 181 b, 182 t, 183, 185, 202, 207 t, 208, 212, 213 t, 214, 216, 221 b, 223 t, 223 b; AAAC: 174

VAL/Artephot: A. Held 92; Silvio Fiore 48

VAL/Bridgeman: 20 b, 62

VAL/Edimedia: 63 t

Werner Forman: 49 t, 66, 67 t, 67 b, 76, 78 b,170 t, 198 l; British Museum 55 b; Dorset Natural History & Archeology Society 46; Haffenpreffer Museum of Anthropology 79; Museum fur Volkerkunde 56 t; National Muesum Copenhagen 47 t; Private Collection Sydney 200 t; Statens Historiska Museum 49 b